they are
what you
feed
them

they are what you feed them

how **food** can improve your child's **behaviour, mood** and **learning**

Dr Alex Richardson

HarperThorsons
An Imprint of HarperCollins*Publishers*
77–85 Fulham Palace Road
Hammersmith, London W6 8JB

The website address is:
www.thorsonselement.com

and *HarperThorsons* are trademarks of
HarperCollins*Publishers* Ltd

First published by HarperThorsons 2006

6

© Dr Alex Richardson 2006

A catalogue record of this book is
available from the British Library

ISBN-13 978-0-00-718225-1
ISBN-10 0-00-718225-2

Printed and bound in Great Britain by
Clays Ltd, St Ives plc

This book includes recipes including nuts, nut derivatives and nut oils.
Avoid if you have a known allergic reaction. Pregnant and nursing mothers,
invalids, the elderly, children and babies may be potentially vulnerable to
nut allergies and should therefore avoid nuts, nut derivatives and nut oils.

This book is proudly printed on paper which contains
wood from well-managed forests, certified in accordance
with the rules of the Forest Stewardship Council. For
more information about FSC, please visit www.fsc-uk.org

contents

part one

food
and
mood

the basics

chapter 1

starting points

Who Will Benefit from Reading this Book?

I've written this book primarily for those of you who are parents and carers, and the information and advice have been tailored accordingly. Parents or guardians are usually the ones who have most responsibility for and influence over their children's development, at least in the early years, and this is particularly true when it comes to food and diet. What parents don't usually have, however, is easy access to reliable information about just how important good nutrition is to their child's development – and especially to their child's brain and behaviour.

Having said that, many of the parents I've met have taught me a great deal about the links between food and behaviour, and in this book I'll be doing my best to share with you the insights I've gained from working with these parents and their children. Many of them know a great deal more about this subject than most specialists in child behaviour, and I've sprinkled quotes from them throughout the book. They have often gained their knowledge the hard way, however, and sadly the professionals officially in charge of helping them and their children have not always been receptive to suggestions that diet could in any way be relevant to these children's difficulties in behaviour, learning or mood.

This book is about you taking charge and helping your child and yourself.

For this reason, although this book is written mainly for parents, I hope that the material here will also be useful to the many practitioners in health, education, social services or other fields who are struggling to help the children in their care, as well as to the many support groups and charities whose invaluable work has been helping to fill the huge gaps left by official research, policy and practice. In my experience, it is parents, along with some professionals and support groups, who have often been the unsung heroes who have actually made some of the most important discoveries about how diet can affect children's behaviour. Science is only just starting to follow up some of these discoveries – and, as usual, government policy tends to lag way behind.

Why I Have Written This Book

For almost 20 years now I've been involved in scientific research into the nature and causes of many common difficulties in behaviour and learning. The children affected may have been labelled with terms like *dyslexia*, *dyspraxia*, *ADHD* or *autism*. In many cases there is no official 'diagnosis' – and even when there is, this doesn't always lead to effective solutions. For those who know what to look out for, the first signs of conditions like dyslexia, ADHD or other syndromes are there from early childhood, but these are not always recognized until much later – if at all – while the effects of the unexpected difficulties with behaviour and learning usually last a lifetime. They can also cause untold distress and misery if not properly identified and treated.

> Early recognition, along with effective help, can make all the difference.

My primary aim as a researcher has always been to find better ways of identifying and helping people whose lives are affected by these kinds of difficulties. From my earlier background in teaching I first became aware of just how many children were actually affected, although most of them were not being given the help they really needed. What was preventing most of these children from achieving anything like their true potential, I realized, was our sheer ignorance of how human brains and minds really work – especially with respect to individual differences. This is what led me out of teaching and into the world of neuroscience research. At first, my scientific research had nothing to do with nutrition … or so I thought! But that view began to change as I recognized that nutritional issues cut across everything I was studying.

What on Earth Is Really Going On?

In both research and practice in health and education, children who have particular difficulties with behaviour or learning are often diagnosed as having conditions such as ADHD (attention-deficit hyperactivity disorder), dyslexia or specific reading difficulties (SRD), dyspraxia or developmental coordination disorder (DCD) or autistic spectrum disorders (ASD). For children with behavioural problems, 'conduct disorder' and 'oppositional defiant disorder' are the terms commonly applied. Learning difficulties may attract diagnoses such as 'speech and language disorder'.

Unfortunately there is still a great deal of controversy over what these labels actually mean. They may do a good job of *describing* specific patterns of difficulties that are common to many children, but they do little or nothing when it comes to *explaining* them. If help is to be effective, then it really is important to know what's actually causing these children's problems, but this crucial information is not something that any of these 'diagnoses' actually provides.

These so-called 'developmental disorders' also lack any clear boundaries. Not only do they overlap considerably with each other, but their core 'symptoms' also occur in milder forms in so many children in every classroom that it is a matter of opinion (and considerable controversy) where the dividing lines should be drawn. In the UK, around one child in every four or five would now meet the criteria for one or more of these 'disorders', leading many people to ask, 'What on earth is really going on?'

Diagnostic labels like ADHD or dyslexia can obviously be very useful in some respects – perhaps most importantly because they provide official recognition that a child is *not* 'lazy', 'careless', 'stupid', 'selfish' or something even worse.

Sadly, these very negative labels are all too often applied by people who know no better. If left unchallenged – and particularly if your child starts to believe them – such labels could obviously do irreparable damage to his or her self-esteem and opportunities in life. Many children and adults have told me what a relief it was when someone finally identified their difficulties as being typical of dyslexia, dyspraxia, ADHD or ASD. A diagnosis may also be invaluable in opening the way to appropriate treatment. In school, it should allow your child access to whatever specialist assistance may be on offer, because the school can probably get extra funding to meet your child's special needs.

The help on offer doesn't usually consider something very fundamental indeed: your child's diet.

Not every child with behavioural or learning problems will necessarily even qualify for any official diagnosis, of course. But even if they do, these officially recognized labels, which parents have often had to fight for years to obtain, don't always lead to the kind of help that parents really want. For instance, if the diagnosis is ADHD, their child will usually be offered treatment with drugs. If the diagnosis is dyslexia, then some special teaching help may be available. If the diagnosis is dyspraxia or DCD, then behavioural therapies or physiotherapy might be offered. And if the diagnosis is an autistic spectrum disorder, parents may well be told that there is nothing anyone can do.

There is always something that can be done. Don't ever believe it if anyone tells you otherwise.

One of the very real and fundamental issues that affects *every* child, and which *every* parent would benefit from knowing more about, is *nutrition*. The problem is that information and advice about food and diet currently feature absolutely nowhere in standard practice for either assessing or treating children's behavioural and learning difficulties. In my view, this situation is simply indefensible.

Over the years I have seen not just hundreds but thousands of children and their parents, as well as many adolescents and adults, all of whom have been struggling with difficulties in behaviour, learning and mood that neither they nor the experts they've turned to for help can really explain. I've also read and absorbed the findings from a huge and diverse range of the very best scientific research. In addition, I've attended and presented my work at many scientific and professional conferences in the UK and abroad, given hundreds of talks and lectures to both public and professional audiences, published numerous peer-reviewed research papers, contributed chapters to several books and written many articles for charities, support groups and the media.[1]

As a result of the high profile my work has achieved, I receive thousands of enquiries and requests for advice from parents and professionals. These parents and professionals all have the same concerns and aims I have: *to help the children they care for, and find some effective, practical ways that can help these children overcome the behavioural and learning difficulties preventing them from achieving their potential.*

In my view, all of these people are being badly let down. They are often being told things that aren't true, and they are not being given the help that they need and deserve. I see huge sums of money being wasted in our health systems, our education systems, our social services and our criminal justice systems (let alone what happens within the worlds of employment and self-employment which generate the tax revenue that pays for most of these systems). It has also become very clear to me that a similarly large proportion of the resources devoted to research in the name of helping people is simply being wasted, because we continue to ignore some of the most basic facts that are staring us in the face.

Nutrition matters!

A Quite Extraordinary Denial

Food and diet are important to all of us at the most fundamental level, because without the right nutrients it simply isn't possible for our brains and bodies to develop properly, to grow properly and to function properly. It is also a fact that the diets of a huge number of children (and adults) in developed countries like the UK simply are not providing all the essential nutrients they need. Official figures from the latest National Diet and Nutrition Surveys bear this out – but oddly enough, the shocking findings have not been given any media coverage.[2]

Results from the most recent official survey of the nutritional status of children in the UK, carried out in 1997 and published in 2000, are not even freely available on the Internet (like the results from the adult survey are), despite this research having been funded by UK taxpayers' money. Perhaps the Government would rather we didn't know? Later in the book, you'll read about some of these findings, and I hope you will agree that they really don't give us any cause for complacency.

We keep being told that 'a well-balanced diet can provide all the nutrients you need'. That may be true, but the truth is that many children's diets are a very long way from being well-balanced … and the effects of this malnutrition on their behaviour and learning can be devastating. What I see going on in almost every sphere is a mixture of ignorance and a quite extraordinary denial of how food and diet can influence our brains and our behaviour.

They Are What You Feed Them

In recent years public concern has finally been mounting about the unhealthy nature of many children's diets, but it took Jamie Oliver's dramatic exposé about school dinners to put the shocking issues right in front of us. The British Medical Association, not usually known for its radical stance, has since joined in and demanded that something be done about children's nutrition.

> The evidence is now undeniable that poor nutrition is putting children's physical health at risk. Many children are now expected to die *before* their parents – as a direct result of their unhealthy diets and lifestyles.

The epidemic of overweight and obesity in children is the most obvious sign that all is not well, and has become rather difficult to ignore. For years, the food industry and its supporters have always got away with blaming the expanding waistlines of our children purely on lack of exercise – but as anyone with half a brain can see, poor diets are equally, if not more, to blame.

The physical health problems that accompany, and in most cases precede, such unhealthy weight gain are not usually so obvious to the naked eye. The underlying problems that are leading to Type II diabetes (in which the body stops responding normally to insulin), even in children, often go unnoticed until this has already caused major health problems. Type II diabetes used to be a rare disease that occurred mainly in old age. If you follow the advice given in this book, however, I can almost guarantee that your child will not fall victim to this 'silent killer'.

The effects of food on behaviour are also invisible, but very real. The brain is part of the body, and it relies on the same food supply to meet its needs. However, despite this obvious fact, almost no attention has been focused on the importance of nutrition for children's behaviour and learning.

Many children's diets are high in sugar, refined starches and the wrong kinds of fats, as well as artificial additives. They are high in calories (energy), but lacking in essential nutrients. The risks to physical health of such a 'junk food' diet are now recognized, but their potential effects on children's behaviour, learning and mood are still largely ignored. The (very limited) research that actually exists into human requirements for different nutrients has never even taken brains and behaviour into account.

Spending on Behaviour Doesn't Include Diet

In the UK, the Government has recently been forced to spend an additional £342 million on school behaviour-improvement programmes, and the World Health Organization predicts a 50 per cent rise in child mental disorders by 2020.[3]

The brain, like the body, needs the right nutrients to function properly.

But scientific research aimed at finding out the extent to which better nutrition could improve children's behaviour and learning is not something that anyone seems prepared to fund – so our ignorance continues.

Nonetheless, as this book will reveal, there is in fact already evidence to show that for many children (and adults) the improvements in behaviour, learning and mood that can follow from some remarkably simple changes in diet can be quite dramatic. The problem is that too many people don't even know about this research. Instead, far too many parents who actually suspect that food may be part of their child's problem – and have good evidence of their own to support this – are often told dismissively by the supposed experts, 'Oh, there's no evidence that diet can make a difference.'

This is simply untrue. There is quite a lot of evidence, and much of it is first-class … but it tends to be in different places, and is rarely pulled together. If you add it all up, the case for doing something to improve the diets of children in the UK (and other countries) is now overwhelming.

This book will tell you how to go about improving your child's diet, with particular emphasis on the impact this can have on mood, behaviour and learning.

In my view, it's actually verging on negligence for any professional to deny to parents that food and diet *can* affect their children's behaviour – although of course there will always be other factors to consider, and dietary approaches should always be complementary to other proven management methods. However, I can't really blame individual professionals for reflecting the training that they've been given and the culture in which they live and work.

We Need to Change Our Legacy

The real problem is that we're dealing with a legacy of ignorance and complacency about nutrition that has now gone on for many decades. In relatively rich, developed countries like the UK, it's simply been assumed that no one is really likely to be at risk of malnutrition. Rising rates of obesity are taken as evidence to confirm this – but of course there is a big difference between being overfed and being well nourished. What too few people seem to recognize and acknowledge is that our diets – and particularly children's diets – have changed out of all recognition during the past few decades. To make matters worse, the education that any of us receives about how our brains and bodies work, and what nutrients we need not just to stay healthy, but to allow our minds and brains to function properly (let alone at their best), is extremely limited.

School syllabuses do cover diet, but there is little time to teach children what they really need to know. What's more, healthy eating messages can easily be subverted by the heavy advertising of 'junk foods' and peer pressure that our children face. Generally speaking, most adult education in this area is limited to information in the media. Sadly, most of this actually comes from the food, supplement and diet industries, and is often little more than marketing and advertising for their latest products and services. This doesn't help anyone to make properly informed choices.

Over the years, many parents have asked me where they can get information that they can really trust on the food and diet issues that most concern them as they try to do the best they can for their children. When you've read this book, if you'd like more information about the scientific research in this area that is *independent* of commercial influences, and any further details on some of the information provided here, you can find it on the website of the charity Food and Behaviour Research (see www.fabresearch.org).

Where to Go Next

I'm not going to pretend that we have all the answers, because we don't. There's still a huge amount that we don't know about how nutrition can affect mental health and performance. Many of the answers to key questions would not actually be hard to find if there were a will to investigate. If this kind of research received just a tiny fraction of the resources that go into pharmaceutical and other approaches that have so far failed to deliver, we would have much of the evidence we need. This is why I've dedicated the entire proceeds of this book (which would otherwise go to me, the author) to the Food and Behaviour (FAB) Research charity.

I hope you enjoy this book, I hope you learn something from it that will be useful to you, and I also hope you decide to act on its guidelines. Please know that I'd prefer it to become 'dog-eared' and covered in highlighter and notes than put neatly on a shelf to gather dust. There are numerous issues I've not been able to include or cover in depth here, and no doubt many corrections that you can help me with. I'm open to your feedback. Please let me know how you get on.

FAQs

My doctor doesn't believe in food intolerances and pooh-poohs what I say. What should I do?

There are some more enlightened doctors out there who keep up with the research in this field; try to seek one out. To be fair – their workload makes it almost impossible for most doctors and other health professionals to find time to read up on nutrition. What's more, most of them still receive very little training in this area – and as you'll see in Chapter 6, the whole area of food allergies and intolerances is a highly complex one that still needs more research. Do tell your doctor about the FAB Research website, though, because many health professionals I know find this a very useful resource, allowing them to see some of the scientific research for themselves. I also don't think many doctors would take issue with most of the dietary advice you'll find in this book, but the decision on what to do has to be up to you. If I were you, I'd get a second opinion from a doctor who does listen – but I'd also read up as much as I could, talk to other people and then make my own choices. In any case, I wish you the best of luck.

I'm a teacher and have three main frustrations: because of the crowded syllabus I have so little time to explore the need for good nutrients with my pupils; we have vending machines that sell soft drinks and sweets (the Head says we need them to fund non-teaching staff); since we were forced to put the school dinners out to tender, they have gone from healthy spreads to mainly junk food.

I hear these frustrations a lot. Show this book to your head teacher, other staff and governors. Write to your local MP and the education minister, and join FAB Research and the many other not-for-profit groups who are campaigning for things to change.

Summary

1. This book is mainly written for parents, but it is also for anyone in the health, education and social services who has children in their care.
2. I've written this book to share my discoveries with you about how food and diet can affect children's behaviour, learning and mood. This may be particularly relevant to those affected by conditions like autism, ADHD, dyslexia and dyspraxia, but the fundamental issues affect all of us – because we all need to get from our diets the nutrients needed for mental as well as physical health.
3. Labels like *ADHD*, *dyslexia* or *autism* can be useful, but they do little or nothing to explain these conditions, and they have many features in common with each other and with what's considered normal functioning.
4. If your child has been given one of these labels, you may have been told there's little or nothing you can do. You *can* do something, and one very fundamental thing that may help is to look at your child's diet.

5. The latest official survey of the nutritional status of children in the UK shows that many of them are lacking in essential nutrients. Little publicity has been given to these findings or their potential implications for physical and mental health. Results from the survey are not even freely available on the Internet, despite this research having been funded by UK taxpayers' money.

6. Many school meals are unhealthy, and the limited education that children do receive on food and diet cannot begin to compete with the promotion of unhealthy foods via advertising and other media. Many of the adults who care for them are no better informed.

7. Rising obesity has been blamed mainly on lack of exercise. This can obviously be a contributory factor, but in most cases diet is equally if not more important.

8. This book will present evidence that children's diets can affect not only their physical health but also their mental health and performance.

9. 'Junk food' diets are now being recognized as a serious risk to the physical health of our children, but their effects on behaviour, learning and mood are still largely ignored.

10. You can help to redress this neglect – starting with your own child.

chapter 2

facing the facts

When it comes to how much we – the public – usually get to know about the foods we eat, and what we've been feeding to our children for years now, I'm afraid it's rather like the old joke about the 'mushroom' style of management, namely: 'Keep them in the dark, and feed them ****.'

For a long time, both the food industry and successive governments have effectively kept quiet about many things they've known (or should have known) about the appalling nutritional quality of much of our food – and children's food in particular. Many of these appalling facts are available to anyone willing to read up about this subject (although, ironically enough, I've found that some of the best books are often in the 'politics and economics' section of bookstores rather 'nutrition').[1] It took Jamie Oliver's stunning TV series on the state of school dinners to bring some of these issues to public attention and make the UK Government finally admit that there is a problem.

A poor diet leads to poor health.

The real trouble is that cheap, low-quality foods and drinks bring big profits to those who get away with selling them. (All the better if the contract is with a Government agency and lasts for years, as some school dinner contracts do.)

Reading through this chapter, have a think about whether there might be a connection between diet and why your child misbehaves, gets moody, is often tired, or has problems learning. If you saw *Jamie's School Dinners*, you may remember that many people interviewed spoke about the dramatic changes in some children's behaviour after 'dumping the junk' and feeding them with real, freshly cooked food. When the media followed up on this, they naturally wanted to track down the 'scientific evidence' for this remarkable phenomenon, and speak to the scientists involved in such research. So on one particularly memorable morning, I got four different phone calls on my mobile as I dashed between meetings in Oxford, London and Cambridge (via Luton airport to pick up a colleague!). When even the *Financial Times* joined in I realized that the 'food and behaviour' issue really had hit home. This was the aspect they all seemed to be interested in – and no surprises there, really. The only trouble was there clearly weren't enough scientists to go around, so I found myself deluged for some time.

Where's the Good Evidence?

The reason so many enquiries came to me is that when it comes to the kind of research that really can provide firm evidence of cause and effect,[2] there are actually remarkably few studies of how food and diet may affect children's behaviour and learning. Fewer still are by researchers in the UK. My own investigations of this kind have mainly involved omega-3 fatty acids (found in fish oils) – belatedly recognized as essential 'brain food' as well as beneficial for your heart, joints and immune system. In our latest study, children given omega-3 showed faster reading and spelling progress, better attention and memory, and less disruptive behaviour than a matched comparison group over a three-month period. We still need more evidence, but I can understand why parents, teachers and the media are interested. You'll hear more about these special fats – and our research findings – in Chapters 8 and 9.

Healthy Strawberry Yoghurt, Anyone?

Check your labels:
- 'strawberry yoghurt': contains some real strawberry
- 'strawberry-*flavoured* yoghurt': there's a tiny bit of strawberry, somewhere
- 'strawberry-*flavour* yoghurt': no strawberries at all

The cheaper ones are usually the last of these three, and some of their ingredients can be dubious: gelatine, pectin/gum, flavourings, colourings, and corn sugar.

Low-fat 'healthy' yoghurts usually contain even more thickeners (corn starch this time) along with plenty of sugar or artificial sweeteners.

Other scientific studies have looked at other aspects of diet. For example, many well-controlled trials have looked into whether artificial food additives might aggravate hyperactivity and related behaviour problems. Many of these were carried out years ago, but variability in their designs and results made it hard to know what to believe. More recently, two important studies have confirmed that some common food additives with no nutritional value really do seem to *worsen* behaviour in many children. Might your child be one of them? How much more evidence will we need before we take action? When you read about these issues in Chapter 6, you can decide for yourself (and your children) what you want to do.

'Cheap Trick' Frozen Chicken Nuggets*

Ingredients
- Chicken carcasses
- Chicken skin
- 'Mechanically recovered' bits of bird
- Artificial additives (colourings, flavourings, preservatives, texture-modifying agents)
- Hydrogenated (bad) fats

Procedure

- Scrape the skin and other bits off the machinery or factory floor.
- Add to chicken carcass and put in high-speed blender.
- Add the bad fats, texture-modifiers and other additives.
- Form into nugget shapes and cover with 'bread crumbs' (more additives).
- Freeze and package attractively.
- Sell to parents to feed to their children.
- Sell to schools and restaurants en masse for the same purpose.

with due credit to J. Oliver and Co for showing that consumers do often change their preferences when you tell them what they're really eating.

It's not just what has been added to our food that matters – it's also what's been taken away. In Chapter 4 we'll look at essential nutrients. As you'll see, there are lots of these – but many are seriously lacking from the diets of children, adolescents and adults in the UK. How would you know? Well, deficiencies in some nutrients lead to well-documented physical symptoms, but these are not always recognized as such – and may be treated with medications that can make matters worse. What about mental symptoms? Can a poor diet alone really cause bad behaviour? Later, you'll hear more about a rigorous study of young offenders carried out in a high-security prison.[3] In this study, giving just the recommended daily amounts of vitamins and minerals (with some essential fatty acids) with no other changes actually *reduced* the number of violent offences by more than 35 per cent. Can you imagine that effect translated into the wider community? What might be achieved in your child's school, or your neighbourhood, if aggression and antisocial behaviour fell by that amount? Given the potential implications, wouldn't you think the Government would be keen to follow up on these kinds of findings? In the UK, sadly the answer is 'No, not yet.' The funding for this particular research (including replication studies now underway) has been provided almost entirely by charities.[4]

Healthy Apples?

Supermarkets force producers to grow larger apples (so people end up buying more) which means the apples' vitamin and mineral content declines.

Want Fries with That?

McDonald's got into trouble for selling their fries as fit for vegetarian consumption when their reformed spuds had been cooked in beef tallow.

So they switched to vegetable oil (which incidentally produces bad trans fats when heated). Now the distinctive taste of the fries comes from an infusion of *synthetic* beef tallow.

In fact, many of the flavourings now used in our foods are synthetic chemicals: you can't smell or taste the difference, but there is no nutritional value in them.

Slowly But Surely …

Even if policymakers are lagging behind, it seems that consumers are beginning to turn. Sales of bagged snacks, sugar confectionery, fizzy soft drinks, frozen meals and pizzas have apparently declined over the last year, while sales of fruit juices, cheeses, bread and drinking yoghurt have increased. McDonald's has had to close at least 25 of its UK branches (even though it began to introduce supposedly 'healthier' ranges – but let's not go there!). The media tell us that confectionery and soft drinks companies such as Cadbury-Schweppes may be planning to put health messages on their packaging (is this to provide them with some defence if they find themselves sued like the tobacco companies?). The makers of sausage rolls and pasties are apparently seeing a large drop in profits. And I know I'm not the only one pleased to see that one of the big supermarkets has finally taken a certain brightly coloured, additive-laden drink pretending to look like orange juice off its shelves. 'Surly Despair' would be a better name for this one, given the amount of sugar and artificial additives it contains. If I had a pound for every time a parent, professional or support group leader has complained to me about the way that this (and similar drinks) can 'send our children up the wall', we could probably fund our whole next year's research programme on the proceeds. As it is, these kinds of companies have been raking in the money and yet few people have seen the need to finance research to see what these and other 'junk foods' might really be doing to our children's brains.

Not All Sweetness and Light

A survey for *Food Magazine* in 2004 revealed that a single drink of Ribena or Lucozade could give your child more than a whole day's recommended sugar intake.

- 500ml bottle Ribena: 70g sugar (equivalent to at least 15 teaspoons)
- 380ml bottle Lucozade Energy: 64g sugar
- 330ml bottle Coca-Cola: 25g sugar

That means a bottle of the soft stuff can give your child the same 'sugar hit' as one to four packets of sweets. In some cases, the sweetener may be in the form of high-fructose corn syrup (which is cheaper to produce than sugar).

'No added sugar' varieties just put in artificial sweeteners instead, which some good evidence shows may carry different kinds of risks.

Regular consumption of fizzy, sweet drinks can lead to a decline in body levels of important minerals

In the news, we hear that 40 per cent of patients in our hospitals are suffering from malnutrition – which can add serious complications to their treatment and care, and significantly slow their recovery.[5] In most cases it probably contributed to their illness too – but at least the links between nutrition and physical health are starting to be acknowledged by our health services. (They have long been recognized by top performers in physical sports!) What we need now is a similar acceptance that food and diet also affect *mental* health and performance. It really should be 'barn door' obvious. The brain is part of the body – and has nutrient and energy requirements of its own. But remarkably little systematic effort has so far been devoted to finding out what those requirements really are – and just how our mood, behaviour and learning really can be affected when these needs are not properly met.

Still, it's encouraging to see that consumers are beginning to wise up to some of what's been going on, and to change their shopping and eating habits as a result. For the sake of your children, I do hope you are one of them – and I hope this book will give you some of the help you'll need.

There Is a Good End in Sight

Before we go any further, let's just consider what's possible, and what isn't. Right now, your child's mood, behaviour and learning (or all three) are probably giving you cause for concern, or you wouldn't be reading this book. I can guess that what you'd really like to find here are some simple, rapid and effective solutions to your child's difficulties. Well, I obviously can't promise that this book will solve *all* your particular problems. But if you choose to act on the information I'll be giving you, the rewards *could* actually be greater than you might think possible. If you're sceptical – I don't blame you. But by feeding your child well, you can at least be confident that you'll be taking some fundamental and necessary steps towards unlocking your child's true potential.

What's more, I hope you'll also apply what you learn here to your own diet. (If you want to improve your child's eating habits, then 'Do as I do' is much more effective than 'Do as I say!'). If you do, expect benefits not only for your child, but also for yourself and any other members of your family who are willing to join in. Better health is one thing that should definitely follow from this plan – and for that reason alone you're unlikely to regret it if you choose to take the advice I'll be giving you. If you understand *why* you need to improve the dietary choices that you and your child have been making, then learning *how* to do it is so much easier – although I'll be helping you with that as well.

> Food and diet really are key to making the most of your child's potential, both mentally and physically. *We are what we eat, and our children are what we feed them.*

I can give you the information, but putting it into practice is clearly up to you, and I'm not going to promise that this will be easy. Quite a lot of people will probably tell you that you are wasting your time. Some of them may do more than that to try to undermine your efforts. Remember that such an attitude is *their* problem, not yours. In Chapter 10 you'll find plenty of tips on how to get in the right frame of mind to move ahead without making it difficult for yourself.

You'll probably find yourself changing a good deal more than your child's diet if you choose to follow the plan completely. Whether you'll want to do this or not is again for you to decide, but presumably what you've been doing so far hasn't been working too well, or you wouldn't still be looking for new solutions. So isn't it worth trying something else? Something that is completely natural, involves no drugs and no special equipment, and costs you very little? You've already taken an important step by picking up this book.

Hopes and Promises

One other thing I want to make very clear at the outset is that this book is not about 'miracle cures'. We are all prone to believing all kinds of things that turn out not to be true, simply because they fit in with what we want to believe. It's called 'the triumph of hope over experience' and we are all prone to it. Our society tends to emphasize the 'quick fix', and the wonders of modern technology have led to a situation in which we're surrounded by all kinds of goods and services – from electronic gadgetry to air and space travel – that seem to 'work like magic'.

Amazing brain-imaging techniques can show you how your brain lights up when you solve a problem; global satellite navigation systems can talk you through the narrowest side-streets in a foreign country; guided missiles are said to need no human intervention to find their target; wonder drugs will apparently rescue men's failing sex lives and turn them into super-studs overnight. Yes, really. Advertising has become so clever and so insidious that we are all prone to falling for promises of things that either couldn't possibly be delivered – or which come at a cost (often a hidden one) that none of us can actually afford.

Against this background, we are all too easily fooled into parting with good money for some miracle treatment that will reverse ageing, cure baldness, allow us to eat all that we like and still lose weight, and more. If you've already fallen victim to promises like these, you are certainly not alone. But perhaps it's time to try a different approach. The plan set out in Chapter 11 really needn't cost you much money, and in fact may turn out to save you a great deal.

Good nutrition (and the avoidance of toxins as far as possible) can of course only provide your child with the basic foundations for better mood, behaviour and learning. Many other factors are important, including general health, physical activity and sleep, as well as a wide range of social, educational and cultural factors. Could parenting skills or the family situation be in need of a rethink? What educational input is your child really getting – and from whom? Does your child seem to be more influenced by his friends, or by what's on TV, than by anything you or his teachers say or do? Children are exposed to all kinds of influences in our modern age – many of them quite pernicious[6] – so your child will need all the help you can give him or her. Only minimal guidance on these issues can be provided here, but plenty of good books have been written on these subjects. You'll find some of these in the References and Resources chapter, which also includes helpful sources of information.

'Miracle cures' are certainly not common, but when the dramatic changes that can attract this label do happen, they usually reflect something very important – and often very simple – that has hitherto been overlooked. The story of Patrick, an eight-year-old boy whose moody and defiant behaviour had his loving parents at their wits' end, is a good case in point.

A highly intelligent and sensitive child, Patrick suffered unpredictable mood swings and temper-tantrums. He was underachieving at school, found it hard to make or keep friends and knew how to manipulate his parents and siblings. Most of all, he was clearly unhappy. Talking about the situation with him just seemed to make things worse.

Patrick also looked unhealthy and tired when I saw him, but, with his mother's help, we gathered some basic information and drew up a plan that he was willing to try. It quickly turned out that he was very intolerant to cows' milk and anything made from it. Once milk products were removed from his diet, Patrick's 'moody' spells simply vanished.

His mother Sarah wrote to me: 'Patrick is a transformed child following your diet. His aunts and uncles just couldn't believe the change in him after such a short time. They want to know how I did it. I can hardly believe it myself, but I will never be able to thank you enough. Keep up the good work.'

The media are very fond of 'miracle stories', of course – and one superb example of how to influence public opinion with no more than anecdotes came from the BBC TV series *Children of Our Time*. Children born in the millennium year are monitored at intervals for the purposes of this popular TV series. Early in 2004, one episode focused on just two of these children, who had been showing serious behavioural problems. 'Miraculous' improvements were reported after their diets were supplemented with fish oils. It certainly made great TV – and the Internet bulletin boards were buzzing for some time afterwards. Sales of all fish oils (many of dubious quality and content, and some quite unsuitable for these purposes) went through the roof, and I found myself on the receiving end of yet another deluge of enquiries from the media, public and professionals, as the only UK scientist who'd actually done controlled trials in this area. As the more responsible journalists pointed out (and as I tried to emphasize), there were many other possible explanations for the improvements shown by these two particular children.

Whenever possible, try not to base any important decisions you make on purely anecdotal evidence. If we want to be able to predict anything with reasonable certainty, we need to adopt 'scientific methods'.

To be confident that any treatment really does 'cause' positive changes, we ideally need what are called 'randomized controlled trials' (RCTs), as explained in the Appendix, page 375. These are very difficult to carry out, however, and are in some cases just not feasible. In these cases, other evaluation methods have to be used. Even then, the best we can do is to assess probability. Your child may be different from the ones studied. In short, there are no miracles and no guarantees, I'm afraid.

Having said this, 'scientific' is the word to describe many of the case studies carefully carried out by parents and practitioners I've met. Often, these people have observed and experimented with dietary changes for years, and many of them have done so despite the scorn of the so-called 'scientific establishment'. Although some of them may be misguided or plain wrong in what they have come to believe, it is my view that we would do well to pay more attention to some of their ideas, as I've always tried to do. In many cases it's their insight and observations that have led to some extraordinary breakthroughs, opening up new and highly fruitful lines of scientific investigation.[7]

Whom and What Can You Believe?

Most of the parents I see have already consulted many other specialists and experts in their search for some effective solutions to their child's apparent difficulties in mood, behaviour or learning. Some of the advice they've received has been helpful; some of it has been anything but. Many have also read numerous 'self-help' books and articles from magazines or newspapers, and these days a good proportion will also have spent hours and hours on the Internet trying to find out how to help their children. The feedback I usually get is that when it comes to food and diet, the amount of conflicting information leaves most people totally confused. People ask, 'What am I supposed to believe when so many people are telling me such different things?'

Well, to start with, just ask yourself, 'Who really benefits if I believe this?' Apart from weighing up carefully the potential risks and costs of any course of action, the best advice I can give you is: always consider who will actually gain from your believing any information you are given. Sadly, I've come across a great many unscrupulous companies and individuals who are happily making money for themselves by exploiting parents' desperation.

Rule number one: don't be too gullible. Always think first about whether anything you are recommended could actually do your child harm, but also be particularly wary when it comes to parting with your money.

Companies' Influence Isn't Always Obvious

You can of course get plenty of information and advice about food and diet for free. Quite enough to drown in! In these cases you want to ask, 'Do the people giving me this information really know any better than I do?' Let's start with the newspapers and magazines. Some are more reliable than others, but sadly, very few allow their journalists time to research a story properly.[8] Deadlines are the name of the game. Press releases, for instance, are often picked up and turned into articles without anyone checking the sources or their credentials. Basically, the fact that you 'read it in the papers' or 'saw it on TV' is no guarantee that it isn't just a cleverly disguised advertisement. I'm sorry to say that much, if not most, of what passes for 'news' on food and health in the media is likely to have come from some company that stands to make money if you'll only believe what they're telling you. Remember, virtually all papers and magazines and most TV channels are supported by advertising revenues, either directly or indirectly.

It's well over 10 years now since my own research first started making headline news, and if it hadn't been for my own personal experience of the media I really wouldn't have believed the extent to which what you see or hear through these channels is influenced by companies who will benefit when you believe their stories. The food and drinks industry is a massively powerful force to be reckoned with. Quite apart from the direct advertising that they do – which is powerful enough – they exert a huge degree of less visible control over the information you are given and the choices available to you. The name of the game for big companies is sending out press releases, holding press conferences, wining and dining journalists and hiring the experts they need to back the stories that will benefit them.

'I was looking at websites which talked about the effects of sugar substitutes, as I'd heard that some of them are bad for you. One site in particular did a very good job of listing everything wrong with artificial sweeteners ... but it was only later that I found out that this site was hosted by a sugar company! Now I know why they said nothing at all about avoiding sugar itself.' – *Sonia*

Worse still, the enormous profits that the big food and drink companies make can allow them to 'buy' only the research they want to see done (as also happens with pharmaceutical products, of course). And if they know they aren't going to like the results, they're just not going to do the study. Truly independent research looking into how food can affect behaviour really has been extraordinarily limited, because, apart from a few charitable trusts, nobody has been prepared to fund this kind of work. There's just no profit in it for the companies – and Government agencies and other conventional funding bodies have been either too blind, too conservative, or maybe too much 'under the influence' to look into this rather important area. As well as the conventional food industries, we have the 'diet industry', the 'health food industry' and the 'food supplement industry'. All of them are in the business of making money, whatever else they may tell you. As long as you keep this in mind, you can actually get a lot of useful information from these sources – but always take care to read around, weigh up the different points of view, and make your own decisions.

Read around, weigh up the different points of view, and make your own decisions.

The Pharmaceutical Industry

The pharmaceutical industry is a major beneficiary from the status quo because impoverished diets which will cause or exacerbate all kinds of diseases and disorders suit the drug companies just perfectly! These huge multinationals have an extremely powerful influence on what you are led to believe, and they really do help to set the research agenda in medicine and other health-related areas. Having worked alongside doctors and within medical schools for many years, and attended numerous conferences in the fields of medicine and psychiatry, I have become appalled at the extent to which the influence of so-called 'Big Pharma' dominates the medical training that our doctors and allied health professionals receive. Their influence on scientific research has also become so great that any line of enquiry that doesn't fit with their preferred 'medical model' (ideally, one that requires you and your child to take their drugs – in the long term if possible), or which could serve to undermine some of their most profitable markets, is likely to go unfunded by conventional sources. If the research does get done anyway, it can then be very difficult to publish if it might upset these vested interests.[9]

The Specialists

Do the specialists advising you know anything about food and diet, and its potential effects on brains and behaviour? Sadly, unlike vets, most doctors in the UK and other Western countries still receive very little training in nutrition and its implications for health. They do learn about the basic 'deficiency diseases' (such as scurvy, pellagra or rickets) and there is now an increasing focus on 'preventative medicine' – which usually includes at least some attention to nutrition and diet. But even though good nutrition is essentially about the body's biochemistry, *medical training usually puts far more emphasis on the way in which drugs can be used to manipulate this.* Synthetic drugs can be patented for profit. With some rare exceptions, naturally occurring nutrients can't.

It's rather ironic that veterinary training involves far more emphasis on nutrition and health than does ordinary medicine – probably because the economic factors surrounding animal health are rather different. When farm animals get sick, for example, dietary considerations and possible nutrient deficiencies or imbalances are usually one of the main factors considered. That said, vets' patients don't usually attend their appointments demanding a course of pills that will make them better! We would do well to learn from this.

What other specialists might you and your child see? Clinical psychologists, occupational therapists, education professionals, and those working in social services or related fields receive little or no formal training in how food and diet can affect behaviour and mental health. For this reason these professionals can often be very sceptical about dietary issues, even when parents try to raise these.

Good nutrition is the essential foundation for health – and poor nutrition is guaranteed to lead to ill-health of one kind or another, sooner or later. This is as true for the brain as it is for the body. Unhealthy children generally do not feel well, do not behave well, do not learn well, and – surprise, surprise – do not perform well.

The same goes for unhealthy parents, so I do want to emphasize that this book is written for *you*, not just for your child. It also applies, of course, to unhealthy teachers, unhealthy doctors, unhealthy social workers or any other unhealthy people whose opinions and decisions are important to your child's welfare! You may already have met some of these.

You may want to look at what the statistics say about health, life expectancy and job satisfaction among members of our education, health, social service and criminal justice systems. Most of the sad facts are easily explicable in terms of the conditions and the culture in which these professionals are expected to work, the ever-increasing targets they are supposed to meet, the training and resources with which they are provided, and the systems and people that govern them. Most of them know very little about nutrition, as I have pointed out already. Those that do are not usually encouraged (or even allowed) to use that knowledge in their work …

It's Up to You to Take Charge

It's easy to blame the health services, your child's school, the social workers or other professionals for ignoring any dietary issues that you think are affecting your child. In the current climate, though, strict financial controls, superficial 'efficiency' criteria and short-term goals have come to dominate. These will obviously colour both the motives and the information available to managers and policy-makers in these areas. I share your frustration – but these are not things that most of us can hope to influence very easily, so there's little point in dwelling on them for long here.

It's your life, and your child's life, that we are focusing on in this book.

You may already have adopted some dietary strategies with your child. If so, I hope you've already seen some benefits. You'll also need some luck, though, because much of what you'll have read or been told about the effects of food and diet on your child's behaviour and performance is not actually supported by any reliable evidence – usually because the studies needed to provide this just haven't been done. This is a real problem that I'll do my best to help you with in this book. Mind you, the same is also true of a remarkable number of 'interventions' (treatments or management methods) that are part of 'standard practice' in medicine – not to mention the education, social services and criminal justice systems.

Some research into how food and diet may be affecting our behaviour is almost impossible to do – either because the 'uncontrolled experiments' have been going on for so long that there is no control group left, or because ethical issues make some types of studies difficult or impossible. For example, in the Western world we have all been consuming 'trans fats' for many decades now. (You can read more about these in Chapter 8.) These artificially twisted fats are found in hydrogenated vegetable oils (used in many cheap margarines, fried foods and commercially baked goods of all kinds), and are now known to damage our physical health. Given that the brain is 60 per cent fat, might these artificial fats alter its structure or function, too? Very probably ... but it would be extremely hard now to find a well-matched control group who have not been ingesting trans fats for most or all of their lives. What's more, extracting brain tissue from living subjects to study how its fat composition may relate to psychological well-being or performance is just not an option!

Similarly, a huge number of different food additives have been permitted following individual 'safety testing' for potential toxic effects. Do these tests look at how these food additives might act in combination? Well, no, actually – that would be far too complicated. With the number of additives now in use, it's just not feasible. In fact, it is only very recently that some careful studies have looked into how the growth of nerve cells may be affected by just two common food additives in combination. Even though more work is still needed, the first results (discussed in Chapter 6) will give every parent cause for concern.

Show Caution and Take Practical Steps

Although the scientific studies needed to answer some important questions simply can't be done, in my view we would often do well to follow the 'precautionary principle', *especially* when it comes to ingredients that are used purely for cosmetic appeal and the convenience and profits of the manufacturers (as is the case with many artificial flavourings and colourings, or hydrogenated fats).

> *My aim is to give you a new way of thinking about your child's health and performance as a whole,* and provide you with a better understanding of the issues surrounding food and diet, and how these can affect your child's well-being.

I'll be giving you some facts that may well be new to you, but I will also do my best to provide a framework that allows you to integrate any new information with what you already know. I'll encourage you to start thinking about the information you get from other sources, so that you don't find yourself confused by the apparently conflicting advice you hear or read about elsewhere. Overall, *I urge you to gather what reliable and relevant information you can, weigh up the likely risks and costs against the potential benefits, and then make your own informed choices.*

'When I told my doctor I thought my son (then 7) was intolerant to cows' milk, he sneered at me and prescribed some drugs. Because it was a short appointment, I held my tongue, but binned the prescription, switched my son to goats' milk and cheese, and his symptoms improved dramatically. You know, apart from the doctor's arrogant belief that his way was the only way, I think the fact I was dressed as a "mum at home" had a lot to do with his not listening to me properly! I find if I'm dressed smartly, I get listened to much more than if I'm wearing jeans and trainers.' – *Sarah*

Ask Questions All the Time

Of course, anything you read here will inevitably be coloured by my views, ideas, beliefs and prejudices, along with the knowledge and experience I've gained over the years that I want to share with you. At the end of the day, you are the only one who can decide what – among all the information you gather – can actually be trusted. If you're not sure, keep asking questions:

- Is this information really independent, or just another piece of advertising?
- What sources are the most reliable if I want a second opinion?
- Is there any alternative explanation that would make sense?
- Are there any approaches – however unusual – that mainstream practice has overlooked, but which could actually be important?
- Are there any risks involved in trying these?
- Are there good reasons to believe this approach could work for my child?
- What are the chances (actual probabilities) that these approaches might help?

Throughout this book, I will try to help you through the minefields by doing my best distinguish between:

1. evidence that can reasonably be trusted to be 'objective' and reliable (based on independent research carried out according to established scientific principles and practice)
2. evidence that comes from research carried out or directly funded by those with a vested commercial interest in its outcome
3. theories and observations that make sense, but which have not yet been backed by much firm evidence, including some of my own personal opinions and beliefs.

Past, Present and Future

'What have I been doing wrong?' is a question I've heard from countless parents – parents who care deeply about their child, and who have tried every which way to solve their child's problems, and still not succeeded. Things have not been turning out as they hoped – and, like most parents, they are prepared to take more than their fair share of the responsibility. They have 'tried everything', following all the best advice they could get – and still things don't seem to be working out.

You, like some of them, may have had no idea of the effects of a poor diet (nor indeed what really constitutes a poor diet) before now. Or you may have read up a great deal on the subject already, and cried 'If only I'd known this before …' Whatever the case may be, you need to *focus on where you are now*. What's past is past: you need to let go of any feelings of guilt or anger towards yourself or 'the establishment', and use today as the starting point.

The most important things for you to focus on are the ones that you can most easily influence, govern and control. Those things really should include what you put into your own and your child's mouth.

Although many other factors are also important, good nutrition is simply crucial to your child's health, well-being and functioning. Your child's eating habits are affecting his or her behaviour, learning and mood now, and they will continue to do so in the future. Please remember it took a long time to get to where you are, so don't expect things to improve instantly. In some cases (for example, after excluding additives to which your child reacts badly) improvements can happen almost 'overnight'. In most cases, however, the benefits from improving your child's diet are far more likely to happen gradually. It may take weeks, months – or even years in very severe cases – but with a diet that actually suits your child, happen it will.

What You Can Do to Improve Things

The advice I give to parents follows broadly the same three stages. These are the steps I'll take you through in detail in this book. They are not difficult, and one or more of them will almost certainly apply to your child. I always emphasize that I am not officially qualified to give individuals advice on nutrition *per se* – and when parents need that kind of guidance, as many of them do, I always refer them to either a dietician or another suitably qualified practitioner who can advise on their child's individual dietary needs.[10]

1. **Your child may be consuming foods or other substances to which he reacts badly.** To my mind, avoiding unnecessary additives that are suspected of causing behaviour problems is a 'no-brainer'. You may be surprised at how many of these additives there are, but we'll look at this issue in Chapter 6. When it comes to avoiding specific foods, then unless it's patently obvious what's causing the problem (and it's not a 'major food') I'd advise you to seek expert advice. Improving your child's diet and digestion should come first, as you'll learn in Chapter 5.

'My friend had mysterious pains since his childhood that no doctor could help. He eventually found a practitioner who advised him to focus on improving his bad digestion, and told him how to go about this. Once he changed his diet, the pains (and the grumpiness!) went away.' – *June*

2. **Your child may be 'hooked' on sweet, sugary and starchy foods.** A diet containing too many refined starches and sugars is guaranteed to wreak havoc with the fuel supply to your child's brain – swinging him or her on a rollercoaster of energy 'highs' and 'lows' throughout the day. The same 'fast-action' foods and drinks are also damaging your child's digestive and immune systems, which can lead to a whole array of health-related problems that may be closely linked to difficulties in mood, behaviour and learning. In Chapter 7, we'll see what foods you and your child can eat (and which ones to avoid) to ensure balanced, calm energy throughout the day.

3. **Your child probably eats too many 'bad fats' and not enough 'good fats'.** This is a very easy one for me to identify, not only because it's even more common than the sugar and 'energy imbalance' problems, but also because my own specialist research to date has been focused mainly in this area. 'Bad fats' are found in many processed foods and margarines. The 'good fats' include the very special omega-3 fats (EPA and DHA) which are found in fish and seafood, and are absolutely essential to brain development and function. In Chapter 8 you'll learn how to 'get the fats right', and in Chapter 9 I'll take you through the latest research into omega-3 for child behaviour and learning, sorting the facts from the myths and explaining what the research has – and hasn't – shown.

Facing the facts isn't always easy – but as we've seen in this chapter, you can't rely on the 'powers that be' to look after your child's interests where issues of food and diet are concerned. However, *there are some simple steps that you can take to help your child* – the first of which is getting informed. In the next chapter we'll look at some of the labels that are often given to children with behaviour or learning problems, and see how diet may relate to these. Then we'll look at essential nutrients and digestion (these really are the basics you need to understand) before moving on to the chapters that will take you through the three main steps I've outlined above. In the last few chapters of the book we'll focus on putting what you've learned into practice.

FAQs

Why is there so much conflicting advice, and how do I know which advice to follow?

Much of the information and advice you get about food and diet is really aimed at *selling* you something. Many news and media stories are actually based on company press releases, so always be suspicious. Look carefully at the results and conclusions of proper trials (many can be found on the Internet with user-friendly summaries – see the FAB Research website for examples). In some areas, reliable evidence really is lacking. The best thing you can do is to keep an open mind – but not so open that your brains fall out, as they say! Read, observe, talk to people, ask questions, weigh up all the evidence and make your own mind up which advice you're going to follow.

I thought doctors say a good diet is important so we don't get fat? My child seems slim and fit even though he eats mostly chicken nuggets and chips, and he won't touch fruit and vegetables.

A poor diet doesn't always make you fat, and your child may look 'slim and fit', but have you seen his insides? It can sometimes take years for the effects of bad eating habits to show, but a diet of highly processed foods and insufficient fruit and vegetables really can damage physical and mental well-being. Some children are more resilient than others – and yours may be one of the lucky ones (so far) – but the time to start making some changes is now.

Surely if what the big companies say is wrong, the Government would ban them from saying it?

I wish! Sadly, economics and politics play a huge role here – for example, look at how long it took for the tobacco industry to be exposed for what they were really doing. The Government can't regulate everything, and their perspective is usually very short term. They are also keen to avoid offending the big players in industry – for many reasons, some good (to try to protect jobs that might be lost, for example) and some not so good.

Why aren't doctors and many other health professionals trained more in nutrition?

In my view, they need to be – and the more enlightened ones carry on studying such subjects after their initial training. In defence of the others, they are often so busy dealing with acute problems that preventative approaches may take second place, and they have little or no time to study. In my opinion, some training in the effects of nutrition on behaviour really would reduce the workload of most professionals in our health, education, social services and criminal justice systems, with benefits all round.

Who am I to question the experts?

Well, for a start, you'll find that the experts usually disagree! As to 'who you are', please try to have a little more faith in your own good sense. If you're a parent, you'll probably know more about your child than anyone, and if you're reading this book then you've got what it takes to find out more. Then make your mind up as to the best course of action. It's usually one based on common sense and grounding in all the facts. I'd say always question the experts. (If they can't handle that – they're no experts!)

Summary

1. The fast food and 'convenience' foods that dominate many children's diets are often of very poor nutritional quality. If you knew what really goes into some of these, it's very unlikely that you'd keep buying them.

2. The big food and drink companies and the pharmaceutical industry have been making huge profits out of our ignorance, although there are signs that you – the consumers – are starting to wise up and 'dump the junk'.

3. It's now accepted that poor nutrition will affect your child's physical health. Recognition of the impact on *mental* health and performance is taking longer, and most professionals in health, education and other public services still receive little or no training in this area.

4. The big drug companies' influence over medical publishing (and most other media) has become so great that the editors of several top medical journals have felt the need to 'go public' about this. Drugs are not the only approach to many common ailments, and aren't always as effective as they're made out to be.

5. Dietary changes can improve behaviour, learning and mood – although these are not a substitute for other approaches, and we still need more research into the brain's nutritional needs.

6. Conflicting information and advice on food and diet has left most people very confused. Beware of hidden advertising, but do seek out and weigh up the information you need make up your own mind.

7. You need to think about your child's health and performance as a whole. Diet is only one aspect, so you will need to look at other areas, too.

8. There are no quick fixes or miracle cures – you must take charge, start from where you are and work slowly but steadily towards a healthier diet and lifestyle for your child.

9. Three basic dietary problems affect many children, and probably yours, too. Your child may react badly to some additives or foods, may be 'hooked' on simple carbohydrates, and is probably eating too many 'bad fats' and not enough essential fats. In this book you'll find out how to improve these things.

chapter 3

what's the problem?

Could Your Child Be Doing Better?

All parents will ask themselves this question at some time or other, and in most cases the answer will probably be 'Yes!' But if your child generally enjoys life, seems happy and fulfilled (most of the time) and causes no major problems for other people either at home or at school, then you should have no serious cause for concern. Nobody's child is perfect – just as there is no such thing as the perfect parent, or the ideal relationship – and every child has her own particular pattern of strengths and weaknesses. All children also go through 'phases' or periods when they seem to have specific difficulties in one or more areas. They may even appear to lose some skills or interests that they'd previously mastered. These are all normal aspects of development and 'growing up'.

However, if you think your child is struggling with real and persistent difficulties that are affecting her behaviour, learning or mood, what can you do? You obviously need to find out what's wrong, but do remember that things aren't always what they seem: the real, underlying problems aren't necessarily the ones you think they are. You have to start somewhere, though – so first, try to identify the broad areas that are causing most concern:

- Does your child have trouble making and keeping friends, or getting on with other family members?
- Does his performance at school fall short of what you'd expect from the abilities he shows in other ways?

- Does your child seem unhappy, or behave in a way that upsets, worries or puzzles others?
- Does he seem genuinely 'different' in some way from other children, to the extent that this is causing difficulties?

Next, discuss your concerns with others who know your child. If you're convinced that there really *is* a problem, always seek professional help. Start with your doctor, to check that your child has no physical health problems that could explain things. Talk to your child's teachers or carers. Referral to other specialists may be appropriate, but will usually come through these routes. If formal assessments are carried out, this may or may not lead to a 'diagnosis' of some kind of recognized behavioural or learning disorder – such as ADHD, dyslexia, dyspraxia, autism or some other label. (There are so many possible diagnoses that I won't even try to cover more than these, which are the most common ones.)

Labelling a child in this way can be helpful – but it can also have its drawbacks. Even if the diagnosis you've been given is an accurate one (which it may not be), there's still a great deal more to be discovered.

A 'diagnosis' is only a *description*; it is not an *explanation*.

These 'diagnoses' tell you nothing at all about the actual *causes* of your child's difficulties, which will vary from child to child and always involve a complex web of interacting factors.

The experts who make these diagnoses rely on checklists of particular features or symptoms, backed up with what they call a good 'case history', and sometimes (but not always) on the results of psychological or other tests. Sometimes the information is gathered mainly from parents, although at least some input from others is usually required – typically teachers or others who are familiar with the child in other settings. Perhaps unsurprisingly, parents often tell me that when they are finally given a diagnostic label for their child's difficulties (often after years of struggle and heartache), in the end this tells them nothing they didn't already know!

A diagnostic label can be very useful, though, for a number of reasons:

- You now have an explanation for yourself, and to give others. It explains that your child's difficulties are not down to 'laziness', 'carelessness', 'stupidity' or any desire to misbehave or otherwise cause offence. Sadly, though, it does not explain why your child has these difficulties.

- Your child now knows it's not his fault .This is worth emphasizing to him, if he's capable of understanding at this level. Most children dislike any label that makes them feel different – but try to help your child to see that this is not a disease, and is something he can overcome with the right strategies and help.

- You now know it's not your *fault*, either. Anything past is past – and you've now opened up opportunities to find out what works best for other children like yours.

- A formal diagnosis can often allow you to access specialist help and resources. Medical or other therapies may be available if needed; your child's school may be able to get funding for him to have extra help, or you may be able to get other assistance you may need with his care or education.

You don't have to just accept a label – let alone things that may be offered along with it. This is not to say that you should ever just dismiss out of hand medications or other treatments that your child's doctor or other professionals may offer, but do always discuss with them any concerns you may have, and get a second opinion (or referrals to other specialists) if necessary.

I'm not going to dwell for long on issues concerning the diagnosis of different kinds of behaviour and learning difficulties. These are beyond the scope of this book, and good information is available elsewhere.[1] What's more, the information I'll be giving you applies to pretty much *all children*, although I'll point out wherever I can the issues that may affect some kinds of children more than others.

It's worth emphasizing that the 'symptoms' or features that define ADHD, dyslexia, dyspraxia or autism are almost all 'dimensional'. That is, they are not categorical things that children do or don't have. They occur to *differing degrees*, and most of them simply form part of normal, individual variations in children's behaviour, learning and mood. There are no 'hard' objective tests and no 'biological markers' for any of these conditions.

The patterns of behaviour or learning that define ADHD, dyslexia, dyspraxia or autism are not 'diseases' or 'disorders' in any conventional medical sense.

This may help to explain why these kinds of conditions now seem to affect, to some degree, around 20 per cent of school-age children in the UK.[2] In most cases these children's difficulties don't even attract a formal diagnosis; and in many cases they go unrecognized by both parents and teachers. For reasons we don't yet know, more boys than girls are affected – though there's growing concern that many girls with these kinds of difficulties are underachieving and suffering in silence, simply because they don't behave the same way that boys with these difficulties do, so the problem goes unrecognized.[3]

So what should you look for? I'll give a brief overview of each of these conditions here, and the Resources chapter will tell you where you can get more information if you need this.

Dyslexia

If your child is dyslexic, this can only be formally diagnosed after he's spent many years struggling (and failing) to learn to read and write to the level expected for his age and general ability. Dyslexia involves more than just difficulties with written language, though. Early clues may include an unusual curiosity and an 'intuitive' kind of intelligence, with a tendency to think 'holistically', 'laterally' or 'divergently' rather than in a linear, sequential way. Dyslexic children are often particularly good at solving complex problems by seeing the bigger picture and using their creativity and logic to find original solutions. By contrast, despite their best efforts they experience failure and frustration in some tasks that other children find (literally) as simple as ABC.

A classic dyslexic area of weakness is 'working memory', especially for verbal, sequential information. Things can seem to go 'in one ear and out the other' – particularly sequences of information with no intrinsic meaning, like telephone numbers, security numbers or the sequence of letters in the alphabet. (If your child is dyslexic, you'll need to make sure that any important information of this kind is heavily 'over-learned', and/or that there are good back-up and reinforcing strategies.) Learning any verbal sequence – like the days of the week, or the months of the year – can be problematic, particularly more complex ones like reciting multiplication tables by rote. (This doesn't necessarily mean that the mathematics isn't understood – just that other ways of determining this will need to be found.) There may be persistent difficulties in telling left from right, and in learning to tell the time from a clock face. Difficulties with phonology (the sounds in words) are often regarded as a core feature of dyslexia, but this argument can be rather circular: We learn many of our advanced 'phonological skills' through learning to read – so any poor readers, including adults who are illiterate for social or cultural reasons, tend to find these tasks difficult.

When it comes to strengths, many dyslexic individuals show unusual talent in business, the visual arts and/or the sciences. A number of top financiers and outstanding business 'visionaries' are dyslexic[4] – and other professions with an over-representation of dyslexic adults include the arts, architecture, engineering, physical sciences and information technology. People with this profile are far less well suited to repetitive clerical or administrative jobs, but – provided they can avoid being judged too harshly on their spelling and punctuation – there's no reason why dyslexic individuals can't succeed in any occupation they may choose. One in 20 children is severely affected by dyslexia, and a further one in 20 has mild to moderate difficulties of the same kind – although the frequency in boys is slightly higher.

Common Indicators of Dyslexia

- Difficulties in reading and spelling that are relatively specific, and which interfere with academic achievement or daily living skills[5]
- Directional confusion (such as difficulty telling left from right)
- Poor working memory (especially for information that carries no obvious meaning in itself – like telephone numbers, or anything learned 'by rote')

- Particular difficulties in segmenting words into their individual sounds, or building up words from their component sounds, when writing or speaking
- May have early delays or difficulties learning spoken language
- Difficulties with ordering and sequencing information
- 'Intuitive', holistic style of problem-solving, using lateral or divergent thinking rather than following a linear, step-by-step strategy

Dyspraxia

Dyspraxia (or Developmental Coordination Disorder) is just as common as dyslexia, and again boys are more susceptible than girls. *Praxis* means 'doing', and the most obvious difficulties are usually in motor coordination, affecting either fine motor skills (like holding a pen), or gross (big) movements like running or throwing. Muscle tone may be poor, resulting in 'floppy' movement, or joints may be unusually flexible and 'bendy', leading to other kinds of postural and movement difficulties. As in dyslexia, left–right confusions are common – with particular difficulties coordinating actions between left and right sides of the body ('crossing the midline'). Thus, complex tasks that involve using both hands together (tying shoelaces, or doing up buttons) can prove frustratingly difficult to learn.

Not all dyspraxic children are overtly clumsy, though. The younger child may compensate for his unsteadiness by using excessive muscle tension, so the problems may go undetected. Later, when he tries to run, jump or dance, or to throw and catch a ball, his lack of coordination becomes apparent. Difficulty or failure in these areas can lead to anxiety or embarrassment, and more tension. He may therefore dislike and avoid team sports and games (or dancing, where he may epitomize the saying about having two left feet!). Dyspraxic difficulties apply more fundamentally to the planning and carrying out of any complex, sequenced actions. Organization and time-keeping are usually poor, and if he's dyspraxic your child may be slow to start and finish tasks. He may be able to do one thing properly at a time, but can easily get distracted and try to do too many things at once, so none gets finished.

As with dyslexia, this syndrome is independent of general ability, and strengths often include good reasoning and creative problem-solving skills, including lateral and holistic thinking. Verbal abilities are usually superior to non-verbal abilities, with particular weaknesses in visuo-spatial and attentional processing. Spelling and copying from a board, as well as handwriting, are usually areas of difficulty, although reading itself may or may not be a problem.

> 'Our son was always a cause for concern amongst his teachers. We cut additives like tartrazine from his diet, and that helped a lot, so he was no longer hyperactive. The other problems remained, though.
>
> In the end, the new Special Needs teacher suggested he might have dyspraxia, which proved to be the case. Yes, it's a label, but now that everyone understands, we have put strategies in place that will help him.
>
> One of those strategies is changing his diet to follow the principles you outline. It's early days yet, but I'm convinced we're already seeing a difference.'
> – Jan and Andrew

Because his verbal abilities may be very good, the discrepancy between these and his written work (particularly when under timed pressure) can lead others to think your dyspraxic child is just being lazy or careless, even when he's trying very hard indeed. When time is not limited, his work may be outstanding, which can add to that impression. No surprises that he may be susceptible to stress and frustration, often appearing irritable and moody as a result. With respect to attention, 'sensory overload' (too much happening at once) is often a problem for the dyspraxic child – but once absorbed in something, he may have an unusual capacity to maintain his concentration, provided that the environment offers few distractions. While naming no names at all, I will say that in my experience dyspraxic tendencies are perhaps over-represented within academia, because in highly able individuals, dyspraxia often manifests as the 'absent-minded professor' syndrome!

Common Indicators of Dyspraxia or Developmental Coordination Disorder

- Motor coordination skills substantially below the level expected from age, education and abilities in other areas[6]
- Delays in achieving motor milestones such as crawling, sitting and walking
- Difficulties with activities such as running, throwing and catching, tying laces, and handwriting (often using undue muscle tension in the efforts to compensate for poor coordination)
- Coordination difficulties interfere with academic achievement or daily living. Attentional and organizational difficulties may compound these problems.
- 'Intuitive', holistic style of problem-solving, using lateral or divergent thinking rather than following a linear, step-by-step strategy
- Verbal abilities usually superior to non-verbal abilities

Moving away from the core defining features, many dyspraxic children seem oversensitive to touch (complaining about 'scratchy' labels in clothes, or the fabric itself) – but like some children on the autistic spectrum, they may respond well to gentle physical pressure (liking tight hugs, and heavy bedclothes, for example). There are often general health issues, too, especially with respect to allergies or poor digestion – although these can affect many other children, too, of course.

Attention Deficit Hyperactivity Disorder (ADHD)

For their age, ADHD children are severely inattentive, or hyperactive and impulsive, or both. These difficulties must also be persistent over time and in different situations, and causing serious problems both at home and at school. If your child has ADHD, he probably has some other problems, too. 'Conduct disorder' and 'oppositional defiant disorder' (breaking rules and having problems with those in authority) are the most common ones, but anxiety, depression or other mood disorders are also linked with ADHD at both the individual and the family level, as are specific learning difficulties like dyslexia and dyspraxia. On the positive side, the energy of ADHD can be very productive when this is suitably channelled – and a willingness to take risks is part of most truly creative achievements in any domain.

Common Indicators of ADHD

In ADHD children, many of the following features or 'symptoms' occur much more than expected for the child's age and developmental level. They also occur persistently, both over time and across different situations.

Attentional Problems
- Makes careless mistakes in schoolwork and other activities, and doesn't give close attention to detail.
- Has difficulty organizing tasks and activities
- Forgetful in day-to-day activities (often loses 'tools' for a job, e.g. pencils, ruler, homework diary)
- Has difficulty sustaining attention in work or play. Even if instructions are understood, and intentions are good, they're not followed through
- Doesn't like sustained mental effort and may try to avoid it
- Often 'daydreams' (may appear to be 'elsewhere' when spoken to)
- Is easily distracted from a task by other things that are going on

Hyperactivity/Impulsivity
- Runs about or climbs when it's not appropriate to do so
- Fidgets, squirms or shows other signs of restlessness
- Has difficulty sitting or playing quietly
- Talks or chatters excessively

- Interrupts questions, conversations or games, and has difficulty waiting for his turn
- Shows impulsive behaviour in other ways: can't restrain himself, and often acts without thinking (may appear unaware or careless of potential dangers)

The consensus is that full-blown ADHD affects around 1 child in every 20 (5 per cent), but in some parts of the US up to 20 per cent of children are medicated with stimulant drugs (such as Ritalin) for the condition. Diagnosing ADHD properly involves ruling out some other medical conditions that can mimic it, including some hormonal and metabolic disorders, infectious diseases, neurological disorders, blood diseases, metal intoxications, cancers, genetic disorders, and various other disorders! In reality, resources are scarce (and stimulant drugs are cheap), so I'm sorry to say that in my experience this kind of detailed examination and testing certainly does not usually happen.

The 'ADHD' label can cover a multitude of different things. Any co-existing conditions can make a big difference; and either hyperactivity-impulsivity without inattention, or attentional difficulties without hyperactivity both fall into this same diagnostic category. (There used to be a separate label for the latter – Attention Deficit Disorder, or ADD.) This huge variability between different children who are given the ADHD label guarantees that no single management approach is going to 'work' with all of them. However, the first thing that's usually offered to parents if a child receives this diagnosis is stimulant medication.[7]

> I am not opposed to medication for ADHD, when it is clearly warranted – as I think it can be for some children – but I do think that it should always be the last resort, not the first.

We often hear that around 70 per cent of children with ADHD get at least some benefits from stimulant medications. That's very impressive, but it still leaves 3 children in every 10 who gain *nothing* from this kind of treatment – and many parents are understandably worried about possible side-effects, which can include difficulties with appetite and sleep, stunted growth, undesirable mental symptoms and increased risks of certain physical disorders. Any 'benefits' are also limited to behaviour, as no advantages for academic achievement have ever been demonstrated from the use of stimulant medications. (If they behave better and concentrate better, why don't they learn better?)

Most children can pay attention in at least some situations – it just depends on what these are, how motivated the child feels (what's the pay-off for him?), and what the child's perception is of the situation and his role in it (what demands does he feel under, and whom is he trying to impress?).

'… all that was needed was to change the "pay-off" [in a test], so that the child who tried to rush through the test without even trying would pay a worse penalty than the one who spent time trying to work out the correct answer. This time, the computer would not move on to the next item until some time had elapsed (the time that most non-ADHD children would spend, on average, trying to solve the problem). For any child who just pressed the button early, their reward was to have to look at a blank screen for the rest of the time period. The next item would appear no sooner that it would have done in any case. Under these conditions, the well-known "deficits" of the ADHD children simply didn't show up!'

What we don't usually hear is that in certain subgroups the proportion who benefit from stimulant medications is much lower. For example, it may drop to 30 per cent for children with anxiety as well as ADHD (and some evidence suggests that negative side-effects may be more likely in these children).[8] In other words, for 7 out of 10 of these anxious, often 'moody' ADHD children, stimulant drugs may be no use at all.

Before accepting any stimulant drugs for your ADHD child, or antidepressants, do make sure that 'bipolar disorder' has been ruled out. A large-scale survey of parents of bipolar children concluded that children with undiagnosed bipolar disorder can sometimes be 'thrown into manic and psychotic states, become paranoid and violent … unstable and suicidal …' if they are given these drugs before their mood has been stabilized.[9] Worryingly, they suggest that one-third of all children diagnosed with ADHD in the US are actually suffering from early symptoms of bipolar disorder. According to the American Academy of Child and Adolescent Psychiatry, '… a third of the 3.4 million children who first seem to be suffering with depression will go on to manifest the bipolar form of the disorder'. If medications are to be used, it's worth making sure they're the right ones.

Autism (ASD)

Autism is the most severe form of what is now recognized as a range of 'autistic spectrum disorders' (ASDs). Features include restricted or absent social and interpersonal skills; a preference for repetition and routine; and interest in objects over people. ASD is much more common in boys than girls (perhaps not surprisingly, given that autism has even been characterized as simply an extreme of the archetypal 'male' brain!).

If your child is autistic, he will show poor social interaction – in fact, this learned skill may be absent altogether. He'll try to avoid interacting through conversation or cuddles, and may be viewed as aloof, withdrawn and 'living in a world of his own'. Autistic individuals generally find objects easier to deal with than people – probably because the behaviour of objects is much easier for them to anticipate. A small percentage of autistic children have islets of high functioning-to-genius abilities and are known as Autistic Savants, but as with all the conditions considered here, ASD can occur in children with any level of general ability. In those with normal or high ability, areas of strength may include computing, engineering and any occupations where good 'people skills' are not essential.

The number of children diagnosed with ASD has increased dramatically in recent years. For example, in Scottish schools, diagnoses nearly trebled between 1998 and 2005. In the US, autism diagnoses in school-aged children rose from 5,400 in 1991–2 to a massive 97,800 in 2000–2001. Better recognition and diagnosis may account for some of this increase, but cannot explain it all away. Something else is going on. As I've emphasized, the autism label is purely descriptive, so looking for any single 'cause' is likely to be fruitless. The real causes are likely to be multiple, highly complex, and will vary between different children. In my view, the simplest broad-brush explanation is the combination of two things: on the one hand, increasing exposure to potential toxins (from synthetic chemicals, heavy metals and other environmental contaminants), and on the other, decreasing intake of many essential nutrients needed to 'defuse' and get rid of those toxins. For genetic reasons, some children may have less efficient 'detoxification' systems, and/or metabolic inefficiencies that increase their need for certain nutrients. It is interesting that the earliest reports of autism show that it was regarded as a metabolic disorder, and special diets were often recommended. (See the Resources chapter for some excellent books on this subject.)

Common Indicators of ASD

Autism is now recognized as having varying degrees of severity, captured by the term 'autistic spectrum disorders'.

- Before the age of three, shows delays or regression (permanent loss of previously acquired abilities) in social interaction and language skills
- May show repetitive movements of part or all of the body (rocking, tapping, head-banging or self-stimulation)
- At any age, shows a lack of spontaneous, imaginative play appropriate to his age
- Shows poor or limited 'non-verbal' behaviours, such as eye contact, facial and body expressions
- Has difficulties making friends and reciprocating socially or emotionally (may not appear interested in showing or telling you things)
- Has difficulties with speech and limited use of gestures (if language skills are developed, conversational skills are still poor)
- Shows restricted patterns of behaviour, interests and activities (preference for repetition and familiarity, and behaviour may be ritualized)
- May be preoccupied with certain objects or their parts (for example, often attracted by things that move or spin)

Alternative labels have been springing up in recent years. Some emphasize the more positive aspects of these conditions, and tend to cross-cut the conventional diagnostic labels. The Highly Sensitive Child (HSC) is a good example, and in her popular book of the same name, Elaine Aaron does an excellent job of capturing many of the qualities that these children show.[10]

Your child may be in august company: Einstein appears to have exemplified the 'absent-minded professor' syndrome. He was dismissed at school as a daydreamer with little or no potential, and he was also sacked from two teaching jobs for his poor spelling – consistent with dyslexic/dyspraxic traits. More recently, he has also been claimed for the autistic genius camp for his supposed obsessiveness and lack of social skills!

Overlaps

Although they're usually regarded as separate conditions, in practice there's a big overlap between dyslexia, dyspraxia, ADHD and the autistic spectrum. Most children who qualify for one of these labels also show features of one or more of the others.

- 30–50 per cent of dyslexic and ADHD children have clear dyspraxic tendencies.
- 30–50 per cent of dyspraxic children have notable dyslexic difficulties.
- Attentional and working memory problems are found in all three conditions.

Always remember that your child is an individual. Reality is much messier than any of the discrete diagnostic labels we may use to 'pigeon-hole' children, so even if your child has one diagnosis already, be aware that this may not give the whole picture.

This is a summary of a letter I received from Jane, a grateful parent:

'As a baby, when Peter started on solid food he became tearful and wakeful, began to projectile vomit and lost weight dramatically. He developed a high temperature and a red rash so bad they thought it was scarlet fever! In fact, he reacted badly to many foods including eggs, wheat, artificial food colourings and other additives. When he started school, teachers said he was hyperactive – but with advice from the Hyperactive Children's Support Group we modified his diet, and Peter improved dramatically.

All was fine until he started falling behind at school, and this time (aged 10) he was diagnosed as dyslexic. I heard about your research and increased his omega-3 fatty acid intake. This seemed to do wonders, and he quickly became an above-average pupil.

Then at 15, Peter started using cannabis, which he reacted to badly. Within a year he was admitted to an adult psychiatric ward and was prescribed powerful drugs (even though he still had easy access to cannabis in the hospital!). His prognosis was said to be poor. The hospital diet contained lots of foods I knew didn't suit Peter, and I explained his history of food allergies, but they wouldn't listen. The doctors just decided he had "mental health problems". At no time was his physical health investigated.

Then I attended an inspiring conference on diet and behaviour. With specialist help, I was able to persuade the hospital staff to put Peter onto a new dietary regime. This made such a difference – and once he himself could understand what had happened to him, he agreed to stop smoking cannabis. Within four weeks he went from being a seriously ill young man to near normal.

Six months later, Peter was back at college and enjoying a social life with family and friends. Without the help of researchers and scientists, I really think Peter would still be a lost child in an adult ward. Thanks to them, I have my son back – the greatest gift anyone could have given me.'

Keeping It in the Family

Conditions like ADHD, autism and dyslexia tend to run in the same families, but the reasons for this aren't always down to genetics. The *predisposition* to these kinds of difficulties is certainly under some degree of genetic influence – and research is starting to tease out some possible 'candidate genes' that may play a part. However, let's get one thing clear: there are no individual genes 'for' any of these conditions. Many different genes can contribute to an individual's risk; these differ between individuals, and some are widely distributed in the general population. What's more, no genes can operate without an environment. This includes other genes, various influences that operate while a baby is still in the womb and many, many others that continue to switch genes 'on' and 'off' during every single moment of your child's life.

These influences include your child's diet – because nutrition interacts with genetics in two main ways:

1. Some genes can affect the way in which your child absorbs and uses (metabolizes) different nutrients. This is just another way of saying that different people have different nutrient requirements.
2. *Nutrients can actually affect the expression of many genes.* This means that you might be genetically 'at risk' for something like ADHD or depression, but you won't necessarily develop the symptoms if your environment (including diet) is good.

Genes are not destiny – and it's worth pointing out that families often share dietary habits as well as genes! How good are yours?

What's Beneath the Surface?

Your child's behaviour and performance at school (or in other things she does) are just the things you can see on the surface. These are often the main focus of programmes aimed at changing or influencing children's behaviour and learning, some of which can be very helpful. But other powerful forces at work are often well hidden. What your child is thinking will affect her behaviour and performance. (If she thinks the teacher sees her as stupid or lazy, for example, she'll be rather less likely to do what she's told at school; or if she doesn't understand why you won't let her stay up late, this could lead to a tantrum.) What she's thinking, though, is usually much harder to tell than what she's doing. It's beneath the surface.

You can help here by doing your best to develop a good relationship with your child. Talk to her and try to find out what she thinks. Even more important – *listen* to her without judging; so that she feels able to tell you what's going on in her mind. With some children, this kind of communication can be hampered by their very difficulties – especially if these are with language, for example, or social interactions. Sometimes a professional with the right experience can help – but keep doing what you can, and always remember that your child's thoughts and beliefs (based on whatever her perceptions and powers of reasoning are) will affect her behaviour and performance.

At the next level, your child's feelings will colour her thinking. If she feels bad about herself, she's more likely to develop negative thought patterns and beliefs, and this can prevent her from trying to learn how tackle her own problems. The same applies to you, of course. If you ever find yourself thinking 'I've failed as a parent' or 'I really can't deal with this', it will be because your own feelings at that moment are negative ones. You may be feeling overwhelmed, but when those feelings pass, you'll think differently. It's the same with your child.

Underneath your feelings (the things you can recognize, identify or put a name to), there is another level at work – and that involves your emotions. We're on the physical level here – because your raw emotions actually reflect the constant shifts and changes going on at the level of your bodily functions, including your heart rate, your breathing, your digestion, and even the workings of your immune system. These things are governed by your 'autonomic nervous system' (which works without your conscious intervention, and usually without even your conscious awareness). They do, however, have a very powerful effect on everything you think, feel and do. In fact, your emotions are literally what 'move you' or motivate you to do anything. Think of them as 'e-motions' – reflecting physical (electrical and chemical) energy in motion.[11]

At the very foundations, then, your emotions are affected by your physiology. In other words, the state of your body affects the state of your mind – and vice versa, of course.

When you use your mind to choose to do something – like going for a walk, talking to a friend, eating something healthy, or hugging your child instead of shouting at him – your decision will affect what happens to you physically. The exercise and fresh air from going for a walk will affect your body chemistry positively (whereas slumping in front of the TV or drowning your sorrows with a drink will have different physical effects). Sharing your concerns with a friend, or showing your child you love him, can also help you (and them) to relax and feel better – so you think more positively, and as a result will probably perform better than you otherwise would. Either eating something healthy or consoling yourself with junk food will also affect your body chemistry – but rather differently in each case.

I hope you can see why nutrition is the real bedrock of this physiological level – because your body's repertoire will be influenced by the chemical raw materials that it has available. And the same goes for your brain. This is why food and diet really are fundamental to your child's development, both physically and in the way his mind works.

Your child's behaviour (and the mind–body links that create it) can be likened to an iceberg: only one small part is showing, but a whole lot more is going on beneath.[12]

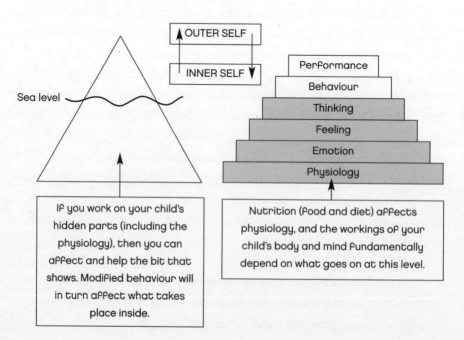

OUTER SELF

INNER SELF

Performance

Behaviour

Thinking

Feeling

Emotion

Physiology

Sea level

If you work on your child's hidden parts (including the physiology), then you can affect and help the bit that shows. Modified behaviour will in turn affect what takes place inside.

Nutrition (food and diet) affects physiology, and the workings of your child's body and mind fundamentally depend on what goes on at this level.

What's Behind the Labels?

As we've seen, the 'diagnosis' of most developmental difficulties focuses only on a few core features of behaviour and learning – as though these exist in isolation from the rest of the child. In fact, some other features seem common to almost all children with these kinds of labels – and many of them are consistent with known nutritional deficiencies and imbalances. I've always pointed this out in my own talks and lectures, and parents and front-line professionals usually recognize the picture (even if many researchers and so-called 'experts' prefer to keep focusing on their artificial pigeon-hole labels).

Then, a few years ago at a conference, I met another speaker whose introduction to her talk was almost exactly the same as mine! Her name is Dr Natasha Campbell-McBride, and you'll hear more about her work in later chapters. When her own child was given the 'autism' label and she was told that nothing could be done, she went and studied nutritional medicine, and worked out a diet that got him doing well at a normal school. What Natasha had recognized – and what my own work was uncovering – is that it's all to do with 'guts and brains', and the links between them – in which your child's immune system plays a major part. But where my talk went on to focus on research into omega-3 fatty acids – which you'll hear more about in Chapters 8 and 9 – Natasha's talk emphasized the critical importance of gut bacteria (often called 'gut flora'), which you'll hear more about in Chapter 5. These are crucial to your child's digestion, helping him to absorb and manufacture key nutrients. What's more, along with omega-3 fatty acids, they also play a vital role in programming and supporting his immune system.

Guts and Brains

Autistic spectrum disorders in particular have been linked with digestive difficulties – but in fact all the conditions I've been describing in this chapter typically involve a history of gut problems, immune dysfunction, and difficulties with mood, arousal and perceptual skills as well as behaviour and learning. In Natasha's book *Gut and Psychology Syndromes*[13] she explains the connections between all these things, and provides details of her special diet for dealing with even extreme cases of autism. I'd recommend this book to any parent or professional dealing with these syndromes, and although the full diet is not necessary or suitable for every child, the principles are – and she includes some great recipes, too!

To illustrate some of the features Natasha and I had noticed in the children we were seeing, ask yourself whether any of the following apply to your child:

- bottle-fed rather than breastfed (for whatever reason)
- prescribed antibiotics at a young age (for repeated ear infections, for example)
- prone to feeding difficulties/a fussy eater from weaning
- suffers from allergies, repeated infections or other immune-system dysfunction
- has other physical health problems (including digestive difficulties, headaches or other aches and pains)
- has sleep problems
- is prone to anxiety, depression or mood swings
- is very susceptible to stress, with low frustration tolerance, possibly aggression
- has perceptual as well as behaviour or learning difficulties, including visual and auditory symptoms.

The immune system has an extremely powerful influence on both our guts and our brains, from early development right through life. It plays a huge part in the connections between mind and body – but to work properly, your child's immune system needs both the right nutrients and a proper balance of healthy gut flora. If your child shows many of the features above, read on.

Breastfeeding

In most cases, breastfeeding provides babies not only with the best possible nutrition, but also with various immune-enhancing substances – including what should be good bacteria from mother to get the baby's own population of gut flora started.[14]

Allergies, Infections and the Immune System

Children with dyslexia, dyspraxia, ADHD or autism seem unusually prone to 'atopic' (allergic) conditions like asthma, eczema and hay fever, indicating immune-system imbalances. Many have ear infections in early childhood, typically treated with antibiotics – which destroy the good gut bacteria along with the bad, weakening the immune system and perpetuating the problems. Other physical health complaints, including headaches, stomach aches and other digestive disorders, all fit the picture of 'gut dysbiosis' (an unhealthy imbalance of gut flora) and a lack of key nutrients including omega-3 fatty acids.

Sleep and Arousal

Disordered patterns of sleep and arousal from early infancy are common in children with behaviour and learning difficulties, and may reflect nutritional imbalances or adverse food reactions. Many parents of children given omega-3 fatty acids in our trials have reported that their child's sleep improves as a result. This is anecdotal evidence at the moment (we were not formally assessing sleep), but it fits with existing evidence and needs investigating further.

Emotional Sensitivity and Mood Swings

If your child is underachieving because of his behaviour or learning difficulties, it's understandable that he may suffer anxiety, loss of self-esteem or even depression. Mood swings or temper outbursts may reflect the sheer frustration he feels. However, some factors – including diet – could contribute to both the behavioural/learning difficulties and the emotional ones. The evidence that nutrition affects mental health has recently been reviewed by two UK charities as part of a campaign to raise public and professional awareness of these links.[15]

> 'I've spent the last few years to-ing and fro-ing between the GP, the specialist and the educational psychologist. They've done their best but at no time has anyone suggested link between his social and physical problems and his diet. Why not? It makes so much sense. My son is changing physically and emotionally for the better since we changed his diet.' – Jo

Susceptibility to Stress

Does your child become easily 'stressed' and show a low tolerance for frustration? (Do you?!) Some children show this as hostility and aggression. Others 'internalize' their stress instead, and may complain of stomach aches and nausea, or generally seem solemn or withdrawn. Stress is a likely consequence of the difficulties any child may experience if he feels 'different'. Repeated feelings of failure and humiliation will only serve to exacerbate symptoms. Do what you can to support your child, but again, that has to include feeding him a nutritious diet (and making sure he gets enough exercise). We'll be looking in more detail at the nutrient deficiencies and imbalances that can add to mental stress in Chapter 4, and you'll find other tips and strategies that may be helpful in dealing with stress in Chapter 10.

Perceptual Anomalies

Perceptual problems can sometimes interfere with the development of communication and language skills (both spoken and written).[16] Standard auditory or visual tests may show your child's hearing and sight are normal, or even super-sensitive, but do get this checked out. If you're still concerned, specialist assessments may be helpful, as the perceptual skills we take for granted are highly complex: literally, your child may not see things the way you do! My interest in omega-3 came from my early work on visual symptoms in dyslexia, because these fatty acids (along with vitamin A and other essential nutrients) play key roles in vision.

What You Can Do

So, your child may or may not have a label. The great news is you can do something for him. In the following chapters I'll explain why a varied diet based around fresh vegetables and fruit, good-quality protein, the right kinds of fats and the right kinds of carbohydrates (starches) could make a big difference to your child – and to you. We'll also look at digestion and how it can go wrong, and I'll point out three main things you can do to improve your child's diet. Some helpful tips and a plan of action are provided in later chapters – but looking ahead, you should be able to ensure better health and well-being for your child (and you!) if you just stick to these essentials.

	Phase out	Phase in
Diet	■ Obvious sugars	■ Complex carbohydrates
	■ Hidden sugars	■ Essential omega-3 fatty acids
	■ Simple carbohydrates	(in oily fish, walnut and flax
	■ Too many saturated fats	oils, and supplements)
	■ Too little protein	■ A wide variety of foods
	■ Protein late in the evening	■ Plenty of deeply-coloured
	■ Too few vegetables	vegetables and fruit
	■ Polyunsaturated cooking	■ Nuts, seeds and beans
	oils (vegetable)	■ Olive oil or butter/ghee for
	■ Additives	cooking with
	■ Sweet drinks	■ Enough protein in morning,
		daytime, and early evening
		■ Some carbohydrate later
		in the evening
		■ Foods that don't contain
		artificial sweeteners and
		unnecessary additives
		■ Plenty of water
Exercise	Little or no exercise	Exercise – at least three times a week, and preferably more. Even walking helps a lot
Sleep	Poor sleep hygiene	A regular sleep pattern. Keeping a diary helps
Structure	Letting your child dictate what happens when	Routine and structure
Environment	Environmental toxins	Do your best to identify them and get rid of their source
Knowledge	Ignorance/uncertainty	Research, read, see health professionals, and always ask questions

If you apply the information in this book, you may well find that your child's mood, behaviour, attention and learning will improve – and with them, his self-esteem. Remember, though, that diet is only one component in the effective management of behavioural and learning difficulties. Make sure you let any professionals dealing with your child know that you'll be adjusting his diet, and discuss this with them if possible. In particular, if your child is taking any medications, the levels may need to be monitored more closely.

Any good doctor should support you in implementing a healthy eating and exercise strategy – but some may be dismissive about 'food intolerances' or the effects of additives. If so, please feel free to show them this book or direct them to the FAB research website where they can read some of the evidence for themselves. Or find another doctor. Always remember that you probably know your child better than anyone, so don't mistrust your own instincts and observations. Become better informed and always keep looking for support and advice from other people who are qualified to provide this – both professional experts and other parents in your position.

'My son (12) has dyspraxia. I've finally worked out his symptoms are worse when he eats a high-carbohydrate diet with little protein or essential fatty acids. It's hard work sometimes to get him to eat and exercise properly, but even he is beginning to see cause and effect, and the strategies are beginning to work.' – Abi

FAQs

The Educational Psychologist says my son is showing some symptoms of ADHD and dyspraxia, but he's not fully in either camp. Can your programme still help him?

Yes, it can. The approach shown in this book should be suitable for almost any child, but always remember that diet is only one component. You're also likely to need other assistance in managing his symptoms, so discuss this with the Educational Psychologist and other professionals if necessary.

My child fits a lot of the criteria you've outlined for dyslexia and dyspraxia. As I can see he probably has both, do I need to see a health professional?

Yes. Ideally you want the help of both health and education professionals (working together) to assess your child and explore with you the best management methods. If your child does get formally 'diagnosed' with either or both of these conditions, his school may also be able to get additional funding so that he can receive any extra help or equipment he may need.

You say there's been a rise in the number of children suffering from these behaviour and learning disorders. Why is that?

Many people have a 'genetic tendency' towards ADHD, autism and other conditions, but these syndromes simply aren't triggered because of their good lifestyle and diet. Children today are often exposed to more potential toxins (synthetic chemicals and pollutants), less exercise, and a poor diet that's lacking in many vital nutrients. These things can damage children's brains as well as their physical health.

Summary

1. Labels like dyslexia, dyspraxia, attention deficit hyperactivity disorder (ADHD) and autism can be both helpful and unhelpful. These diagnoses are descriptions, not explanations – but they can provide reassurance and should open the way to effective help.
2. These conditions affect around 20 per cent of school-age children in the UK to some degree, although more boys than girls are affected.
3. Most of the 'core features' used to define these kinds of behavioural and learning difficulties simply reflect extremes of normal individual differences.
4. There are substantial overlaps between all of these conditions. Children who only show symptoms of one of them are the exception, not the rule.

5. Genetic factors play some part in a child's risk developing ADHD, dyslexia and autism, but environmental factors – including diet – are equally if not more important, and much easier to change.

6. Any child's behaviour and performance are only the 'tip of the iceberg'. These are affected by what that child is thinking and feeling, his emotions and, fundamentally, his physiology. Diet works at this fundamental level.

7. Our brains often reflect what's going on in our guts – and the two are closely linked by the immune system and other chemical messenger systems.

8. Children with behavioural and learning difficulties often show other features and physical health symptoms (including allergies) that indicate digestive and nutritional imbalances.

9. A healthy balance of gut flora and the right dietary fats (such as omega-3) are needed for good digestion and a well-functioning immune system. A healthy, well-balanced diet (and exercise) can help to ensure this.

10. Dietary approaches should never be regarded as the only way to manage behaviour and learning difficulties, but good nutrition is fundamentally important and may enhance the effectiveness of other therapies.

part two

the good,
the bad
and the
unhealthy

chapter 4

essential nutrients and your child's diet

Whatever his specific difficulties may be, a balanced, varied, wholesome diet that provides all essential nutrients really can make a big difference to your child. Poor nutrition contributes to infections, inflammatory problems (like asthma) and obesity (with all of its knock-on effects); it can also affect your child's sleep, mood, behaviour and learning. As you saw in Chapter 2, the facts about the food children are eating aren't good, but until you – the parents – really take charge, there's little sign that the Government or the big food-producing companies are going to look after you or your loved ones.

In this chapter I'll outline the basic dietary components your child needs, and point out some of the ones most likely to be lacking. In later chapters we'll look at some of these in more detail. Briefly, your child must have enough:

- water
- protein
- fats (in the form of essential fatty acids)
- carbohydrates (in the form of complex carbohydrates and fibre)
- vitamins
- minerals
- antioxidants
- moderate exercise – yes, this is part of a good diet!

A Long Time Ago

Our hunter-gatherer ancestors ate a very wide range of nuts and seeds, edible roots and leaves, wild animals (usually small, and very occasionally a big one), fish, shellfish, berries and wild beans.

So: plenty of protein, vitamins and minerals and complex carbohydrates, little saturated fat, and equal proportions of omega-6 to omega-3 fatty acids.

↓

Agricultural Revolution

Smaller variety of foods eaten, a much greater proportion of cereals (grains), and less fruit and vegetables. Meat consumption decreased as well.

So: decreased vitamin and mineral intake, and a higher proportion of omega-6s than omega-3s.

↓

Industrial Revolution

This began in the late 18th century, so we needed lots of cheap food for workers who arrived in droves to work in towns and cities. New preservation and production methods were introduced, meaning foods could be transported long distances in bulk quite cheaply. The use of vegetable oils, refined starches and sugars rose sharply. Consumption of farmed meat rose by about 200 times per person per year!

So: white flour goods became the norm ... and carried less than a quarter of vitamins B_6 and E, magnesium and zinc than their wholemeal counterparts.

Sadly, most of our children eat diets lacking at least some key nutrients. Even for those of you trying to avoid the obvious junk, some of the dietary advice you've been getting from governments and their agencies has been positively misleading. In the US, government agencies offered the so-called 'Food Pyramids' as guidelines for planning a 'balanced' diet. Nutrition experts at the Harvard School of Public Health (HSPH)[1] have pointed out some serious flaws in these – and in the contribution of the food industry

The Twentieth Century

This saw an increase in global food trade, and also discoveries about how to make synthetic vitamins. Foods began to be 'fortified' with vitamins and minerals.

The irony was, during the two World Wars, we began to eat more healthily once again! Rationing meant poorer families received more proteins and micro-nutrients, and richer people ate less fat (from meat and processed foods) and sugar. At the same time, it was discovered how to dehydrate vegetables and eggs, and to produce processed meat.

After WWII, policies were introduced to make sure we could produce our own food, and not rely too much on supplies from other countries. Ready-prepared foods took off.

Buying flour and other ingredients plummeted, and meat consumption rose again. A decrease in the amount of fruit and vegetables eaten began, and there was a dramatic increase in the consumption of hydrogenated (including trans) fats, refined starch and sugar, and numerous artificial additives.

The Twenty-first Century

Where are we now? Well, eating more than ever, and suffering more diet-related problems such as obesity, mental ill-health and behavioural problems. In the last 60 years, there's been a 34% decrease in UK vegetable consumption, and a 59% drop in consumption of oily fish (omega-6/omega-3 ratios have reached an all-time high).

We are eating far more processed foods (and thus more saturated and hydrogenated fats, salt and sugar, more artificial additives and fewer micronutrients), especially those on low incomes.

in helping to build these dodgy pyramids. In the Appendix you'll find a more appropriate 'Healthy Eating Pyramid' which the Harvard experts have designed. (You may also find it educational to look at their website and play 'spot the difference'!)

If you really don't feel you need to know about all the details of the different nutrients your child needs, don't worry. Just use the HSPH guidelines and the plan you'll find in Chapter 11, and you shouldn't go too far wrong. But understanding *why* the different nutrients are so important may help to motivate you, and your child, so in this chapter we'll take a look at them (and then in Chapter 5 we'll look at what actually happens to food once your child has eaten it).

Water

Is your child drinking enough water? Fizzy, sweet drinks (or tea or coffee) are not acceptable substitutes; most have undesirable ingredients and may even cause you to *lose* water. Your body is 50–70 per cent water (and your brain 85 per cent) – but you lose it constantly through breath, sweat, urine and faeces. You can only survive a few days without water, as its remarkable properties help to mediate every function in your brain and body.

Without enough water your child will become dehydrated, which can lead to headaches and tiredness. His concentration and his digestion will be impaired, along with most other functions. Make sure your child drinks enough at home, and that he takes water to school with him if the school doesn't provide this. Your child can also get water from food, especially fruit and vegetables, or fruit juices (best diluted – by you) or herbal teas. Unfortunately, vending machines that sell fizzy drinks are found in most schools. Most soft and fizzy drinks can upset blood sugar levels, but schools often depend on the income the vending machines generate.

Macronutrients

Macronutrients is the term used for the three main food groups: proteins, fats and carbohydrates. Each fulfils a particular nutritional need, and in a 'balanced' diet all of them must be present – within limits. It isn't the overall *quantity* of protein, fat or carbohydrate that really matters, but the *quality*. We'll discuss protein briefly in this chapter – but children's consumption of carbohydrates and fats is so often 'wrong' in quality terms that we'll look at these topics separately in Chapters 7 and 8.

What's the right balance?

The most suitable dietary balance of macronutrients depends on your child's lifestyle, current health and metabolism. Both 'low-fat' and 'low-carbohydrate' (high-protein) diets have been popularized in numerous 'miracle' weight-loss programmes. Most of these are aimed at adults, but each usually claims to 'cure' all kinds of ills at the same time. Generally speaking, none of these diets is suitable for children (or you!), unless prescribed for medical reasons.

A 'reasonable' balance of macronutrients includes around half of total energy (calories) from carbohydrates, one-fifth from protein and one-third from fat – but don't even think of spending your time trying to calculate this! Some sensible ground rules about what kinds of foods your child should be eating (and which ones to avoid) should be enough, and those are provided, with recipes, in Chapters 10–14.

> The **type and quality** of proteins, fats and carbohydrates that your child consumes matter infinitely more than the overall quantities.

Proteins

Proteins are the main building-blocks of living things, so a regular supply of protein is essential for brain and body growth and maintenance. The very structure of most of our tissues – like muscles, tendons or bones – depends on proteins. The enzymes that assist or enable almost all biochemical reactions are usually made of proteins; the receptors and other channels for signalling within and between cells are mostly made of proteins. Many of the messenger-molecules that carry information via those channels are also proteins, or fragments of proteins called 'peptides'.

When we eat and digest proteins, they're broken down into their component amino acids. There are 20 types of amino acids we use. When we need a new protein, it's assembled from specific amino acids arranged in a particular sequence (a sequence dictated by your genes). The resulting chain of amino acids then folds up in a special way to achieve the proper structure of that protein. Peptides, which are used as important signalling molecules in many brain and body systems, are simply shorter chains of amino acids.

There are eight 'essential amino acids' that we can't make for ourselves, so they must come from our diets. You can make the other 12 amino acids your body needs.

> The eight essential amino acids go by the names of: isoleucine, leucine, lysine, methionine, phenylalanine, threonine, tryptophan and valine. Some lists include a ninth: arginine.
> Don't worry about learning the names – just make sure your child eats a range of protein-rich foods.

We need a regular intake of good-quality protein to build, repair and run many body systems, so make sure your child gets enough. Don't overdo it, though – because too much protein can affect your kidneys – but most people don't eat too much protein unless they're on some diet that leaves out much of another food group (like carbohydrates), and that's not recommended. Your child needs to eat only a handful of protein (a quarter or less of the plateful) at any meal, but just *vary the type*. This could include lean meat, fish, eggs, cheese, nuts, or beans and pulses.[2]

Animal and Vegetable Protein

Vegetarians need to be aware of the essential amino acids. Most animal foods contain 'complete protein', meaning that it provides all the essential amino acids we need. By contrast, most vegetarian foods contain only some of them,[3] so the others must be obtained by eating the right combinations of legumes, pulses, nuts and grains.[4]

Protein – Summary of Key Points

Proteins play numerous roles. They are:

- a source of amino acids/peptides
- key building-blocks of tissue
- used to translate DNA codes so the correct new proteins can be assembled
- what most enzymes are made from
- signalling molecules (e.g. neurotransmitters)

Either too much or too little protein can have damaging effects on health.

Fats (Lipids)

Fat is not just a convenient store of energy. Certain dietary fats are absolutely essential to your child's physical and mental health, being needed for:

- the structure and flexibility of *all* cell membranes
- regulating the transport of all substances into and out of cells
- supporting the immune system, heart and circulation and hormone balance
- maintaining the structure and function of your brain and nervous system.

Fats are dealt with in detail in Chapter 8, but in summary, saturated (hard) fats like those found in butter, cream and meat fat are not a problem *in moderation*. In fact, it's better to use these for cooking than vegetable oils (which can produce toxic fats when heated). Olive oil and other monounsaturated fats (found in nuts and seeds) have some health benefits, but the fats your child needs most are the natural polyunsaturated fats, particularly special ones called omega-3 fatty acids (found in oily fish and flax oils) and omega-6 (found in vegetable oils, grains, meat, eggs and dairy produce). You and your child are far more likely to lack omega-3 than omega-6 fats – which could even be increasing stress, anxiety or depression in both of you.[5]

Carbohydrates

Carbohydrates are dealt with in detail in Chapter 7, but basically fall into three types:

1. Sugars – used for energy and found in fruits, some vegetables, milk and most processed foods and drinks
2. Starches – used for energy and found in all grains (including rice), all vegetables (especially potatoes) and most refined foods
3. Fibre – used to help digestion and bowel function and found in vegetables, whole grains and unrefined foods

Sugars occur naturally in fruit and milk, but can also be man-made (like sucrose or table sugar). *We have no dietary need whatsoever for manufactured sugars*, and these can play havoc with your child's blood sugar levels, energy levels, health and well-being, and behaviour.

Starches are made of many sugar molecules joined together. The body usually breaks them down into simple sugars (mainly glucose), which we use for energy. Some starches (like those found in mashed potatoes or chips, and the 'refined' starches in many processed foods) break down very quickly, causing your blood sugar levels to rise too fast. Adding protein (like cheese with your baked potato) or fibre (eating the potato skin too) can help to slow this process down. In Chapter 7 we'll see why complex carbohydrates, which we digest more slowly, are *much* better for your child than simple starches or sugars.

Micronutrients

'Micro' means *small* – so this term simply refers to nutrients that we generally need in much smaller quantities – vitamins and minerals, antioxidants, flavonoids and some others.

Vitamins

Vitamins are substances we absolutely need for health, but which must come from our diet, along with certain essential minerals. Unfortunately, many 'fast' foods are devoid of both. Let's look at some of the main vitamins and minerals your child may be lacking, and see why they're so important.

Fat-soluble Vitamins

Deficiency states are recognized for all vitamins, but let's start by making clear that in some cases too much can make you ill, too. If you ate polar bear liver, for example (it has happened!), you'd end up dying a nasty death, as just 500g (about half a pound) of polar bear liver will send a lethal dose of vitamin A into your body.

Fancy Trying Polar Bear Liver? Think Again

You'll suffer from:

- a throbbing headache
- stomach cramps
- diarrhoea
- drowsiness
- irritability
- dizziness
- hair loss
- enlargement of your spleen and liver ...

... and to cap it all, before you die, your skin will peel off!

Why is polar bear liver so rich in vitamin A? Well, vitamin A originates in marine algae, and then passes up the food chain in ever-increasing concentrations until it reaches carnivores such as polar bears, seals and arctic foxes.

Being stuck in the arctic with only a dead polar bear to eat is unlikely for most of us, but be aware of the risk of vitamin A poisoning. Don't misunderstand me: vitamin A's vital for your health, but it isn't water-soluble, so an excess can't be excreted in your urine (as happens with vitamins B and C). It gets stored in the body instead. As with all nutrients, you need a balance.

Vitamins A, D, E and K are all fat-soluble, so any excess is stored in fat-rich body tissues, mainly the liver. Between them these vitamins are responsible for a vast array of functions. You can get them directly from organ meats, some fats (including those in dairy products and eggs) and nut or seed oils, but we make most of our vitamin D from sunlight (if we get enough!), and a healthy gut (if we have one) will house bacteria that produce vitamin K. Let's see what these vitamins (should) do for your child.

Vitamin A (Retinol)

Vitamin A is critical for your immune system, vision, the brain and nervous system, the linings of your gut and lungs, and your bones and teeth. It's also essential for reproduction and growth.

In the developing world, vitamin A deficiency accounts for more infant blindness (and thus mortality) than any other single nutrient deficiency. Insufficient vitamin A can stunt your child's growth, weaken his immune system, damage the delicate linings of his guts and lungs, and impair his vision (particularly in dark conditions). It's essential to numerous cell-signalling systems in your child's body and brain.

Deficiency can reduce appetite and taste, and has been implicated in various autistic-type symptoms, including visual perceptual problems.[6]

Relatively few foods contain the active form of vitamin A (retinol). Organ meats (liver, kidneys, heart and brain) and oily fish are the richest dietary sources, but egg yolks and full-fat dairy products contain some. An artificial form (vitamin A palmitate) may be added to skimmed and semi-skimmed milk, but in anyone whose gut may be unhealthy (as we'll discuss in the next chapter) this might not be absorbed properly. Vitamin A can also be made within the body from beta-carotene and other carotenoids. These substances help give carrots and other orange, yellow or green vegetables their natural colours. There's no danger of accidental overdose with this route, as you only make what vitamin A you need from carotenoids. (As we've seen, active vitamin A can be toxic in excess – which is why warnings are issued to pregnant women to be careful about their intake – especially from supplements.)

According to the latest UK survey, your child is far more likely to get too little vitamin A than too much. In every age group, between one-half and two-thirds of all children were found to be getting less than the official daily 'adequate intake' of vitamin A from their diets. For those aged between 11 and 14 years, frank dietary deficiency was found in more than one in eight boys, and one in five girls.[7] If you think your child's intake may be too low, you could encourage him to eat more oily fish, liver, pâté or cod liver oil – but only in moderation, as these all provide active vitamin A. You can be more liberal with the carrots, oranges or other sources of beta-carotene from fruits and vegetables, as it's hard to overdo it on these. The worst that's likely to happen is that your child's skin might temporarily turn a harmless shade of orange! (This did actually happen once to someone in my lab who adored tangerines, and ate them by the netful! She was a little alarmed, but came to no harm and learned her lesson: *Vary* what you eat.)

Vitamin D

Vitamin D is critical for building strong bones and teeth, and has extremely wide-ranging influences on most of your bodily systems – and your brain.

Vitamin D is the 'sunshine vitamin', formed naturally by your skin when it's exposed to the ultra-violet light that accompanies bright sunlight. In summer, you should make enough to last you through the darker days of winter. It's fat-soluble, so we can store it – but only if we're exposed to enough sunlight to build up a surplus, or get plenty in our diets. Few foods provide much vitamin D directly. Organ meats (liver, kidneys, etc.), oily fish or full-fat dairy produce are the main dietary sources.

A severe lack of vitamin D causes rickets (softening of the bones, leading to physical deformities). Less obvious deficiency is a major cause of osteoporosis, and is implicated in unexplained muscle and bone pain. That's because you need vitamin D – along with magnesium – to actually get calcium into your bones.

Active vitamin D is also one of the most powerful pre-hormones in the human body. Deficiency can contribute to heart disease, stroke, hypertension, various autoimmune diseases, diabetes, depression, chronic pain, osteoarthritis, muscle weakness, muscle wasting, birth defects, periodontal (gum) disease, and 17 varieties of cancer![8] There's also some evidence that vitamin D deficiency in pregnancy may contribute to hyperactivity and mental health problems in the next generation.[9]

This being so, it's not good news that almost one in four children and adults in the UK are seriously deficient in vitamin D each winter, and those who rarely go outside are at risk all year round. What's more: people with dark skins need up to 10 times the exposure to UV light that fair-skinned people do to make the same amount of vitamin D. This needs to be recognized, as indoor lifestyles (and even some habits of dress) can make it difficult to achieve enough exposure to sufficiently bright sunlight in the UK (or any other countries at a similar, or greater, distance from the equator).

If more than a quarter of our children and adults are frankly vitamin D deficient for large parts of the year, why haven't we heard more about this? Could it be because no one can patent sunshine, and there are no big profits to be made from selling vitamin D? Looking on the bright side (sorry) – at least sunshine is free: just make sure that you and your child get enough. Take care never to burn (if skin turns even slightly pink, that's more than enough), but the evidence suggests that *moderate* exposure can bring real health benefits, with no serious additional risks of skin cancer, which we *have* all heard plenty about.

TB and Vitamin D

During the Industrial Revolution, many people worked inside for long, long hours and were never out in the sunshine. TB (tuberculosis) was prevalent then, and sufferers were sent off to sanatoriums, where the medicine given was good food and sunshine. Many recovered. Incidentally, the better food alone didn't cure TB; the daylight really made a difference.

Vitamin E

Vitamin E has powerful antioxidant properties. It particularly helps to protect important fats that your brain and body need.

Vitamin E is actually a whole family of substances (different tocopherols and tocotrienols) which act as 'antioxidants' – discussed later in this chapter. Vitamin E helps to protect fats and fat-like substances from going rancid. It's needed by all our cells, but particularly those in the brain, nervous system and vital organs, because these are rich in essential omega-3 and omega-6 fatty acids, which are easily destroyed by 'oxidation'. Deficiencies of vitamin E and these fatty acids usually go hand in hand – and can contribute to some movement and coordination disorders.[10] Vitamin E deficiency may also result in fragility of the red blood cells which carry oxygen around your body.

More superficially, you may have seen vitamin E added to skin care products – aimed at helping keep your skin looking and feeling younger, or minimizing scar tissue. It's probably more effective to provide it from the *inside*, via a healthy diet that provides many other skin-nourishing nutrients! And you need to know that unless you have enough vitamin C with it, vitamin E won't work – and could even have the opposite effect. Basically, a whole range of different antioxidants work together – so you need them together, in the way they are usually provided by many natural foods. Vitamin E is found in wheatgerm, whole grains, seeds and nuts (including nut butters), *unrefined* vegetable oils and some fruits and vegetables. (Commercially produced bread without whole grains contains virtually no vitamin E, as milling destroys it. The same goes for refined oils – and Chapter 8 will give you more good reasons to avoid these.)

Vitamin K
Vitamin K is needed to help with blood-clotting.

Vitamin K activates some of the proteins involved in bone growth, and helps your blot clot when you cut or bruise yourself. It's found in soya, broccoli and spinach. If you have 'good' gut flora, some of these bacteria produce vitamin K for you.

Water-soluble Vitamins
Vitamin C and the B vitamins are water-soluble. Unlike A, D, E and K, they can't be stored by your body, so regular supplies are needed each and every day.

Vitamin C

Vitamin C is an all-round antioxidant and also essential to help build healthy bones, cartilage and teeth, to heal wounds, and a whole lot more.

A deficiency of vitamin C results in scurvy, a nasty disease that probably killed more than 2 million sailors on long voyages until it was discovered that a little lemon juice (or home-grown cress!) could prevent this completely. Vitamin C helps your immune system to protect you from viruses and bacteria. It's also a natural laxative. If your child is deficient in vitamin C, you might notice she's tired, may be prone to infections, any wounds are slow to heal, and her gums bleed easily.

Vitamin C is found in fruit (especially citrus fruits) and vegetables (especially leafy green ones). Don't be fooled by artificial vitamin C (ascorbic acid) added to soft drinks: many contain negligible amounts, and these drinks may also contain sodium benzoate – a common preservative that reacts with vitamin C to produce the toxic chemical benzene. (See Chapter 6 for more details on how this brain poison has been found in many soft drinks at up to 8 times the maximum that's legally permitted in drinking water.) The message is: get vitamin C from fresh fruits and vegetables – as many different types as possible!

Vitamin B

Vitamin B is actually a whole range of vitamins. All are used as co-enzymes – that is, they help other enzymes to perform numerous tasks around your brain and body. They're important for energy-production, maintaining a healthy heart, growth and reproduction of cells, and various mental functions including attention, thinking skills, coordination and memory.

The B vitamins all work together, so they're known as the 'B Spectrum'. I can't begin to do justice to them all here, although I've singled out a few for illustration. You can find plenty of details elsewhere if you want more information on individual members of the B family.[11]

Vitamin B Complex is essential for:

- normal growth and development
- energy-production
- functioning of the brain and nervous system

- functioning of the liver, kidneys and other organs
- health of the heart and circulation
- maintenance of other body tissues
- digestion
- immune function
- protein, fat and carbohydrate metabolism
- manufacture of red blood cells
- endocrine and hormonal systems
- cell division and DNA repair
- numerous enzyme systems

Better Nutrition Can Reduce Antisocial Behaviour

Results of a study by my colleague Bernard Gesch,[12] funded by the charity 'Natural Justice', revealed the remarkable effects of micronutrients on behaviour. This was the most definitive study yet showing the impact of diet on antisocial behaviour, including violence: a rigorously controlled trial involving 231 young offenders at a high-security prison in the UK.

Half the young men received daily multivitamin and fatty acid supplements (providing micronutrients only at doses close to recommended daily intakes). The others received identical-looking placebo capsules. Each prisoner was followed for up to nine months of dietary treatment, and his rate of offending during that time was compared with what had prevailed over the preceding nine months.

Offences fell by more than 25 per cent in the group receiving active supplements. When analyses were restricted to those who actually took the supplements for at least two weeks, the reduction was 34 per cent; and for violent offences, it was 37 per cent. In each case, there was no significant change in offending rates for those on placebo.

We Have a Choice

The food provided by the prison in Gesch's trial met official dietary requirements. The problem was that 'poor food choices' by prisoners compromised their nutritional status.[13] *Exactly the same problem applies to children, mental health patients and a very large proportion of the general population.*

Previous research had already indicated that improving diet could improve the behaviour of young offenders. In one study more than 20 years ago involving 3,000 imprisoned juveniles,[14] snack foods were replaced with healthier options, reducing the inmates' consumption of refined and sugary foods. *There followed a 21 per cent reduction in antisocial behaviour over 12 months, a 100 per cent reduction in suicides, a 25 per cent reduction in assaults, and a 75 per cent reduction in the use of restraints.* Although this study didn't use the rigorous placebo-controlled design employed by the Natural Justice trial, why weren't these findings followed up earlier? And why won't the Government – even now – put funding into doing something about this?

I hope you can see that the B vitamins (all of them) are *vital* to your child's overall health and well-being – and yours. General tiredness or lack of energy, lack of concentration, loss of appetite or skin problems are among the first signs of B deficiencies.

Some New Names for Pellagra?

Pellagra is a nasty disease caused by *lack of vitamin B_3* (sometimes known as niacin or 'nicotinic acid'). In its extreme form, pellagra is characterized by what doctors have nicknamed 'the three Ds' – dermatitis (burning or itchy, scaly skin, sometimes with mouth inflammation), diarrhoea and dementia. *Mental function can be seriously impaired.*

Children who in the past were diagnosed with mild or 'sub-clinical' pellagra showed signs of hyperactivity, inappropriate social behaviour, moodiness and problems with perception. Today children with these symptoms are often given labels like ADHD, ASD or dyspraxia/dyslexia, without anyone even thinking of assessing their nutritional status.

The early signs of vitamin B_3 deficiency are digestive problems, sometimes eating difficulties, muscular weakness and skin problems.

Vitamin B_3 is found in meat, poultry and fish, nuts and yeast extract. Your body can also make B_3 from an amino acid called tryptophan (found in eggs and dairy products).

- Dermatitis (dry, itchy or scaly skin) and diarrhoea, along with attention or memory problems, can indicate a lack of vitamin B_3.[15]
- Without B_6 you can't make serotonin (that feel-good neurotransmitter, a lack of which is usually the rationale for prescriptions of Prozac and other 'SSRIs'),[16] Recognized B_6 deficiency signs can include dermatitis (skin inflammation), depression, confusion and convulsions (and, as one drug company website puts it in a rare but laudable display of honesty, *'an outbreak of convulsions in infants did follow the inadvertent destruction of vitamin B_6 in infant formulas'*).[17] Incidentally, if you drink a lot of alcohol, use contraceptive pills or take oestrogen supplements (such as HRT), any of these can increase your chances of B_6 deficiency. As can a poor diet – although some people may need more B_6 than others for genetic reasons, as with any nutrient.
- Folate or folic folic acid (vitamin B_9) is present in almost all natural foods, but processing destroys up to 90 per cent. It's needed (with B_{12}) for DNA synthesis – required whenever you make new body or brain cells. Lack of folic acid during pregnancy can cause spina bifida – a serious developmental defect. In the US, flour is now re-fortified with folic acid. In the UK in April 2006 the Food Standards Agency sanctioned a consultation exercise, alongside consumer research, to decide on a recommendation to Government ministers about adding folic acid to some flours used in bread production.

- B_6, B_{12} and folic acid all work together to keep down levels of homocysteine. High levels of this substance are thought to be an important risk factor for heart disease and stroke.
- Deficiencies of B_{12} can lead to memory loss, disorientation, hallucinations and tingling in the arms and legs. Vegetarians, and particularly vegans, need to take B_{12} supplements because this nutrient is found only in animal products. Others – particularly the elderly – may have trouble absorbing B_{12} as they lack the 'intrinsic factor' needed to do this. Some people diagnosed with dementia or Alzheimer's disease may be suffering from vitamin B_{12} deficiency – which is rather more easily reversed.[18]
- Research is only just starting to explore the potential of B vitamins in managing depression (and other mood-related disorders), dementia (and other disorders of memory and thinking) and other mental health conditions. At present, the most rigorously controlled trials show only marginal evidence of benefits in depression and dementia[19] – but following pharmaceutical tradition, most studies use only a single B vitamin in isolation (usually B_6, B_{12} or folate). *Foods usually provide the whole spectrum – and other nutrients, too.*

Because we can't store B vitamins, anyone who's under stress or leads a hectic lifestyle runs the risk of depleting their supplies unless these are topped up regularly. Some medications can also deplete B vitamins – as can *eating processed foods*. Children with ADHD are often deficient in B vitamins, and several studies – including controlled trials – show some benefits from giving vitamin B_6 (with magnesium) to autistic children.[20]

So does your child get enough B vitamins? National surveys show that many children in the UK don't.[21] The diets of more than one in five girls between 11 and 18 years of age were seriously lacking in vitamin B_2 (riboflavin). Fewer boys and younger children had such low intakes, but blood tests of the *functional efficiency* of B_2 gave no cause for complacency. These showed B_2 deficiency in 75 per cent of boys and 87 per cent of girls between the ages of 4 and 18, and the risk increased with age. In girls aged 15–18 years, almost *all* of them (95 per cent) were B_2 deficient on this measure. Riboflavin is needed for normal cell function, growth and energy-production. Your teenage daughter may benefit rather more from knowing that a lack of B_2:

- will impair her coordination on the dance floor
- can also prevent conversion of vitamin B_6 to its active form (see above for what *that* could do); and
- can cause both fatigue and some nasty skin lesions – including dry, cracked or sore skin around the mouth or elsewhere, including some embarrassing places.

It's another sad fact, but appeals to your child's vanity are likely to work far better than concerns about her health. You could try adding (to both her and her brother) that early signs of B_1 (thiamine) deficiency include fatigue, irritation, poor memory, sleep disturbances, anorexia, abdominal discomfort and constipation. (Sound familiar? And that's all well before the full syndrome of beri-beri kicks in. Do look that one up before they start drinking too much alcohol).[22] Serious dietary deficiency of B_1 affects one in eight of both boys and girls aged between 15 and 18 years – and 70 per cent of this age group consume less than the 'reference nutrient intake' (or RNI – the amount needed to keep most of the population healthy). And we wonder why our teenagers have problems with mood, behaviour and learning!

These figures – and many others from these UK national surveys – are worrying enough, but it's worth pointing out again that *none of our official recommendations for 'adequate' nutrient intakes has ever considered the possible effects on our brains or behaviour.* As my colleague Bernard Gesch is fond of pointing out, the current 'nutrient intake' recommendations are estimates of the *minimum* you need just to 'stop bits dropping off you'! We really don't know, without more research, whether higher intakes might lead to better functioning, but there's certainly evidence to suggest this for at least some nutrients. For example, more Vitamin B_1 seemed to improve attention and reaction times in young women in controlled trials.[23] Even though they weren't initially deficient on standard tests, they performed better with extra thiamine, and reported feeling more clear-headed, composed and energetic. (See also Chapter 9 for evidence that more omega-3 fatty acids – for which 'reference nutrient intakes' haven't even been established yet – could benefit mental performance.)

The B range of vitamins is found in eggs, meat, dairy products and a wide range of grains and vegetables. Some forms of yeast can be a very good source, but may not be suitable for everyone, as discussed in the next chapter.

Food for Thought

In a study of patients with biochemical evidence of thiamine (B₁) deficiency *related to junk food diets*, the adolescents especially were found to be quick to anger, irritable, aggressive and impulsive.[24]

Just one reason why refined sugars (for example, in soft drinks) are so bad for your child is that they help deplete his body of B vitamins and essential minerals such as magnesium and zinc. Lack of these can lead to mental and physical disorders – which may then get treated with drugs ... which may deplete B vitamins further!

Minerals

Your child needs the full range of vitamins for her body and brain to function properly – and these can't be absorbed without minerals to help them. Minerals also help build your body cells (bones, teeth, muscle, blood, soft tissue, nerves and so on) and are vital in other ways. Important in digestion and in the use of other nutrients, they're also needed to catalyse (speed up) reactions such as hormone production, muscle response and nerve transmission. We can't make minerals, so we must get them all from a healthy, balanced and varied diet. *Junk food diets often don't contain enough minerals to meet your child's needs.*

A table of essential minerals and some of their roles is in the Appendix (page 375). It's not important to learn these, just to be aware of why minerals are so important to your child's health. Here I'll describe a few that are known to affect brains and behaviour, but may well be lacking from your child's diet.

Advertising Junk Food to Children

Massive advertising of foods and drinks that lead to childhood obesity and behavioural problems is part of our 'free, civilized' society. Who is looking at the costs to our children, our future economy (less able work force), and the cost to our health and education services? Help your children become aware of what advertising aimed at them is really doing. Lobby your MP – and meanwhile the *Which?* kids' food campaign website is a great place to start. See www.which.net/campaigns

Iron

Iron deficiency leads to anaemia, because iron is needed (with copper) to make the red blood cells that carry oxygen around your body. Even a mild lack of iron can cause physical fatigue and lack of energy, and can also impair mental performance.

Many children in the UK, especially teenage girls, don't get enough iron. Around 10 per cent of children under 4 years of age and almost one in two girls aged between 11 and 18 years had seriously iron-deficient diets, and biochemical measures of iron status and metabolism painted a similar picture.[25] One study from France reported low ferritin (used by your body to store iron safely) in children with ADHD,[26] but controlled trials are still needed to find out if more dietary iron might help in this condition. As we saw in the last chapter, different children with this diagnostic label can vary greatly, and in another study from Taiwan, both dietary and blood measures indicated *increased* iron in children with ADHD.[27]

The frequent occurrence of 'restless legs syndrome' and disturbed sleep patterns in children with ADHD may be because of a deficiency in iron.[28]

Only about 10 per cent of dietary iron (mainly from meat) is in a readily absorbed form called 'haem' iron. The other 90 per cent comes as 'non-haem' iron (found in fruits, vegetables, dried beans, nuts and grains); how much of this you absorb varies with your iron status and other factors.

Vitamin C helps considerably (giving yet another reason why your child should eat her fruits and vegetables!). The presence of any haem iron (or even the use of cooking pots made of cast iron) can also boost absorption.

By contrast, substances called 'phytates' – found in bran, soya, whole grains and legumes – can *reduce* absorption, as they bind to iron (and other metals like zinc and calcium). Tannin and other substances found in tea and coffee can also reduce iron absorption, so don't let your pale, tired child try these for 'energy'.

As meat is the best source of absorbable iron, vegetarians need to take care to get enough, particularly as some staple vegetarian foods are rich in phytates. Some foods (like breakfast cereals) are fortified with iron – but do weigh this against the rest of their content! If they're high in sugar, for example, don't bother. Find some healthy sources instead.[29]

If your child does seem pale, listless and lacking in energy (and/or unduly inattentive or hyperactive), try asking your doctor to test for iron deficiency. Iron supplements aren't necessarily the best solution, though. This is because if there's an imbalance of gut bacteria (see the next chapter) some of the 'bad' bacteria love iron, and may gobble this up so it doesn't even reach your child. Discuss this with your doctor, and take further advice if needed.[30]

Calcium

You've probably heard that you need calcium for strong bones and teeth, but this mineral does a good deal more for you as well. Calcium helps contract your muscles, regulates your blood flow, produces hormones and enzymes and helps the body send and receive messages throughout your brain and nervous system. In fact, calcium is so important for these jobs that your body will take it from your bones if it has to, in order to keep your blood calcium levels up to speed.

Again, many children (and adults) in the UK don't get enough calcium from their diets. Milk, cheese and other dairy products are rich sources of easily absorbed calcium, but other sources include tofu, green vegetables (particularly broccoli, kale and spinach), canned salmon and sardines, shellfish, almonds, Brazil nuts, sesame seeds and dried beans as well as grains and dried fruits. Remember, too, that your child also needs both magnesium and vitamin D to get calcium into her bones.

Magnesium

Magnesium carries out hundreds of biological functions for you, and is absolutely essential for good health. It helps keep your bones and teeth strong, and your heart rhythms steady. It also helps you to make proteins, is important in energy metabolism (including blood-sugar control) and helps regulate muscle and nerve function, immune reactions and control of blood pressure.

> If your ADHD or ADD child suffers from light or restless sleep and daytime sleepiness, try adding calcium and magnesium-rich foods to his diet. These include: milk products, cocoa, sardines, green leafy vegetables, tofu, brown rice, whole grains and beans.
>
> See also: *10 Effective Ways to Help Your ADD/ADHD Child* by Laura Stevens, and her excellent website with dietary tips at http://www.nlci.com/nutrition/.

Magnesium powerfully affects 'nervous excitability', and deficiency states are characterized by tension, agitation and stress. Lack of magnesium is linked with many psychiatric conditions, including anxiety and panic disorders, Tourette's syndrome (involving involuntary movements or speech utterances known as 'tics'), autism and ADHD.[31] There's preliminary evidence of benefits from magnesium supplementation in ADHD children, although this still needs confirming in rigorous randomized controlled trials.[32] Early signs of magnesium deficiency include loss of appetite, fatigue, weakness, nausea or vomiting, muscle contractions and cramps, numbness and tingling. Severe deficiencies can lead to seizures, personality changes and heart rhythm abnormalities.

Unfortunately, magnesium deficiency in the diets of UK children is even more common than lack of calcium. As the national surveys show, average daily intakes of magnesium fall short of 'reference nutrient intake' levels in all except those under 6 years of age. In boys aged between 11 and 18 years, one in every four or five has a frankly deficient intake of magnesium; for girls of the same age, it is more than half of them.[33]

All green vegetables provide magnesium (it's in the chlorophyll that gives plants their green colour), as do most nuts, seeds and grains. A wide range of different foods containing magnesium is needed, though, as no one food is a particularly rich source. Along with a lack of fruit and vegetables, this is where many children (and adults) go wrong, of course – but I hope you can see once again why it's so important that you encourage your child to eat a *wide variety* of whole, fresh, *unprocessed* foods.

Copper

Copper, along with iron, helps form your red blood cells – so a lack of this mineral can actually be another possible cause of 'iron-deficiency anaemia'. It's also very important in keeping your bones, blood vessels, nerves and immune system healthy, as well as your skin. Copper deficiency has been implicated in thyroid abnormalities, cardiovascular disease, thrombosis, poor glucose tolerance, some immune system abnormalities and the formation of collagen (an elastic substance important in tissue health and healing). We're told that copper deficiency in the UK is rare (mainly because our water is usually delivered in copper pipes), but some researchers in the field would strongly disagree. No official 'dietary deficiency' levels have even been established, but at least one-third, and in some age groups four-fifths, of UK children get less than the 'reference nutrient intake' of copper from their diets.[34]

Copper is found in green leafy vegetables, dried fruits (like prunes), beans, nuts and potatoes, but the amount in our vegetables has been declining owing to mineral depletion of our soils.[35] Other sources include kidney and liver, shellfish, yeast and cocoa (so there's even a little in chocolate – but please don't let that be your child's main dietary source, will you?).

Copper and zinc in the body must be very carefully balanced, because they compete for absorption, and in many other ways. (For this reason, zinc can play a key part in the treatment of Wilson's disease – a rare genetic syndrome in which copper can't be excreted, and the build-up can lead to progressive poisoning and death.) Many children with hyperactivity, attentional problems and poor impulse control seem to show an elevated copper-to-zinc ratio on biochemical testing. However, some children with similar symptoms have exactly the opposite pattern – raised zinc and low copper.

If your child is fatigued, pale, has skin sores, oedema (fluid retention and swelling), slowed growth, hair loss, anorexia, diarrhoea or dermatitis, these *could* all be symptoms of insufficient copper (although all of them could have other causes). Infants fed almost exclusively on cows' milk products without a source of copper can be at particular risk.

Is the Government Listening? Are You?

In January 2006, the Mental Health Foundation (MHF) issued a new report *linking mental ill-health to changing diets*. It said that poor-quality food can have an immediate effect upon someone's behaviour and mental health – and that there can be lasting effects if the diet isn't changed to a healthy one.

One finding is that the rate of depression in the UK has not only increased, but the age of onset has decreased. The MHF went on to say that complementary health services which focus on diet and nutrition are showing promising results, but that they need more funding to conduct full-scale trials.

They spoke of a clear link between the rate of depression and the sort of diet followed: those eating 'convenience' foods rather than freshly prepared ones. In other words – *people eating junk food are more likely to suffer from depression*. The lack of fish oils and micronutrients was highlighted.

Changing Diets, Changing Minds, published by Sustain, an organization that campaigns for better food, warns that the British National Health Service's bill for mental illness will keep rising unless the Government focuses on diet and the brain in its policies on education, farming and food.

For the full report and others, visit www.mentalhealth.org.uk.

Zinc

Zinc is needed for more than 200 different biochemical reactions in the body and brain. Your child needs it for normal growth, sexual development, a working immune system and brain and healthy skin, nails and hair. With insufficient zinc, he'll be open to infections and more prone to allergies, night blindness and skin problems. He may have a poor sense of smell and taste (which will keep him wanting the highly flavoured, salty, sugary junk foods), mental lethargy, thinning hair, shortage of breath when exercising, stunted growth and slow sexual maturity. Phew! Zinc deficiency is also associated with fertility problems in adolescents and adults (and it's worth knowing that sperm are very rich in zinc, so adolescent boys – and men – can sometimes lose significant quantities of zinc through this route!).

White spots on your child's fingernails (or yours) are good clues to zinc deficiency, as is proneness to infections. So are stretch marks on the skin (which may appear during growth spurts, or during pregnancy), although a lack of vitamin E and essential fatty acids will exacerbate these; as usual, these nutrients all work together.

In terms of behavioural problems, zinc is also crucial. It's needed to make complex omega-3 and omega-6 essential fatty acids in the body (see Chapters 8 and 9), so if your child doesn't have enough zinc, his brain – 20 per cent of which is made from these fats – is unlikely to function properly. Both zinc and copper are also found in your brain's hippocampus region. This is best known for its role in memory and learning, but has many other functions – like helping to regulate your emotions, stress responses and sensitivity to pain.

Once again, the UK national survey data don't give good news. Serious dietary deficiencies of zinc were found in 5–37 per cent of our children, depending on their sex and age; 70–90 per cent of children consumed less than the 'reference nutrient intake'.[36] Perhaps we could teach our children something about nutrition before they have their own children, as apart from the 'unexpected' fertility problems they might have, there's also evidence to suggest that maternal zinc deficiency may lead to immune system impairments that persist for three generations.[37] Just what sort of legacy have we been creating with our junk food diets?

Several studies indicate low levels of zinc (and high copper) in children with ADHD, as already mentioned. Many nutritional therapists, therefore, automatically recommend zinc supplements for hyperactivity, as well as for dementia and other behavioural disorders. Some of them recommend zinc to pretty much everyone – and, given the vague but comprehensive list of potential deficiency signs above, it's easy to see why. However: *I would warn against supplementing with zinc alone until we have further evidence that the benefits outweigh the risks.* Two small controlled trials did show short-term benefits from zinc supplementation in ADHD, but both involved Middle

Eastern children, and these findings may not apply to children elsewhere. What's more, there's some disturbing evidence to suggest that zinc supplementation alone can cause cognitive *decline* in dementia patients, and the same has been reported in animal studies.[38] Some researchers think *these effects could be due to an undetected copper deficiency* (which standard blood tests may not pick up).

Because zinc and copper compete in so many ways, a high intake of one can deplete the other. As ever, my advice would be to *try to get both of these micronutrients in ample quantities from good food*, as most foods that provide one will also provide the other. Micronutrients delivered in their natural food packaging are extremely unlikely to give rise to unexpected and possibly toxic reactions or nutrient imbalances (well, OK – there is polar bear liver!). With individual micronutrients, we really do need more research in most areas before anyone can say with confidence what their effects may be. (Please get in touch with FAB Research if you'd like to help us do the studies: www.fabresearch.org.)

- Fat-soluble vitamins are needed to make minerals work – they can't perform in isolation. For example, iron can't be used unless there's adequate vitamin A present as well, and calcium and potassium need vitamins A and D before they can start their work.
- Parts of nerves (and all cell membranes) are made from omega-3 fatty acids, which will go 'rancid' (because of oxidation by free radicals) if they're not protected by antioxidants, including vitamins E and C.
- The nervous system also needs B vitamins, magnesium, zinc and vitamin C to help make the neurotransmitters that are used to cross the gaps (called synapses) between the nerves.

Some Other Minerals – in Brief

- Iodine is added to table salt because deficiency causes such serious mental and physical problems.
- Chromium, manganese and probably vanadium (as well as zinc) are needed for blood-sugar regulation, and lack of them is often linked with mood swings, inattention and carbohydrate cravings.

- Cobalt is involved in nervous function because it's needed for vitamin B_{12}.
- Selenium is important for immune function and antioxidant defences, but soil levels in Europe are low, reducing the content of locally grown produce.
- A fascinating study in Texas showed that areas where lithium concentrations in the drinking water were highest had the lowest incidence of suicide, rape and murder. Higher doses of lithium have long been used to treat bipolar depression, but the Texas study suggests that even very low doses can affect human behaviour.[39]

Did You Know?

- Historically, copper, iron, manganese and zinc deficiency have each been associated with mental impairment such as confusion, violence, feeling 'dull' … and sometimes even death. On the other hand, too *much* lead can lead to brain damage, and too *much* copper or zinc can cause behavioural problems.
- Vitamin B deficiencies and magnesium deficiencies have frequently been associated with anxiety, depression and other neuropsychiatric disorders.

What Else Children Need from Their Diet

In addition to the nutrients we've considered, your child also needs some other substances for good health – and once again, fruits and vegetables are the best sources.

Phytochemicals

'Phytochemicals' are plant compounds that help protect you from many diseases, including cancer and many disorders of the heart, circulation and immune system. They include 'flavonoids' (found in fruits, vegetables and red wine), isoflavones (in soya and some other vegetables) and lycopene (in tomatoes). I only have space to deal very briefly with flavonoids here, but most phytochemicals have antioxidant activity, so we'll have a quick look at antioxidants again before we finish this overview.

Flavonoids

Flavonoids are a group of phytochemicals found in plants, and are vital components of a healthy diet. They help protect your child against bacteria, viruses and fungi, and many have anti-inflammatory, anti-allergic and immune-boosting properties. They're found in the leaves, skin and pips of vegetables and fruit – so washed and pulped whole (preferably organic) these will provide your child with very healthy 'shakes' or 'smoothies'. You'll find them especially in dark fruits such as blueberries, dark cherries and prunes, as well as in cooked tomatoes, some forms of soy and green tea.

Antioxidants

Chemical reactions go on all the time in our bodies and brains. Some of the by-products are 'free radicals', dangerous substances that can attack any parts of our cells and tissues, and play a direct or indirect role in most major diseases and disorders, as well as the deterioration we've come to associate with 'normal' ageing.

Environmental pollution also exposes us to free radicals. (Smoking gives you millions of free radicals in every puff. Give up if you can – and don't expose your child to smoky atmospheres.)

Antioxidants are our defence against free radicals, so a diet low in antioxidants means your child is more vulnerable to cellular attack. Different antioxidants act in different and complementary ways, and we need them all. For example, vitamin E is needed to stop important fatty acids from 'oxidizing', but it won't work without vitamin C. The only way to give your child the full mix of antioxidants is with a diet rich in a variety of nuts, seeds, whole grains, fruits and vegetables.

Antioxidants that come straight from the diet include vitamins A, B, C and E – and also flavonoids and co-enzyme Q10. You can make some of your own antioxidants in the form of enzymes and other compounds. However, to do this you need certain minerals (for example, copper, zinc and selenium), as well as compounds such as glutathione (a peptide), oestrogen (a hormone) and melatonin (produced when you sleep).

The Antioxidant Vitamin C – For the Final 'Mopping Up'

You really must have a mixture of antioxidants present in your body at once, as they all help each other. When an antioxidant 'mops up' a harmful free radical, it can in turn become a free radical itself, and then needs to be 'neutralized' by another antioxidant … and so on! Fortunately the end of the chain often lies with vitamin C (if you have enough of it!), which turns into a water-soluble free radical and is lost from your body when you urinate. Vitamin C is therefore a real 'master antioxidant'. Make sure your child gets enough.

Why Don't Dogs Eat Oranges?

Dogs and most other animals can make their own vitamin C, and it's very handy for them. There are a few animals that can't, and we're one of those species. Guinea pigs can't, either.

Your dog doesn't need to eat fresh oranges and other sources of vitamin C, but it's essential your child does. Incidentally, you'll get more natural vitamin C out of fresh fruit than you will out of a carton of juice.

Practical Steps You Can Take to Prevent Malnutrition

Tackle the Dietary Issues

First and foremost – start feeding your child better! This will take time and effort, but the next few chapters will give you more information on what to do (and what not to do), and there are some tips and a plan for you to follow in Chapters 10 and 11.

Also, always ask your doctor about possible effects of any medications on your child's nutritional status.[40] Likewise, tell your doctor about any complementary or alternative approaches you may be using, including dietary supplements or any other dietary strategies. *This is very important.* There could be interactions – positive or negative – between any different 'treatments' your child may receive. Be alert for these, because anything you notice may be relevant not just to your child's health and well-being, but also to many other children – and unless you report any suspicions you may have, potential interactions may never even come to light.

Exercise

There's more on this in Chapter 10, but diet alone won't make your child healthy. Moderate exercise is essential a few times each week, if not daily. Too little (or too much!) exercise can impair immune-system functioning, but your child may not feel like exercising if she's been eating a poor diet. It's always sensible to build up exercise gradually.

Exercise helps to alleviate depression, aids sleep, helps your child develop coordination and helps your body burn fuel more efficiently. The doctors who prescribe exercise (usually in conjunction with the local council-run leisure centre) have got it right: exercise encourages brain cells to multiply, thus strengthening their connections and protecting them from damage. When you exercise, your brain and nerve cells release a chemical called brain-derived neurotrophic factor (BDNF), which in turn triggers other chemicals that promote brain health – so exercise really does help you get smarter. If you choose the activities that are right for you and your child, you'll both find it's fun – and you might even get a period of quiet or rest after it.

Supplements Are Not the Solution

Food supplements can be useful – but as with drugs, my view is that these should be a last resort, not the first option. Remember that your child's physiology has been shaped by evolution. It's used to dealing with foods, not isolated nutrients, and natural foods always contain numerous different ingredients in combination, as a package.

That combination can be critical to the body's ability to absorb and use the nutrients themselves without an adverse reaction. As we've seen, supplementing zinc without copper might actually make some mental symptoms worse. There are many other examples. Beta-carotene was expected to improve health, but in controlled trials it actually appeared to *increase* rates of lung cancer in smokers. This might have been because the smokers were low in vitamin C, for example. (Foods that provide beta-carotene usually have plenty of vitamin C in the same package. The pills used in the trials didn't.)

The principle of 'synergy' is a crucial one in physiology – which is the study of biological *systems*. Not parts, but highly complex systems. Modern medicine often tries to explain things in terms of their component *parts*. We're led to believe that there will be some 'magic bullet' (ideally a single compound that can be patented for profit) – and that this will somehow undo any damage caused by diet, lifestyle and environment that simply don't suit us. Even when they help to reduce symptoms, *drugs are never the whole answer to difficulties in behaviour, learning and mood. Nor are food supplements* – however persuasive the marketing 'hype' may be.

Having said all this, I do know that supplements are sometimes the only realistic option. I also think these can be worth while if used judiciously, and if the alternative really is an ongoing state of malnutrition. Here are some useful ground rules:

- *Never use supplements as a substitute for a good diet* – they are *supplements* – with many potential limitations and drawbacks.
- *If you are determined to use supplements, learn something about them first.* Seek expert advice, but do your own homework, too.[41] Read around, talk to other people. In particular, talk first with your doctor or a qualified dietician about what would be best for your child, especially if she has any physical complaints. (For example, if she has kidney problems, she may be advised not to take magnesium.)
- *Don't ever be swayed by people who are 'selling' you something* – whether that's advice, supplements or both. At the moment, no formal qualifications are needed before almost anyone can set up in private practice, calling themselves a nutrition therapist or nutritionist, let alone a dietary advisor. Check they're at least registered with one of the professional organizations trying to improve this lack of regulation.[42]
- Many supplements use synthetic rather than natural forms of vitamins. These may not always work in the same way as the natural forms in food. Ask about this, or check the research yourself.
- Even if you know which nutrients you want to use, there are many brands to choose from. Don't just go for the cheapest ones – but don't think the expensively packaged ones are the best, either. You can't judge a book by its cover.
- Some supplements contain fillers that your child may be intolerant to, so look for ones that are 'yeast and sugar free', for example. Watch out, too, for artificial sweeteners and flavourings in any supplements – but particularly the ones aimed at children.
- If they need anything in supplement form, most people usually need a *combination* of nutrients. This is where a good dietician can be very helpful, as they know what foods could provide this naturally – and what works best with what. For example, vitamin E works better when vitamin C and selenium are present too, and vitamins B_6, B_{12} and B_9 (folic acid) work better together than separately.
- A broad-spectrum multivitamin and mineral supplement (providing minimum daily requirements of most or all essential micronutrients) can be a good insurance policy.[43] People's needs vary, though – so always check with your own doctor first. Also be careful what you choose, as

some multi-supplements don't contain enough (and often none) of some important micronutrients.

One area where supplements *are* usually essential is for research into cause and effect. This really needs randomized controlled trials (see the Appendix); matched supplements containing 'active' and 'placebo' treatments are ideal to for ensuring the trial is 'double-blind', as well as controlling the doses delivered.

Wise Up to the Bigger Picture

You've already heard about the dramatic improvements in behaviour that followed when young offenders were given both multivitamin and fatty acid supplements in a rigorously controlled trial.[44] Much earlier, no fewer than 13 similarly well-controlled trials had already been carried out to see whether giving vitamins and minerals alone to school children could boost their general intelligence, or 'IQ'.

These studies were expertly reviewed not long ago by one of the leading researchers in this field, Professor David Benton of Swansea University.[45] Overall, the findings showed that yes – many children's reasoning ability could indeed be improved by increasing their intake of vitamins and minerals. Ten of the 13 studies showed a positive response in at least a subgroup of children – those who were most poorly nourished to start with. Well, we'd hardly expect significant benefits if their diets already gave them enough nutrients. But as we've seen in this chapter, this isn't the case for many children in the UK today. When these 'vitamins and IQ' studies were carried out, children's nutrition (and their sheer ignorance of food, which Jamie Oliver and half the nation found hard to believe!) hadn't got quite as bad as it is now. So if these trials were re-run today, I think the effects would probably be even more significant. If essential fatty acids were given, too (as in the young offenders' trial – and see Chapter 9), the results would probably be more striking yet – but omega-3's critical importance to the brain was hardly yet recognized when these pioneering vitamin and mineral studies took place. That alone should tell you how little we've known, and how complacent we've been, in letting the fast food industry have their way for so long.

We really do need to know more about nutrients – and what they
can do for us – but the answer is always going to lie in the quality
of the *whole diet*, not just this nutrient or that nutrient.

As it is, progress in recognizing the fundamental truth that diet matters is
either non-existent or very slow. In some cases, vitamin and mineral recipes
'borrowed' from veterinary practice are now belatedly being trialled (with
promising preliminary results) in children with extreme behaviour
problems which decades of human drug research haven't been able to
solve.[46]

But why have we forgotten or ignored the results from the important
research that's already been carried out,[47] and let things get as bad as *Jamie's
School Dinners* showed us they are? I'll tell you why.

- The media just loves to swing a story from 'Hey, what a miracle!' to
  'There – told you so, it doesn't work after all!' They build a story up just
  to knock it down. The truth is almost always somewhere in the middle –
  but 'grey areas' and details don't sell newspapers, do they? After the
  initial 'hype' over the 'vitamin and IQ' studies that had middle-class
  parents clearing the supermarket shelves of 'vitamin pills', the media
  couldn't be bothered to follow up with any serious commentary.
- For researchers, this whole area of 'food and behaviour' is almost a no-
  go. It attracts almost no funding and plenty of scorn from the
  establishment. Both can seriously damage researchers' career prospects –
  so most of them don't go there. However, some of them – like Professor
  Michael Crawford, whom you'll hear more about in Chapter 8 – have
  warned for a long time that 'brain disorders' would be next.
- Our education and health systems haven't concerned themselves with
  nutrition. Why should they? It's not their job. What's more, in the face of
  tight budgets catering responsibilities have been contracted out to the
  lowest bidder by schools and hospitals – with dire consequences.
- Linked inextricably with these other reasons, economic and political
  forces have been at work. The big food company bosses and the big drug
  company bosses preside over industries that have grown shockingly
  rich, and more powerful than governments, on the junk we've been
  peddled. They can usually buy what media stories they want, and

finance what 'studies' they want – while suppressing others that don't suit them. Except that even those people aren't winning, you know – because some things matter rather more than money. I've actually met quite a few such people whose own children have been diagnosed with conditions like ADHD, dyslexia or autism – or more severe mental and physical disabilities. Some of them have recognized that the industries they work in have helped to create some of the apparent epidemics we're now seeing – not just in these conditions, but in the wider problems our society is now facing, including antisocial behaviour and drug abuse. (It's easy to see why malnourished youngsters would look for something to make them feel better – and Bernard Gesch of Natural Justice has some tragic cases to illustrate this from his previous work as a probation officer.) But when it comes to doing something about it, these parents also recognize that it's up to them – as it's up to each one of us – to decide what to do about it.

The supplement industry has become big business too, of course – but quite honestly, you'll probably find that you don't need to worry too much about individual vitamins and minerals if you follow the three main steps explained in Chapters 6, 7 and 8, namely:

- Get rid of the artificial additives and anything else to which your child may be reacting badly.
- Ditch the sugary stuff that's probably destabilizing his mood and behaviour (and setting him up for diabetes, too).
- Dump the junk fats – which are found in more processed foods than you'd believe possible.

Once you've decided to do these things, your child's diet – and yours – will start to consist of real, fresh foods that should provide all the micronutrients and energy you both need to make the most of life.

FAQs

If most vitamin A is found in animal products, where do vegetarians get their vitamin A?

Many orange, yellow or green vegetables and some grains provide beta-carotene (or other carotenoids). The carotenes are widely regarded as an acceptable substitute for vitamin A, because the body can convert this into the active form (retinol). What's more, there's no risk of 'overdose' from this route – whereas pre-formed, active vitamin A can be toxic in excess.

Be aware, though, that individuals can differ quite substantially in their ability to convert beta-carotene to vitamin A. What's more, some so-called 'vegetarians' I've met don't actually eat many fruits and vegetables at all. That way trouble lies! – and not just for their vitamin A status. With no animal products and no fruit and vegetables, the kind of junk these folk do eat can create multiple nutritional deficiencies and imbalances very quickly, with serious consequences for their physical and mental well-being. It's perfectly possible to be a healthy vegetarian – but you do need to eat vegetables, and to know something about food. The same goes for non-vegetarians!

Why was our ancestors' diet better than today's?

First, let's be clear that the diet was better only when the hunter-gatherers could get it! Many would have starved or suffered nutritional deficiencies, too. The difference is that today, in First World countries at any rate, we don't have an excuse. Hunter-gatherers ate a huge variety of plants and seeds, which weren't covered in pesticides and were full of nutrients, and the occasional (not daily) animal – including insects and grubs. (To survive, you couldn't afford to be squeamish – as applies in many countries to this day.) The animals were wild and not farmed, so had a different nutrient composition. River and seaside dwellers ate lots of fish and other marine foods – and there is good evidence that humans actually evolved 'at the water's edge' – so foods rich in omega-3 were plentiful. During last century's world wars many people went without, but more food was home-grown, and less sugar and meat were consumed. The diet was better balanced – and the nation's health improved. See also the website of the McCarrison

Society: He was an army doctor who realized more than 100 years ago that refined foods caused disease – and did the studies to prove it.

I've read that a 'Mediterranean' diet is healthier, but I also know 'food miles' are a bad thing. What's the answer?

Healthier than what? If you avoid processed foods, and eat local foods that are in season (go to markets and farm shops), you're more than halfway there. A Mediterranean-type diet *is* healthy – but it's the principles that matter, and if you don't want to use imported goods, then go for your own version here: oily fish, local vegetables and fruit, and lean meat or game. (There's a recipe for a Greek salad in Chapter 13, and you can make moussaka using locally bought ingredients.) Whether you use 'high air mile' foods is up to you, but I'd say that you can eat a healthy diet using mainly or exclusively British ingredients if you seek out good local produce.

Are there any 'safe' fizzy drinks? My children won't drink enough water.

In general, fizzy drinks just aren't good for your children. They contain sugars (bad for their blood sugar levels), additives (can cause ill-health and behavioural problems) and acidic chemicals (erode their teeth enamel). Don't force a ban overnight, but do use the tips in Chapter 11 on ditching the squash. Make sure your children eat plenty of fruits and vegetables too (these contain lots of water), and keep them away from diuretics like tea and coffee.

If they don't like the taste of your tap water, try filtering this, or add a squeeze of lemon juice to make it taste more interesting. It could be that your children aren't really rejecting water, but are craving sugar: once they follow a diet that regulates blood sugar, they'll lose their constant taste for sugary things. Children push – try to stick to your plan, and let them know what you're doing and why.

Is organic produce better and worth the extra money?

This depends on the produce, and your income. Organic fruits, vegetables and meat generally taste better (so less wastage), and aren't covered with pesticides or fed with hormones, but the quality of non-organic produce varies greatly in this respect. Soil composition also matters, because even pesticide-free produce can lack some nutrients (like selenium) if grown in depleted soils.

We don't exercise much and don't really like it. Do we really need to do it as well as changing our diet?

Yes. Once you start eating well, you'll find it easier to exercise, and when you exercise you'll feel better and want to eat healthily, and so on. Exercising doesn't have to be hard – just go walking together, and maybe take a ball with you to kick or throw and catch ... all easy but fun stuff.

Can you recommend any supplements?

Sorry – I can't do this, for three reasons. First – my aim here is to get you to see that the right foods, not supplements, are the best way to give your child the vital nutrients he needs. Second – I can't possibly know, without much more information, what anyone's individual nutrient needs may be. Third – I've always taken great care (and made huge sacrifices) to keep my own research free of any commercial influences, but I'm well aware that I might be accused of bias if I recommended particular products. I obviously choose particular supplements for my own research, and I also do some advisory work, both for individuals and for some companies I believe really are trying to provide the best-quality products in their domain. However, I always refuse to do commercial endorsements – which is what any citation in this book could be seen as, I'm sorry to say.

I hope you can appreciate my position. I'd love to be able to help you, but if you really feel your child needs supplements, I'd advise you to read up, ask around, if needs be find a qualified specialist you can trust, and in the end make up your own mind. Let me warn you, though: supermarkets and other large outlets generally demand such huge profit margins from suppliers (70 per cent of the purchase price in some cases) that you're unlikely to find the best-quality supplements there – although there are always exceptions. Also be aware that many nutrition practitioners receive commission from companies for supplements (or tests) that they recommend. That doesn't necessarily mean they're bad supplements (or bad tests, or bad practitioners), but do ask whether and why you really need what anyone may suggest, and why they recommend any particular versions. You can find more general guidelines to assist you via the FAB Research website (www.fabresearch.org).

Summary

1. Your child needs a varied, balanced diet including macronutrients (focus on complex carbohydrates, good-quality proteins and essential fatty acids), micronutrients (vitamins, minerals, antioxidants and other phytochemicals found mainly in fruits and vegetables) and water.
2. What we eat today is very different from our ancestors' diets. Industrialization has stripped much of our food of its vital micronutrients, and replaced these with artificial (synthetic) ingredients and other additives, leading to widespread malnutrition.
3. It's essential to drink enough water, as your body is mostly made from it.
4. We need proteins to help build and repair our bodies and carry out numerous vital functions. There are 20 amino acids (protein components), and your child must get eight of these from her diet. Animal foods provide all of these, but few vegetarian foods do, so vegetarians must carefully combine their foods.
5. Fatty acids are a source of energy. They're also vital for cell membrane structure and numerous vital functions. Chapter 8 provides more details.
6. Carbohydrates (starches and sugars) are a source of energy – but complex, unrefined carbohydrates also provide essential nutrients and fibre (carbohydrates we can't digest, but that we need to help food and waste move through the gut). Refined sugars and simple carbohydrates are no substitute (see Chapter 7).

7. Your child absolutely needs a wide range of vitamins, minerals, antioxidants and other phytochemicals for his brain and body to work properly. Surveys show that many children in the UK eat diets that are lacking in many of these essential micronutrients. (Most also consume far too much sugar, saturated fat and salt.)

8. Antioxidants help protect your body and brain from free radical damage. These include vitamins E and C as well as numerous substances found mainly in fruits, vegetables, nuts and seeds. Antioxidants are needed in combination, because some help recycle others.

9. Exercise is a vital part of your child's diet!

10. Food supplements are just that – supplements. They should *never* be seen as an alternative to a healthy diet of fresh, wholesome foods. Individual micronutrients taken in isolation can sometimes have unexpected (and negative) effects. Nutrients work in synergy, and more research is needed to understand their interactions and effects on health. Expert advice can be helpful, but unfortunately many nutrition practitioners may not know or understand what research there is. Always check that they have appropriate qualifications to advise you – and do your own homework, too.

In the next chapter we'll take a quick look at digestion – because the real issues lie not just in *what* your child eats, but *how* he eats it, and what his body actually *does* with it!

chapter 5

digestion: they are what they absorb

In this chapter we'll look at what actually happens to the food your child consumes. Even if the food itself is potentially 'nutritious', its effects on your child's body may be good news or bad news depending on the state of his digestion. (And if the food isn't nutritious, it's simply *guaranteed* to make his digestion worse.)

Good digestion is the route to good health. Without this, we can't properly absorb what nutrients there may be in our food – and if we don't digest our food properly, we may also suffer some very unpleasant side-effects. What goes in must be dealt with somehow – and if this isn't done properly, it will cause trouble sooner or later. If you're one of the many people who really doesn't want to contemplate all that slimy piping that's part of your 'insides', think of it this way: bad drains really can ruin the whole house! But it's more than the drains you should be worried about.

As we've already seen in Chapter 4, many different kinds of nutrients are simply essential – but for your child to get them into his body is not as simple as it may sound. As we'll see, your body digests the major macronutrients (proteins, fats and carbohydrates) in different ways and at different stages. When it comes to vitamins, minerals and other 'micronutrients', these too need the right 'carriers' and the right conditions for absorption if they're going to nourish your child as they should.

Who Else Is Living with Your Child?

As I also mentioned very briefly in the last chapter, some vitamins are actually manufactured in your body by 'friendly' bacteria. Trillions of microbes inhabit the whole length of your guts – from your mouth to your bottom. (They also live in your ears, nose and throat, and on your skin.) Think of them as friendly housekeepers and servants – because if you've got the right ones, they don't just feed you by making vital micronutrients (including the vitamins K, B_1, B_2, B_3, B_5, B_6, B_{12}, folate and some amino acids[1]), they also silently and invisibly get on and do unbelievable amounts of 'housework' for you, just in exchange for the free board and lodging. And they do even more: They also act as security guards – forming a protective line of defence against any 'pathogenic' (harmful) organisms that might try to gain entry or do damage. Crucially, they also help feed and train all the soldiers in your various immune-system armies.

Up to 2 kilos of bacteria actually live in your guts – and unless they're the right kind, neither your digestion nor your immune system will work properly. That's a recipe for trouble. Can you imagine what could happen if you gave free house room to the wrong kinds? Worthless layabouts who'd eat all the food and not give anything back? Vandals who'd 'party', get drunk, fill the house with drugs and wreck the place? Not to mention the real criminal types who'd hijack any system they could get into, and subvert your own immune troops so that they join in the rampage, attacking the body instead of defending it?

Sad to say, the 'wrong' gut flora have probably already made themselves at home in your child's gut – and in yours. The only good news is that there is still something you can do about it. You can get the intruders to leave (although it may take time, and they may put up a fight), and you can encourage back the loyal servants of your child's welfare instead. You've probably already heard something about these good bacteria, or 'probiotics' – because the idea of 'good' as well as 'bad' gut bacteria is becoming familiar to many more people now that various products containing just some of these microbes are being advertised on TV.[2]

I mentioned in Chapter 3 my first meeting with Dr Natasha Campbell-McBride, and her remarkable book *Gut and Psychology Syndromes*.[3] In this book she explains why she thinks that a whole range of what are diagnosed as 'behavioural' or 'mental' disorders actually start with (and are then maintained by) an abnormal balance of gut flora. I think she's absolutely right – although that's not to say that there aren't other elements, too, including some genetic and many other environmental risk factors.

In my view (and Natasha's), it's no coincidence that so many children with behaviour and learning problems, and so many adults with so-called 'psychological' disorders, seem to suffer from allergies, intolerances or auto-immune disorders of various kinds.[4] All of these indicate an immune system that's malfunctioning or 'out of balance' – and in turn, that usually reflects at least some degree of 'gut dysbiosis', the term given to an unhealthy balance of gut flora. Immune-system disturbances could well contribute directly to some of the 'mental' symptoms these children and adults experience, because we now know that the immune system provides powerful links between mind and body (with heavy traffic in both directions).[5] Of indisputable importance to everyone, though, is the fundamental business of digestion and the absorption of essential nutrients; these processes also depend on the very special microbes that should live in our guts.

I promise it will repay you well if you take just a little time and effort to understand the basics of how your digestion *should* work. Unfortunately, very few people have 'perfect digestion' (the sales of indigestion tablets alone tell us that – and I'll have more to say about those later). And if your child has difficulties with behaviour, learning or mood, it's almost certain that she's not one of the lucky few.

In this chapter I can only take a very quick look at the highly complex topic of digestion, and how your child's guts can affect her brains. I hope, however, that it will encourage you to think about not just *what* your child eats, but *how* she eats it, and what happens to it after that.

The diagram opposite gives you a simplified outline of the stages of digestion. Let's look at each of these briefly in turn.

The Digestive System

Your Mouth

Your mouth is the starting point for digestion – and is often the place where things first starts to go wrong. Chewing your food well is *essential* if the later stages of digestion are to work properly when they get their turn. I'm quite frankly appalled at how many people don't seem to realize this. They just 'hoover' their food down so it hardly has time to touch the sides: gulp, swallow and it's gone! Unless you grind your food into small pieces by chewing, it will reach your stomach in lumps that are far too big to be tackled effectively. Chewing also stimulates the production of saliva; mixing your food with enough saliva is another key to good digestion, because

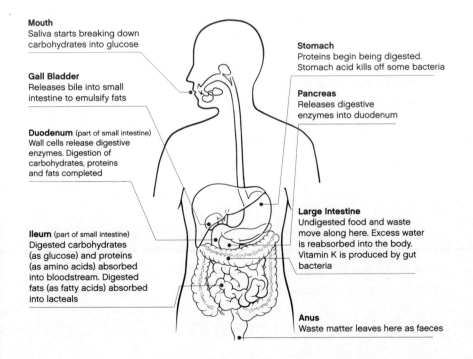

Mouth
Saliva starts breaking down carbohydrates into glucose

Gall Bladder
Releases bile into small intestine to emulsify fats

Duodenum (part of small intestine)
Wall cells release digestive enzymes. Digestion of carbohydrates, proteins and fats completed

Ileum (part of small intestine)
Digested carbohydrates (as glucose) and proteins (as amino acids) absorbed into bloodstream. Digested fats (as fatty acids) absorbed into lacteals

Stomach
Proteins begin being digested. Stomach acid kills off some bacteria

Pancreas
Releases digestive enzymes into duodenum

Large Intestine
Undigested food and waste move along here. Excess water is reabsorbed into the body. Vitamin K is produced by gut bacteria

Anus
Waste matter leaves here as faeces

enzymes secreted with this should actually start the digestion of starches and fats. Ideally, solid foods should be chewed to a liquid before you swallow them. You can set your child a good example, and practise this together.

Chewing also helps you to taste your food (you can't taste it dry), as well as to send 'get ready' messages to your stomach, and 'we'll soon be full' messages to your brain. If you bolt down your food you're far more likely to overeat, as well as suffering bad digestion. (Those two things go together for many reasons – as the 'fast food', 'weight-loss' and 'drugs' industries know all too well, to their profit and your cost.)

Saliva Starts Off Starch Digestion

When you chew, a chemical called *amylase* in your saliva begins to digest any starch you've eaten, turning it into maltose (a sugar).

To illustrate this, force some saliva into your mouth, put a piece of a dry, savoury cracker onto your tongue and wait for a couple of minutes: you'll notice that the cracker soon starts to taste sweet. Get your child to try it, too.

Talk to your child about chewing food properly – and set him a good example. It really is vitally important.

Your Stomach

Your stomach is an amazing organ. One way to explain its workings to your child is to liken it to a cement mixer that has an added 'kneading' function. (OK – I know we hardly want to be producing cement! But it'll do as a metaphor.) Obviously you'll need to adapt it to his age and understanding, but the story goes something like this:

- Your stomach takes the food you've chewed and swallowed and begins to grind and churn it up.
- At the same time, it begins to start digesting the proteins you've eaten, using a mixture of 'digestive juices' and enzymes.

- Proteins are broken down by enzymes (proteases) from the stomach wall. These need an 'acid' environment to work, so strong (hydrochloric) acid is squirted in from the stomach walls, too. This acid also kills off some bacteria.
- Imagine your cement mixer is churning away happily, and then you add three pails-full of pebbles (too much at one go), slabs of concrete (under-chewed meat) and a couple of buckets of water (your drink) – the whole process will go horribly wrong.

This allows you to explain to your child three very important 'rules of thumb':

1. **Don't overload your stomach:** The amount of food you can hold loosely between your cupped hands is enough for any one sitting.[6]
2. **Chew your food thoroughly:** If you swallow big lumps of meat, for example, the enzymes just can't digest it properly.
3. **Keep drinks mainly for 'in-between' meals:** If you drink a lot at meal times, your digestive juices (acid and enzymes) may get too diluted to work effectively.

Key Facts about Protein Digestion

- As we learned in the last chapter, proteins are made from very long chains of amino acids. During digestion, proteins from your diet are broken into shorter chains (peptides), and then (given the chance) they're broken down fully into their individual amino acids.
- Amino acids are single units that can act as building-blocks for new proteins. The same amino acids can be used to make different types of protein, depending on the order in which they're arranged. (Your DNA gives the instructions for these sequences.)
- Fully digested proteins (amino acids) can therefore be used to repair and build your body, or to make new digestive enzymes. They won't look like possible parts of some other 'foreign' organism that could trigger your immune system to launch an attack.

- If you don't digest your dietary proteins properly, you can end up with two unsavoury consequences:
  - Undigested protein, such as meat, can begin to putrefy (rot) in your large intestine, which can cause you health problems.
  - If peptides, rather than amino acids, get too far down the gut (or into the bloodstream via a leaky gut – see page 122), your body may see them as invaders and attack them. This can be the basis for some food intolerances (see Chapter 6 for more details) or even autoimmune diseases. Some protein fragments or peptides – particularly those from gluten (in wheat and other grains) or casein (in milk and dairy products) – can actually have an effect like morphine, an opiate drug. This observation has led to some leading theories that could explain some symptoms of autism and the associated cravings for these foods (which many other people also experience).[7]

So: incompletely digested proteins = less replenishment of your amino-acid stock = fewer enzymes produced = less able to digest your food properly, and possible triggering of food intolerances = ill health … and the whole sorry process can carry on in a downward spiral. It's worth getting digestion right!

Your Small Intestine, Part I

Your 'small' intestine is only called that because it's narrower than the large intestine. It's actually around 6 metres long, coiled up inside you like a very flexible tube, and it does the most amazing things – if you'll only let it. Let's follow that food.

As it moves from your stomach into the first part of the small intestine (the duodenum), more juices are added to the acidic mush (chyme) that emerges from your stomach. These come from the pancreas and duodenal walls. One important function of these new juices is to neutralize the powerful acid, to stop it from hurting the walls of your small intestine.[8]

These new juices also contain various enzymes, produced by your pancreas. These carry on digesting the carbohydrates and proteins and start digesting fats and oils. Bile is also released at the same time. (It's made by the liver and stored in the adjacent gall bladder.) Bile 'emulsifies' fats and oils, causing them to split into tiny globules. It acts like the detergent that helps to dissolve grease when you're washing up – but bile is even more powerful, more like 'drain cleaner'! The digestive enzymes (lipases) that work on fats and oils (lipids) will do the job much more effectively if they're dealing with tiny particles – not great lumps of fat.

Your Small Intestine, Part II

The food matter now carries on along the small intestine to the next section, called the ileum. This part of the gut has an enormous surface area (about the size of a football pitch) because it contains millions of tiny, finger-like projections called *villi* – which are there to 'catch' nutrients from as much of the digested food as possible before it passes into the large intestine.

Glucose (simple sugar), amino acids, fatty acids and some other substances can pass through the lining of the villi and straight into your 'hepatic' portal vein, part of the bloodstream that goes straight to the liver ('hepatic' means to do with the liver). Your liver is an amazing factory with many, many functions; one is to process what's come in from your gut (including any medications or other drugs). Fatty acids can also pass into a system of specialized vessels that are part of your lymphatic system, to join the bloodstream at a later stage.

You Need Good Gut Flora to Absorb Nutrients

The finger-like *villi* (and their little hair-like projections, called *microvilli*) are absolutely key to the absorption of nutrients from food, and the right gut bacteria are critical to their health. The cells on the surfaces of the villi work so hard in absorbing nutrients for you that they must be constantly shed, and replaced by new ones. But without the right balance of beneficial gut flora to look after them, protect them and feed them, these special cells (called *enterocytes*) become disorganized and weakened, don't regenerate properly, and the whole system starts to fail. (If they stay around longer than they should do, some of these cells can even become so damaged they could turn cancerous.) Basically, nutrients just won't be absorbed properly if this very special 'skin' that lines your gut doesn't have the right bacteria around to help.

One way to get this across to your child is if you describe these villi and the microbes that support them as 'living turf' on his 'football pitch'. The right bacteria will provide the nourishing soil and nutrients for the 'grass' (those villi and their microvilli) to grow lush and strong. With the wrong ones – fizzy drinks and sugary or additive-laden snacks – he could quickly turn that lush green turf into a derelict wasteland where nothing will grow … polluted, strewn and clogged up with rotting rubbish like an abandoned industrial yard or an urban wasteground! Perhaps you can find examples near you of each of these to show him? You could also try explaining to him that living things deserve respect – especially if they're his guardians and servants, and his health depends on theirs.

In coeliac disease (the classic form of intolerance to dietary gluten, found in wheat and other grains) the villi can become damaged in another way, by ongoing auto-immune reactions triggered by an allergy to gluten. That's why it's so important for anyone with true coeliac disease to keep gluten out of their diet, otherwise serious malnutrition can result as the villi become 'worn away'. You'll hear more about this in the next chapter, and how nine out of ten people whose immune systems react badly to gluten are likely to be unaware of this.

Macronutrients: What Happens

Food type	Digested into:	Goes from the ileum into:	Used for:
CARBOHYDRATES (polysaccharides)	Disaccharides and then monosaccharides (GLUCOSE)	Bloodstream, which goes first to the liver	■ Energy for the body's cells
PROTEINS (chains of amino acids)	Shorter chains (peptides) and then individual AMINO ACIDS	Bloodstream, which goes first to the liver	■ To repair damaged cells ■ To make new cells
FATS (LIPIDS) Fatty acid and glycerol in combination	FATTY ACIDS and glycerol	Bloodstream and lymphatic system, which both go to the liver	■ Energy ■ As a source of vitamins A, D, E and K ■ To help build healthy cells, including brain cells and other nerve cells

This is a highly over-simplified outline of what happens, although there's a little more detail later in this chapter. I want you to have a broad understanding of digestion, but not get bogged down in specifics. If you'd be interested in more details, see any school biology textbook, or check on the Internet.

Your Large Intestine

At only 1.5m long, your large intestine (also known as the colon, or large bowel) is somewhat shorter than your small intestine, but it's much bigger in diameter (width). Basically, it's responsible for:

■ reabsorbing water and some other substances (the liquids added to your food during its digestion include up to 2 litres of stomach acid, 2½ litres of pancreatic juices, and ½–¾ of a litre of bile per day. That's a lot of liquid – and it doesn't include what you drink with your food!)

- absorbing vitamin K and a range of B vitamins that your gut bacteria ('flora') have made (if you're lucky and have enough of the right kind of gut flora)
- compacting and storing waste (as faeces) before it passes from the body.

The presence of undigested fibre (from plant matter) is important for giving bulk to your stools; it literally helps the large intestine to push things along. It also helps to feed your 'good' gut bacteria. In turn, these bacteria produce waste products which can be used as nourishment by the cells lining the large intestine.

Vitamin K

Vitamin K is needed to coagulate (clot) your blood and maintain proper bone density.

We can get vitamin K from leafy green vegetables, but if your child doesn't eat much of these, he has to rely on his beneficial gut bacteria for his needs. Broad-spectrum antibiotics can destroy these bacteria. If your child has had antibiotics, he needs to have some probiotics and a healthy diet to replace them and prevent potentially harmful organisms from taking their place.

Too much aspirin can cause stomach and intestinal bleeding, as it blocks the clotting effects of vitamin K.

More details about vitamins are found in Chapter 4.

Your Stools

'Stools' is the term health professionals use for faecal matter, or 'poo'. In Britain we're not usually encouraged to look at our stools, never mind mention the subject. But paying some attention can give you a good indication of the state of your digestion. (This is why in Germany and some other European countries, toilets have a little platform so that your stools land there for observation before being flushed away.) Please don't read the rest of this section now if you're eating, or feeling queasy, but it is important that you understand the significance of certain signs that stools can provide.

Your stools are made up from fibre, water, dead intestinal cells and dead bacteria. Stools are usually brown because your gut bacteria create brown pigments as a waste product. They may change in appearance (colour and form) from day to day, but if you see any dramatic or lasting change, then *you need to see your doctor*. Your child needs to observe his stools, too, and let you know of any changes; if he's young, look for yourself. For example:

- If you've eaten a lot of beetroot, cherries or iron pills, your stools might briefly appear reddish or even black. However, black or red stools can indicate bleeding in your gut, so if this persists – or if blood ever looks like it's mixed in with stools – see your doctor without delay.
- If stools are loose and a yellowish or greenish colour, it might be from eating lots of green foods, but otherwise check for infection or intolerance. After taking antibiotics, the strange colour might be because your bowel has effectively been sterilized – and that's bad news! Probiotics can help to compensate for the damage antibiotics can do to your good gut flora.
- If your child isn't digesting or absorbing fats properly, stools can be soft, pale and smelly, and will float or stick to the sides of the toilet bowl. This is known as 'steatorrhoea'. It can occur as a one-off after a particularly fat-rich meal,[9] but if it persists – take your child to the doctor. (This could reflect gluten intolerance, or even a blocked bile duct or other problem.)
- Normal stools should be about 75 per cent water, reflecting a good amount of fibre. Fibre absorbs water, giving your stools bulk and keeping them soft enough to pass without straining (and thus damage). Small, dry stools can mean you're eating too much meat and not enough fibre, and/or not drinking enough water.
- Narrow, ribbon-like stools can indicate Irritable Bowel Syndrome, or worse: old faeces may be impacted and glued to the sides of the bowel – so only a little is getting through the middle. This so-called 'overspill syndrome' – along with other bowel problems – is found in many autistic children.
- If there are more than a few undigested food particles in his stools, your child may not be chewing food properly, may have low stomach acidity, or may be lacking in crucial enzymes.

- Stools always smell, but they should be easily bearable and not foul in odour.

There are many more possible signs, but I hope these examples show you why it's important not to ignore completely what comes out at the other end. If your child isn't passing well-formed stools daily, or if he has to strain, then look closely at his diet and drinking habits, and also check for food intolerances. If you're concerned, see your doctor, and ask for referral to another specialist if necessary.

How Digestion Can Go Wrong

As we've seen, a failure to chew food properly, eating too much at once, and drinking too much with your meals can all get things off to a bad start. Get your child to take time over meals, and eat in a relaxed manner. Try to make sure you set a good example. Encourage him to drink a glass of water half an hour before meals – so he won't be so thirsty when eating. Teach him to chew and savour his food, so he learns to enjoy its tastes and textures (instead of shovelling it down as if it were just fuel at a hasty 'pit-stop'!).

Another problem many people suffer from is low stomach acid – which can be a direct result of the overgrowth of some 'bad' bacteria and yeasts (notably *Candida albicans*) that also live in your guts. Your stomach needs to be highly acidic if it's going to break down proteins and many mineral compounds properly – and also to kill off potentially harmful bacteria.[10] Antacids are *not* the answer to most people's 'indigestion'.

Low stomach acid can lead to feelings of fullness, bloating or belching after meals, and many other unpleasant symptoms. There may be nausea (particularly after taking supplements), and undigested food may appear in your child's stools. Large, protein-heavy meals and/or fried foods are likely to cause the biggest problems for people with low stomach acid. When the stomach can't cope (particularly if its contents have been diluted by large quantities of drink at the same time), its distress can trigger an excess of bile to be produced, which can add to the discomfort. This explains the so-called 'bilious attack' that has many people reaching for their antacid tablets … But if there's still food in your stomach, just ask yourself what effect those will have. Yes, quite. There may be some temporary relief, but the main problem (lots of undigested protein) is simply pushed further along the system.

An insufficiency of digestive enzymes can also be a problem, leading to incomplete breakdown of proteins, fats and/or starches, depending on which enzymes are lacking. We've already seen that absorption of nutrients can be compromised if you don't have the right gut flora. This in turn can create a lack of raw materials to make enzymes. It's easy to see how things can get worse and worse once your child's digestion starts to go wrong. But before you get too discouraged, remember that the opposite also applies. If you start doing the *right* things, you really can expect his digestion to get better and better – and with it, his health and well-being.

When it comes to disposing of waste, if you don't eat enough foods rich in fibre (a very common problem), then the 'transit time' of food through your colon gets too slow. Too much water is reabsorbed, leading to constipation. (The effects are magnified if you haven't been drinking enough water in the first place.) If you've still got undigested protein in the mix, it can just sit there and start to putrefy. Not a problem? Think of it this way: would you voluntarily eat rotting meat?

'Move Along, Now …!' Transit Time – and Why Ignorance Isn't Always Bliss

One of the young offenders in Bernard Gesch's 'prison trial' of micronutrient supplementation (see Chapter 4) appeared to be complaining: 'Don't know about these capsules, guv… they're making me **** myself all the time.'

To check whether the treatment might perhaps be causing any adverse side-effects, Mr Gesch took the young man aside to a private space to discuss things further.

It transpired that prior to the trial – and for most of his life – this young man had been used to a solid bowel movement only *once every week or two*. (Just try not to think about the state of his insides.) With the nutrients, things were apparently now moving along more regularly and frequently – albeit not yet at the regular, reliable 'once a day' that really should be everyone's minimum target!

With a little basic information and reassurance, the young man was happy to carry on with the trial (the results of which showed that antisocial behaviour fell by more than a quarter in those who received the active supplements).

One is left wondering how many more of our young people really don't know that 'once a fortnight' isn't enough. Don't let your child be one of them.

Leaky Gut

I'm afraid it can get worse still. As you'll know, your skin is an important protective barrier. If your child has a cut, or severe eczema that's flaky or 'weeping', for example, harmful bacteria can sometimes get into the body and cause infection. Your gut is lined with its own 'skin', and it's there to do a similar job. It provides a physical barrier to keep invading particles out of your body.

The other major function of the gut lining is to help you digest your food. As we've seen, it allows glucose (from carbohydrates), fatty acids (from fats and oils) and amino acids (from proteins) to cross into the bloodstream and lymphatic system, where appropriate. They can then be carried around the body and used for energy, building new cells, repair and maintenance. It should allow us to absorb vitamins, minerals and other micronutrients into the body for use in maintaining health and vitality. But it needs to keep less desirable substances confined to the gut, to be 'dealt with' and/or escorted off the premises as soon as possible.

Now, *healthy* intestinal cells are closely packed together, and they only allow fully digested food particles to pass through. In addition, they contain special 'carrier' proteins that bind to certain nutrients and transport them across into the bloodstream.

'Gut dysbiosis' can damage the actual structure of your gut wall. Spaces between the cells can become enlarged, so substances that shouldn't normally get through may escape into the bloodstream. The rather frank term Leaky Gut Syndrome has therefore been coined to describe this unhealthy state of affairs. Factors that can contribute to (or exacerbate) gut dysbiosis and leaky gut syndrome include:

- A poor diet (high in sugary foods and drinks, high in processed foods and artificial additives, and lacking in essential fatty acids and other nutrients)
- Many prescription drugs, including:
    - antibiotics – especially if used recurrently
    - aspirin and other non-steroidal anti-inflammatory drugs (like ibuprofen – but there are many other so-called NSAIDs)
    - antacids
    - the contraceptive (birth control) pill or other hormones (such as steroids)
- Too much alcohol or caffeine over a long period (these are both irritants)
- Insufficient digestive enzymes (exacerbated by poor diet and a failure to absorb what nutrients there may be in it)
- Chronic (long-term) stress
- Poor liver function (inflammatory toxins can be released into your gut via bile)
- Some physical disorders, including Crohn's disease – an autoimmune disease in which the gut wall gets inflamed and damaged by inappropriate immune attacks.

Broad-spectrum antibiotics in particular can wipe out your 'friendly' gut bacteria (along with the ones you wanted killed off). Yeast can quickly take over, along with other 'nasties' that are resistant to standard antibiotics. (Clostridia is among these 'nasty' bacteria – and while one form is now causing trouble in NHS hospitals, others have recently been identified as unusually common in children with autism.[11]).

A host of problems can arise from gut dysbiosis and the Leaky Gut Syndrome that can follow this. A simplistic version of these is illustrated in the diagram overleaf.

Increased absorption of:

- Large (part-digested food particles that may trigger adverse reactions
- Toxins
- Bacteria and other harmful micro-organisms

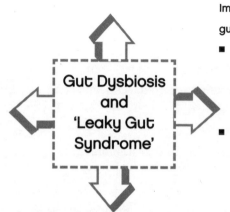

Discomfort

- Bloating
- Flatulence
- 'Tummy ache'
- Allergies and intolerances
- Fatigue (physical and mental)
- Irritability/mood swings

Gut Dysbiosis and 'Leaky Gut Syndrome'

Impairment of the gut's immune function

- Reduced ability to fight off 'bad' bacteria and yeasts
- Vicious spiral of more gut dysbiosis, and more damage to the gut wall

Nutritional deficiencies

Fewer nutrients get absorbed owing to:

- Weakened enterocytes and/or damaged villi
- Depletion or damage to 'carrier' enzymes that transport nutrients

Leaky Gut Syndrome Can Increase Absorption of:

- Large (part-digested) food particles that may trigger adverse reactions – your child's immune system may 'see' undigested food particles as invaders and attack them with substances called antibodies. If the particles resemble any of your child's body cells, antibodies could attack these too, leading to auto-immune disease.
- Toxins – the liver is put under great strain, not least because lack of nutrients can reduce its ability to make enough of the

right 'detox enzymes'. As a result, more toxins may get back out of the liver (instead of being neutralized) and circulate around the body. Symptoms could include 'foggy' thinking, inflammation of body tissues (including the skin, in the form of rashes) and damage to organs, including the liver itself. It can be another vicious spiral.

- Bacteria and other harmful micro-organisms – 'gut dysbiosis' and 'leaky guts' may be implicated in a large number of illnesses, because inflamed gut walls can allow bacteria to get through into the bloodstream. Poor health of one kind or another will inevitably result.

The Trouble with Yeast

Various types of yeast inhabit the gut, but the most common is *Candida albicans* – usually known as 'candida' for short. If your body is healthy, these yeasts are kept under control by your immune system and by competition for space with the 'good bacteria' that should populate your gut. Under some circumstances, though (especially if antibiotics or other drugs have killed off the competition and lots of sugar is available to feed them), yeasts can proliferate and spread, with some highly unpleasant consequences.

Yeasts produce alcohol (ethanol) as a by-product when they digest sugar, which the body processes in a series of steps. Acetaldehyde is one of the products, and is the chemical responsible for the main symptoms of a hangover.[12] There are some wonderful (probably apocryphal) stories about strict teetotallers being pulled over for drink-driving and testing positive for alcohol, simply because they'd eaten so many sugary, yeasty foods that their insides had become a brewery! Even if those anecdotes aren't exactly trustworthy, they do make a good point. Any child who's infected with candida overgrowth could be expected to display poor behaviour and learning if even just a little of this kind of thing is going on.

Signs and Symptoms of Possible Candida (Yeast) Overgrowth

- Hypoglycaemia (low blood sugar – the yeast is getting your sugar instead!)
- Stomach aches (especially with bloating)
- Food cravings (especially for sweet things)
- Reduced tolerance to alcohol (your yeast is making lots already)
- Feeling 'hung over' – without having been drinking! (ditto)
- Food intolerances (from poor digestion and 'leaky gut')
- Feeling 'feeble', weak or tired all the time with no obvious cause
- Irritable Bowel Syndrome (IBS) – obvious bowel irregularities – often alternating between diarrhoea and constipation
- Itches and rashes
- Thrush (oral or vaginal)

Not surprisingly with this little lot, depression, anxiety, irritability and mood swings are usually present. The mental symptoms may feel like 'brain fog' – short-term memory may be poor, and it may be hard to concentrate.

Do bear in mind, though, that each of these signs and symptoms could have other causes – see your doctor first.

These symptoms are often shown by children with behaviour and learning disorders like autism and ADHD (discussed in Chapter 3).

Unfortunately, candida has two different identities. In its simple *yeast* form, it has no roots, but given the chance to grow into a population that really feels at home (as it can in an under-defended gut with plenty of sugar to eat) it will change into its *fungal* form, growing roots that can actually penetrate the gut wall. This is a very easy way to achieve the unpleasant Leaky Gut Syndrome.

Your doctor may be able to prescribe an antifungal drug such as nystatin if there's reason to think that your child has a serious yeast infection.

Otherwise, follow the dietary guidelines outlined in Chapter 11, and do all you can to take sugar out of your child's diet, even if she's craving it – as she probably will be. (Avoid using sugar substitutes, as these can have unwanted side-effects of their own, as we'll see in the next chapter.) Other anti-candida tactics could include supplementing her diet with probiotics and B vitamins (biotin, one of the B vitamins that 'good' bacteria produce, is particularly thought to help control candida) – but as I've emphasized throughout this book, most supplements are best used with the guidance of a well-qualified practitioner (see the Resources chapter on how to find one).

Improving Digestion

In the same way that growing a new garden or lawn will take time (particularly in a space bigger than a football pitch!) you can't expect instant results when you start to tackle the effects of long-standing neglect of the digestive system. You will need to be patient, because if bad bacteria and yeasts have taken hold in your child's gut (or yours), they aren't going to give up their comfortable home overnight. What's more, if they did you could be very ill indeed, because as they become dislodged and 'die off', this too can release various toxins that the body has to deal with. (For this reason, doctors who prescribe nystatin or other antifungal drugs are usually aware of the need to proceed carefully, and to caution you that things may appear to get worse before they get better).

Slowly and gently is the way to get these intruders off the premises. If you simply follow the dietary changes recommended in Chapter 11 (which won't happen overnight either!) you'll be creating the conditions for the friendly, helpful bacteria to re-establish themselves – and they should start to crowd the bad ones out themselves. As your child's body and brain become better nourished, his immune system should also start to reassert itself and deal with them more effectively.

One point I should mention here, though, is that if your child's gut flora really have been 'pathological' from the outset,[13] it's possible that his immune system may have learned to tolerate these 'baddies' instead of attacking them on sight. If so, you and he will need to be even more vigilant about his diet, and a regular supply of the right bacteria from probiotic supplements may be needed on a long-term basis.

FAQs

What can I do to improve my child's ill-health? He's always 'under par', gets every cold there is, and often complains of stomach aches, headaches or other pains – but the doctor says there's nothing wrong with him. Could he be making it up?

Well, he could – but that's not the most likely explanation. He's probably more than anxious and stressed by now, so try to find out from him or others if anything else may be bothering him (is he being bullied at school, for example?), but mysterious aches and pains can often stem from a poor diet, poor digestion, or both. I'd also say that colds are pretty hard to fake, so it sounds as though his immune system is under-performing – which it will do if his diet or digestion isn't good.

Stomach aches can sometimes indicate adverse reactions to specific foods or additives (see Chapter 6), but poor digestion underlies many of these. A bad diet over time, or a single course of antibiotics, can seriously deplete his 'good' gut bacteria, allowing 'bad bacteria' and yeasts to take over. That can stop him digesting his food properly, which can lead to all kinds of unpleasant feelings and symptoms. His bowel movements may give you some clues: if he doesn't easily pass a daily stool that's well-formed and not too smelly, then his digestion could definitely be better!

If his guts are the problem, the good news is you can do something to help him. (The less-good news is that it can take a while!) You've done the sensible thing in checking with your doctor first. Now take on board the information in this book: gradually dump the junk, get your child eating a wide variety of fresh, unadulterated foods, drinking plenty of water, and exercising more. (If need be, ask for a referral to a dietician or other specialist if you need help. Probiotic supplements can also help to restore proper balance to his gut flora.) Once you just get going on a healthier diet and lifestyle, you and your child will find it gets easier and easier. And when your child's better, make sure you tell the doctor how you did it!

I think my child might have a leaky gut or perhaps candida. What should I do next?

First, you *must* visit your doctor to rule out other possible causes of your child's symptoms. Self-diagnosis, or diagnosing your own child, can be very dangerous, as there are always many possible causes for any particular set of symptoms. You haven't told me what those are – but your doctor is always the best person to decide if any other tests or treatments may be needed.

Do discuss your own views, but don't be surprised if the doctor takes a different approach. If you don't agree, you can always get a second opinion. Whatever your doctor recommends, there should be no conflict with feeding your child a healthy diet, limiting foods or drinks high in sugars and refined starches to a minimum. These would just feed any excess yeast, destabilize your child's blood sugar levels and deplete him of vital nutrients at the same time. Plenty has been written about candida and Leaky Gut Syndrome, but the right balance of 'good' bacteria is what you should aim to achieve. This will improve your child's digestion and immune system, so he should be able to keep yeasts and other 'baddies' in check for himself. Once you've seen the doctor, he or she may be able to refer you to a dietician or other specialist if you need individual dietary advice. If you use a nutrition therapist, do check that they're registered with one of the organizations that tries to regulate professionals in this area.

Summary

1. Poor digestion can cause as many problems as poor diet – but the two are inseparable, so they always need to be tackled together.
2. 'Good' bacteria that live in our guts do much of our digestion for us, as well as numerous other 'housekeeping' jobs. In addition, these beneficial gut flora are critical in 'programming' the immune system and keeping it working properly.
3. Digestion takes place in the mouth, stomach and duodenum (part of the small intestine). Faulty digestion can be caused by numerous things: a bad

diet, not chewing properly, eating under stress, low stomach acid, a lack of the right enzymes, and/or some physical diseases.

4. *In all cases of bad digestion there will also be an imbalance of gut flora – known as gut 'dysbiosis'.* This can result in a vicious spiral with increasingly negative consequences for health and well-being.

5. Chewing food thoroughly is essential to good digestion. If things go wrong here it can have knock-on effects on the rest of the system.

6. The stomach mainly deals with digestion of proteins. Some breaking down of fats takes place there, but most digestion of fats needs the help of bile (from the liver) and special enzymes released by the pancreas at the next stage. Starch digestion should have started in your mouth – and resumes again after the stomach, as this needs a less acid environment.

7. A poor diet, lack of sleep and stress can each cause indigestion or 'heartburn'. Take time and relax over meals; don't overload the stomach by eating too much at once, and don't drink too much with meals. Antacids may give temporary relief – but they can make the underlying digestive problems worse. (The stomach needs strong acid in order to break down proteins properly.)

8. Absorption of digested food mainly takes place in the ileum (the last part of the small intestine). Special cells on the *villi* (finger-like projections from the gut wall) need the support of the right gut flora to stay healthy and do their job. Nutrients and special 'carrier proteins' are also needed to help the absorption process.

9. The colon mainly passes on waste for excretion, reclaiming water to produce a solid 'stool' (poo). Looking at your child's stools can give you a good idea of what's going on his gut. Teach him to do this for himself as soon as he's old enough – and if there are any obvious abnormalities, see the doctor without delay.

10. Antibiotics and many other common medications can *seriously* upset the balance of the good gut bacteria your child needs to stay healthy, and may encourage the overgrowth of bad bacteria and yeasts (like Candida) in the gut. This kind of 'gut dysbiosis' can lead to so-called 'Leaky Gut Syndrome' – in which the gut walls allow through substances that shouldn't reach the bloodstream. These could help to trigger some food intolerances, auto-immune diseases and/or other adverse reactions, including undesirable effects on mental well-being and performance.

11. The 'wrong' balance of gut flora can affect every aspect of digestion, as well as the competence of the immune system. These failures are self-reinforcing. The only way to correct such dysbiosis is by changing your child's diet.

12. Improving digestive health can be a slow process, but will pay you big dividends. Establishing and maintaining healthy gut flora really is the key to a well-functioning body and brain, as modern science and medicine are only just starting to recognize.[14]

In the last chapter we saw how important it is that your child gets a good dietary supply of *all* the essential nutrients he needs. You've now seen how important it is to develop and maintain a healthy digestion. In the next chapter we'll look at what foods or substances your child may be consuming that simply don't agree with him, so that you can take the first crucial step. This is to *stop feeding him things that could actually be causing his ill-health, low moods, bad behaviour and learning difficulties.* In Chapter 7 we'll take a closer look at how his eating habits are affecting his energy levels (and yours), so you'll see what you can do to improve this fundamental aspect of his well-being and capabilities. Then, in Chapters 8 and 9, I'll tell you everything you should need to know in order to 'get the fats right' once and for all. When you do this, you'll know how to feed his brains (and your own) with what they really need to make the most of their potential, but have probably been missing out on until now. Then, in Part 3, I'll show you how you can put all this knowledge into practice and improve your child's guts and brains, so both of you can reap the benefits.

chapter 6

what to avoid

additives, anti-nutrients, allergies and addictions

So far we've focused on what your child's diet should be providing (and may not be) in the way of essential nutrients. I've also emphasized how important it is to make sure that what children eat – and the way they eat it – also promotes a healthy digestive system, so that children can break down food properly, absorb what they need from it and neutralize or eliminate all the other substances that are not needed or wanted.

Now it's time to focus on the first of the three main steps I recommend to any parents seeking dietary advice to improve their children's behaviour, learning and mood – as well as general health. This concerns *what your child should avoid*. Before you start adding new foods or drinks to your child's diet, let's first consider what he or she is already eating or drinking that might be doing harm.

There's No Such Thing as a 'Healthy' Food

The good news is that a *huge* variety of different foods can be recommended as part of a healthy, balanced diet – but that variety itself is very important. Your child's diet needs to provide *all* the essential nutrients discussed in

Chapter 4. This is difficult to achieve from a restricted range of foods – and a repetitive diet can also makes food intolerances more likely, as we'll see later in this chapter. To achieve the right balance between different types of foods, check out the revised 'Healthy Eating Pyramid' provided by the Harvard School of Public Health (Appendix, page 386).[1] This helps to correct the highly misleading messages promoted in earlier 'healthy eating guidelines' put out by governments (and their friends in industry), which failed to distinguish between different kinds of fats, or different kinds of carbohydrates. You'll be learning more about how important these distinctions are in Chapters 7 and 8.

With the exception of some truly 'junk' foods (or drinks), most basic foods should cause no problems for *most* individuals. However, it's worth keeping an open mind on this, because it really is true that 'one man's meat is another man's poison'. Some people really can react badly to certain foods that are otherwise nutritious, and which cause most other people no ill-effects at all.

There really is no such thing as a universally 'healthy food' that can be recommended to everyone.

This is why you should at least *consider* whether your child might be having adverse reactions to any of the foods and drinks that he or she regularly consumes, even if these are usually thought to be 'healthy' ones.

Interestingly enough, it's now well recognized that *some food intolerances actually lead to cravings for the very foods that are causing problems*. So if there is anything that your child eats – or wants to eat – at every meal, or every day, do bear this in mind. Prime examples of common, otherwise nutritious foods that can cause problems for *some* children include cows' milk (and dairy products derived from this), wheat (and some other grains), or oranges and other fruits, to name just a few. We'll be taking a look at these later in this chapter.

Some Foods and Drinks Really Are 'Junk'

If there is no such thing as a universally healthy food, then what about 'unhealthy' ones? Surely there are some prime candidates here? We often hear people arguing that no individual food is 'unhealthy', and that the real issue is the overall balance of the diet. Well, quite frankly, listen carefully when you next hear this kind of comment, because I think you'll find that these people are usually representatives of the food industry (or its supporters – which sadly include many people within the Government and its agencies, as well as some professionals in the field of nutrition).

I'd certainly agree that what matters most is the overall balance of the diet, and that means the *combination* of nutrients and energy that your child consumes.

A combination of nutrients and energy is important both in the short term (at the level of each meal or snack, and over the course of a day), and the longer term (weeks, months and years). For this reason I am not one of the killjoys who will say that you and your child should *never* enjoy chocolates, some sweets or other 'snack foods'. However, I will tell you that foods high in sugar, salt and saturated fats (not to mention hydrogenated and trans fats), along with an array of artificial colourings, flavourings and other additives, shouldn't form a regular part of *anyone's* diet if they want a healthy body and mind.

Sadly, these poor-quality foods are just the kinds most heavily advertised to children – and they make up a shocking proportion of some people's diets. No wonder, when they also make up such a scandalous proportion of what's on the supermarket shelves.

Artificial additives, accompanied by too much sugar, salt and the 'wrong' kinds of fats, are found in so many common foods these days that you really need to check the labels. If in doubt, leave it.

Does your child eat many sweets, biscuits, cakes and soft drinks? How about crisps or other savoury snack foods, fast foods and takeaways? Do you buy highly processed 'convenience' foods for the main meal … and if so, do you check the ingredients?

In my opinion, if you are concerned about your child's behaviour, learning or mood, there really are some substances and foods that I think should play little or no part in your child's diet. What's more, you and any other family members could well benefit from avoiding these, too.

The same kind of diet that is good for the body is also good for the brain. Two for the price of one, as it were!

The main things I'd advise you to help your child avoid include:

- **Unnecessary food additives.** Examples include artificial food colourings, artificial sweeteners, some flavourings and even some preservatives, as we shall see. Good-quality, fresh food doesn't need these kinds of additives. They are usually there to make non-nutritious foods look and taste appealing.
- **Other 'anti-nutrients'** – including environmental contaminants such as lead, mercury and other 'heavy metals', pesticides and other synthetic chemicals. Unfortunately, many of these find their way into our food supply as well as getting into our bodies through the air we breathe or physical contact with the skin. Without becoming obsessive about this, do what you can to minimize your child's exposure to these kinds of potential toxins.

Other things I'd recommend any parent to keep 'down and out' of their child's diet – but which are dealt with in the next chapters – include:

- **Foods or drinks rich in sugars or refined starches.** We'll look at this issue in Chapter 7, showing you how to feed your child in a way that avoids the dramatic energy 'highs' and 'lows' that can underlie many rages, tantrums and other behavioural problems, as well as impairing attention, memory, learning ability and sleep.

- **'Junk' fats (hydrogenated and trans fats).** In my opinion, it's more important to avoid these artificially saturated and twisted fats than to avoid natural saturated fats. In Chapters 8 and 9 we'll clear up some of the confusion (and explode some myths) about dietary fats. You'll learn about the essential fats your child really needs if his brain is going to work properly, and what you need to do to 'get the fats right'.

In this chapter we'll look at these first two issues in more detail, because in my view they apply to *all children*. Later in this chapter we'll go on to consider individual differences and the challenges of allergies, intolerances and related gut problems.

There may well be some other foods or substances that *your child in particular* would do well to avoid. Detailed discussion of these issues is beyond the scope of this book, but I'll be offering you some tips on what you can do if you suspect (or already know) that specific food allergies or intolerances are a problem for your child. As we saw in the last chapter, your child's eating habits can seriously affect her digestion. Difficulties at this level (particularly so-called 'leaky gut syndrome') can increase the chances of various adverse food reactions, and could even be the underlying cause of some kinds of weight problems.

Food Additives

Additives are usually included in a product to lengthen its shelf life (preservatives and some unhealthy fats), or to make it look, taste or feel more 'appealing' (colourings, flavourings, emulsifiers or other texture-modifying agents, including those unhealthy fats again!).

Are They Safe?

All food additives that are permitted by UK law have been tested for safety – but I find it rather disturbing that the UK still allows some additives in children's foods and drinks that have long since been banned in other EU countries. There is already good evidence that some food additives can have negative effects on children, including changes in behaviour or mood, as we shall see shortly. The trouble is, behavioural changes aren't usually considered by the experts who advise governments on food-safety issues and regulations. In the same way, the brain's nutritional needs have never really been properly investigated. So whenever you hear someone say, 'Oh, but there's no evidence …', please remember that the key question is: 'Has anybody really *looked*?'

In fact, when we consider what the safety tests and regulations governing food additives actually consist of, they do seem rather ludicrously inadequate when you compare them with the real-life situations they're supposed to be modelling. The standard tests for finding out if food additives may be harmful are usually carried out on *each individual substance in isolation*. But we don't consume these additives in isolation, do we? No, far from it. In foods and drinks, they're usually found in combinations. Typically there may be up to half a dozen additives in just one food or drink. In extreme cases, 30 or more have been noted in some processed foods and drinks that are aimed at children.

Why?

'… nowadays our tastebuds are being fooled by fake flavours, smells and colours. Modern scientists have cooked up over 4,500 chemicals to do just that …

'Natural flavourings don't have to come from the plant or animal you might expect. For example, strawberry flavour products can contain natural flavourings that have never been close to a real, natural strawberry. They have been made in a laboratory and are so chemically similar to real strawberry extract that they are allowed to be called natural. They are sometimes described as "nature identical".'

This quote comes from an excellent website posted by the Food Commission and designed for children and teenagers: www.chewonthis.org. You can also take a look at their website: www.foodcomm.org.uk.

Synergy: When One Plus One Equals Seven

What current regulations ignore is the fact that food additives may have a 'synergistic' effect when they're consumed together. In other words, their effects in combination may be many times more powerful than their separate individual effects would suggest. This was exactly what was found in a recent study at Liverpool University,[2] which tested some common food additives that are regarded as 'safe' in UK law (that is, when tested individually, they all meet current regulations). Four common food additives were studied for their effects on nerve cell development, both individually and in combinations of just two at a time. The additives were:

- Monosodium glutamate (MSG) or E621 – found in many noodles and 'pasta with sauce' products, many crisps and savoury snacks, some processed cheese products, sausages and prepared meals
- Quinoline Yellow or E104 – found in some sweets and confectionery, smoked haddock, scotch eggs and some pickles. It's banned in Australia, Norway and the US.
- Brilliant Blue or E133 – found in sweets, tinned processed peas, some soft drinks, canned and baked goods, confectionery, desserts and edible ices. It's banned in the majority of EU countries.
- 'Aspartame' (containing L-aspartyl-L-phenylalanine methyl ester), or E951 – found in diet/'lite' drinks and foods, and some sweets.

The researchers found that, even individually, each of these additives prevented immature nerve cells from branching out as they otherwise would. But the *combined* effects of these additives in stunting nerve-cell growth were indeed synergistic, causing up to *four times* the effects that would be expected from simple addition in the case of Brilliant blue + MSG, and up to *seven times* the expected effect for Quinoline Yellow + Aspartame.

Rather worrying, don't you think?

When you're told that something is 'safe', just remember that no 'safety testing' procedures are perfect, and the ones currently used to approve any new chemicals are far from it.

Leading developmental toxicopathologist Dr Vyvyan Howard (senior scientist on the Liverpool study) had already highlighted the 'synergy' problem in an earlier study.[3] He pointed out then that to test the 1,000 most common toxic chemicals in unique combinations of three would take at least 166 million different experiments – and that's ignoring the need to study varying amounts or doses!

In my view, none of the additives in the Liverpool study should need to be in our foods and drinks in the first place – and certainly not in those aimed at children, whose nervous systems are still developing. My advice is: try to avoid foods with non-essential additives and, whenever possible, buy fresh, basic ingredients to make your own simple yet nutritious and tasty meals. (Chapters 12–14 have some great recipe ideas.)

Can Food Additives Really Cause Bad Behaviour?

In the 1970s a US paediatrician called Ben Feingold suggested that hyperactivity and related symptoms could be reduced in many children by eliminating artificial food colourings (AFCs) from the diet. He also recommended avoiding salicylates (substances found naturally in many fruits and vegetables) and some preservatives.

Many parents and teachers have long insisted that certain food additives affect their children's mood and behaviour, and many leading support groups and other professionals who work with children agree. But the full Feingold diet is a very restrictive one, and to date only some of its recommendations have been backed by rigorous scientific study, as we shall see.

The thing is, neither 'anecdotal' reports nor survey data count as reliable scientific evidence for cause and effect. 'Randomized controlled trials' are always needed for that, in order to avoid the influence of the researchers' expectations or other possible sources of bias. These kinds of trials are certainly not easy to do, and they are not always even feasible for some kinds of 'treatment', including complex changes in children's diets. (There's a full explanation of randomized controlled trials in the Appendix, page 375.)

The good news is that in the decades following Feingold a number of rigorous trials of this kind were in fact carried out and their results published – some of them in top medical journals such as the *Lancet*.[4]

Many of these studies did show that removing certain additives from children's diets could improve their behaviour ... but others didn't. The substances that triggered adverse reactions also varied considerably between individuals, and for some children these included specific foods as well as – or instead of – additives. Over 20 years ago, a statistical summary (or 'meta-analysis') combining the results from different trials was published, and this concluded that the 'Feingold Diet' had only a small and non-significant effect on ADHD symptoms. Many parents and support groups continued to apply or recommend the Feingold approach, and a few health professionals remained sympathetic, but by and large the medical establishment pretty much decided that the case was closed.

Another Look at Artificial Food Colourings

Two important new studies have recently re-opened the debate. The first was an updated review and meta-analysis published in 2004, which told a rather different story from the first one.[5] This was more tightly focused, looking only at artificial food colourings (AFCs). According to the US researchers who carried out this new review, an update was needed for several reasons:

1. The earlier statistical summary included too broad a range of studies, involving different kinds of dietary interventions. This unfocused approach could well have concealed genuine links between *some* dietary changes and ADHD symptoms.

2. It failed to include some relevant studies that were available at the time.

3. Several more good-quality trials had been published since then.

For the new review, the authors first searched systematically for all published double-blind, controlled trials of AFCs on the behaviour of children with hyperactivity or similar syndromes. They found 15 trials involving a total of 219 children. When all the results were combined in the meta-analysis, the result was clear: overall, the behaviour of these children *did* improve significantly when AFCs were eliminated from their diets. In fact, *simply removing these unnecessary additives led to benefits that were, on average, between one-third and one-half of those that would usually be expected after taking stimulant medications.*

Of course, averages are just that: for some individual children the effects were quite dramatic, while for others the dietary changes made little difference to their behaviour. It also didn't seem to matter whether or not the children had been officially diagnosed with hyperactivity or ADHD. Parents noticed the differences more than teachers and, not surprisingly, the children whose behaviour improved the most when AFCs were withdrawn from their diet were those whose parents already suspected that their child was a 'responder'.

The authors of this review were understandably very cautious about the implications of their findings. They noted that the restrictive nature of AFC-free diets may 'place a burden' on children and families. (Well, only because these artificial colourings are permitted in children's foods and drinks, when there is really no good reason for this at all that I can see!) They therefore suggested that 'imposition of the diet should be done "reluctantly" until more certain methods have been developed to identify AFC-responsive children'. (In my view, parents usually do a pretty good job of predicting this if they are alerted to the possibility. Instead, many are told that what they regularly see with their own eyes just can't be true!) The authors did, however, emphasize the need for additional research in this area. Hear, hear!

The Isle of Wight Study

By coincidence, additional research was already on its way. Although too late to be included in the US meta-analysis, the biggest controlled trial of food additives and behaviour to date was also published in 2004, this time by a group of UK researchers.[6] This landmark study was initially funded by the Ministry for Agriculture, Fisheries and Food (MAFF), but when this organization was disbanded, responsibility for the trial then passed to the Food Standards Agency. Most of the previous studies concerning food additives had involved children with hyperactivity or other 'ADHD-type' difficulties, leaving unanswered the very important question of whether similar effects might apply to children more generally. Another suspicion was that perhaps children who suffered from allergies might be particularly vulnerable. This new study of 277 3-year-olds from the Isle of Wight was designed to address these issues.

The researchers looked into the effects of artificial colourings (E102, E110, E122, E124) and a preservative (E211). First, with advice from a dietician, parents removed foods and drinks with these additives from their children's diets for a whole month. (Almost immediate improvements in behaviour were noticed by parents – but of course they knew the additives had been removed, and so these improvements could have been affected by what the parents were expecting to happen.) Then for one week during that month the children all drank a special fruit drink every day. All these drinks looked and tasted identical, but half of them contained the additives being tested, and half didn't, and no one knew which was which (this is what's known as a 'double-blind' trial – as neither the researchers nor the participants, and in this case their parents too – could know who was taking what). The results were telling:

Additives Used in the Isle of Wight Test

ARTIFICIAL FOOD COLOURINGS (AFCS)
Tartrazine (E102): a synthetic yellow azo dye ('azo' is the name used for a particular class of food colourings) found in sodas, ice cream, sweets, chewing gum, jam and yoghurt. It's commonly used in the UK but banned in Norway and Austria.

Sunset yellow (E110): a synthetic yellow azo dye found in orange jelly, apricot jam, packet soups … and canned fish and hot chocolate mixes! It's banned in Norway and Finland but not in the UK.

Carmoisine (E122): a synthetic red azo dye found in jams, sweets, sauce, yoghurts, jellies and cheesecake mixes. It's banned in Japan, Norway, Sweden and the US, but not in the UK.

Ponceau 4R (E124): also known as Cochineal Red, this is a synthetic red azo dye found in dessert toppings, jelly, canned strawberries and fruit pie fillings, salami and seafood dressings. It's banned in Norway and the US, but not in the UK.

PRESERVATIVE

Sodium Benzoate (E211): an antibacterial and antifungal preservative that can also be used to disguise the taste of poor-quality food. It aggravates the symptoms of asthma, particularly when ingested in conjunction with tartrazine. Sodium benzoate can also react with vitamin C to form the aggressive cancer-causing compound benzene.

The parents of children who got the 'additive cocktail' noticed a significant increase in their child's hyperactivity and related behaviour problems (for example, poor concentration, temper-tantrums, fidgeting, disturbing others and difficulty going to sleep) compared with parents whose children were given the ordinary fruit drink. A particularly striking finding was that the negative effects of AFCs on behaviour applied to *the whole group of children*, not just those who showed hyperactive behaviour or allergies before the tests started.

To safeguard children's health, countries like Norway, Denmark and the US have already restricted or banned the artificial colourings tested in the Isle of Wight study. So why is that not happening here? And why not worldwide? The official response of the Food Standards Agency (FSA) to the Isle of Wight study was to declare the results 'inconclusive', mainly on the grounds that on some other measures (namely computer games designed to assess the children's 'impulsivity' or 'inattention') the children's behaviour wasn't affected by the type of drink they were given. In my view, when it comes to assessing the behaviour of 3-year-olds accurately, I'd back the parents' observations over a computer game every time. The FSA has, however, commissioned more research.

Meanwhile, many children's foods and drinks continue to include these additives, so if you want to play safe and rule out one possible cause of your child's behaviour problems, don't expect the regulatory agencies to help you just yet! It still remains up to you to check food and drink labels carefully, and avoid them.

FSA Awaits More Results Before Considering Action

After the Isle of Wight study indicating that some common food additives could trigger bad behaviour in *all* 3-year-olds (not just certain groups), the FSA has now funded a follow-on study to look into how artificial food additives may affect the behaviour of children. Results are expected in spring 2007.

You can wait until then if you like – or do something *now* to reduce your child's exposure to these additives.

You'll find further information and details of studies in this area on the Food and Behaviour Research website.[7] Unfortunately, there really are lots of additives that can cause problems for some children. You can find 12 of the 'worst offenders' in the Appendix, but for information on many more additives, and children's foods and drinks that contain these, visit the Food Commission's website.

To get you started, we'll look at just five different additives in a little more detail here:

- MSG (a commonly used flavouring)
- tartrazine (an artificial colouring that is banned in other countries)
- sodium benzoate (a commonly used preservative)
- 'sulphites' (also used as preservatives in many foods)
- artificial sweeteners (used instead of, or in addition to, sucrose and other sugar substitutes)

Monosodium Glutamate (MSG)

Glutamic acid is a naturally occurring amino acid (a precursor to a protein), and MSG is a sodium salt derived from glutamic acid. The glutamate, not the sodium, is the active ingredient in MSG. Glutamate is an 'excitatory' signalling molecule used by many of your cells, and known to be toxic to brain cells in excess, but most of the glutamate in your body and brain is chemically bound up so that it doesn't over-excite nerve cells. 'Free' (unbound) glutamate is found in many foods such as kelp, parmesan cheese, peas, tomatoes, grapes and plums, but usually in small enough quantities for your body to deal with it. MSG is used as a flavour enhancer because it stimulates taste buds, and in fact this chemical lies behind the 'fifth taste' that's now been identified (in addition to the basic tastes of salt, sweet, sour and bitter). It's a meaty, cheesy, savoury kind of taste that's been given the Japanese name of 'umami'.

The problem with MSG is that your child can get too much glutamate in its free form all at once from some foods, such as some Chinese foods, ready meals, flavoured crisps and savoury snacks. Most people are not affected by MSG in the diet, especially in small doses, but if your child is intolerant to it he or she may suffer from physical symptoms like asthma, sneezing and a runny nose, or behavioural reactions including hyperactivity and fatigue. Other symptoms of what was once called 'Chinese Restaurant Syndrome' can include headaches, flushing, heartburn, palpitations, chest pain, numbness or burning in or around the mouth, a sense of pressure around the jaw and face, and sweating.

As we saw earlier, new evidence shows that MSG can have 'synergistic' effects with some synthetic food colourings when it comes to damaging the development of young nerve cells. It may make 'empty' snacks and foods taste better … but are the possible risks to your child really worth it?

Tartrazine (E102)

Tartrazine is one of a group of brightly coloured 'azo' dyes derived from petroleum products. Tartrazine closely resembles the colour of oranges, so it began to be used in drinks in the early 20th century. It was later adopted for use in a wide variety of foods such as 'bread crumbs', fish fingers, cakes, sweets and biscuits, milk shakes, fish fingers and canned vegetables.

As we've seen, tartrazine and other azo dyes were not only the main additives tested in the Isle of Wight study, but they are also classic 'AFCs' used in many of the other studies that showed negative effects on children's behaviour.

> 'My friend inadvertently gave my son (5) an ice lolly with tartrazine in it. She apologized profusely when she dropped him back at home, saying that he'd been "hyper" since he'd had it an hour previously. He was running around, leaping on furniture and beating up the walls. It took another two hours for him to calm down. Ice lollies without tartrazine in have no such effect.' – Debbie

We still don't know the exact mechanisms by which azo dyes can disrupt some children's behaviour, but in a pioneering early study the UK researcher Dr Neil Ward and the Hyperactive Children's Support Group found that drinks containing tartrazine triggered an excessive loss of zinc in the urine of children with ADHD.[8] As we saw in Chapters 3 and 4, children with behaviour and learning difficulties often lack zinc in any case (as do many other children), and this trace mineral is needed for at least 200 different enzymes in the brain and body to do their jobs properly. More orange drink, anyone?

Good Reasons to Avoid Many Artificial Food Colourings

Many rigorous scientific studies have now shown that the artificial food colouring tartrazine and other 'azo dyes' can worsen the behaviour of hyperactive children.

In one such double-blind, placebo-controlled trial, 54 children were tested with 6 different dose levels of tartrazine, and parents rated their reactions over the next 24 hours.[9] 24 of the children reacted badly to tartrazine (19 of 23 'suspected reactors', 3 of 11 'uncertain reactors' and 2 of 20 'control' children). The negative effects increased systematically with higher doses of tartrazine.

All of these children had a history of allergies, asthma, eczema or allergic rhinitis (runny nose).

Different children reacted in different ways, but the effects varied between younger children (2 to 6 years old) and the older ones (aged 7 to 14 years).

- **Younger children** showed constant crying, tantrums, irritability, restlessness, and severe sleep disturbance and were described by their parents as 'disruptive', 'easily distracted and excited', 'high as a kite' and 'out of control'. Their parents were exhausted through lack of sleep and the constant demands of their children, who couldn't be comforted or controlled.
- **Older children** showed behaviours described as 'irritable', 'aimlessly active', 'lacking self-control', 'whiney and unhappy' and 'like a bear with a sore head' – but their sleep difficulties were less likely to disturb the entire family.

Sodium Benzoate

'Soft drinks', including fizzy drinks, squashes and some fruit juice drinks, rarely have any real nutritional value. As we've just seen, many contain artificial colourings, along with far too much sugar and/or artificial sweeteners. (We'll have a word to say about artificial sweeteners shortly – and sugar deserves a book all to itself, but we'll look at this in the next chapter.) Most soft drinks also contain preservatives, often including sodium benzoate (or its close relative, potassium benzoate) to help prevent bacterial growth. This is why sodium benzoate was also included in the Isle of Wight study cocktail.

A new worry about benzoate preservatives is the fact that manufacturers often add some vitamin C to soft drinks, in an attempt to make them appear healthier. Why should this be worrying? Well, the benzoates have long been known to react with ascorbic acid (vitamin C) to produce benzene, which is an aggressive carcinogen (it causes cancer).

Earlier this year (2006), 230 drinks on sale in Britain and France were found to contain eight times the level of benzene that is legally permitted in drinking water. This issue was investigated after similar findings in soft drinks in the US, where the US Food and Drug Administration registered its concern about the possible long-term effects on people's health. The UK Food Standards Agency said that finding these traces at eight times the level permitted in drinking water didn't pose an immediate health risk.[10]

We seem to have some double standards here! If drinking water can only have one part per billion of benzene, why on earth should soft drinks be allowed eight times as much, especially when they're so heavily marketed to children? Some helpful commentators suggested, 'Just take the ascorbic acid out again' (I think this slightly misses the point!), and 'We drink much more water than soft drinks, so it's not a problem.' (Not for them, maybe – but in fact many children actually consume more of these kinds of soft drinks than they do water.) It's obviously your decision, but I know what I'd choose to do!

Think about this carefully: soft drinks used to be a rare treat, and they are not in any way necessary. The evidence is mounting that many of these kinds of drinks could damage your child's brain as well as body. What could you do to 'treat' your child instead?

Sulphites

Sulphur dioxide and other sulphite compounds are used as preservatives in many foods. Sulphur dioxide, for example, is an antioxidant used to prevent browning (the process you see when you leave a cut apple exposed to the air); it's that which keeps dried apricots looking, well, 'apricoty'. Organic dried apricots are brown.

You need to look for 'sulphur dioxide' and 'sulphite' on food labels (it might be hidden in longer words such as 'sodium metabisulphite'), or any of the E numbers from E220 to E228.

It's well known that sulphites may aggravate symptoms of asthma, and they have also been linked with dizziness, nerve problems, blurred vision, stomach problems and reduction in levels of vitamin B_1 (thiamine) in the body. Less well known is that sulphites can aggravate symptoms in children with autism and other behavioural disorders. This is because these individuals have a problem with a process called 'sulphation' where sulphites are oxidized into sulphates.[11] One of the side-effects is that the 'arousal' neurotransmitters are not deactivated very well, so the child involved stays in a state of arousal/hyperactivity.

And that's not all: consider the *hidden* sulphites – those in corn syrup and cornstarch: sulphites are added in during the production process, and as such aren't included in the labelling. Be aware that corn syrup and cornstarch are used in many, many commercial food and sweets. So it's a double whammy – sugar and those sulphites.

Artificial Sweeteners

Artificial sweeteners are the subject of huge controversy, with some protesting their safety (usually food industry supporters) and others seriously questioning them (usually parents and many professionals who work with parents and children, and also scientific researchers who have studied them). Some artificial sweeteners have been linked to behaviour or mood changes, and some are implicated as being carcinogenic (cancer-causing). Even the argument that sugar replacements are good for people on special diets for weight loss or diabetes is questionable in many cases.

Probably the least controversial of the sugar-substitutes are certain alcohol sugars, including xylitol, manitol and sorbitol. There is even evidence that these can help to prevent the growth of bacteria that can cause tooth decay. Taken in excess, however, xylitol can have a laxative effect – so don't let your child chew too much 'sugar-free' gum in a day! And ideally, you really want to be steering your child away from wanting too many sweet things, rather than looking for foods or drinks with a sugar substitute. Hints to help you here are included in Part 3.

By far the most controversial of all the artificial sweeteners is Aspartame (NutraSweet™). Do a search on the Internet for 'aspartame' and be prepared to stay there for a week. It is one of the most contentious dietary issues around. Basically, there are two main camps: the food industry, backed by various governmental bodies in different countries, with plenty of corroborative research; and thousands of individual reports attesting to the detrimental effects of aspartame, also backed up by some good research – but oddly, most of it not funded by industry.

As always, in the end it is up to you to read, listen, analyse and decide for yourself and your child. But do ask yourself if your child really needs to ingest anything that has been implicated in at least 92 different health problems, including hyperactivity, aggression, anxiety, depression and migraine. (Aspartame also isn't recommended for use by people who have the rare genetic syndrome called phenylketonuria, as it contains phenylalanine, which they can't process safely.)

Aspartame isn't actually marketed as a diet aid, but being very low in calories it's used in many 'low-sugar' foods and drinks – so of course people will make the assumption that it could help them lose weight. In fact, overweight or not, your child is best served by a varied diet that contains relatively little sugar (the World Health Organization recommends a maximum of 10 per cent of total energy) and provides enough proteins, complex carbohydrates and essential fatty acids – along with other essential micronutrients (vitamins, minerals and antioxidants) and plenty of exercise. Aspartame and other artificial sweeteners are typically found in foods and drinks with very little nutritional benefit, and a range of other suspect additives in them, too. My advice would be: 'If in doubt, leave them out.'

I am also horrified that *many vitamin and mineral supplements aimed at children contain artificial sweeteners*. Unsuspecting parents can easily be caught out here. Don't be one of them.

Aspartame by Any Other Name ...

Aspartame has many aliases. Look at labels for:

- NutraSweet™
- Equal™
- Canderel™

- Benevia™
- Spoonful™
- Misura™
- E951
- 'Contains a source of phenylalanine'

Food for Grim Thought

Think of what additives – with their synergistic effects – your child might be eating in one day. Next time you're in the supermarket, look carefully at the ingredients labels, and keep a tally sheet (see Appendix, page 389) of the additives they contain. And don't just look for additives; note how much sugar, processed starches and fats are involved. The lists below outline a typical day's food for two children from a real survey.[12] On the face of it Chloe's diet looks much healthier, but *both* of these children are getting too much salt and saturated fats – and way too much sugar – and analyses showed that Chloe is consuming 48 different additives in one day, while Jordan's diet contains no less than 80 different additives, and is lacking in every nutrient included in the analyses.

Jordan
- Breakfast: yoghurt, two glasses of milk
- Lunch: bread and butter, chips and spaghetti hoops
- Tea: sausages and bacon, ice-cream and chocolate cake
- Snacks: packet of savoury snacks, soft drink, yoghurts, Swiss roll, chocolate

Chloe
- Breakfast: crumpet with savoury spread, 2 glasses of milk
- Lunch: bread and butter with savoury spread
- Tea: 2 fish fingers, mashed potato, sweetcorn, carrots
- Snacks: banana, cheese snack, fromage frais, two chocolate bars, sponge cake, blackcurrant juice drink, apple, tangerine, packet of crisps

	Recommended Daily Intake	Jordan	Chloe
Salt	5g	7g	5.8g
Saturated Fat	23g	29g	44g
Sugar	54g	142g	153g
Portions of fruit and veg	5	0	5
Fibre	15g	10g	18g
Folate	150mcg	86mcg	282mcg
Vitamin A	500mcg	290mcg	1,021mcg
Vitamin C	30mg	19mg	200mg
Iron	9mg	6mg	9mg
Zinc	7mg	6mg	9mg
Calcium	550mg	800mg	884mg

'When I changed my son's diet, it was a real struggle at first – he was addicted to junky foods. Eventually his tastes changed … and so did his behaviour. He still has ADHD symptoms to a degree, but is so much better and happier.'
– Daisy

On the face of it, Chloe was being given a healthier diet than Jordan, but her mother was still unaware of just how many additives and sugars were present in the food. The good news is that once you realize why additive-laden, processed foods are worth avoiding, it really isn't too hard to replace these with healthier options.

Why Do We Still Have Unnecessary Additives?

The researchers in the Isle of Wight study estimated that if problem additives were taken out of children's diets (food and drink), the rate of hyperactivity would drop substantially – from 1 in 6 to 1 in 17.

If the manufacturers aren't going to lead the way, then you can. Read labels carefully and don't let your child eat or drink these additive-laden products. Write and tell the manufacturers why you're no longer buying their product.

Talk this over with your child, pointing out cause and effect, because once he's old enough not to be under your supervision he must be informed enough to read labels for himself and say 'No.'

Other Anti-nutrients

Unfortunately, exposure to synthetic chemicals is now a fact of life – and we all have many substances in our bodies that simply didn't exist 100 or even 50 years ago. Rather alarmingly, children generally seem to have higher levels of these chemicals in their bodies than their parents and grandparents do, as their systems may be less able to prevent these substances from gaining access in the first place, or to get rid of them once they do.

Heavy Metals and Other Potential Toxins

Toxic metals are bad news, and include mercury, lead, cadmium and aluminium. You've also probably heard plenty of 'scare stories' about pesticides and other toxic chemicals, including organophosphates and organochlorides, PCBs and dioxins among many others. These powerful chemicals are known to be capable of causing adverse neurological (brain) symptoms. Unfortunately they've been used so widely that traces have accumulated in our environment, including the food chain. This means that diet can certainly play *some* role, but major exposure to these kinds of toxins *usually* comes primarily from other sources. I can only go over them briefly here; you can read up on them in more detail on the Internet. Medline Plus is a respectable and trustworthy source that's a good place to start: http://www.nlm.nih.gov/medlineplus/poisoningtoxicologyenvironmentalhe alth.html.

Lead

There are no safe levels of lead. That is one thing everyone is agreed on, although it took many years of pioneering work by Professor Derek Bryce-Smith and others to get our Government to accept the damage it can cause to mental development and function. Lead is a broad-spectrum toxin, meaning that it can disturb almost every metabolic function in the body and brain. It interferes with nerve function and can mimic and inhibit calcium in cells. It can reduce the availability of (the body's access to) both serotonin and dopamine – key brain chemicals needed for impulse control and the suppression of violent behaviour.

Not everyone will react in the same way to lead exposure, of course, so it could make some children appear 'dull' and others 'hyperactive'. High levels detected in blood, teeth and hair could reflect excessive exposure or inadequate detoxification mechanisms – in other words, individual effects will depend on your child's genetic make-up, as well as age and diet. More is absorbed through inhalation (for example, from petrol fumes) than ingestion, although some old houses do still have lead pipes carrying drinking water – the main 'dietary' source of exposure. Children absorb much more than adults, and you should make sure that no toys or furniture they can access contain lead-based paints. There have been extensive studies on the toxic effects of lead[13] that you may find interesting to read in detail.

Mercury

Mercury is another heavy metal, and in the form of methyl mercury it is well known as a neurotoxin, meaning that it can damage the brain and nervous system. Unborn babies and children are particularly vulnerable, and exposure to methyl mercury can damage vision, hearing, attention and memory, or cause muscle weakness and poor motor coordination, problems in acquiring speech and language skills, and poor cognition (thinking and reasoning).

Apart from accidental ingestion (from broken thermometers, for example, or industrial contamination), other potential sources of mercury include amalgam ('silver') dental fillings and some vaccinations. Some types of fish can also be contaminated with mercury – and advice from government agencies about this to pregnant women in the US and UK has led to a fall in their fish intake. Unfortunately, the vast majority of pregnant women weren't actually consuming *enough* fish in any case, because fish and seafood are major sources of the omega-3 fatty acids that their baby's brains need in order to develop and function normally. In fact, the latest evidence suggests that the real risk of mercury toxicity from fish has probably been grossly over-estimated, and that there is actually more risk of exactly the same list of problems if children don't get enough omega-3 fatty acids.[14] You can find out more about fatty acids and their benefits in Chapters 8 and 9. Meanwhile, use these checkpoints to minimize your child's exposure to mercury:

- Check that tuna and salmon, marlin, swordfish and shark are from sources that guarantee they're mercury free, particularly if you're pregnant or trying for a baby. If you're not sure, switch to sardines or high-quality, purified fish oil supplements, because *not* having the key omega-3 fatty acids that fish oils can provide is even more harmful to your health.
- Ask your doctor to give vaccinations that don't include the mercury-containing preservative thimerosal. Numerous studies link thimerosal with oxidative stress, which causes cell damage.
- Get your dentist to check your child's fillings are not cracked, and ask for non-amalgam ones the next time these may be needed. (If you cut down on the sugary foods and drinks, your child shouldn't need so many fillings in any case.)

Pesticides

Numerous studies link the use of pesticides to various neurological (brain) disorders. Some of the most controversial pesticides have been banned, but sadly their residues – and other pesticides with toxic potential – are all around us. Without becoming obsessive about this, do what you can to minimize your child's exposure to them. Children are particularly vulnerable because they take in more food and drink per body unit of weight than adults, and they have relatively immature 'detoxification' systems. It's not easy: on the one hand you're told to encourage your child to eat fruit and vegetable skins (where practicable!), and on the other to discard the skins because they're covered in pesticides.

Foods which are more likely to have pesticide residues include strawberries, nectarines, peaches, apples, pears and cherries. Some other foods, such as bananas and oranges, don't seem as vulnerable, and we don't usually eat the skins in any case. Current Government policies on the residues that fruit and vegetable produce are allowed to contain are fairly strict, and these are based on avoiding any possible toxicity risk according to the best evidence we have. But as we've seen, no safety testing system can ever be perfect.

Avoid Pesticides As Much As You Can

The Ontario College of Family Physicians (OCFP) is strongly recommending that people reduce their exposure to pesticides wherever possible after releasing a comprehensive review of research on the effects of pesticides on human health.[15]

The review (April 2004) shows consistent links to serious illnesses such as cancer, reproductive problems and neurological diseases, among others.

The study also shows that children are particularly vulnerable to pesticides.

You can do several things to help reduce your child's exposure to pesticides, such as:

- Make sure your child has a healthy, well-balanced and varied diet. This will help to maintain the body's natural defences against many potentially harmful chemicals.
- Wash food thoroughly, scrubbing harder skins.
- If possible, choose organic fruit, vegetables and grains and/or grow your own. Although organic foods are often more expensive, they are likely to contain more nutrients and taste better, so they usually get eaten rather than half-left.
- Avoid exposing your child to all pesticides whenever and wherever possible. Stay clear when parks or fields are being sprayed, and try to avoid using pesticides (or choose organic ones) in your own home and garden.

Once more, you need to become informed so that you can make the decisions you believe best for your child.

Food Allergies and Intolerances

We've already seen that various artificial food additives could be having damaging effects on your child's behaviour. Now it's time to consider whether some foods might also be a problem. Adverse reactions to foods or drinks can come in a wide variety of different forms, including:

- simple food poisoning (from eating contaminated or spoiled food)
- 'toxic overload' from consuming 'too much' of a substance at once (alcohol hangovers are a prime example in grown-ups …)
- food allergies (in various forms)
- so-called 'food intolerances'

Unfortunately, the issues surrounding food allergies and intolerances are immensely complex, and can't be addressed in detail in this book. All I can do is to give you some very basic guidelines, but two books I'd recommend to anyone wanting to know more about these subjects are *Was It Something You Ate?*[16] – which provides a very sensible and balanced coverage of many common adverse food reactions (and how to avoid them), and *The Complete Guide to Food Allergy and Intolerance*[17] – which really does live up to its title!

Although they're certainly not confined to these groups, food sensitivities of all kinds seem particularly common in children with autism spectrum disorders, ADHD, dyslexia, dyspraxia or other kinds of behaviour and learning difficulties. In this area, by far the best book I've come across for explaining these apparent links is *Gut and Psychology Syndromes* by Dr Natasha Campbell-McBride, which I drew your attention to in Chapter 5.[18] Years ago, when her own son was given the 'autistic' label, Dr Campbell-McBride was told that there was 'nothing that could be done'. Fortunately, being a doctor already she knew how limited the existing medical knowledge in this area really was. So, with the true dedication of a mother, she went and found out for herself what could be done, and she did it! Her book explains clearly how modern medical practices (particularly antibiotics and other medications, including the contraceptive pill) have acted along with 'junk food diets' to actually 'set us up' for the apparent explosion in the prevalence of gut and brain-related conditions such as autism. If your child falls anywhere within the 'autistic spectrum' (or has any of the associated conditions – which are many), *make sure you read Dr Campbell-McBride's book* before you adopt any of the 'special diets' recommended by people who haven't got Natasha's qualifications.

Let's now take a quick look at the subject of food allergies and intolerances – but before we do, I want to offer two important words of warning:

1) Don't get carried away with 'exclusion diets'

I've met numerous parents who've become preoccupied with excluding all kinds of foods from their children's diets, on the grounds of supposed 'allergies' or 'intolerances'. There may sometimes be good reasons for this, but quite often, excluding major foods or groups of foods (such as wheat and other grains, milk and other dairy products, or most fruits and vegetables) is not only unnecessary, but could actually put your children at risk of nutrient deficiencies. I cannot emphasize strongly enough that in my view, **you should always seek specialist advice** *(from someone who really does have suitable qualifications to provide this advice[19])* **before you start excluding major foods or food groups from your child's diet.**

Unduly Restrictive Diets Can Sometimes Make Matters Worse

One study compared autistic children on 'gluten-free, casein-free' (GF-CF) diets (excluding many cereals as well as milk products) with another group of autistic children who were allowed to eat what they wanted.[20] They found that:

- Both groups had more signs of protein malnutrition (deficiencies in the levels of essential amino acids in their blood) than a control group of normally developing children.
- Many of the autistic children in both groups lacked the amino acids needed to make important neurotransmitters (chemicals involved in brain cell signalling).
- These nutrient deficiencies were slightly *more* pronounced in the autistic children following the GF-CF diet.

These findings show clearly why it is always worth investigating the nutritional status of children with these kinds of behaviour and learning difficulties. But the findings also highlight the possible drawbacks of strict exclusion diets (particularly with children who are 'fussy eaters' anyway, as so many autistic children are).

So: *if you want to try excluding major food groups from your child's diet to see if this may help, do get advice first from a dietician or other suitably qualified specialist.*

2) Start with the guts of the matter

Many so-called 'food allergies and intolerances' reflect much more complex issues concerning digestion, immune-system balance and general health, as well as the overall 'toxic load' to which any individual is exposed. As the book *Gut and Psychology Syndromes* explains so well, many disturbances of behaviour, learning and mood can also be the result of an unhealthy gut and an impaired digestive system. As we saw in Chapter 5, your child's digestion is an exquisitely complex affair that can be 'upset' by numerous things. A poor diet, along with many common medications (most notably antibiotics) can easily impair digestion and disrupt the healthy 'gut flora' that should inhabit the digestive tract from top to bottom.

These good bacteria are essential for your child to be able to digest and absorb nutrients properly. They also help to *make* many essential nutrients, and they play a crucial role in protecting the delicate lining of the gut wall. Together with certain key nutrients that children's diets often lack (omega-3 fatty acids, vitamin A, zinc and selenium, to name but a few), a healthy population of gut flora will help your child to maintain a healthy, balanced immune system. A balanced and varied diet, and a healthy digestion, can therefore help to keep at least some potential 'allergies' and 'intolerances' in check.

So before you start blaming your child's problems on sensitivities to foods that could otherwise make a valuable contribution to his diet, take a step back and consider *first* the state of his digestion. If you work on improving that, you may find that the symptoms you thought were 'allergies' will go away in any case. Many people claim miraculous improvements following the exclusion of certain foods from their diets. They often don't realize that these could easily be the result of *other* dietary changes they've been making – either alongside or as substitutes for the foods they are now avoiding. Don't be one of those parents who falls for all the latest fads, paying out money for expensive tests (often of dubious merit), or seeing all kinds of alternative therapists until you've done some homework. Before you think about depriving your child of his favourite foods, make sure you consult with someone who really *is* qualified to help you decide whether 'food intolerances' are the primary problem. Although such intolerances can be very real, why not make some of the more obvious improvements to your child's diet and digestion first?

Food Allergies

An allergic response happens when your body responds to something you inhale, touch or ingest as if it were a threat. Substances provoking this kind of reaction are known as 'antigens' or 'allergens'. Your body produces special proteins called *antibodies* to fight antigens, and the type of antibody produced in the case of any 'classic' allergy is an immunoglobulin called IgE. Tendencies towards high IgE levels can run in families. If your child has any food allergies, you might have noticed that she or other members of the family are prone to other allergic reactions like hay fever, asthma or eczema.

Also involved in allergic reactions are 'mast' cells, which are found in all body tissues, but especially in the nose, throat, gut, lungs and skin – just the places where you usually notice the effects of allergic responses. IgE is found in these places, too, where it can cause mast cells to release chemicals like histamine which produce the symptoms of an allergic reaction:

- Histamine released from skin mast cells can produce intense itching or hives (raised, red welts).
- Histamine released from gut mast cells can cause abdominal pain or diarrhoea.
- Histamine released from the nose and throat can cause an itching mouth or tongue, and possibly problems with breathing or swallowing.

Classic allergy symptoms usually occur almost immediately after exposure to the offending substance, so they are *usually* fairly obvious. The diagnosis of a true food allergy should not in any way be left to chance or experiment, however, and should always be carried out by a medical consultant. The most common foods that children may develop allergies to are eggs, milk, wheat, peanuts (and some other nuts), fish, shellfish and soy. Severe allergies can be life-threatening if not properly treated, but once identified they can usually be managed by avoiding the substance in question, and making sure that the right kind of treatment is available if accidental exposure should occur.

Food Intolerances

'Intolerance' reactions usually involve different mechanisms from those involved in so-called 'classic' food allergies. These are still not well understood, but immunoglobulins called IgA and IgG are thought to be responsible, rather than IgE. To give an extremely simplified outline:

- IgA act as an 'unarmed' first line of defence, and their job is to prevent foreign (unrecognized) molecules from escaping from the gut into the bloodstream.

- IgG circulate in the blood, and like IgE, they can launch a full-blown immune attack if they come across something that they think shouldn't be there – like a fragment of protein from partly digested food.

This explains why food-intolerance reactions are not usually immediate (it takes time for substances that you eat to get down to your guts, and into your bloodstream). It also explains why *poor digestion is usually the starting point*, because if you digest your food perfectly, all proteins are broken down to their individual amino acids. Our immune systems are mainly primed to react to proteins or protein fragments – because these are usually what signal the presence of foreign invaders such as viruses or bad bacteria.

What's more, this kind of 'indirect' mechanism also explains why poor health and repeated infections can increase the chances of developing food intolerances. Many common medications can actually lower IgA defences, and some infections (including measles and some other viruses) can compromise the integrity of the gut lining (as can some allergic reactions, including coeliac disease – the classic form of gluten intolerance).

I hope you can now see why the information in Chapter 5 about how your digestive system works is so important. Make sure you address this issue *first*, or you could be making your child avoid foods unnecessarily as well as failing to solve the real problems. As we've seen, poor digestion can be triggered by numerous factors, including failure to chew food properly, eating when highly stressed or 'on the run', low stomach acidity, poor enzyme production, gut 'dysbiosis' (an unhealthy imbalance of gut bacteria), yeast infection or a 'leaky' or damaged gut lining. Various disorders of the gall bladder or pancreas can also cause unpleasant reactions to foods, but these usually produce other symptoms, too. As ever, if your child has any persistent symptoms, your first port of call should *always* be your doctor.

With food intolerances, your child won't necessarily show symptoms immediately after eating the food in question, so unlike classic allergies, these kinds of reactions can be difficult to spot.

An 'exclusion/reintroduction' diet is the only truly reliable way to determine whether any food or substance may be triggering adverse reactions. This means you cut out any suspect foods, and then gradually reintroduce them one at a time, keeping a careful diary of symptoms. Make allowances for possible time delays (up to 36 hours in some cases, although 2–12 hours is more common) and *be particularly suspicious of any foods that your child particularly craves.*

Given the practical difficulties of this kind of detective work, expert advice is likely to be needed. In my view, dietary experimentation or other testing for allergies or intolerances should be carried out under the guidance of a registered medical practitioner as well as a dietician or other suitably qualified nutrition specialist with proper experience in the complex field of food allergy and intolerance.

Milk Intolerance? It Could Just Be the Sugar

Intolerance to milk (and dairy products derived from this) can happen either for classic allergy reasons – meaning your immune system reacts to the protein in milk – or because of more subtle forms of food intolerance. Lactose intolerance is extremely common in some ethnic groups. *Lactose* is milk sugar and is found in all animal (including human) milk. A baby secretes the enzyme *lactase*, which breaks down this sugar. After weaning, the production of lactase falls and may stop altogether, so drinking milk later on can cause an intolerance response.

Milk and dairy products form almost no part of the traditional diet in China, Japan, other parts of Eastern Asia, India and Africa. Many individuals with ancestors from these regions can't digest lactose, and if they do consume milk products, this sugar ferments in their gut, causing an uncomfortable range of digestive problems from excess wind to stomach cramps and 'irritable bowel syndrome'.

When milk is found in the traditional diets of people from these regions, it's had special bacterial cultures added that turn it into yoghurt (such as the traditional kefir[21]) and also break down the lactose in the process. Some cheeses are low in lactose for similar reasons.

In fact, only a minority of the world's population can tolerate milk as adults – and these are generally people of Northern European descent whose ancestors were probably mainly 'herdsmen'. It's easy to see why an unusual tolerance to milk as an adult food might confer a survival advantage in these population subgroups.

If your child is intolerant to lactose, you could try nut milks, oat milk or soya milk. Alternatively, versions of 'lactose-free' or 'low-lactose' dairy milk are now available from health food shops and some supermarkets.

The good news is that even if you do identify a genuine intolerance reaction, your child won't necessarily be intolerant to that food for ever. If the food is avoided and reintroduced in small quantities (usually after a few months), your child's body might be fine with it – just don't overdo it! A diet of healthy, fresh and varied foods will help to repair and restore the gut lining, and can help to prevent many intolerances from recurring – or even from starting in the first place.

Some Possible Symptoms of Food Allergies and Intolerances

Many different parts of the body, including the brain, can be affected by food allergies or intolerances, and the sheer variety of symptoms that have been documented is one reason why many people still remain sceptical about these issues.

Here are just some of the ways that adverse food reactions could affect your child – but always remember that each of these symptoms could easily have other causes, and check with your child's doctor *first* before you assume that any specific foods must be 'the problem'. It's also important to recognize that even if your child's diet *is* contributing to these kinds of health or behaviour problems, imbalances or deficiencies of particular nutrients may be to blame, rather than any particular foods or substances. In other words, the *pattern* of your child's overall diet should be your first focus of attention.

Food allergies or intolerances can affect the nose, ears, bladder, central nervous system, digestive system, eyes, heart, skin and musculo-skeletal system.

They *can* also cause a wide range of mental symptoms, including those listed here. Once more, always remember that *there may be other causes, including a* lack *of the right nutrients.* Check every other possibility.

- **Anxiety and mood disturbance**
Panic attacks, depression, mood swings, premenstrual tension, irritability, tearfulness, self-destructive thoughts or actions
- **Oppositional defiance**
Being argumentative, touchy, resentful, defiant of rules and authority, blaming of others, losing temper easily, annoying others deliberately
- **Social**
Being easily bored, unmotivated, demanding, disruptive, ill-disciplined, destructive, hyperactive, fighting (especially with siblings), having difficulty making friends
- **Coordination**
Poor motor coordination, poor handwriting, frequent clumsiness leading to accidents
- **Memory**
Often unable to concentrate, vague, forgetful, little motivation, disorganized, difficulty in reading
- **Speech and language**
Loud voice, selective mutism (not speaking), stammering, hard-to-understand speech, constant chatter, repetitive noises
- **Sleep**
Difficulties getting to sleep or waking up, and night-time sleep disturbances (including bedwetting beyond the expected age)

Allergies and Addictions?

A puzzling feature of many allergies or intolerances is that sufferers often experience powerful cravings for the very food or substance in question. The reasons for this are not yet well understood, and any 'addictive' behaviour always has multiple causes, but in my view three possible mechanisms could help to explain these 'food cravings', either individually or in combination. Let's take a very quick look at these.

1) Partly Digested Food Proteins

The first reason is that some partly digested food proteins can bind to special receptor sites and have an opioid-like effect. It's been suggested that gluten (from wheat and other grains) and casein (from milk and dairy products) can do this, and that autistic individuals may be particularly vulnerable. Anyone wanting to know more about his should check out the work of Dr Paul Shattock and colleagues at Sunderland University, who have pioneered the 'Opioid Excess Theory of Autism'.[22] Once again, the scientific studies remain scarce, so we urgently need more research in this area. However, one systematic review has looked at the effects of gluten- and casein-free (GF-CF) diets on autistic children.[23] Only one study was sufficiently well controlled to meet their strict criteria, but this did show a significant reduction in autistic-like symptoms in children following this exclusion diet.

A Wheat-free Diet

One UK school for dyslexic children reported benefits after adopting a wheat-free diet for all of its pupils.

This was done following remarkable improvements shown by one child who'd been put onto a wheat-free diet for his digestive problems. According to his teachers and parents, there was a dramatic reduction in his dyslexic 'symptoms': he no longer mirror-reversed letters when trying to write and spell, his handwriting improved dramatically, and he suddenly started making dramatic progress in his reading.

Wheat and other grains containing gluten always come high on any list of common foods that can cause 'adverse reactions'. Wheat-free or gluten-free diets are therefore popular with many nutritionists, other health practitioners and companies who sell various tests purporting to diagnose allergies or intolerances. Some people do seem to benefit from removing wheat and other grains from their diet – but the exclusion of *any* major foods or food groups (particularly grains or dairy produce) should never be done without good reason. I would *always* recommend that you seek advice from a suitably qualified practitioner before attempting such diets.

Suspected Wheat and Milk Intolerances?

Don't rush into a 'faddy' diet. I have seen parents remove wheat and milk from their children's diets ... and replace them with additive-laden corn chips and cola! Always seek advice from a suitably qualified professional.

- If you think your child may be intolerant to gluten (the protein found in wheat and some other grains), ask for a simple blood test from your doctor to confirm this.
- If your child is intolerant to milk, it could just be the lactose (milk sugar), and not the casein (milk protein), that's causing the problem.
- If so, try some of the lactose-free or low-lactose milks now available (and find out which cheeses don't contain lactose).
- If you think it's milk protein your child reacts badly to, try him first with goats' milk or sheep's milk products rather than cutting dairy out altogether. Or you could try Guernsey milk. Anecdotal evidence suggests that so-called 'A2 milk' may be better tolerated by some people with autism and related conditions, although research to confirm this is still needed. Breastmilk

contains a milk protein called A2, but much cows' milk
(particularly from Friesians) is high in the variant A1, and it's
thought that this may be what causes some intolerances. Jersey
milk has a much higher proportion of A2 to A1, and Guernsey
milk even more. Channel Island milk also has a high fat content,
so it's a good source of vitamins A, D, E and K.

Some interesting reports that still need formal investigation suggest that intolerance to certain grains containing gluten may perhaps be unusually common in children with dyslexia, dyspraxia, ADHD and autistic spectrum disorders. The classic form of gluten intolerance is coeliac disease, in which gluten triggers the immune system to cause actual damage to the gut lining. The resulting digestive symptoms and malabsorption can often take years to be properly recognized, and formal diagnosis of coeliac disease requires a gut biopsy.

However, blood tests have now been developed to show the presence of anti-gliadin and endomycelial antibodies (AGAs and EMAs) in people with the intolerance. These have shown that 10 times more people than originally estimated (one in 150 rather than one in 1,500) have an immune reaction to gluten. Sufferers may not ever get full-blown coeliac disease (in which case they're known as 'silent coeliacs'), though it's possible that their guts and brains could still be affected.[24] In my view, this area urgently needs more research. Meanwhile, if you have a family history of coeliac disease, or suspect that gluten grains are a problem for your child, ask your doctor for these tests.

2) False Fat

A second possible reason why people may 'crave' the very foods they are intolerant to is explained in Dr Elson Haas's book, *The False Fat Diet*[25]. 'False fat' is swelling and bloating caused by food reactions: it looks like the real thing and is just as uncomfortable. I can't begin to do justice here to his excellent explanation of this phenomenon, but in a nutshell, the false fat problem goes like this:

1. Your child eats a food she's reactive to.
2. She ends up with a rapid drop in blood sugar, serotonin, adrenaline and endorphin levels.
3. She gets grumpy, tired and upset, and craves simple carbohydrates (sugary things) to remedy this.
4. Her tissues swell up because of the reaction to mast cells releasing their histamine, and she starts feeling 'heavy' and tired.
5. She also begins to store fat because she's eaten too many sugar-based foods; as a result of this and lack of exercise, she burns up her fat stores more slowly.
6. She gets even more fed up and binges further on simple carbohydrates (particularly in the week before her period, if she's old enough).
7. Her gut lining begins to react: inflammation means more allergens can get into the blood; at the same time, she absorbs fewer vital nutrients.
8. Candida (yeast) and other infections start to take hold, exacerbating the gut problems. She gets bloated (from wind), tissues swell even more, and she becomes even more sensitive to the food or foods she's reactive to.
9. Thus the cycle continues, until you change her diet for a varied, balanced and nutritious one.

The drop in blood sugar, serotonin, adrenalin and endorphin described here would set anyone up for feeling rotten and behaving in an impulsive, 'cranky' manner. It's easy to see why the response would be to grab one of those junk foods or snacks you think might make you feel better. Well, for a short while it might – but that snack probably contains wheat, milk and eggs (all common intolerance triggers) along with heaps of sugar and a handful of artificial additives! So that tactic will very soon backfire, and will just help you pile on the weight while you feel and behave in a worse and less controlled (or controllable) manner.

Does this kind of pattern sound familiar? I will say that I think this particular issue – intolerances and cravings – affects not just many children I come across, but a large number of their stressed-out mums and dads, as well as many other people in our eating-disordered society. If you're one of them, do read *The False Fat Diet* and try doing something about it. If you've ever seen the simply extraordinary film *Super Size Me* (showing what can happen to a healthy young man who eats nothing but McDonald's food for a month), you may also see that there are some common elements here. In addition to the appalling weight gain and health problems he suffered, even in such a short space of time, Morgan Spurlock also found himself with mood disturbances and cravings that didn't go away for a very long time afterwards.

3) Sugar and Additives

The third reason why people may 'crave' foods that really don't 'agree' with them is, in my view, plain and simple: most of the 'problem' foods and drinks that cause such cravings don't just contain wheat, eggs, milk, chocolate or other common 'intolerance triggers'. They are usually laden with sugar as well, and often a cocktail of artificial additives. It's possible that some of these additives (particularly MSG and similar flavourings) might cause cravings in some people because of the 'excitatory' nature of the chemicals they contain. And certainly, if the foods your child craves are savoury snacks that contain this, you should already know what to do! In general, though, the foods or drinks that most people crave are more often the sweet ones. And in my personal opinion, sugar is very often the key issue for people who have an 'addictive' relationship with food (and associated difficulties with mood), although I know that the sugar, soft drink, confectionery and fast-food industries would have you believe otherwise. We'll take a look at this issue in more depth in Chapter 7.

Many children are overweight now, and some are obese. If this applies to your child, a conventional, restricted-calorie diet is not necessarily a good idea, and especially not if he doesn't appear to be overeating. You've learned in this chapter why artificial sweeteners may cause problems of their own, and you'll hear more in the next two chapters that will also help to explain why conventional 'weight-loss diets' don't usually work. First, you'll learn more about why it's the sweet and sugary junk that you really need to dump. Then we'll take a serious look at fats – which should explode some of the myths you may have come to believe about 'low-fat' diets being the healthiest. If your child has got a serious weight problem, or an eating disorder (or if you have), you should first get some professional help: Start by asking your doctor for advice. Then follow the guidelines in this book and you should find that much of the real fat, together with any 'false fat', will come off too.

FAQs

I've been exposed to more pesticides than my child has – so am I likely to get the same kind of problems?

Because they're still developing, babies and children are more vulnerable to harm from toxic chemicals, not least because their nervous systems, immune systems and main detoxifying organs (the kidneys and liver) aren't fully developed for some years. Adults can usually cope better with exposure to things like pesticides – but you've obviously been alerted to the fact that *no one* should take unnecessary risks with these or any other potential toxins. If you're worried about your own past exposure, do talk this through with your doctor. If you still think you need additional help, there are some good support groups who can point you to properly qualified specialists in this area who will take your concerns seriously (see the References and Resources chapter, page 397).

If food additives are so dangerous, why haven't they been banned?

Not all food additives are 'dangerous' by any means, though the evidence does suggest that *some* artificial food colourings, flavourings, sweeteners and preservatives can contribute to health or behaviour problems in many children. As outlined in this chapter, particular concerns have been raised about tartrazine and other 'azo' dyes, MSG, aspartame, sodium benzoate and the 'sulphite' preservatives, among others. All of these are currently permitted in the UK, but many campaign groups would like to see them banned – as some already are in other countries. Additives approved by European law carry an 'E' number, indicating they've been tested for safety. The trouble is that current safety tests have their limitations. They don't take into account individual differences, and for practical reasons they can only look at additives one at a time. Your child may not react in the same way as others, and additives can have 'synergistic' (multiplied) effects when consumed together.

How will I know if some foods or additives are affecting my child's behaviour?

You can do two things: get your child assessed by a properly qualified specialist and/or eliminate the food in question from her diet, and keep careful note of the results. When it comes to non-essential additives, I'd say just cut them out, replacing additive-laden foods and drinks with healthier alternatives. Avoiding all 'suspect' food additives can be difficult, though – and remember that diet is almost never the only issue that needs tackling when children have behaviour problems. If you need help or want to find out more, talk to other parents who've tried this, and then make your own decision. For further details on useful sources of information and support, see www.fabresearch.org.

If I cut out foods or additives he's reacting to, how soon will I see a difference in my child's behaviour?

In some cases (such as tartrazine or other artificial additives) improvements can be almost immediate if this has been the main problem. But for other substances it may take longer: for milk and dairy, for instance, a week or two should make a difference, but for wheat it can sometimes take months. If you're excluding major foods, always get specialist advice first so that your child doesn't miss out on any essential nutrients. You'll also need to look at other possible contributory factors (such as stress) in your child's life.

Summary

1. Individual differences mean that there really is no such thing as a 'healthy food' that will suit everyone. By contrast, there are some truly 'unhealthy foods' in my opinion – but eating these *occasionally* is unlikely to do serious harm to *most* children, *provided that the overall diet is well balanced.*

2. Some food additives, especially artificial food colourings (AFCs), can have negative effects on children's behaviour. These are found in many processed foods, and in my view should be avoided. (So too should foods high in sugars, refined starches and 'junk' fats.)

3. There are long-standing controversies over whether aspartame (and some other artificial sweeteners) may be harmful to physical health and/or behaviour. Avoid these where possible.

4. Combinations of food additives can have a 'synergistic' (multiplied) effect. This is not taken into account in official testing for their 'safety'.

5. Do what you can to reduce your child's exposure to any environmental toxins such as heavy metals and pesticides.

6. Food allergies and intolerances can manifest in many different ways – both physically and in behavioural changes. Many food sensitivities seem to be unusually common in individuals with autism, ADHD and related conditions.

7. If you suspect that your child has food allergies or intolerances, *always talk to your doctor first,* and seek referral to a properly qualified specialist. 'Elimination-challenge' diets are the only truly reliable test, but these are not easy to implement and may require medical supervision.

8. Lactose (milk sugar) intolerance affects many people, and is particularly common in people with Asian or Afro-Caribbean rather than Northern European ancestry.

9. *Some* children may benefit from a gluten-free and/or a casein-free diet (or from excluding other foods) – but 'healing the gut' and improving digestion should be your first priority. If you do want to try excluding any major foods or food groups, always get advice from a dietician or other properly qualified specialist, or your child may not get all the essential nutrients he needs, and this could make matters worse.

chapter 7

eating for balanced energy

putting the right fuel in the tank

You can get energy (fuel) for your body from three broad dietary sources: proteins, fats and carbohydrates. As we saw in Chapter 4, though, each of these 'macronutrients' has very different functions, so it's worth considering each of them again briefly here.

Proteins

Proteins generally contain as much energy (calories) per gram as carbohydrates do, but they're vital for building, maintaining and repairing your actual body tissues, *and* the enzymes needed to carry out most functions (including helping you to digest your foods). For this reason we don't use proteins primarily for energy. Carbohydrates or fats are usually our main sources of fuel, but if not enough of these are available, your body will burn protein for energy – sometimes breaking down (or failing to repair) its own tissues in the process. This happens in severe anorexia, for example, or any prolonged period of starvation, when carbohydrate and fat intake is too low to provide the energy needed to keep vital functions going.

The dietary advice on proteins is fairly simple: they're essential, and best obtained from a range of foods such as fish, eggs, lean meat, milk and cheese – or nuts, seeds, whole grains, pulses and beans for vegetarian options. Remember too that, in general, only animal-derived foods provide 'complete protein' (containing all the essential amino acids together), so vegetarians will usually need to combine different protein sources at each meal.[1] Protein-rich foods are best eaten at breakfast, lunch and early evening, and not just before bedtime (they take a while to digest and can sit heavily in your stomach while you're trying to sleep).

Fats

Fats give you twice as much energy, gram for gram, as proteins or carbohydrates. They're a compact and convenient form of energy storage, and as you probably know all too well, those calories that aren't 'burned off' in fuelling your daily activities get stored as fatty deposits around your waistline, hips, thighs or elsewhere! You need fats for much more than just fuel, though, and your brain can't actually use fats for energy at all. (The brain's fuel is glucose – a form of sugar that we'll be looking at in detail in this chapter). In fact, some *very special types of fat* are needed to build and repair your brain, other nerve cells and your immune system – and to allow these to function properly. We'll look at these in detail in Chapters 8 and 9. Meanwhile, be aware that you can't just rely on fats to provide all the energy you need, because you'd rapidly become obese and unhealthy – and very sick of your diet! Fats promote 'satiety' – that sense of fullness and satisfaction after eating – and we all know that fat-rich meals can be very 'heavy' and difficult to digest properly. So you do need enough of the right type of fats in your diet, but when it comes to 'food as fuel', you must get a large part of your total energy requirements from carbohydrates.

Carbohydrates

Carbohydrates include all sugars, a wide range of different starches, and dietary fibre. We use them primarily as energy-givers – but *it really does matter a great deal which kinds you and your child eat.*

In this chapter we'll look at what different kinds of carbohydrates there are, and what effects these different types can have, not only on your child's body but also on his behaviour, learning and mood. The types of carbohydrate that your child eats can profoundly affect not just his energy levels, but his physical and mental health.

All Carbs Are *Not* the Same

You may well feel confused by how often the word 'carbs' is bandied about in diet books, newspaper 'health' columns and magazines. Many so-called 'low-carb' diets have attracted media attention. Any sensible ones are really 'low refined-sugar-and-processed-starch diets' – because some carbohydrates (the unrefined starches and natural sugars found in fruits and vegetables in particular) are simply essential to any healthy diet. The worst of these 'low-carb' diets will encourage you to eat fat and protein to excess (absolutely *not* a good idea) while making all 'carbs' sound almost deadly. I repeat: You and your child should actually get most of your energy from carbohydrates – but *please make sure they're the right kind.*

Good Carbs

These are found in most natural, unrefined plant foods such as vegetables, fruits, potatoes in their skins, beans, pulses and whole grains. These foods are superior sources of energy, because they:

- supply you with numerous essential micronutrients, other vital substances and dietary fibre
- break down slowly in your body, leading to a steady release of energy throughout the day.

Bad Carbs

These include all refined sugars and highly processed starches, including white flour, white rice or other cereals, instant mashed potato and the starches and sugars found in most sweets, snack foods and fizzy drinks. They also include various 'modified starches' (emulsifiers, stabilizers and thickening agents), found in a huge range of refined and processed foods (particularly biscuits, cakes, pastries, breakfast cereals and children's snacks). These are distinctly inferior sources of energy, because they:

- contain few if any of the original nutrients, such as vitamins, trace minerals and antioxidants – many of which are actually needed by your body to digest the sugars and refined starches and access the energy in them
- break down very easily when you consume them, so the sugar they provide gets into your bloodstream very fast. That may be great for a 'quick energy fix' – it's why serious athletes may use glucose to keep up their energy levels throughout intense, prolonged exercise, for example. But if you're not running a marathon, these 'fast-burn' foods and drinks can seriously destabilize your blood-sugar levels, and rob you of essential nutrients. This can create irritability, mood swings and concentration problems in the short term, and a host of serious physical and mental health problems in the longer term.

The failure to help people distinguish good starches from bad starches is (in my opinion) one of the most confusing and misleading aspects of the official dietary advice that we've been getting from Government agencies in the UK and the US[2] – let alone the food industry. (The other is the failure to distinguish between good fats and bad fats, which I'll be telling you about in the next chapter.) If you care about your child's health and well-being (and let's face it, you wouldn't be reading this book if you didn't), then I'd strongly advise you to learn the difference, remember it, and act on it.

Learning From History

More than 100 years ago, it was shown that eating a diet of processed foods rich in refined sugars and starches (and lacking the nutrients and fibre found in whole grains and fresh fruits and vegetables) could produce a whole range of degenerative diseases such as diabetes, heart disease and cancer.[3] These diseases afflict every country that has adopted the modern, 'Western-type' diet; wherever it goes, they follow. In the old days, only the rich ate refined foods and took little exercise, so they were the main victims of these diseases. Now we can all afford them.

More recently, the eminent British psychiatrist Professor Malcolm Peet, who has pioneered much of the scientific research into how nutrition affects mental health, has shown how closely the dramatic rise in severe mental health problems such as schizophrenia followed the dramatic rise in sugar consumption after the Industrial Revolution. He's also shown that when comparisons are made between different countries, the number-one dietary factor explaining most of the variability in rates of depression and schizophrenia is a high average intake of sugar.[4]

Although this kind of study can't be taken as evidence of cause and effect, neuroscientific studies do back up his findings: a high-fat, high-sugar diet can stunt brain growth and learning capacity.[5]

> Some 'Supersize' servings of cola contain up to 48 teaspoons of sugar. If you're letting your child drink this kind of stuff, presumably you've not read *Pure, White and Deadly* or *Sugar Blues?*[6] (You certainly can't have seen the film *Super Size Me*.)

History lessons are one thing, but I know that what you choose to do with your child's diet (and your own) will depend on whether you can personally understand and believe how much difference it can make to you. So in this chapter we'll first take a look at how sugars and starches are digested. A key issue is how quickly different types of food release their sugar into the bloodstream, because it helps to explain the powerful effects that carbohydrates can have on mood, behaviour and learning.

The terms 'glycaemic index' and 'glycaemic load' are often used to describe the way in which foods can affect blood-sugar levels, so we'll also take a quick look at those, but understanding the basic principles is always more important than getting hung up on numbers and values.

We'll then focus on why some people find it particularly difficult to keep their energy balanced, and why it is that some children and adults find it much harder than others to avoid the temptations of the unhealthy, 'quick fix' foods and drinks that can destabilize mood and concentration (sometimes with devastating consequences for behaviour). This will take us into the more controversial areas of 'sugar sensitivity' and 'sugar addiction'.

Carbohydrates in Brief

Glucose is used in your cells as fuel. While our bodies can also use fats and proteins as fuel when needed, our brains can only use glucose.

Single sugars are called **monosaccharides**; that is, they are made solely from one sugar molecule. The most important ones are glucose (also known as dextrose), fructose (fruit sugar) and galactose (from milk sugar).

We also get two-sugar molecules, which are called **disaccharides**:

- Table sugar (sucrose), made up of one molecule of glucose and one molecule of fructose
- Malt sugar (maltose), made of two molecules of glucose
- Milk sugar (lactose), made of one molecule of glucose combined with one molecule of galactose.

Chains of three to nine sugar units are known as **oligosaccharides**, and those of 10 or more are called **polysaccharides**, which include starch and fibre.

Monosaccharides are absorbed straight into the bloodstream. The rest of the 'available carbohydrates' from food need to be broken down by enzymes before they can be digested (but see Chapters 5 and 6 for details of this process, and how it can sometimes go wrong).

Some carbohydrates from food are resistant to digestion. These 'unavailable carbohydrates' are called 'dietary fibre' – sometimes known as 'non-starch polysaccharides' (NSP).

Certain forms of **refined** or **processed starches** are ingredients in many 'convenience foods' and are often found in products like breakfast cereals, savoury snacks, crackers, cakes, bread and biscuits. They are added to foods to help extend their shelf-life, or to 'improve' the taste, texture and appearance of foods. Look for 'extruded starches' and 'modified starches' on the labels.

- Refined sugars and starches are digested into glucose very quickly, which is not good for anyone's blood-sugar levels.
- In people with severe 'gut dysbiosis' (see Chapter 5), the digestion of *any* sugars and starches except the simplest monosaccharides may be

compromised. Under these circumstances, a very special diet may be needed to restore health – excluding all grains, many starchy vegetables, and all disaccharide sugars (like table sugar and milk sugar) until this condition is corrected. This kind of extreme diet is not easy to follow, and expert professional advice may well be needed.

Digesting Carbohydrates

As we saw in Chapter 5, the digestion of starches and sugars starts in your mouth, where an enzyme called amylase breaks these down into smaller molecules. Food then travels through your stomach (where very little further digestion of starches takes place) to the small intestine, where starches and disaccharide sugars are normally broken down into glucose by other enzymes. I say 'normally' with very good reason, because I'll come back to this important point shortly.

From here, the glucose passes into your bloodstream, ready to be taken to your cells, which burn it to produce energy. Some simple sugars like fructose (fruit sugar), galactose (a milk sugar) and sugar alcohols can also pass straight into the bloodstream and get taken to the liver to be turned into glucose. (From there the glucose is either released back into the bloodstream for transport to any cells that need more fuel, or it can be kept in reserve and stored as 'glycogen'.)

Starch Really Can Be Dangerous For Some People

Some people with severe 'gut dysbiosis' (as explained in Chapter 5) can't break down disaccharide sugars properly. Their intestinal flora and their gut lining have become so unhealthy that they just can't produce the enzymes needed. For these people – who often have serious mental problems such as autism or schizophrenia, and/or serious digestive problems that resist other treatments) – all starches and most sugars in the diet really are a 'no-no'. The only way to restore full health is via a diet that allows only very specific carbohydrates to be eaten (monosaccharides –

found in fruits, vegetables and honey – and in natural live yogurt). In this respect, this diet is similar to the one our hunter-gatherer and herdsman ancestors would have eaten.[7]

This important discovery was first made by doctors investigating coeliac disease – the classic form of gluten allergy.[8] Coeliac disease involves an auto-immune reaction that can progressively destroy the gut lining, leading to poor absorption of many nutrients.

Some time later, it was found that true coeliac disease can be halted in its tracks provided that gluten (found in wheat and some other grains) is avoided. What has now been all but forgotten is that the 'hunter-gatherer' type diet 'worked' for many other conditions, too – including serious gut disorders like ulcerative colitis and Crohn's disease (another in which the immune system attacks the gut wall). In these conditions, *all* grains and disaccharide sugars – not just gluten – were a problem. Until these too were removed from the diet, many patients with these and some other health problems simply didn't get better. But when they were, they did. What's more, once the gut had 'healed', these people could usually tolerate some grains and starches once again, at least in small amounts. But while they were in their initial digestive mess, then eating starchy foods and most sugary foods would serve to keep them there. Undigested starches (which couldn't get broken down beyond the disaccharide maltose) would simply ferment in their guts, creating unpleasant physical symptoms like wind and bloating. Even more important, this fermented starch would keep making the gut dysbiosis worse by feeding the 'bad bacteria' such as *Clostridia*, which we heard about in Chapter 5. As we saw then, a vicious cycle can be set up, involving:

- impaired digestion (so you can't absorb nutrients properly)
- an impaired immune system (which not only fails to defend you but may attack you instead), and
- the full Leaky Gut Syndrome (so that toxic molecules can get from your gut into the rest of your body and brain).

This combination could clearly serve to make someone very ill indeed; *Clostridia* and some other bad bacteria can produce highly toxic substances that have long been known to be capable of affecting the brain.

182 they are what you feed them

In my view, it's nothing short of scandalous that there isn't more awareness of – and research into – these areas. I have personally met several mothers who've completely 'lost' their teenage or young adult children to locked psychiatric wards because the supposed 'care staff' and doctors in charge have pooh-poohed what these mothers have told them about certain foods to which their children react very badly indeed. The foods in question are almost always sugary and starchy ones – but many artificial additives (like the ones I told you about in Chapter 6) were also found by these mothers to have very damaging effects. So they read up what they could, worked out their own diets and, while they were in charge, their children stayed well. But in one particularly tragic case, even though this mum had travelled the country to find a suitable care home for her now adult son who had social and learning difficulties, she found the staff ignored everything she told them – and all the written information she provided – about her son's dietary needs. She was cast as an interfering busybody, and told that it was her son's 'human right' to eat chocolate, biscuits, cakes and every kind of fast food. When I first met this mum, Laura, she was sobbing over the kitchen table at a friend's house, having just come away from the psychiatric hospital where her son was now in a straitjacket, dosed up with very strong (and highly toxic) psychiatric drugs, and with a prognosis from the doctors that he had 'atypical schizophrenia' and was not expected to get any better. Unlike the story I told you of another mother in Chapter 3, Laura never did get her son back, to my knowledge, but when I last heard from her she was setting up a support group to try to help other mums in a similar position.

Your child probably doesn't have this kind of very severe gut dysbiosis – but be aware that this can occur to some degree in any of what Natasha Campbell-McBride calls the *Gut and Psychology Syndromes* in her book of the same name – including not just autism and schizophrenia but also conditions like dyslexia, dyspraxia, ADHD, depression and other mental health problems. So if your child does have very extreme digestive symptoms in keeping with the 'gut dysbiosis' patterns described in Chapter 5, do find out more about special dietary approaches to tackle this.[9] It could help to prevent a lifetime of misery – but it's not an easy diet to follow in today's fast-food world, so you may need help from a suitably qualified and experienced nutrition professional to make sure your child doesn't miss out on any essential nutrients.

The Importance of Dietary Fibre

Some forms of carbohydrate just can't be broken down by your digestive enzymes; we call these 'dietary fibre'. One example is the string on runner beans, which is made from cellulose. This is what gives plant cells their structure (just as our bones do for us), so it's pretty resilient stuff. It does, however, provide important nourishment for the good bacteria that should inhabit your child's guts.

There are two main types of dietary fibre, and most 'high-fibre foods' contain both in varying proportions. These are:

Soluble Fibre

This is found in oat bran, pulses (beans, peas and lentils), fruits and vegetables. Soluble fibre helps digestion: It slows the rate at which food leaves your stomach and then travels through the gut. It can help to control blood glucose levels and help reduce blood fats.

Insoluble Fibre

This is found in stringy vegetables and foods such as wholewheat cereals. It used to be known as 'roughage'. Fibre adds volume to your stools (faeces or 'poo') and reduces the amount of time that foods stay in your gut. It's essential to have plenty of insoluble fibre so you don't get constipated, and foods rich in fibre help to keep your intestines healthy.

In general, whole grains, vegetables and fruits that contain fibre as well as complex starches will take longer to be digested than simpler, refined starches and sugars, so your blood-sugar levels won't rise so quickly. That's a good thing. If your blood-sugar levels rise too quickly, that can lead to the body producing too much insulin. This can cause an equally sudden drop in blood-sugar levels, so that in a short time you're back where you started, or worse.

A Word about Insulin

I've made it sound as though the sugar (glucose) that you absorb from digesting carbohydrates will automatically give your cells more energy. In fact, the hormone *insulin* is essential in helping sugar to get out of your bloodstream and into those cells. It 'opens the cell doors' for glucose, as it were. But if you can't produce enough insulin (which happens in people with Type I diabetes), or if the receptors on your cells have become insensitive to insulin (a key stage in the development of Type II diabetes), then you can be in trouble here. Plenty of glucose may be circulating in your bloodstream, but you still can't get it into your cells to be burned for energy. More about this later.

The Glycaemic Index (GI)

One measure of how easily foods release their sugar is the 'glycaemic index' or GI. Generally speaking, we should avoid foods with a high GI (which release sugar very quickly), or eat them alongside foods that have a low GI. That way, sugar reaches the blood at a slower, more sustainable level.

The following diagrams show what happens to your blood sugar when you eat a high-GI meal and a low-GI meal, and what happens if your blood-sugar levels are out of control.

Please do note that GI is calculated in different ways by different people. There are now *books* of these tables available in the shops, but in my view you really only need to grasp the general idea. Battling with numbers (especially if you're tired and/or hungry and your child is throwing a tantrum for the same reasons) is the very last thing you should be worrying about! The same goes for counting calories, in my view. Yes – know what they are, and be aware of them, but if you use the plan in Chapter 11 you won't have to bother with number-crunching calories or GI numbers. The whole point is to *improve* life for your child and you, not to struggle even more. Just keep in mind that high-GI foods, especially if eaten on their own, may cause your child's mood and

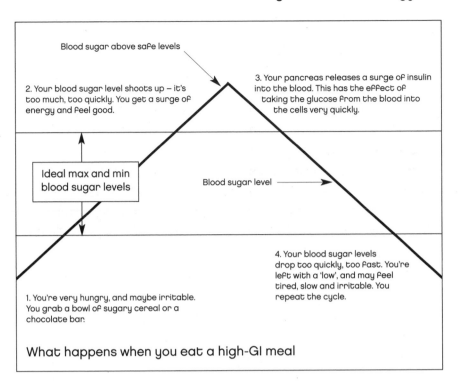

Blood sugar above safe levels

2. Your blood sugar level shoots up – it's too much, too quickly. You get a surge of energy and feel good.

3. Your pancreas releases a surge of insulin into the blood. This has the effect of taking the glucose from the blood into the cells very quickly.

Ideal max and min blood sugar levels

Blood sugar level

4. Your blood sugar levels drop too quickly, too fast. You're left with a 'low', and may feel tired, slow and irritable. You repeat the cycle.

1. You're very hungry, and maybe irritable. You grab a bowl of sugary cereal or a chocolate bar.

What happens when you eat a high-GI meal

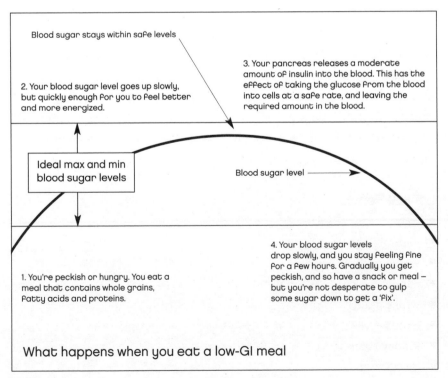

Blood sugar stays within safe levels

2. Your blood sugar level goes up slowly, but quickly enough for you to feel better and more energized.

3. Your pancreas releases a moderate amount of insulin into the blood. This has the effect of taking the glucose from the blood into cells at a safe rate, and leaving the required amount in the blood.

Ideal max and min blood sugar levels

Blood sugar level

4. Your blood sugar levels drop slowly, and you stay feeling fine for a few hours. Gradually you get peckish, and so have a snack or meal – but you're not desperate to gulp some sugar down to get a 'fix'.

1. You're peckish or hungry. You eat a meal that contains whole grains, fatty acids and proteins.

What happens when you eat a low-GI meal

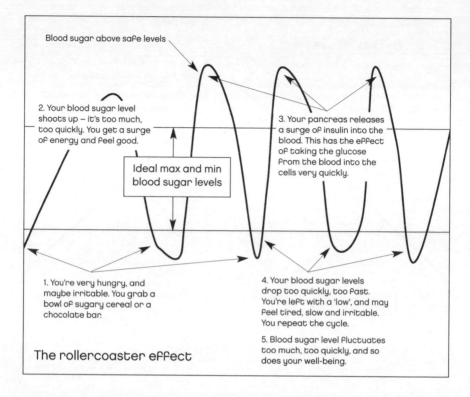

Blood sugar above safe levels

2. Your blood sugar level shoots up – it's too much, too quickly. You get a surge of energy and feel good.

Ideal max and min blood sugar levels

3. Your pancreas releases a surge of insulin into the blood. This has the effect of taking the glucose from the blood into the cells very quickly.

1. You're very hungry, and maybe irritable. You grab a bowl of sugary cereal or a chocolate bar.

4. Your blood sugar levels drop too quickly, too fast. You're left with a 'low', and may feel tired, slow and irritable. You repeat the cycle.

5. Blood sugar level fluctuates too much, too quickly, and so does your well-being.

The rollercoaster effect

behaviour to fluctuate along with his levels of energy and the fuel reaching his brain.

Some common foods categorized by their usual broad GI range (low, medium or high) are shown in the lists below. You won't find proteins and fats here, as the GI concept only applies to carbohydrates. These other macronutrient types do, however, help slow down the rate of carbohydrate digestion (which is a good thing).

Low-GI Foods
- nuts
- natural yoghurt
- whole milk
- barley
- whole grains
- lentils
- kidney beans
- butter beans

- chick peas
- plain chocolate
- dried apricots
- apples
- cherries
- grapefruit
- pears
- whole fibrous vegetables (including green, leafy ones)

Medium-GI Foods

- All Bran
- muesli
- oats
- buckwheat
- bulgar wheat
- brown basmati rice
- wholemeal pasta (made with durum wheat)
- pitta bread
- rye bread
- carrots
- peas
- sweetcorn
- sweet potatoes
- new potatoes (boiled)
- potato crisps
- fresh apricots
- bananas (slightly green ones)
- grapes
- kiwi fruit
- peaches
- plums
- sultanas
- oranges

High-GI Foods

- processed breakfast cereals
- sugar
- couscous
- rice other than basmati
- white bread
- pizza bases
- crackers
- rice cakes
- corn crisps
- biscuits
- sweets
- flavoured yoghurts
- chips and other potatoes (especially if baked or mashed)
- broad beans
- parsnips
- swedes
- ice-cream
- soft drinks
- most fruit juices
- alcohol
- milk or white chocolate
- cereal bars
- raisins
- melons
- pineapples
- ripe bananas

Some foods can have a high GI (like carrots), but as they also have a high water content and you're not likely to eat a kilo at a time, it really doesn't matter ... it's the overall glycaemic total or 'glycaemic load' (GL) at any one time that counts.

If you eat a high-GI food, precede it and accompany it with low- and middle-range GI foods, and non-GI foods (proteins and essential fatty acids).

If you reach for a food because you know it'll give you an instant hit, it'll probably be a high-GI food. Try to find something else if you can.

Do remember the nutrients and fibre! A parsnip is a high-GI food, and so is a bar of toffee, but one is rather healthier than the other. You're after foods that are less refined and processed, remember?

Keeping Some Energy in Reserve

If you absorb more glucose than your cells need, some of the excess is stored in your liver and muscles as *glycogen*. This provides an 'emergency supply' of energy that can be called on as needed. Glycogen reserves can be 'mobilized' (turned back to glucose) very quickly if you need to raise your blood-sugar levels. Anything that triggers a surge of adrenalin, cortisol and other so-called 'stress hormones' (the so-called 'fight or flight' reaction) will release sugar into your bloodstream from this source. (For our ancestors, the most likely reason for needing a sudden surge of energy would have been for running away from, or fighting, some unexpected threat.)

If you continue to absorb more glucose after your glycogen stores are full, the rest will be turned into fat and stored – first around the thighs, belly and breast areas, and then around the active organs like your heart and kidneys. If this 'fat attack' carries on for too long, the functioning of these vital organs is eventually compromised. In the end, blood pressure and circulation can be affected, your tissue building and immune system capabilities slow down, and your nervous system itself can be affected. *Being seriously overweight or obese really is something to be avoided.*

If your child is overweight or 'fat-phobic' when it comes to food, do explain clearly to her about how excess sugar gets converted into fat. This is why 'low-fat' foods and drinks laden with sugar are such a complete con! But as we saw in the last chapter, artificial sweeteners are not the answer, either. You need to adjust your child's tastes slowly away from sweeter things – and it is possible, honestly!

Cinnamon

- Do you use cinnamon in your apple pies? Studies show that cinnamon helps reduce blood-sugar levels, which is especially helpful for people with diabetes. This is because cinnamon mimics insulin, activates insulin receptors, and then works synergistically with insulin in cells.
- If you use cinnamon, nutmeg and other spices in your puddings, you'll find they add to the taste, so that you don't need to have as much sugar in the recipe.

Hidden Sugars and Empty Calories

You'll find a remarkable amount of sugar hidden in many processed foods (see the Appendix, page 390, for a list of the many forms and disguises it can take). Frankly, they're all best avoided as far as possible.

The term 'empty calories' is often used to describe highly refined sugars and starches. These foods certainly provide energy (calories) – but *your body can't actually use the energy without certain micronutrients*. In their natural forms, these starches or sugars are eaten as part of the whole grain, vegetable or fruit, so you also get the vitamins and minerals needed to digest them. But if your child eats highly processed carbohydrates, he doesn't get the full 'nutrient package'. *Refined sugars and starches can rob your child of essential nutrients*, as well as making it difficult for him to control his blood-sugar levels.

Can Sugar Be Addictive?

Insofar as some people crave sugar and then get grumpy and unsettled (or worse) when they can't have it, I think that sugar can be said to be addictive. If you look up the definition of 'addiction' (itself rather a slippery concept, actually – but we do all think we know what it means!), you'll find that for some people sugar can meet the criteria with no trouble at all. Not that the companies peddling the stuff to you and your child will ever want to admit this.

Experimental studies have shown that, in animals, *intermittent excess sugar consumption can lead to agitation, anxiety and an inability to concentrate*. Their physiological symptoms are equivalent to those experienced on withdrawal from morphine or other powerful opiate drugs (including heroin).[10] These effects were found in rats fed on a diet of just 25 per cent sugar. *Some of the most popular children's breakfast cereals contain more than **40 per cent** sugar*, as do many of children's favourite daytime snacks and soft drinks.

In fact, the World Health Organization recommends that sugar should provide less than 10 per cent of energy intake, yet it's more like 30 per cent in the diets of many UK children.

Naughty but Nasty

Too much sugar consumption in children can lead to:

- tiredness
- 'foggy brain'
- inability to concentrate
- irritability
- nervousness
- depression
- allergies and intolerances
- blood-pressure changes.

In adolescents, this can become even more marked. Underachievement and delinquent behaviour are very often linked with excessive sugar consumption, which also lowers the body's ability to handle alcohol.

If your child craves sugar-rich foods, it's worth knowing that sugar can have opiate-like effects on the so-called 'reward areas' of the brain that influence and motivate behaviour.[11] Basically, this means the sugar can give your child an artificial 'high'. Remember, as we evolved our sources of sugar were primarily fruits and some vegetables; these contain numerous essential vitamins, minerals, antioxidants and fibre, all of which have important health benefits. Their availability was also restricted by what could be found. In stark contrast, the sugars your child is having often come from sugary foods and drinks with no nutritional value whatsoever. They're also so easily available that many children (and adults) consume them way in excess of anything that the body could be expected to handle.

> Apart from seriously destabilizing the fuel supply to your child's brain, sugary foods can also disrupt the entire digestive system in ways that prevent the absorption of essential nutrients – and can imbalance your child's immune system into the bargain. Is that really a price worth paying for those sweet treats?

If your child craves sweet and sugary foods, ask yourself if this is affecting his mood and health:

- Could it be causing your child to behave in ways that are rude and offensive to you or other people?
- Could it be contributing to your child's difficulties with attention and learning?
- Could it be causing your child's moods to swing from sweetness and light on some occasions to bitterness or tears, mood swings and angry tantrums on others?

> Poor blood sugar regulation should be suspected in anyone who experiences rapid mood swings, is prone to inattention ('brain fog') and irritability, or who has obvious cravings for refined carbohydrates.

Blood-sugar Regulation

The brain is fuelled by glucose (a simple form of sugar), which gets to the brain via the bloodstream. Blood-glucose levels must be kept within narrow limits, as any failure to do this can have serious consequences. If your blood-sugar levels fall too low (*hypoglycaemia*) this can be dangerous. The symptoms of mild hypoglycaemia, though, are familiar to all of us, because they usually start to occur in anyone after a few hours without food or drink. Feelings include low mental energy, 'fuzzy' thinking, irritability and/or low mood.

To avoid this unpleasant state, the easiest 'quick fix' is of course to consume something that will quickly release its sugar into the bloodstream – so we reach for some sweets, biscuits or a piece of cake, or we drink something that contains sugar. (The healthier option would be a piece of fruit, preferably with a handful of nuts or seeds to slow the sugar release.) Fruit juices, soft drinks or alcoholic drinks will all do the job quickly – as will a spoonful of the white stuff in our tea or coffee.

A Sweet Tooth?

A high intake of sugar and refined carbohydrate (sweets, soft drinks, biscuits, cakes, pastries, etc.) can be damaging:

- Rapid blood-sugar swings can affect attention, memory and mood.
- There's a high risk of deficiencies in essential micronutrients (because refined foods often have very little nutritional value).
- You run a long-term risk of 'metabolic syndrome', which is a precursor to Type II diabetes and cardiovascular disease.
- High-sugar, high-fat diets can stunt brain growth and connectivity.

Even if they contain no sugar at all, be aware that tea, coffee, cola and other stimulant drinks will help to lift blood-sugar levels in another way: They trigger the release of adrenalin (the 'flight or fight' chemical), which in turn triggers the release of glucose into the blood.

Blood-glucose levels that are low and still falling could quickly lead to unconsciousness and even death. In its wisdom, the human body has therefore developed ways of keeping your blood sugar from falling too low, even if no food or drink is available. Increased arousal – achieved by the release of adrenalin and associated 'stress' chemicals like cortisol – will do the job nicely, triggering the release of glucose from the temporary stores kept in your liver and muscles.

Glucose Intolerance and Antisocial Behaviour

As yet, there's little firm scientific evidence that consuming sugar *directly* causes behavioural problems in children. That said, poor control of blood sugar is frequently reported in connection with ADHD, and in young offenders. My colleague Bernard Gesch found that the majority of youngsters on probation were actually 'flat-line hypoglycaemic' when tested. This means that their *blood-sugar levels would fall too low and stay there* unless they were constantly consuming sugary foods and drinks – including alcohol, of course – or engaging in activities that stimulated a huge release of adrenalin.

You can probably imagine for yourself what sorts of activities might do that. There *are* some healthy ones – but once blood-sugar control is blunted and the adrenal system starts to weaken, too, a stronger and stronger stimulus will be needed to get the same 'high'. For this reason children may engage in increasingly reckless behaviour, often deliberately courting fear or danger in order to achieve a 'comfortable' level of blood sugar and the feelings of alertness and focus that go with that. For those already on the 'young offenders' track, this might be stealing and racing cars, the 'thrill' of breaking and entering to commit burglary, or starting a fight, perhaps. Alcohol and many illegal drugs will similarly boost adrenalin – and with it, blood sugar, if only for a short time before the effects wear off. At that point they'll be in a worse state than when they started – not to mention the damage and distress caused to others by their behaviour.

Signs of Hypoglycaemia

- Feeling
  - 'clammy'
  - hungry
  - dizzy
  - irritable
  - shaky
  - nauseous
  - confused/'foggy'
  - headachy
- May experience
  - light-headedness
  - blurred vision
  - loss of co-ordination
  - nightmares
  - heart palpitations (raised heart beat)
  - tingling/numbness in the lips or tongue

Could Low Blood Sugar Contribute to ADHD Symptoms?

How many ADHD children 'acting out' in the classroom may be caught in this pattern too, we wonder? The fact is – your blood-sugar levels need to be kept within a narrow range just to keep you alive (that's why uncontrolled diabetes can be so dangerous). So when your body senses that your blood-sugar levels are falling dangerously low (you had no breakfast – or maybe a chocolate bar and a sugary fizzy drink on the way to school or work), it's pretty easy to see why an inexplicable adrenalin surge might 'kick in'. From your perspective you just suddenly feel restless and 'antsy' for no apparent reason. It's the 'fight or flight' response (so which is that child in the classroom going to do, do you think?).

The fact is, anyone eating a diet high in sugar and refined carbs is likely to experience dramatic swings in blood sugar throughout the day. That will lead to corresponding fluctuations in attention, memory and mood (glucose is the brain's only fuel, remember). To me, it seems beside the point that the sugar industry keeps telling us that there's no direct effect of sugar on behaviour. I'll quite happily believe that very few individuals will react badly to sugar *per se* in a one-off 'challenge' (although some will and do). The thing is – the negative effects don't necessarily have to be direct or immediate to set up the patterns I've described above. The ideal conditions – involving almost unregulated consumption of sweets, sugary soft drinks and snacks – now apply to literally millions of our children, although some individuals will be more vulnerable than others.

Equally important is that if your child keeps eating these foods, she'll run a high risk of developing deficiencies in a range of essential nutrients. Let's go over it again:

- High-sugar foods usually have very little nutritional value themselves.
- They replace other, nutrient-rich foods that children could otherwise be eating.
- They deplete your child of nutrients (used up in digesting the refined sugar).
- They can feed yeast in the gut, adding to unhealthy 'dysbiosis', impairing digestion and immune function.
- Long term, there is a risk of your child developing 'metabolic syndrome' (sometimes called 'Syndrome X'), a precursor to Type II diabetes, and cardiovascular disease.

Diabetes – a Modern-day Disaster

Blood sugar that remains high for any length of time (hyperglycaemia) is as dangerous as very low blood sugar. It's associated with diabetes, of which there are two distinct types, with different initial causes.

1. Type I diabetes is caused by the body's failure to produce enough insulin (owing to auto-immune damage to cells in the pancreas), so you can't get the sugar out of your bloodstream and into the cells where it's needed.
2. Type II diabetes is caused by a failure of your cells to respond to the insulin you do produce. You've become 'resistant' to insulin. Your body tries producing more and more, but you still can't get that sugar into the cells. Still feeling the 'brain fog', you may well reach for yet another sugary snack …

The 'blood-sugar rollercoaster' described earlier can be a direct cause of Type II diabetes, which is becoming alarmingly common, even in children. This used to be a fairly rare disorder, and a disease of old age. Now we're told that it affects one person in five living in New York City. (More fast food, anyone?)

The complications and potential disability associated with diabetes can be substantial – particularly if it's not picked up early. Be alert for possible signs of persistent high blood sugar (hyperglycaemia), which include:

- excessive thirst
- frequent urination
- fatigue
- weight loss that's unexplained
- blurred vision
- increase in occurrence of thrush and other infections.

If you think you (or your child) may be hyperglycaemic, visit the doctor for a check-up without delay.

Individual Differences

Remember that sugar cravings can take different forms in different people. Susie, for example, is a child whose parents were horrified when she was given the 'ADHD' label. The foods she craved were the classic ones, so that everyone who knew her would say, 'Oh yes, she has a very sweet tooth.' Susie would devour chocolate, sweets and biscuits whenever these were around. She also adored almost all cakes and desserts, which made her very popular with her grandmother, who loved making them. Of course, this further reinforced Susie's eating behaviour.

'A High-sugar, High-fat Diet Stunts Brain Growth – It's Official!'

No – oddly enough I haven't yet seen this headline, but the research to justify it is emerging, and could provide a powerful incentive to many people who just can't kick their unhealthy dietary habits. Brain-derived neurotrophic factor (BDNF) is a substance that is essential to the growth of brain cells and the connections they make with one another. Mice engineered to lack this substance hardly develop any brains at all ... and low levels of BDNF have been linked with serious mental health conditions such as schizophrenia.[12]

Susie's father hardly touched those kinds of foods. He was adamant that he didn't have a sweet tooth at all. But what he did do was add several spoons of sugar to the teas or coffees that he consumed throughout the day (occasionally interspersed with a can of cola). After work he'd pour himself a beer, and usually have a few more over the course of the evening. All of these drinks, of course, will satisfy sugar cravings too.

As in this case, males and females often deal with their sugar-cravings in different ways – and these differences are largely reinforced by society. To alleviate the discomfort of low blood sugar, girls and women are more likely to go for sweet and sugary foods (especially chocolate). Boys and men tend to choose high-sugar stimulant soft drinks or alcohol for the same purpose.

This pattern appears to be changing somewhat as society becomes more tolerant, or even encouraging, of females drinking alcohol. However, the combination of a poor diet and excessive alcohol consumption is a particularly dangerous one, for both men and women. One has to wonder how much of the reckless and criminal behaviour associated with 'binge drinking' might be avoided if these young people were better nourished.

Sugar Sensitivity

Many people, possibly including you or your child, are what's been called 'sugar sensitive'. This condition (thought to have a genetic basis), means your blood-sugar levels will rise much more quickly than would happen for some other people when you consume food or drink with a high GI.

If you're sugar sensitive, not only does your blood-sugar level rise too quickly when you eat something sugary, but your insulin responses are also excessive, bringing your blood sugar down again too quickly, and overdoing it so it can fall too low for comfort. Your brain then sends frantic signals asking for quick fuel, so you go for something sweet again, or equally fast-acting (like white bread, coffee or cola). The cycle continues, so you can feel up one minute, and down the next. If your child is suffering this, she may be feeling tired, irritable and grumpy a lot of the time.

The story doesn't end there. Each time you get a blood-sugar 'rush', you release adrenalin from your two adrenal glands (placed atop your kidneys). Adrenalin helps you prepare to fight or run for cover (the blood sugar gets taken to the muscles to fuel them) … and it's designed for emergencies only – not many times a day! What can happen over time is that your adrenal glands become depleted, as they can't recharge quickly enough.

As a result, when your blood sugar 'spikes' quickly, the adrenal glands may act too slowly. Too much sugar in your blood is dangerous, so your pancreas releases even more insulin, making your sugar levels plummet. Then you look for more instant-energy-fix foods … and the whole cycle develops bigger peaks and troughs, with smaller intervals between highs and lows.

There are no studies that show eating refined sugar has any benefits.

Watch your child carefully to see if maybe he fits this pattern. Remember, this tendency to sugar sensitivity is genetic, so if either you or your parents have a sweet tooth or drink a lot of sweet tea, coffee or cola, or alcohol, your child is more likely to show sugar sensitivity. With a balanced, varied and healthy diet that is as free as practicable from simple sugars and processed carbohydrates, you can help your child learn to control this and become more settled and even-tempered.

Unfortunately, just handing over a quick-fix sugary snack doesn't help: your child will stay in this loop, run the risk of developing diabetes, and may become very overweight when the excess sugar is stored as fat. There are other effects, too. We've talked about the signs of hypoglycaemia – and anyone can suffer from that if they don't eat regularly – but people with sugar sensitivity also suffer from low serotonin and beta-endorphin levels.

Sugar, Proteins and Serotonin

What does this mean? Well, you need serotonin to feel relaxed, calm and content about things, and you need it to sleep well. If you are prone to low serotonin, this could *make* you grab for a cake or biscuit (and you thought it was lack of will-power!). Low serotonin is associated with impulsivity, depression and some other conditions you really don't want, for yourself or your child. Serotonin is made from tryptophan, an amino acid. Your brain will steer you towards eating carbohydrates because they help tryptophan to get into the brain, where it's used to make serotonin. If you've not eaten protein some time before the carbohydrate (with enough time to digest it down to its amino acids, so that there's tryptophan available), then this ploy doesn't work. You may feel briefly high from the sugar (until the insulin kicks in), but you won't produce more serotonin.

Tryptophan, found in all complete proteins, is sometimes portrayed as a 'weak' amino acid because it 'loses the race' against the others to get across the blood-brain barrier if they're all there together. If your child eats some protein earlier in the day, this should be fully digested to amino acids by bedtime. Eating some complex carbohydrate such as a small potato with its skin shortly before bedtime can make sure most of the amino acids get quickly escorted to the muscles (to prepare for fight or flight) … leaving the tryptophan behind so it can cross into the brain unopposed, to be made into serotonin, which should help mood and sleep. This strategy was first put forward in Kathleen DesMaison's best-selling book – *Potatoes, not Prozac*.[13] People tell me the bedtime-potato trick works (and certainly the competition between tryptophan and other amino acids to get into the brain is a well-established phenomenon) – but, perhaps unsurprisingly, controlled trials of the nightly-baked-potato experiment haven't yet been done, at least not to my knowledge!

Sugar and Beta-Endorphins

Beta-endorphins act like opium, so they're your body's natural heroin and morphine. When your beta-endorphin levels are up at a normal level you feel peaceful, your self-esteem levels are good, you cope with pain better and you may even feel on top of the world. On the other hand, if your beta-endorphin levels are low you can feel depressed and anxious, and your self-esteem dwindles. Does your child swing between low and high more than might be accounted for by adolescence, for example?

If your levels are naturally low (this aspect of 'sugar sensitivity' is again thought to have a genetic basis), your cells build more receptors so that they can capture any beta-endorphins that go by. Sugar, like alcohol, causes a release of beta-endorphins, which is why sugary-based foods and drinks give you this feel-good factor. This is all well and good, but if your child is one of those who has many more receptors than normal, the sugar has a drug-like effect and can set up cravings. As a result, your child can develop the high–low rollercoaster cycle talked about earlier.

The needs for sugar-fixes can't be controlled by will-power alone, but you can help your child's cravings and mood swings by introducing a balanced diet that also contains complex carbohydrates, proteins, essential fatty acids and micronutrients including chromium and zinc (see Chapter 4).

Breakfast is a must (see Chapter 12 for recipes), even if your child says he doesn't feel like it. In fact, the very people who 'can't face breakfast' are often the sugar-sensitives who need it most. What can happen is that their blood-sugar levels fall so low during the night that it takes a surge of adrenalin to wake them up at all – so a shockingly loud alarm clock or some other powerful stimulus may be needed to get them out of bed in the first place. Then they're usually slow, groggy and grumpy until the adrenalin really starts to kick in – when the stress of missing the bus, being late (or that bucket of cold water you threw over them) may finally get

them going … but they'll be out of the door without eating anything yet.
Sound familiar?

If your child really doesn't feel like eating at breakfast time, you may
need to work on this. Try a little natural yoghurt, or fruit smoothies (into
which you can smuggle some protein) initially. Eggs make an excellent
breakfast food, particularly if eaten with wholegrain toast, but if those
would take too long to cook or eat, find an alternative that your child will
eat – or at the very least will take with him to eat on the way to school.
(Having a ham salad sandwich ready in the fridge might do the trick.)
However you do it, aim to get your child to *eat breakfast, with some protein,
every day.*[14]

Basic Tactics For Steady, Sustained Energy

As you've gathered in this chapter, balancing brain energy is primarily
about controlling blood-sugar levels. The type of carbohydrates you feed
your child can profoundly affect his ability to do this, which in turn will
affect his mood, behaviour and future health.

1. **Exercise!** Not only is it essential for good overall health, exercise also
   helps regulate your blood-sugar levels and cut down cravings. It also
   raises the levels of feel-good chemicals in your body. Rather than letting
   your child eat a slice of white bread and cheap jam, or a cake, encourage
   him to have a healthy snack and then go out and kick a ball around.
   He'll be happier and healthier for it.
2. **Have a better diet!** Eat a wide range of unprocessed foods, or you're
   missing those very things that'll give your blood-sugar levels a chance:
   minerals like zinc, chromium and magnesium and other key nutrients.
   So:

- Always eat breakfast, and make sure it includes some protein.
- Avoid white foods: sugar (and synthetic sweeteners), highly processed
  'plastic' white bread, cakes, sweets, and so on.

- Drink water regularly throughout the day, though preferably not with your meals.
- Eat a range of fresh, unprocessed foods (and make them organic if you can).

Among the key nutrients your child must get from his diet for brain and body health are the so-called *essential fatty acids* (omega-3 and omega-6), which play a very important part in helping to balance his brain and body chemistry in many different ways. In the next chapter we'll look at these and other types of dietary fat, finding out which ones to choose, and which ones to avoid whenever possible.

FAQs

One sugar and health study shows one result, and the next one seems to suggest something else. Why? What's the truth?

You have to bear in mind the economics and politics of the sugar issue: big companies don't want to see definitive reports that denounce sugar as a white poison, and they have a huge degree of control over what you see and hear. Basically, the evidence that diets high in refined sugar damage human health is pretty difficult to deny. Refined sugar destabilizes blood-sugar control, robs the body of vital nutrients, upsets the balance of natural gut flora that's needed for good digestion and can damage the immune system. Enough said?

When it comes to its effects on behaviour, and whether sugar can be 'addictive', for example, it's always difficult to pin anything on just one substance – and sugar usually comes in foods and drinks that have other non-nutritious and/or harmful ingredients. We still need more scientific studies that stand up to scrutiny, as much of the evidence that sugar alone can destabilize mood, for example, is anecdotal.

As to why you hear such different things. First, the media loves to play a story one way and then the other, because dramatic headlines sell. Remember, too, that most research on this issue is funded by the food industry – and they have a huge interest in keeping us all eating sugary products. By contrast, some studies by independent researchers have produced disturbing findings.

My personal view is that for some sugar-sensitive people, sugar really can be a major issue, and its effects really can be described as 'addictive' (insofar as that word means anything, because it's harder to define addiction than you'd think). But I also believe that it's not the only culprit – any diet lacking in essential vitamins and minerals, good-quality protein and dietary fibre can contribute towards ill-health and mood swings. It's just that the people 'hooked' on sugary foods and drinks are usually missing out on just those things because of their food choices – which they often don't feel they can control. 'Cravings' are always a warning sign – and by far the most common type of craving is for sugary stuff. But rather than focusing on any one ingredient, I'd advise anyone to learn about the role food and nutrition play in general health and well-being, and learn about digestion, too (which refined sugar will damage).

Until the big food companies change their ways – which some of them are starting to do in response to consumer pressure – I'd also advise anyone to learn how to prepare and eat their own meals, and take regular exercise. These are likely to be essential for anyone who feels they're caught in a 'sugar addiction' cycle.

So, if I stop buying my son sweets today, will he turn from a little devil into an angel overnight?

I wish I could say 'Yes', but of course it's never going to be that simple, as I'm sure you know! For starters, even if sugar sensitivity and dietary issues are his only problems (which is unlikely), you'll have to face the effects of some 'withdrawal symptoms' if he's used to having lots of sugar. Yes, do reduce his intake of sweets (and soft drinks or other foods rich in refined sugar), but you'll have more success if you do this gradually. Before you even start, I'd say make sure he eats a good breakfast each day, and include a small amount of good-quality protein at this and every other meal (except bedtime snacks). At the same time, feed him a well-balanced diet, using fruits and vegetables instead of sweets to satisfy any sugar cravings as you cut the junk down gradually, and make sure you get him out for some exercise – all these things help.

Also, if he's able to understand, do tell him what you're doing and why. Explain that as he's being so grown up about it, you'd like to reward him: what would he like? (Play more together, go to a football match together, buy a new book or comic, get a bicycle – whatever.) And obviously, there may be numerous non-diet issues affecting his behaviour that also need addressing. If so, some of the support groups listed in the Resources chapter may be able to help you with those – and/or you may need some help from your doctor, or your child's teachers. In any case, I wish you the best of luck.

My teenage daughter is trying to lose weight. She's obsessed with counting calories and has got into this 'GI' thing, but she really likes potatoes – are they fattening or not?

This questions deserves a long answer, because you and your daughter really do need to get the priorities right. First – your daughter needs to focus on eating and living healthily, not on losing weight. If she eats a healthy diet and gets regular exercise, the weight really will come off anyway (if she needs to lose it). You say 'obsessed' – and that isn't a good sign, but sadly our whole society (driven by those parasitic industries that make money from other people's misery) encourages this kind of obsession – and teenage girls are particularly at risk here. There may well be other issues that are making her unhappy, in which case these need addressing first – but if excess weight really is the main problem, do try to get her to see that counting calories and calculating GI really is to miss the point.

She does need to be aware of which foods to avoid (mainly refined sugars and starches, many artificial additives and hydrogenated vegetable oils). Most of these are found in 'high-GI' foods – but that's not the main reason to cut them out. The fact is, highly processed, refined foods, and either sugary drinks or so-called 'diet' drinks laden with artificial sweeteners, can effectively poison her body and brain, leading to all kinds of physical and mental health problems in the longer term, if not now.

Turning to 'GI': This is in danger of becoming another 'diet craze', because the GI of an individual food (basically, how fast it releases its sugar) actually matters much less than the *balance* of each meal or snack as a whole. Generally speaking, the GI business relates to the *type* of carbohydrates (starches or sugars) she's eating. Foods that are naturally 'low GI' do tend to be healthier – but her focus should be on eating plenty of fresh fruits and vegetables as well as whole grains for their nutrients and fibre, as well as the slow-release energy these provide. It makes no sense to judge potatoes as 'fattening' or not – because this depends on how they're prepared and eaten – and with what other things. (Eating potato crisps and chips more than occasionally, for example, is worth avoiding for anyone, but particularly if you're overweight. This is because they usually provide 'bad' fats as well as 'bad carbs', because the potato is so highly processed. Crisps also usually have too much salt, and may contain artificial flavourings that can upset mood and behaviour in some people.)

- 'Sweet' potatoes, paradoxically, have a lower GI than white potatoes, and if she likes spuds, she may like dishes made with these instead.
- New potatoes have a lower GI than old ones.
- Boiled spuds have a lower GI than baked or mashed. But variations on mashed potato – such as including carrots, parsnips, swede or other root vegetables – can give her a good supply of carotenoids and other valuable micronutrients (see Chapter 4).
- She can lower the GI of her baked potatoes by adding a little fat (make sure this is natural fat – like butter, olive oil or even fresh nut or seed oils), and good-quality protein (maybe cottage cheese). If she accompanies them with some oily fish and a salad or plenty of non-starchy veg, all the better.
- A small baked potato in the evening – eaten with its skin – may help her sleep better (provided she's had some complete protein earlier in the day), and better sleep will help her health and her ability to follow a well-balanced diet.

Why do doctors say a 'low-carb' diet isn't good for me or my child?

What the doctors mean is that we all need some carbohydrates to provide us with energy. In fact, carbs should normally make up around half of your child's energy (calorie) intake. But the key point is that these do need to be *the right kind of carbohydrates*. You and your child also need to eat these as part of a balanced diet that provides enough good-quality protein and the right kinds of fats. (You'll hear about which fats these are in the next chapter.)

Basically, it's only the highly refined sugars and starches that are bad for everyone and can cause ill-health. They're empty of nutrients themselves, and digesting them can deplete you and your child of what nutrients you do have. The foods that contain these refined carbs (such as sweets, soft drinks, biscuits, cakes, pastries and savoury snacks) often have other nasty ingredients, too – such as artificial colourings and flavourings, and the wrong types of fats. To top it all, sugar can feed the yeasts that live in your gut, allowing them to replace the good bacteria that you need to keep your digestion and your immune system healthy. Enough said? If you're following a diet that's low in *these* kinds of refined carbs – that's great. Keep it up. But you and your child both need a good supply of *complex, unrefined* carbohydrates – found in vegetables, fruits and whole grains. These break down into glucose sugar much more slowly when you eat them, so they won't put you and your child at risk of mood and energy swings in the short term, and diabetes and other health problems in the long term, the way that refined carbohydrates do. These kinds of foods rich in complex carbohydrates also provide lots of essential micronutrients, including vitamins, minerals, antioxidants and phytonutrients (see Chapter 4), as well as important dietary fibre that helps your digestion and feeds the good bacteria that are vital for health. So don't avoid all carbs – just sugar and the highly refined starches.

Summary

1. Of the three main macronutrient types, it is carbohydrates (rather than proteins or fats) that we primarily use for energy. In the case of brain cells, glucose (a simple sugar) is the *only* fuel they can burn for energy.
2. There are three broad types of carbohydrate: sugars, starches (made up of many sugar molecules joined together) and fibre, which is indigestible starch.
3. 'Good carbs' are the more complex carbohydrates (unrefined starches found in whole grains, vegetables and fruits). These release their sugar

slowly, and also have many other nutrients and fibre. 'Bad carbs' include highly refined sugar and starches (found in most processed foods), which have the opposite characteristics.

4. Sugars include monosaccharides (consisting of a single sugar molecule, such as glucose itself) and disaccharides (consisting of two sugar molecules). Ordinary table sugar is a disaccharide.

5. Monosaccharides (found in fruits, honey and yoghurt) need almost no digestion and can pass straight into the bloodstream. Disaccharides and starches have to be broken down by digestive enzymes and turned into glucose first.

6. Some people with severe 'gut dysbiosis' (abnormal gut flora) can't make the enzymes needed to break down disaccharide sugars or starches. Undigested, these will ferment in the gut and cause health problems. These people can often benefit from a very special diet that permits only certain carbohydrates. (This may require professional help.)

7. Once absorbed, glucose is used for energy or stored (as glycogen or fat) for future energy. Carbohydrates work best for us when the glucose from them is released slowly into the bloodstream.

8. Too much sugar at once can cause blood-sugar levels to rise too fast. The excess is removed by insulin (released from the pancreas unless a person has diabetes), but when blood sugar rises quickly, insulin can over-compensate and drive it lower than it was to start with.

9. Not eating for a long time, or too much insulin at once, causes blood sugar to drop too low (hypoglycaemia). This results in feeling tired and irritable, and finding it hard to concentrate. Eating refined carbohydrates will make this worse, and could set up a 'rollercoaster' cycle of highs and lows in blood sugar, mood, behaviour and capacity to learn.

10. A high-sugar diet can cause attention and behavioural problems in some children, and can also deplete your child of vital nutrients, as these are used up in extracting and using the glucose. (Refined, sugary foods and drinks provide few if any nutrients themselves.) Sugar can also encourage overgrowth of yeast in the gut, making digestion and immune function worse.

11. On food labels, sugar comes under many names – look for hidden sugars, and avoid foods that have these. Sugary snacks may also contain additives which can affect your child's behaviour.

12. Low-GI foods release their sugar more slowly – which is desirable – but even high-GI foods, if eaten with some fats and proteins, can behave like low-GI foods – so there's no need to be obsessive about GI values once you've absorbed the principles.

13. If your child is sugar-sensitive, levels of serotonin and beta-endorphins will be lower than usual, which will add to sugar cravings. A balanced diet will help control this.

14. Diets high in refined sugars and starches can cause serious physical and mental health problems, particularly when linked with consumption of the wrong kinds of fats, too, which are present in many of the same foods.

chapter 8

getting the fats right

Probably no single aspect of our diets has generated more confusion, controversy and misleading information than dietary fat. The word itself doesn't help – because at some level, we don't really want to know! 'Fat' and 'fatty' are ugly words, let's be honest – and yet we love the foods that contain the stuff! It's time to face up to some fat facts – but the news isn't all bad, I promise you.

In this chapter we'll look at why we eat fats, the different types of fats there are, and what effects these can have on your child's physical health as well as his behaviour, learning and mood. This will introduce you to some very special dietary fats – the so-called 'omega-3' fatty acids which are sadly lacking from the diets of many children (and adults) in the UK today. Then, in Chapter 9 we'll be focusing specifically on what scientific research has revealed about the links between omega-3 and children's behaviour and learning. As that's been my specialist research area for many years, I can promise you a more realistic appraisal of the evidence than you may already have picked up from elsewhere – particularly the tabloid media. I'll also be giving you my own opinions on the practical implications of this research for you and your child.

First, then, let's see why most of us (including the supposed experts) just *haven't* been 'getting the fats right' in our diets, even if we think we've been trying hard.

Dietary Fat – Why Have We Got It So Wrong?

At the personal level, no one wants to be carrying around a lot of fat (no matter what they may say), and we've all come to associate 'eating' fat with 'being' fat. For decades we've all been told we must cut the total amount of fat we consume – and that fat is responsible for obesity, heart disease, strokes, cancer and most other diseases of the Western world. Experts have told us our diets should contain no more than 30 per cent fat (although the average for UK children is 35 per cent[1]) – so anyone trying to lose weight or improve their health has been striving to follow tasteless 'low-fat' (and sometimes almost 'no-fat') diets.

Wrong! When research showed which of the world's diets was the healthiest, the winning country was Crete. There, people were living the longest, with the lowest rates of heart attack, stroke and cancers – and their traditional diet turned out to have a whopping 40 per cent fat.[2] *But it was of a very special kind.* So before you and your child start cheering and rushing off to buy that burger and full-fat milkshake, let's be very clear about this: it's the *type* of fat you eat that matters, not the overall quantity (within reason!).

> The typical modern American fast-food diet (which the UK has sadly chosen to follow far more than any other European country) is probably the one that has got it most wrong of all.

Even at the level of research, fat seemed to most scientists a pretty boring and 'un-glamorous' issue to study … until very recently. In the glorious post-war period last century, when all kinds of new discoveries were being made in medicine, it seemed clear that genetics and drug discovery were the fields where all the big prizes were to be won. Fats (or 'lipids', to give them their more scientific name) were hardly even on the map. After all, proteins are the structural building-blocks of most body tissues (along with the enzymes needed to carry out most of our vital functions); and the genetic code – DNA – is actually a blueprint for assembling amino acids into proteins. The receptors for neurotransmitters (chemical signalling molecules) are also made of special proteins; and what's more, some protein fragments (peptides) function directly as signalling molecules. So the search for new drugs was largely focused on these, and not on the lowly fats. 'Let's find a new chemical that might fit the receptor' (like a key fits into a lock) was the main preoccupation in pharmaceutical research – and still is.

A similar pattern was also reflected in the science of nutrition and diet. Vitamins and minerals obviously got a look-in, but throughout most of last century, dietary advice for babies and children was focused mainly on making sure they got enough protein (with the essential amino acids we can't make for ourselves) in order to support their physical growth. Carbohydrates? Well, those are just burned for body and brain fuel. Fats? Very boring – they're just for energy storage. Sadly for us, it was really only the food industry that paid much attention to researching these areas in any detail. Oddly enough, the promotion of health was not very high up on their agenda.

We are all now paying the price for this neglect.

The Eccentric Scientists – Genius Doesn't Always Mean Mad

Within medicine, only a very few 'eccentric' scientists could see from early on the vital importance of fats to human health and disease. Among them was Hugh Sinclair, of Magdalen College in Oxford. Although he and his work were almost ignored by mainstream scientists at the time, he actually helped to make the key discoveries that explained why the Inuit (Eskimo) people rarely suffered from heart disease – even though their diets contained huge quantities of fat. (The answer? Because it was the right kind of fat, containing lots of those omega-3s.)

Early in my own research career, I was very fortunate to meet one of the few people who 'picked up and ran' with Hugh Sinclair's ideas about the vital importance of fats. He was a self-confessed 'maverick' scientist and medical doctor called David Horrobin. A controversial figure in some circles, he was a truly brilliant man.[3] From conversations with him I began to realize how important omega-3 fatty acids might be for my own research into dyslexia and related conditions. I was also very fortunate to be working with Professor John Stein at Oxford (as I still do), who knew Hugh Sinclair and had admired him greatly. He also knew David Horrobin, and agreed with me that David probably had one of the brightest minds on the planet![4] The 'omega-3 revolution' that you'll learn more about here and in the next chapter had hardly begun to reach public awareness at that time.

> I was lucky to have met the right people, at just the right time, to inspire me to carry out the first controlled treatment trials to see if omega-3 could improve children's behaviour and learning.

We Were Warned

Back in the 1970s, another brilliant and far-sighted scientist, Professor Michael Crawford (founder of the Institute of Brain Chemistry and Human Nutrition in London), issued serious warnings. Rates of heart disease and stroke were already rising and, like Hugh Sinclair, he knew why. He predicted then that unless we made some dramatic changes to our dietary fat intake, the next (non-infectious) major epidemic of the Western world would involve 'brain disorders'. Well, we didn't make those changes, and guess what? He was absolutely right. That epidemic is now upon us. Rates of depression and other mental health disorders, aggression and other forms of antisocial behaviour, and a whole array of childhood developmental disorders of behaviour and learning (including, but not confined to, ADHD, dyslexia, dyspraxia and autism) have climbed relentlessly since then.

> According to the World Health Organization, mental health problems are now among the top four 'disease types' accounting for the 'global burden of ill-health' (our dietary habits have been spreading further afield, aided by our multinational industries).

Within Europe, 'brain disorders' have already overtaken heart disease and stroke, with simply astronomical cost estimates attached (and that's just counting the money, not the human misery). Michael Crawford could see all of this looming back in the 1970s because he already knew, from his own pioneering work, about the crucial importance of dietary fats for the brain.

Believe it or not, governments are still hardly taking much notice – and regulations to help you choose the good fats and avoid the bad fats are (as usual) lagging way behind the science. But if you read on, you really won't find it difficult to learn what you can do *now* to make the healthy choices for your child, yourself and the rest of your family and friends. If you really don't want the details, don't worry – just follow the dietary advice.

Fats Are Essential – Particularly to the Brain!

Ignoring its water content, *the dry mass of your brain is actually 60 per cent fat.* This simple fact alone should tell you that *the type of fat in your diet can affect the way your brain works.* All your body cells use fat as part of their membrane structure, but your brain and nerve cells need very special kinds of fats, and if the wrong type gets used, they just won't be able to function properly.

There are good fats and bad fats.

It really is *critical*, both for your physical health and your mental health, for you and your child to know the difference. The trouble is, most people still don't (and sadly, that includes many health professionals). Much of the information we've all been getting about dietary fats has been coming from the food and diet industries, along with the pharmaceutical industry. Most of these have been doing rather well from our ignorance. Naturally, they have more interest in their profits than your health, or your child's brainpower – and so their messages have usually only served to create more confusion. We need to clear that away.

The Fats in Our Diets

Let's start by looking first at why we choose to eat fats, and then at why we actually need them in our diet. You and your child both need to understand the importance of 'getting the fats right'. If you do, it will not only help you both now, it will also pay you huge dividends later on in life.

Why We Eat Fats

They Can Taste Very Good

Fats can help to blend other flavours together. Many aromatic compounds don't dissolve in water, but will dissolve and mingle easily in fat – which is why many recipes start with mixing flavours together in a little oil. (For example garlic, onions, herbs and spices usually go in together when starting soups or casseroles; see the recipe chapters for some good ideas.)

They Give Us Energy

Fats are burned for energy by many cells – but interestingly, not those in the brain. As we saw in the previous chapter, the brain can only use sugar (in the form of glucose) for energy, which is why it is so important to keep blood-sugar levels stable.

Body fat provides us with a highly concentrated *store* of energy, acting as a reserve in case of famine. Excess sugar – that is, more than is needed to fuel our short-term activity – will mainly be converted into fat.

They Fill Us Up

Fats give us a pleasant feeling of fullness ('satiety') after eating. They do this by triggering the release of certain hormones that help to regulate our appetite.

Unfortunately, these signals can sometimes get over-ridden, so we keep eating more than we need without thinking. 'Bad fats' are often hidden in cakes and biscuits, for example, as well as ice-creams and desserts, sauces and salad dressings, and many highly processed savoury snacks like crisps. In fact, we can easily get 'addicted' to many foods that are rich in 'bad' fats – because these often contain:

- sugar (a real problem for the sugar-sensitive among us)
- artificial additives (as we saw in Chapter 6, some of these have been shown to cause behavioural problems in many children)
- foods which many people have some degree of allergy to or intolerance for (such as wheat and other grains containing gluten, or cows' milk and other dairy products).

Why We Need Fats

We've generally been led to think that 'all fat is bad'. Nothing could be further from the truth.

In fact – some fats are absolutely essential.

- Fats are vital to the structure of all your cells, because they form a large part of the cell membranes ('walls').
- Some very special fats are needed for the structure of your nerve and brain cells (and also for the cells in your heart and other vital organs).
- Fats can influence almost all cellular functions, including the transport of substances into and out of cells, and information signalling between cells. Some fats can even regulate your genes, increasing or decreasing their activity.
- Some very special fats are needed to produce substances that regulate your blood flow, your hormone balance and your immune system.
- Dietary fats are a source of vitamins A, D, E and K (see Chapter 4 for why we need these vitamins).
- Fats provide a concentrated source of energy, and a convenient form of storing surplus energy.

So, as you can see, we really do need fats in our diet for lots of very important reasons. Dietary fats are much more than just a compact and 'slow-burning' source of fuel – but they do come in different kinds, so you and your child need to know which kinds to eat, and which kinds to avoid.

The Main Types of Dietary Fats

Edible fats and oils all contain 'fatty acids'. There are three main types, each group with its own properties:

1. saturated
2. monounsaturated
3. polyunsaturated.

It's really worth taking time to understand what these words mean – because once you do, it's much easier to identify the bad fats and learn how to avoid them. The very basic chemistry honestly isn't that complicated! (See the diagram below.)

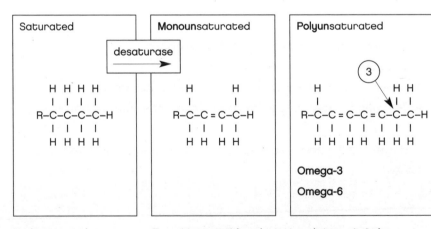

Types of Dietary Fats

Fatty Acids – Chains and Bonds

Why Bonding Is Important
Every fatty acid has a 'backbone' made up of a chain of carbon atoms, to which hydrogen can be attached on either side.

Each carbon atom has four 'free hands' that can form a single bond (link) with another particle:

- When a carbon atom is in a fatty acid chain, two of those four possible bonds are used to 'hold hands' with its carbon neighbours on either side. The other two free 'hands' (one on each side of the chain) can form a bond with hydrogen.
- If two neighbouring carbon atoms have no hydrogen to bond with, they can hold hands with each other, forming a 'double bond'.

The number (and position) of double bonds in the carbon chain determine what type of fat it is:

- **Saturated fatty acids have no double bonds.** (They are saturated, i.e. full up with hydrogen.)
- **Monounstaurated fatty acids have one double bond.**
- **Polyunsaturated fatty acids have two or more double bonds.**

Omega-3 and omega-6 are special kinds of polyunsaturates (see below).

'Straight' and 'Kinky' Fats

Saturated fats with no double bonds have straight chains. This means they can pack closely together in the cell membranes. But wherever there's a double bond, a fatty acid chain can 'kink' or bend. This means they don't pack so closely, making your membranes more 'springy', fluid and flexible. That's one reason why you need polyunsaturated fatty acids in your body's cells – they're flexible!

Why the Funny Names?

- A fatty acid chain can be between 4 and 28 carbon atoms long.
- 'Alpha' is the first letter of the Greek alphabet, and is used to label the first carbon in the chain.
- 'Omega' is the last letter of the Greek alphabet, and is used to denote the last carbon in the chain:
  - Omega-3: the first double bond (kink) occurs between the third and fourth carbon atoms (counting from the omega end).
  - Omega-6: the first double bond (kink) occurs between the sixth and seventh carbon atoms (counting from the omega end).

(Much more detailed drawings can be found in the next chapter.)

Sadly, it's not always so easy to identify the good fats – because food labelling regulations really don't help you with this at the moment. In fact, the way fats are labelled can actually *distract* your attention from what really matters most, as we shall see.

Saturated Fatty Acids (SFAs)

Saturated fats have the following characteristics:

- They are solid at room temperature.
- They have no double bonds (*saturated = 'full' – meaning hydrogen is bonded to every available link on the carbon atoms in the chain*).
- **The main dietary sources** are animal fats, including milk, butter, cream, cheese, lard and the fat attached to meat. Some tropical oils (such as coconut and palm oil) also contain a large proportion of saturated fats.

- **You can also make saturated fats for yourself.** This is what usually happens when you consume more calories than you burn for energy. It's how excess sugar can be turned into fat (as most of us know all too well!).

For a long time, we've been warned to avoid eating too much saturated fat. Being solid (like butter, lard or meat fat), these fats tend to make cell membranes stiffer and less flexible, and they can effectively 'clog up' your arteries, raising your risk of heart attack and stroke. Eating too much saturated fat can also overload your liver and digestive system. (As we learned earlier, your liver helps by producing the bile needed as a 'detergent' to break fats down.)

You may have heard the famous greasy, cooked British breakfast (such as fried bacon and sausage, with fried eggs and fried bread) described as a 'heart attack on a plate'! This is mainly because of the overload of saturated fats it can provide. Similarly, eating too much cream and butter (often hidden in cakes, puddings, ice-cream or rich sauces) can easily take you over the recommended intake of saturated fats.

> Saturated fats should make up no more than 10 per cent of the total energy provided by your diet.

Having said all this, *natural* saturated fats found in natural foods are not deadly *in moderation*. In fact, they're an important source of slow-burn energy and key nutrients, including the fat-soluble vitamins A, D, E and K. What's more, most of the *natural* foods that contain saturated fats also contain other types of fat (including some of the essential fats we'll hear about in a moment), along with other important nutrients.

Monounsaturated Fatty Acids (MUFAs)

These differ from saturated fats in many important ways:

- They are liquid oils at room temperature.
- They have one double bond (*just two hydrogen atoms are missing from adjacent carbons – which use those free links to make an extra bond with each other*).
- **The main dietary sources** are olive oil, some other vegetable oils (including rapeseed and peanut oils), many nuts and seeds, and some fruits and vegetables (notably avocados).
- **You can also make monounsaturated fats for yourself.** (If needed, our enzymes can create a double bond in the carbon chain 7 or 9 carbons from the 'omega' end. This creates omega-7 or omega-9 fatty acids.)

Monounsaturated fats – and the foods that contain them – are usually regarded as fairly 'healthy' fats. They can make membranes more fluid and flexible (think of olive oil versus lard), and we can also use them to make some important chemical signalling molecules. In fact, 'oleic acid', an omega-9 monounsaturate found in olive oil, can be converted into substances that have a calming, relaxing, sleep-inducing effect.[5] That might be worth thinking about the next time your child is bouncing off the walls!

Charlie and the Mediterranean Diet

Charlie's father was at his wits' end. His school in the UK was insisting that Charlie had ADHD and should be on medication. But in Crete, where the family had a business and spent several months each year, Charlie's sleep problems – and his 'hyper' behaviour – always just vanished. Could it be something to do with the differences in diet?

His father really didn't want to give powerful drugs to his child if there was an alternative. We talked about the different kinds of fats, and he agreed to keep Charlie on the 'Mediterranean type' diet when in the UK. Out went the fast foods, fried foods, chips and crisps, and in came the olive oil, nuts, seeds, fresh vegetables and plenty of fish, all of which the family enjoyed when in Crete.

The difference amazed Charlie's teachers in the UK. He stopped disrupting classes and fighting in the playground, settled down and concentrated on his work, and became one of their star pupils. His father easily won the battle to keep his son off medication – and the whole family benefited from Charlie's better sleep patterns.

The healthiest 'Mediterranean diets', such as the diet of Crete, contain plenty of natural monounsaturates from olive oil, nuts, seeds and some vegetables and fruits (as well as plenty of omega-3 polyunsaturates from fish and seafood, which we'll hear more about in a minute). Monounsaturates are generally 'good fats', but, if needed, we can make them for ourselves, so they are not dietary essentials.

'Trans Fats' – The *Real Junk* We've Been Eating

One of the most worrying aspects of the diets of UK children today is not so much the amount of fat, but the *type* of fat they contain. We have long been warned about the risks from diets high in saturated fats – but in fact, the 'trans fats' found in most processed foods are potentially a far worse problem.

Trans fats are by-products of 'hydrogenation', a process that has allowed the food industry to use cheap solidified vegetable oils instead of expensive animal fats.

Trans fats are warped, twisted, unnatural versions of healthy polyunsaturated fats. They are found in crisps, biscuits, cakes, pastries, almost all commercially baked goods, fried foods, takeaways and many 'ready meals', as well as most shop-bought sauces and salad dressings.

After reviewing all the evidence emerging on trans fats (after we've all been eating them for decades), the medical advisers to the US Government concluded that **the upper safe level of trans fats in the diet is ZERO.**

For further information on trans fats, and which foods they are lurking in, check out the websites www.bantransfats.com and www.tfxorg.

Polyunsaturated Fatty Acids (PUFAs)

These are the type of fats that cause by far the most confusion. This is because there are crucial differences between natural polyunsaturates (which are generally 'good fats') and ones that have been highly processed (which can contain some '*very bad* fats').

To start with their basic characteristics:

- Natural polyunsaturates are liquid oils – even at very low temperatures.
- They have two or more double bonds (*corresponding to lots of missing hydrogen, so many carbons can 'hold hands' to form double bonds*).
- **The main dietary sources** are natural vegetable oils, nuts and seeds, whole grains, meat, dairy produce, eggs, fish and seafood.

Now, we need to focus on the all-important distinction between good and bad PUFA. Let's start with the good ones: the natural omega-3 and omega-6 polyunsaturates. These are both *essential* in your child's diet (although you do need the right balance between these two types, as we shall see later).

Omega-3 and Omega-6 Fatty Acids
- Omega-3 and omega-6 are both special kinds of polyunsaturated fats.
- They get their names from the fact that their first double bond is positioned at either 3 or 6 carbon atoms from the far (omega) end of the fatty-acid chain. We don't have enzymes that can put a double bond in this position, so we have to get these special polyunsaturates from our food.
- We need both omega-3 and omega-6, but we can't make them for ourselves. This why they are often called **essential fatty acids** (EFAs).

Let's now look at the 'bad' polyunsaturates. These are 'unnatural' ones that have been warped and twisted out of shape by modern food-processing technologies. They are widespread in our food supply *and are the ones that you and your child should avoid as much as possible.*

I've already explained that saturated fats are solid at room temperature, while natural polyunsaturates (found in most vegetable oils) are liquid. Early last century, the food industry learned how to 'hydrogenate' (artificially saturate) vegetable oils to make them more solid. This way, they can be used as a cheap substitute for butter or lard. The problem is, this hydrogenation process can create some really nasty, twisted fats called 'trans fats'. These are 'warped' versions of natural polyunsaturated fats.[6]

Hydrogenated and Trans Fatty Acids

- Hydrogenated fats are *artificially saturated* fats.
- Trans fatty acids (or trans fats) are *artificially twisted versions of natural polyunsaturates.* They are formed through *partial hydrogenation* of unsaturated oils.
- **The main dietary sources** of hydrogenated and trans fats are ordinary margarines and 'shortening'; biscuits, cakes, pastries and other commercially baked goods; crisps and other snack foods, fried foods and takeaways; and many shop-bought sauces and salad dressings. It's a long list! But any foods made with 'hydrogenated' vegetable fats and oils can contain trans fats (which don't have to be declared on food labels).

Trans fats hardly occur in nature, and despite the fact that we've been eating increasing amounts of them for decades, they are only now starting to be publicly recognized as a serious health hazard. As usual, most food manufacturers don't want you to know, and governments have been very slow to warn the public about their potential dangers. In the US, Government medical advisors concluded a few years ago that there really is *no safe level* of trans fats in the diet. As from this year (2006), all foods sold in the US must be labelled for their trans fat content, so that at least the informed consumers can make their own minds up. In Norway, Denmark, France and other European countries, governments are now taking steps to reduce or eliminate (as far as possible) trans fats in their foods. In the UK, we are still waiting for any announcements on what our Government plans to do about this.[7]

If you take the time to read up on this subject, I think you will be horrified at the way public health has once again been sacrificed to the profits of powerful industries. If you'd like to learn more about this and help get trans fats out of our food supply, join the UK campaign.[8] Meanwhile, if you want to stop clogging up your child's brain with artificial, potentially toxic fats, then once again I'm afraid it's up to you!

To look on the bright side, though, changing your shopping habits to avoid trans fats can make trips to the supermarket a whole lot shorter, because there really are whole aisles that you just won't need to go down any more!

Hydrogenation of Oils: A Gruesome Tale

Hydrogenation is used to change polyunsaturated (liquid) oils into solid fats such as margarine and vegetable 'shortening'. Basically the process, which is usually carried out at high temperatures (150–180°C) and under high pressure, involves bombarding vegetable oil with hydrogen over a period of time (using nickel to speed up the process) until it changes into a semi-solid consistency. As a result, some of the molecules get twisted into harmful trans fatty acids.

Complete hydrogenation converts unsaturated fatty acids to saturated ones, but the process usually stops short of this, in order to keep the resultant 'spread' easy to use. 'Partial hydrogenation' means the resulting mixture usually contains lots of twisted trans fats as well as some of the original, natural polyunsaturates.

Because they're cheap, can be made in a range of consistencies and have a long shelf-life, partially hydrogenated vegetable fats and oils are used in all kinds of commercially baked and processed foods ... and don't have to show up on the label. Manufacturers who have taken trans fatty acids out of their products boast about it on the packet – so if you see the word 'hydrogenated', but nothing else is mentioned, always assume they're in there!

Trans fats have no known nutritional benefits and many health risks:

- *They make 'bad' (LDL) cholesterol levels go up, and 'good' (HDL) ones go down.*
- *Evidence indicates that they can increase the risk of heart disease, stroke, diabetes, inflammation and some forms of cancer.*
- *They can soak up antioxidants in the body, leaving too many free radicals, which can cause all kinds of damage to cells and speed up ageing.*
- **In brain cells, hydrogenated and trans fats can make membranes far less fluid and flexible. This in turn can affect the functioning of all cell-signalling systems.**

What the Food Labels Don't Tell You

Even if you do try to read food labels, the current system really isn't very helpful when it comes to fats. You do get some useful information: as well as the total fat content, detailed labels will usually tell you what proportion may be saturated, monounsaturated or polyunsaturated. So far so good. But what they *don't* tell you (and I think they should) is *what type of polyunsaturates* are in there! So it's very hard indeed for you to know whether these are 'good' or 'bad' polyunsaturates unless you've wised up to the real issues. Very simplistically, the real questions are:

- *Are these natural polyunsaturates (good) or does the product contain 'trans fats' (bad)?* Look at the list of ingredients to help you decide. If you see the words 'hydrogenated' or 'partially hydrogenated' vegetable fats or oils, put it back on the shelf.
- *What proportion of the total polyunsaturates are omega-6 or omega-3?* This is another important question that most processed food labels don't help you with at all, and again, I think they should.

Before you'll be able to make at least an educated guess at this second question, we'll need to look at these very special fats in a bit more detail. Now that we've learned about the bad fats, it's time to focus on the good ones.

Essential Fatty Acids (EFAs)

Both omega-3 and omega-6 fats are *vital* (you literally can't live without them), but you can't make them for yourself, so must get them from your diet. For this reason, they're often called 'essential fatty acids' (EFAs).

There are several different kinds of omega-3 and omega-6. The simplest forms are called alpha-linolenic acid, or ALA (omega-3), and linoleic acid, or LA (omega-6). If you eat these, your body can (in theory at least) use them to make all the other forms of omega-3 and omega-6 that it needs. The pathways for doing this are shown in the diagrams below.

	omega-6		omega-3	
EFA	LA (Linoleic)	18:2	ALA (ALA (A-linolenic)	18:3
	GLA	18:3		18:4
	DGLA	20:3		20:4
HUFA	AA (Arachidonic)	20:4	EPA	20:5
	Adrenic	22:4	DPA (n-3)	22:5
	DPA (n-6)	22:5	DHA	22:6

Different Types of Omega-3 and Omega-6 Fatty Acids

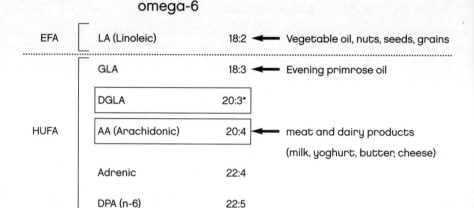

Dietary Sources of Omega-6

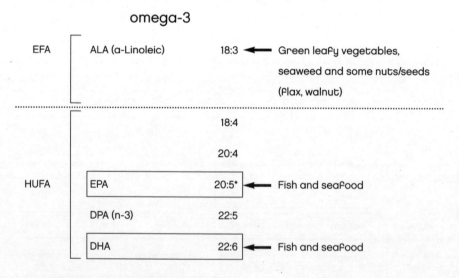

Dietary Sources of Omega-3

EFAs, PUFAs and HUFAs

I know the terminology really can be confusing! But it's worth taking a moment to sort this out. Polyunsaturated fatty acids are often called 'PUFAs' for short. As you've seen, omega-3 and omega-6 are special kinds of PUFAs that you can't make for yourself, but a dietary source of at least the simple forms – ALA and LA – is absolutely essential. In theory, you can make for yourself all the other forms of omega-3 from ALA, and all the other forms of omega-6 from LA. So if we're being very strict with our terminology, then only these two are the truly 'essential fatty acids'(EFAs). But the thing is, *ALA and LA aren't actually the forms of omega-3 and omega-6 that your brain and body need the most.*

The forms of omega-3 and omega-6 with more double bonds tend to be more biologically active – so they are actually much more useful to you than the simplest ALA and LA forms. To distinguish them from the simple forms, they are sometimes called highly unsaturated fatty acids (HUFAs):

- *The ones your brain particularly needs are all HUFAs.*
- They include DGLA and AA from the omega-6 family, and EPA and DHA from the omega-3 family.
- Two of them (AA and DHA) are crucial for the actual structure of your child's brain.
- Three of them (DGLA, AA and EPA) are needed to make other key substances that regulate the way his brain actually functions – as well as your child's hormone balance, immune function and blood flow.

Later we'll look at their effects in more detail, but first let's see what foods will provide them.

Dietary Sources of Omega-3 and Omega-6 Fatty Acids

FOODS THAT PROVIDE OMEGA-6
In LA form (so needs to be converted by the body into the more important forms):
- most vegetable oils (especially corn, sunflower, safflower and soy)
- most nuts and seeds, and
- most grains

Already in GLA form (which converts easily into DGLA and others):
- evening primrose oil, borage (starflower) oil, blackcurrant seed oil

Already in required AA form (very important for brain, heart and immune system):

- all types of meat
- dairy products, including milk, cream, butter, cheese and yoghurt (whole-fat rather than skimmed-milk products)
- eggs

FOODS THAT PROVIDE OMEGA-3

In ALA form (so needs to be converted by the body into the more important forms):

- flax seeds and flax oil, walnuts, some other nuts and seeds (only buy cold-pressed flax seed oil, and only in small amounts; it degrades with exposure to light, heat and air, so is best kept refrigerated)
- green vegetables (the darker and leafier, the better)

Already in required EPA and DHA forms:

- All fish and seafood (oily fish such as sardines, anchovies, pilchards, mackerel, herring, salmon and tuna are the richest sources, but any fish or seafood makes a valuable contribution)
- Wild game/organic meat (animals fed naturally – on fresh grass, or foraging for their own herbs and seeds in the wild – usually produce meat, milk and eggs with at least some omega-3 content, providing some ALA and a little EPA. Grain-fed, intensively-reared animals generally don't.)
- Fortified eggs (various products fortified with 'omega-3' are now available, but you need to check the labels carefully to see how much these actually contain – and what form it is in)
- Fortified milk and dairy products (again, you need to check labels carefully to see how much omega-3 these actually contain and what form it is in)

Converting EFA to HUFA – Not an Easy Job

Some foods (mainly from animal sources) will provide 'ready-made' the HUFA that your child's brain, heart and immune system really need to function properly (see diagram on page 228). Anyone who doesn't eat these foods has to build their own HUFA from the simple EFA (ALA and LA) – but I must emphasize that this is *not* an easy job: unfortunately, studies have repeatedly shown that these conversion pathways are just not very efficient in humans.[9]

Many diet and lifestyle factors can reduce the conversion of EFA to HUFA, including poor diets that don't provide enough vitamin and mineral 'co-factors'. These include vitamins B_1, B_3, B_6, vitamin C, zinc, magnesium and manganese. So if your child is lacking any one of these micronutrients, she may be unable to make enough of the key HUFA, even if she has the right raw materials (ALA and LA). Too many saturated, hydrogenated and trans fats in the diet can also block these conversion pathways (yet another reason to dump the junk food!). Other things that can block the process include high levels of stress, and some viral infections. Age matters, too: these pathways don't work well in young infants or older people.

Sex differences deserve special mention here, because for hormonal reasons *males are at a disadvantage when it comes to making their own HUFA from EFA.* Two careful studies showed that although young women could manufacture at least some DHA from ALA, the young men studied made no DHA at all.[10] These findings are rather worrying for any boys and men who don't eat fish! These sex differences in fatty-acid metabolism might also help to explain why more boys than girls tend to develop behaviour and learning difficulties such as ADHD, dyslexia, dyspraxia and autism – but more research is still needed to find out how dietary fatty acids may influence these conditions, as we'll see in the next chapter.

Fatty Acids for the Brain – is Your Child Getting Enough?

As we've just seen, converting the simple EFAs (ALA and LA) into the HUFA that your child's brain really needs isn't easy, and can't be guaranteed. This actually doesn't matter so much for omega-6, because unless your child is following a very strict vegetarian or vegan diet he can get plenty of AA (the main omega-6 HUFA the brain needs) directly from meat, dairy produce or eggs.

It *does* matter for omega-3, because unless your child regularly eats fish or seafood (the main dietary sources of ready-made EPA and DHA), he is relying almost completely on the 'do-it-yourself' conversion pathway – and yet studies show that less than 5 per cent of the ALA we get from our diets is usually turned into EPA, and even less into DHA.

This is why the Vegetarian Society of the UK recommends a daily intake of at least 4 grams of flax oil, to be sure of getting enough EPA and DHA. That's quite a lot. What's more, the reason they recommend flax oil is that you can't rely on all those green vegetables that your child eats (!) to give him enough omega-3. Think about it: there really isn't very much fat in a piece of broccoli, cabbage or lettuce, is there?

For these reasons, adequate supplies are much more difficult to guarantee unless EPA and DHA are provided ready-made – in other words, unless your child eats plenty of fish or foods specially fortified with EPA and DHA, or takes fish oil supplements. Strict vegetarians need to be particularly careful – and should do everything they can to minimize the possible 'blocks to conversion' outlined above. If your child is vegetarian, make sure he doesn't have vitamin and mineral deficiencies, and make sure he doesn't eat foods containing too much saturated or hydrogenated fats, as many vegetarian 'ready meals' are actually very unsatisfactory in this respect.

Omega-3 or Omega-6 Fatty Acids?

The ratio of omega-6 to omega-3 fats in our diets has increased dramatically over the last century (from around 4:1 to more than 15:1 by most estimates). This dietary shift away from omega-3 has now been linked with increased rates of many physical and mental health disorders, ranging from heart disease, stroke, arthritis and cancer through to depression, antisocial behaviour and suicide.[11]

Your child is much more likely to be lacking in omega-3 fatty acids than omega-6, along with most children and adults in the UK.

See the information below on 'Keeping the Balance' for some practical tips to help you and your child – but the main message for most people is: increase your intake of omega-3! Most people's dietary omega-3 intake falls well short of the level now recommended by experts just to maintain a healthy heart: 500mg of EPA and DHA per day.[12]

Keeping the Balance – Omega-3/Omega-6

Most people are at far greater risk of relative deficiencies in omega-3 than omega-6.

Too much omega-6 relative to omega-3 can upset the balance of your body chemistry – increasing the risk of inflammatory disorders and heart disease, and raising the chances that your brain won't be as sharp and well-balanced as it could be.

To keep a healthy omega-3/omega-6 balance, the main rules are:

- **Eat plenty of food that's high in omega-3**
  - All fish and seafood provide EPA and DHA directly, as do some fortified foods. (Organic meat and eggs may sometimes contain useful traces of omega-3, but they'll provide much more omega-6 at the same time.)
  - ALA is found in flax seeds and green leafy vegetables. (Some other seeds and nuts contain ALA, but they contain even more of the omega-6 LA, so won't help you to redress the balance.)
- **Avoid refined vegetable oils.**
  - These are a major source of the omega-6 LA – and they've been stripped of other useful nutrients in the refining

process. If used for cooking, they can also produce harmful trans fats when heated.

- Most people can get all the omega-6 fatty acids they need from the rest of their diet. (Nuts, seeds and whole grains and unrefined vegetable oils will give you the omega-6 LA, while meat, dairy produce and eggs are all direct sources of AA.)

FRYING AND ROASTING

Saturated fats (in moderation) are actually best for these purposes, because they are stable when heated to high temperatures. Use butter or animal fat sparingly – but try to keep down the amount of fried foods your child eats.

Olive oil contains monounsaturated fats. These are more stable than polyunsaturates (thus producing fewer damaging free radicals when heated) and don't upset your O-6:O-3 ratio.

Don't use polyunsaturated vegetable oils for cooking. Heating will destroy the double bonds, and could produce dangerous trans fats.

SALAD DRESSINGS

Commercial versions need a long shelf-life, so these often contain hydrogenated/trans fats. Check carefully and, if in doubt, *make your own.* This only takes a minute, and you can keep a jar ready-made in the refrigerator:

- Use flax oil or olive oil (or special mixes that also include evening primrose oil – but look for versions that *don't* have lots of the parent omega-6, LA).
- Mix the oil with a bit of lemon juice or balsamic vinegar (or raspberry vinegar for a fruity flavour).
- Use mustard (with a little honey if desired) or plenty of fresh herbs for flavouring.

Why Omega-3 and Omega-6 Fats Are Essential

Your child needs both omega-3 and omega-6 to develop his brain and nervous system in the first place, and he then needs a good dietary supply all his life to keep them functioning properly – along with his heart and other vital organs, and his immune system. Remember, though, it's the HUFA forms that our brains and bodies really need most, not the simple EFA. Omega-3 and omega-6 both help to keep cell membranes flexible (allowing efficient signalling between and within cells). They also have direct and indirect roles in numerous other signalling systems in the brain and body. In fact, these fatty acids are important for so many aspects of physical and mental health that it's impossible to list more than a few of them here.

A Healthy Heart

Omega-3 fatty acids are particularly important for a healthy heart and circulation, with EPA and DHA both playing important roles. (The omega-6 AA is needed, too – but this is much less likely to be lacking from your child's diet, as we saw earlier.) EPA relaxes blood vessels and prevents your blood from clotting too easily. DHA and EPA both help to keep your heart beating properly, so that it can pump enough blood to nourish every part of your body and brain.

Did You Know? Fats and Flexibility

- Omega-3 and omega-6 fatty acids increase the fluidity (flexibility) of cell membranes.
- The proteins that act as receptors and channels for cell signalling are embedded in (or attached to) cell membranes.
- Membrane fluidity can therefore crucially affects the efficiency of cell signalling.

- Saturated fats, artificial fats and cholesterol all decrease cell membrane fluidity.

Building Brains ...

Omega-3 and omega-6 fatty acids are both needed to build a baby's brain and nervous system in the first place (as well as her heart and other vital organs), so a good supply in early life is essential, and the foetus will take the fatty acids it needs from its mother. As a non-maternal colleague of mine was fond of saying, 'Babies are very efficient parasites!' This is well worth remembering if you're planning for a baby or are pregnant. In fact, make sure your diet contains enough of *all* the essential nutrients, or you may run short before your baby does, and obviously, neither of those options is a good idea. Take care also to avoid alcohol and smoking during pregnancy, as it's well known that both of these can have harmful effects on a developing baby. They are also a very effective way to deplete your own fatty acid stores.

Did You Know? Essential Fats

- Fatty acids affect neuronal (brain and nerve cell) migration, growth and connectivity, so they're crucial in early life – but a regular dietary supply is needed to maintain brain function at any age.
- Fatty acids (and substances made from them) have very powerful effects on cell signalling all over the brain and body:
  - They act as 'second messengers' for some neurotransmitters.
  - They regulate hormonal balance, immune function and blood flow.

… And Avoiding 'Baby Blues'?

If you're pregnant, it's particularly important to keep up your own intake of omega-3 fatty acids (getting enough omega-6 is not usually a problem). Pregnant women whose diets include more omega-3 are likely to have healthier babies and fewer premature births.[13] Research also shows links between omega-3 deficiency and other forms of depression,[14] so it's thought that lack of omega-3 in a new mother might increase her risk of 'baby blues', which 10–15 per cent of mums suffer. Controlled trials to investigate this are underway.

If you're breastfeeding, fatty acids are delivered to your baby via your milk, so it's still very important to keep your intake up throughout this stage. If you're using formula feed, make sure this contains both omega-6 and omega-3 HUFA ready-made (in the forms of AA and DHA, not just LA and ALA). Young babies can't do their own conversion very well (if at all), and controlled trials have shown benefits for children's vision, attention and problem solving from supplementing infant formula with the ready-made versions.[15]

Did You Know?

Breastfed babies get omega-3 and omega-6 through their mother's breastmilk. If you're giving your child formula milk, supplementation with these HUFA can boost visual perception and cognitive development.

Good Vision

Omega-3 fatty acids, especially DHA, are particularly important for the development and function of the visual system. No other fatty acid can substitute for this without dramatically reducing the efficiency of visual information processing.

In fact, it was the importance of omega-3 for vision that first drew my attention to the possible importance of these fatty acids in dyslexia and related conditions. With colleagues in Oxford, I'd been studying the visual symptoms reported by many dyslexic children and adults when a small study published in the *Lancet* suggested that DHA could correct poor night vision in dyslexic adults.[16] That study had no proper control group, and only looked at visual measures, but once I'd found out more about omega-3, controlled trials seemed well worth while.

Did You Know?

- The retina is the part of your eye that receives light signals; nerves then transmit these signals to your brain. Some 30–50 per cent of your retina should be made from the omega-3 fatty acid DHA.
- Without DHA, the signalling capacity of the retina can be reduced by more than 1,000 times.
- Omega-3 deficiency is associated with poor night vision and other problems with visual, spatial and attentional processing.

Preventing Inflammation

Inflammation, usually signalled by pain, redness or swelling, is a sign of immune system reactivity. Sometimes our immune systems are over-reactive, and can mistakenly attack either substances that are otherwise harmless (producing allergies) or our own tissues (causing auto-immune diseases). Omega-3s, and particularly EPA, have 'anti-inflammatory' effects, helping to protect against diseases such as arthritis, coronary artery disease, and other conditions in which an overactive immune system causes damage. Too much of the omega-6 fatty acid AA can promote inflammation. To keep joints well oiled, a good intake of omega-3 is needed.

An Inflammatory Issue

If your child suffers from allergies or other 'inflammatory' conditions (such as asthma, psoriasis, inflammatory bowel disease or rheumatoid arthritis), be aware of the different effects of omega-3 and some omega-6. For instance:

- **EPA has anti-inflammatory properties**
  - EPA is provided directly by fish oils – or via limited conversion of ALA from flax oil and green vegetables.
- **DGLA has anti-inflammatory properties**
  - DGLA is easily made from GLA, which is supplied directly by evening primrose and some other seed oils, or via limited conversion of LA from most vegetable oils.
- **AA has pro-inflammatory properties**
  - AA is provided directly by meat, dairy products and eggs.

Generally speaking, substances made from omega-3 (particularly EPA) will:

- reduce inflammation (and some other forms of immune system over-reactivity)
- improve blood flow (they relax and widen blood vessels)
- prevent thrombosis (they reduce blood clotting).

Generally speaking, substances made from omega-6 (but particularly AA) will:

- increase inflammation (and promote other forms of immune system reactivity)
- reduce blood flow (they constrict and narrow blood vessels)
- increase tendencies to thrombosis (they increase blood clotting).

This link between the immune system and the omega-3/omega-6 balance may well underlie some of the effects fatty acids can have on mood and behaviour. A relative lack of omega-3 has been linked to immune-system abnormalities in both depression and chronic fatigue syndrome.[17] Similarly, some of the features of conditions like autism, ADHD or dyslexia may reflect immune-system changes that affect the way the brain functions, but more research in these areas is needed.

In this chapter, we've seen that not all dietary fats are the same. In the next one, we'll look at the evidence suggesting that some of them might actually help to improve behaviour and learning in children.

Chicken – A Healthy Food?

Before you decide to eat chicken every day because it's been pushed at you as a lean meat, just consider these things first ... and then, if you can afford it, source your own supply of organic chickens that *haven't* been fed on high-energy food.

In 2004, Professor Michael Crawford and Yoqun Yang of London Metropolitan University found that chicken contains twice as much fat as it did in 1940. Gram for gram, the chicken they tested contained as much fat as a Big Mac! Today's chicken also has a third more calories and a third less protein. Now, much of the fat drips out when you cook the chicken, so you're not eating it all, but consider what you're spending your money on! You thought it was good-quality protein, maybe?

If the chicken product you're buying has a slightly spongy texture, then it may have been adulterated by hydrolysed beef waste (designed to retain water in the chicken, so making it weigh more). You can read more about this in the book *Not on the Label* written by investigative *Guardian* journalist Felicity Lawrence.

I'm not saying don't eat chicken: but do be informed (and if these facts bother you, join campaigns to improve farming and food-production methods). Remember too that the content of 'chicken nuggets' is usually much, much worse! I'd also say that eating any food every single day isn't a great idea, as you and your child need a much more varied diet.

FAQs

Answering questions on this topic can be complicated, and my publisher tells me that the answers I wanted to give here would take me over the word limit for this book! Please visit our website (www.fabresearch.org) for further details on all aspects of essential fatty acids.

I thought eating fat made you fat.

Not necessarily! This is overly simplistic – it all depends what *kind* of fat you're eating, and also how much of it, as well as how much exercise you get. Even good fats eaten in excess will cause you or your child to put on the pounds – but sugar and refined starches are more likely to give you excess calories, which your body then turns into fat. Keep your saturated fat intake low, eat monounsaturated fats in moderation, and don't touch hydrogenated or trans fats if you can help it. Essential fatty acids like omega-3s can actually boost metabolic rate, so you burn more energy, which can help you to lose weight. Above all, follow a balanced diet, and my advice would also be to avoid 'low-fat' foods and drinks that are laced with sugar or artificial sweeteners.

I thought margarine was better for you than butter.

Unless it's very special margarine, I'd say it's not. Ordinary margarines usually contain hydrogenated fats, and often trans fats. Use butter, home-made mayonnaise or olive (or walnut) oil to put on your bread. If the butter is too hard for your child to spread when it comes out of the fridge, blend it 50–50 with some olive oil.

Were you saying that hydrogenated fats don't have to be listed on food labels? Does that mean that anything saying 'vegetable oils' could potentially be hydrogenated unless it specifically states otherwise?

Trans fats are the ones that don't have to be listed on food labels. 'Hydrogenated' fats or oils usually *do* have to be declared (although whether this is actually compulsory depends on the type of food. Some snacks, etc., or any foods in which fat is only a small proportion of the total ingredients, can be exempt.) Only the partially hydrogenated fats may be twisted trans fats – but the labels don't always tell you whether 'hydrogenated' means fully or partially, so you may want to avoid both to be on the safe side. The foods to check carefully are margarines and spreads, processed foods and all commercially baked cakes, biscuits, pastries, etc. If they *don't* have hydrogenated or trans fats, the manufacturers usually boast about it! You can also contact companies directly and ask them.

Is cod liver oil as good a source of omega oil as the other more expensive brands?

No. If you're trying to reach the recommended daily 500mg of omega-3 HUFA, don't try this with cod liver oil. This popular 'omega-3' supplement is not a very concentrated source of EPA or DHA, but it does contain the fat-soluble vitamins A and D. These are essential nutrients, but can be toxic in excess. The high doses of cod liver oil that would be needed to provide 500mg EPA and DHA are therefore NOT advisable on a long-term basis.

A teaspoon or so per day should present no problems and can make a valuable contribution to omega-3 intake as well as vitamins A and D (provided the diet is not already too rich in these vitamins). If in any doubt, seek expert advice. The *quality* of the oil is also important, as liver oils can be particularly prone to contamination.

Summary

1. Not all fats are bad for you: in fact, some are essential. Dietary fats are needed for much more than just a convenient source of energy.

2. Your brain has a higher fat content than your body (about 60 per cent of its dry mass) and the type of fat in your diet really matters for its structure and function.

3. Leading researchers predicted over 30 years ago that unless we changed the type of fat we were eating, the epidemic of heart disease would be followed by an epidemic of brain disorders in countries eating an American-style fast-food diet. That's exactly what has happened.

4. The worst sort of fats are the 'trans fats' found in hydrogenated (artificially saturated) vegetable oils. They are found in cheap margarines and many commercially baked goods (such as cakes, biscuits, pastries, fried foods, crisps and takeaways). These are so bad for you that medical experts have said they shouldn't be in human diets at all.

5. Natural saturated (hard) fats are not harmful *in moderation*, but the healthiest diets include more monounsaturated fats (as found in olive oil) or natural polyunsaturates (found in unprocessed vegetable oils and fish oils). Omega-3 and omega-6 are special types of polyunsaturated fats known as 'essential fatty acids'.

6. Your body can make its own saturated and monounsaturated fats, but you can't make omega-3 and omega-6 polyunsaturated fats, even though you need them. That's why they're called 'essential'.

7. You need both omega-6 and omega-3 fatty acids in your diet, but most people get more than enough omega-6 fats. So focus on making sure you and your child have enough omega-3s.

8. Theoretically, your body should be able to make your own highly unsaturated omega-3 and omega-6 (the ones you need most) from the simple essential fatty acids of these two types, found in flax or ordinary vegetable oils respectively. However, humans aren't very good at this – so eating fish or seafood at least once or twice a week (or taking supplements) is a good way to guarantee enough of the key omega-3, EPA and DHA.

9. These omega-3 fatty acids are needed to maintain a healthy heart and circulation, to prevent inflammation, and to support eye and brain function at all ages. They can also improve skin and hair quality and boost metabolic rate – but their benefits to mental performance are what has attracted most recent interest. The old folk wisdom was right – fish really is good for the brain.

chapter 9

the omega-3 revolution

food for thought

In the last chapter we looked at the different kinds of dietary fats – and why it matters so much that you 'get the fats right'. Now it's time to address the burning question that so many parents have been asking me for years, namely: *Can omega-3 fatty acids help my child?*

The short and slightly flippant answer is, 'Yes, they can, and already do!' The longer answer I will give you in this chapter, so that you can arrive at your own conclusions, based on the best evidence we have at the moment.

As I hope Chapter 8 made clear, omega-3 fatty acids need to be in your child's diet just to keep her alive – they are essential! Solid research has shown that an adequate dietary intake of omega-3 is needed to:

- allow the brain and nervous system to develop and function normally
- support the heart and circulation
- regulate the immune system, and keep joints well-oiled and supple
- maintain good vision
- keep hormonal systems balanced
- produce numerous other substances crucial for cell signalling in almost every part of the brain and body.

Unfortunately, as we've already heard, omega-3s are relatively lacking from the diets of both children and adults in the UK, whereas omega-6s usually aren't. A dietary imbalance in favour of omega-6 can promote inflammation, allergies and auto-immune diseases, and make thrombosis (blood clots) more likely. By contrast, a higher omega-3 intake appears to reduce the risk of most of these physical health disorders and, as I mentioned in the last chapter, experts now recommend 500mg per day of EPA and DHA just for maintaining heart health. The average intake of children in the UK is less than half of this amount[1] – and even that average is misleadingly high, because most children eat little or no fish at all. Your child may perhaps be one of them – in which case more of these omega-3s could certainly help his physical health.

If it's your child's behaviour, learning or mood you want help with, then the first thing I must emphasize again is that you're likely to need other kinds of assistance too. Don't expect *any* dietary changes to act like a magic wand. Remember, too, that there are different kinds of omega-3. It's the highly unsaturated ones, EPA and DHA – found in fish and seafood – that are most important for both physical and mental health – not the ALA that flax oil and green vegetables can provide. (This needs to be converted within the body to EPA and DHA – a difficult job that it seems not everyone's body can do.)

When it comes to brain function, controlled trials involving adults have provided promising evidence that omega-3 highly unsaturated fatty acids (HUFAs) from fish oils – and particularly EPA – may help in the treatment of a wide range of mental health problems, although more research in these areas is still needed. Significant benefits have been reported for depression and other conditions involving disturbances of perception, attention, cognition (thinking), mood and sleep.[2] Will the right omega-3s help your child in these ways? Can they improve his behaviour and learning, too? Let's take a critical look at the evidence together.

First, we'll look at some signs that *might* help to tell you if your child is lacking in omega-3 (or other) essential fats. Then we'll see what biochemical studies of children with behaviour and learning problems have shown, and finally, results from controlled trials of omega-3 'treatment' in such children. After that, we'll be in a better position to consider what omega-3 might do for *your* child – and to offer some practical tips that may help you to decide whether or not to try this approach.

By the Way …

You may have heard that if you leave a bunch of children in a room with a variety of foods (including sweet stuff), they'll eventually eat what their body *needs*. Don't try this with your child!

Look carefully at the information in this chapter and the rest of the book, and give your child healthy choices. Also educate him as to what you're doing and why.

Dyslexia and Dandruff?

When I first became interested in the idea that fatty acids might help in dyslexia and related conditions, I searched the published literature, as you do. 'Essential fatty-acid deficiencies' as a possible cause of hyperactivity had first been suggested by the UK Hyperactive Children's Support Group,[3] and backed up by some experimental support from the US that we'll hear about shortly. But only one paper I could find anywhere had taken a 'biochemical approach to the problem of dyslexia' – in fact, that was its title!

This paper was published way back in 1985.[4] It told the story of Michael, a boy with dyslexia for whom conventional (educational) management methods had done nothing to help. In desperation, his parents took him to see Sidney MacDonald Baker, a US doctor who specialized in biochemical and nutritional approaches. Dr Baker carried out some detailed blood tests, but was in fact able to make the key 'diagnosis' before this was confirmed by the results. He could tell just by looking at the boy. As he put it:

Michael had very dry, patchy, dull skin. Like a matte finish on a photograph, his skin, as well as his hair, failed to reflect light with a normal lustre. His hair was easily tousled and when pulled between the fingers it had a straw-like texture rather than a normal silky feel. He had dandruff. The skin on the backs of his arms was raised in tiny closed bumps like chicken skin. His fingernails were soft and frayed at the ends.

What Dr Baker knew – and what I wish every doctor, parent and teacher were aware of – was that these are classic physical signs of 'essential fatty-acid deficiency'.[5] When the boy's diet was adjusted to include more of the right fats:

> *Improvement in Michael's schoolwork coincided with the return of normal lustre and texture to his skin and hair. If he had been a cocker spaniel his family would have accepted the connection between his 'glossier coat' and better disposition more readily. The timing was convincing. Although it is never enough to establish 'proof' in a given person, Michael was convinced. He saw and felt the changes together, and he understood the idea behind the work we did with him. With a twinkle in his eye, he told his grandmother that dandruff had been the cause of his dyslexia.*

It's a lovely story – and I wish all of them had such happy endings. But if this 'mirror test' (as Dr Baker called simply looking at this boy with an informed eye) were something that teachers, parents and health professionals could all do whenever they saw a child with behaviour or learning difficulties, we might perhaps save a lot of private misery as well as a lot of public money.

Dr Baker did not overstate his case. He made clear that of course he hadn't in any way 'discovered *the* cause of dyslexia'. But it's a shame that he was forced to add: 'We had, however, raised the ire of many specialists, who chided Michael's parents with somewhat barbed advice, to the effect that "Nutrition has nothing to do with dyslexia".' Many so-called specialists still say this kind of thing to parents today. Do these people really not realize that brains – like bodies – need feeding properly if they're going to perform at their best? Clearly not.

Michael's was only one 'single case study' – but further research has shown that the classic physical signs consistent with fatty-acid deficiency (including excessive thirst and frequent urination, along with rough, dry skin and hair) are unusually common in children and adults with ADHD, dyslexia and autism compared with those with no such difficulties. The more severe their behaviour, learning and sleep problems, the more of these signs they've been found to have.[6] There could, however, be many other possible causes for these kinds of physical symptoms, so firmer evidence is still needed.

Boys with Low Omega-3 Have Behaviour, Learning and Health Problems

In 96 boys with or without ADHD, blood concentrations of omega-3 and omega-6 fatty acids were examined in relation to their parents' ratings of these children's behavioural, learning and health problems.

Low omega-6 status was related only to physical health measures (such as dry skin and hair, frequency of colds, and antibiotic use), not to parental ratings of either behaviour or learning.

Low omega-3 status was associated with physical signs consistent with fatty-acid deficiency (such as excessive thirst, frequent urination and rough, dry skin and hair) and also with both behavioural problems and learning difficulties. Children with the lowest omega-3 levels showed more:

- conduct disorder
- hyperactivity-impulsivity
- anxiety
- temper tantrums
- sleep problems[7]

Biochemical Studies

Biochemical studies followed, showing reduced blood concentrations of omega-3 (and sometimes omega-6) HUFAs in several studies of children and adults with ADHD or autistic-spectrum disorders, although the precise pattern of results varied.[8] With respect to dyslexia, initial results have actually shown no overall group differences in blood fatty acids between adults with and without this diagnosis – but higher omega-3 concentrations are associated with better reading in *both* groups, and with better working memory in dyslexic adults.[9]

We don't yet know whether these low levels of key fatty acids in blood reflect differences in dietary intake or metabolism. It could be that many people with these conditions have difficulty converting fatty acids into usable forms, or maybe they break them down too quickly. Further investigations are going on, but high levels of an enzyme called PLA2, which removes highly unsaturated fatty acids from cell membranes, have already been reported in both dyslexia and autism.[10]

So biochemical studies have provided additional evidence that a lack of omega-3 *could* play a role in behaviour and learning difficulties, but these kinds of studies still don't deal with cause and effect. This is where randomized controlled trials (RCTs) are needed.

Controlled Treatment Trials

Two early trials assessed the effects of evening primrose oil (providing the omega-6 fatty acid GLA) in hyperactive children,[11] but found few if any benefits. Attention then turned towards omega-3 fatty acids, because these are far more likely than omega-6 to be lacking from modern diets, and there was also increasing evidence for omega-3 deficiencies in some adult psychiatric disorders.

So far, only five properly controlled trials of omega-3 fatty acids as a treatment for ADHD and related conditions have been published (see Appendix, page 375, for details). Most of the ones you may have heard about in the media were probably supplement adverts, not proper trials, I'm afraid.

The majority of the controlled studies have been small, and each involved different populations, outcome measures and treatment formulations, making it difficult to draw any firm conclusions at this stage. Nonetheless, the balance of evidence does suggest that supplementation with highly unsaturated omega-3 fatty acids (EPA and DHA) may improve behaviour and learning in at least *some* children with dyslexia, dyspraxia or ADHD. Let's look at the details a little more closely.

ADHD

There have been three studies of omega-3 supplements in children selected for ADHD-type difficulties. Two showed no benefits at all,[12] while one showed modest but significant improvements in teachers' ratings of the children's attention and parents' ratings of their behaviour.[13] What might explain the differences in results between these studies? Many things, actually – but the main one in my view is probably the type of supplements used. In the two studies showing no benefits, the supplements used contained primarily or exclusively DHA, while the 'positive' study used 80 per cent fish oils (containing both EPA and DHA) with a little evening primrose oil and vitamin E.

Dyslexia

The only controlled trial published in this area was a pilot study of 41 children with dyslexia who also showed features of ADHD.[14] They were all attending a special school for help with their specific reading difficulties, but the focus of this study was on their ADHD symptoms. Every day for 3 months, half of these children took supplements containing mainly fish oils (again with a little evening primrose oil and vitamin E), while the others took an identical-looking placebo. According to ratings from their parents, children who took the real fatty-acid supplement showed significantly greater improvements in their behaviour, concentration and other ADHD-type symptoms (such as hyperactivity and impulsivity) compared with children given the placebo.

Dyspraxia/Developmental Coordination Disorder (DCD)

The largest study to date was the Oxford-Durham Study involving 117 children from mainstream schools, all aged between 5 and 12 years of age.[15] They all met the diagnostic criteria for Developmental Coordination Disorder (dyspraxia) – but the study was interested in more than just their motor coordination. Testing showed that around 40 per cent also had specific reading and spelling difficulties (dyslexia), and that just over 30 per cent had severe ADHD symptoms – the usual overlaps between these conditions. For 3 months, half of the children took a supplement containing mainly fish oils (this time enriched with EPA, but still with a little evening primrose oil and vitamin E) while the others were given a placebo.

At the end of the treatment period, *both* groups had significantly improved their motor coordination, but there was no difference between them. This was obviously great for the children – but very disappointing for the researchers (this author among them!). Any possible effect of the fatty acids was drowned out by a huge 'placebo effect'. But this highlights why it's so critical to do properly controlled trials. If you don't, then *any* improvement seen is always credited to the treatment, when in fact (as in this case) it might well have happened anyway. This is why you should ignore most of those media stories that are really just advertisements, and always ask: 'Was it a randomized, double-blind, placebo-controlled trial?'

The motor skills results may have shown nothing,[16] but it was a very different picture for other measures we'd chosen – reflecting the 'dyslexia' and 'ADHD' domains. No placebo effects whatsoever were found here – but the children who received the fatty-acid supplement showed highly significant reductions in ADHD-type symptoms, as well as simply remarkable improvements in reading and spelling progress. Their working memory performance also improved dramatically. No wonder they were so keen to tell their stories on TV![17]

In the children receiving the fatty-acid supplement for 3 months:

- **Reading progress was three times greater than would be expected** for normal children of the same age. By contrast, children receiving placebo treatment made progress only at the expected rate for their age.
- **Spelling progress was twice as great as would be expected** for normal children of the same age. By contrast, children receiving placebo treatment made progress at less than half the normal rate, falling further behind their normally achieving peer group.

- **ADHD-type symptoms fell markedly** (this was true of difficulties in attention and concentration as well as hyperactivity and impulsivity). The size of this effect was similar to the reductions usually achieved by stimulant medication.

In summary, then, three out of five controlled studies have shown that at least some children with ADHD and related disorders can benefit from dietary supplementation with mainly omega-3 fatty acids. But I hope you can see that many important issues still remain to be explored. Why did two studies of ADHD children fail to show any effects? (Was it something about the children studied or the measures used, rather than the choice of supplement?) Did the small quantity of evening primrose oil make any difference? (We don't think so, but we're doing studies now to find out!) What about the vitamin E? This is added to most good-quality fish oil supplements, as it helps to protect highly unsaturated fatty acids (HUFAs) from breakdown (and vice versa, as it turns out). For that reason alone it's worth considering what vitamin E might do on its own! Plenty of other questions still need answering as well, such as:

- Within ADHD, might omega-3 fatty acids be particularly (or only) beneficial for children who also show features of other conditions such as mood disorders, oppositional defiance and/or specific learning difficulties?
- Within dyslexia or dyspraxia, do visual symptoms help to predict benefits?
- Is omega-3 more helpful for children with milder difficulties in behaviour and learning than for those with more extreme symptoms?
- What proportion of children in the general population might benefit from an increased dietary intake of omega-3 fatty acids?
- What quantities and formulations are optimal for behaviour, learning and mood, and do the effects vary according to
  - Age (existing studies have only involved children aged 5 and 14 years)?
  - Gender (most studies have included far more boys than girls)?

I think you can see why a researcher's work is never done! Most of these questions would be best addressed by large-scale studies, ideally drawing from samples representative of the general population. For those, significant funding is needed, but policymakers and funding bodies still don't seem too interested. If you are, please contact FAB Research!

Food versus Supplements

You'll have gathered by now that there's no simple answer to the question 'Will omega-3 fatty acids help my child?' But you don't necessarily need to wait for more research studies before doing something practical which will at the very least be good for his physical health (and *might* help his mood, behaviour or learning, too): Make sure that his diet isn't lacking in the key fatty acids.

In my view, it's always better to get nutrients from food rather than supplements, but I know that isn't always practicable. What's more, concerns about possible contamination with mercury, PCBs or dioxins in fish have put some people off what is otherwise one of the healthiest foods you can eat.[18] If you do want to try omega-3 supplements, always check out their quality and purity for the same reasons; make sure the manufacturer uses the best extraction methods and quality-control procedures. High-quality oils should also have little or no fishy aftertaste! Omega-3s are extremely delicate and easily damaged, so packaging must protect the contents from light, heat and air (I would always choose capsules over liquid fish oils for this reason). Always make sure you use any supplement before its expiry date – and if in doubt, throw it away.

Do Omega-3 Fatty Acids Have Any Risks?

With anything concerning your child, safety should always be your first concern. Fortunately, omega-3 fatty acids have very few limitations in this respect (although be careful to avoid possible contaminants in either fish or supplements, as I've just mentioned). No adverse side-effects have been found in treatment trials of fatty acids for ADHD and related disorders, nor in the studies of adult mental health. Any substance could trigger allergies in some individuals, however, and fish and seafood are no exception. (If your child reacts badly to these you may well know about it already.) Otherwise, just be aware that taking too many fish oils can cause 'digestive intolerance' in the form of nausea, belching or loose stools. In addition, do *be careful if you're taking any anticoagulant medicines*, as EPA in particular can have similar actions at high doses. My advice is always: *See your doctor first* before you take *any* supplements (or make major changes to your child's or your own diet). The Food Standards Agency recommends 2 portions of fish per week for everyone (one of which should be oily), and up to 4 portions for males. Omega-3 from fish oils is generally regarded as safe at doses of up to 3g per day,[19] but my advice would be not to give your child more than 1g daily without expert monitoring and supervision.

Does It Have to Be Fish Oils?

Unfortunately, humans aren't very efficient when it comes to converting the simple omega-3 essential fatty acid ALA, found in some nuts, seeds and green vegetables, into the forms needed by the brain (EPA and DHA) that fish and seafood provide. Males are at a particular disadvantage here, and the same may be true of people with diabetes, eczema or other allergic conditions. Inefficiencies could also arise for constitutional (genetic) reasons, and this is suspected (but not proven) in dyslexia, dyspraxia, ADHD and some other disorders. However, just because you have a genetic tendency to something, you can still control environmental triggers. There are some diet and lifestyle factors that make it more difficult for you to convert EFA to HUFA:

- excess saturated fats
- hydrogenated and trans fats
- vitamin deficiency (especially B1, B3, B6 and C)
- mineral deficiency (especially zinc, magnesium and manganese)
- excessive consumption of caffeine or similar stimulants
- stress

Do what you can to avoid these – and also *avoid alcohol and smoking*, both of which can destroy the HUFAs you've got.

Are Some Fish Oils Better than Others?

Yes, they are! I've already mentioned the key issues about quality and purity – but as with foods, it's also crucial to read the small print on the labels.

- How much EPA and DHA does the supplement actually contain? (You'd be amazed how little this can be. Sometimes it can take 20 capsules to provide a 500-mg daily dose!)
- Are there any artificial colourings, flavourings or other undesirable additives? (Again, you'd be unpleasantly surprised to find what some of the 'omega-3' supplements aimed at children actually contain. Check before you put them into your child's mouth.)

The ratio of EPA to DHA is also worth checking. Standard fish oils usually have three parts EPA to two parts DHA. I've chosen a high-EPA fish oil for our latest studies because, as we've seen, the existing evidence suggests that EPA is more effective than DHA in reducing the difficulties in attention, perception and memory associated with ADHD, dyslexia and dyspraxia. For younger children, or for pregnant mums, a high-DHA supplement may be more appropriate, as this is the omega-3 needed for the actual structure of the brain.

Cod liver oil is probably the best-known source of omega-3 fatty acids. Provided it's 'clean' (the liver is the body's main 'detox' organ, remember) a teaspoon or so per day may be a helpful supplement. However, all fish-liver oils also contain significant levels of vitamin A, which can be highly toxic itself in excess, as we saw in Chapter 4. What's more, they're not actually very rich in EPA or DHA. So if you're aiming to get the daily recommendation of 500mg EPA + DHA for heart health, or any higher doses, *don't try to do this with fish-liver oils* (especially if you're pregnant).

How Do I Know If My Child Needs More Omega-3?

At this stage I can only offer you our best guesses – but if your child suffers from any of the following, more omega-3s in his diet may help:

Physical signs consistent with deficiencies of either omega-6 or omega-3 fatty acids (although these can all have other causes) are:

- excessive thirst
- frequent urination
- rough or dry patches on the skin – especially if this has a 'bumpy' appearance or feel (this is 'follicular keratosis', and is usually most noticeable on the upper arms and legs)
- dull or dry hair ('straw-like' rather than silky)
- dandruff
- soft or brittle nails.

Atopic (allergic) conditions like eczema, asthma or hay fever may indicate an imbalance of fatty acids. The omega-3 EPA has anti-inflammatory properties, as does the omega-6 DGLA; in fact, evening primrose oil was found beneficial for atopic eczema in controlled trials.[20] No controlled trials have used omega-3 for this purpose, but there is plenty of anecdotal evidence. Many individuals report that supplementing with fish oils helps to relieve some of their allergic symptoms.

Visual perceptual problems may reflect omega-3 deficiency, as DHA in particular is essential for good vision. Despite having no 'overt' visual problems that ordinary eye tests would detect, many people with dyslexia and associated conditions report visual symptoms when trying to read, such as blurring, apparent movement of letters and words, eye strain or 'glare' from text on the page. Other visual problems include:

- unusual sensitivity to bright light in general
- poor night vision
- broader difficulties with visual attention and visuo-motor control.

Attention and concentration problems could indicate a lack of omega-3. Controlled treatment trials have shown improved attention and concentration in many children with dyslexia, dyspraxia or ADHD – and I know many adults who say that omega-3 helps them to 'clear the brain fog'. If your child is easily distracted, has real difficulties 'screening out' things that are irrelevant to the task in hand, or 'daydreams' (even without obvious distractions), it's possible that increasing his omega-3 intake might help.

Mood swings, undue anxiety and a low 'frustration tolerance' could indicate that your child might benefit from more omega-3 in her diet. In controlled trials, fish-oil supplements reduced the susceptibility to stress-aggression in ordinary students under pressure,[21] and omega-3s are showing promise for helping to alleviate depression and related mood disorders in adults.[22] Results from our studies also suggest a good response to omega-3 in those with a 'short fuse' (the ones prone to either emotional outbursts or undue anxiety-tension when things don't go as planned – recognize that?).

Sleep problems might also reflect a lack of omega-3, because these and other HUFAs help regulate the chemical signalling that determines when your child falls asleep and wakes up. Fatty-acid imbalances *could* therefore be a factor in some kinds of sleeping problems, but the controlled trials needed to confirm this haven't yet been done. We've had numerous anecdotal reports that omega-3s help with sleep and, perhaps unsurprisingly, those who say this usually report other benefits, too. This issue clearly deserves further study.

Summary of Problems that May Be Due to Lack of Omega-3

- *Physical signs:* excessive thirst, frequent urination, rough or dry skin and hair, dandruff, soft or brittle nails
- *Allergic tendencies:* especially eczema
- *Visual symptoms:* poor night vision or sensitivity to bright light, and visual disturbances when reading – e.g. letters and words move, swim or blur on the page
- *Attentional problems:* distractibility, poor concentration and working memory
- *Emotional sensitivity:* especially excessive mood swings or undue anxiety
- *Sleep problems:* especially difficulties in settling at night and waking in the morning

These features are common in dyslexia, dyspraxia and ADHD, but anyone can have them.

From this chapter and the last one, I do hope you can now see why omega-3 fatty acids are a very important part of your child's diet. In Part 3 I'll help you take the next steps to changing your child's life for the better, and improving your own in the process.

FAQs

This FAQ section is a long one, but still I can't begin to cover everything that parents usually ask. By all means email me with your questions, but *first check out* www.fabresearch.org as there's a lot more information there, and it's constantly updated. You are also welcome to sign up for free email alerts about ongoing research.

My child takes Ritalin, but I'm interested in trying omega-3. Is it safe to take both, and how long will it take to find out if the supplements are working?

First, talk to your child's doctor before starting any kind of dietary supplementation. I'd recommend this to anyone, but it's essential if your child is already taking any medications (or receiving other medical treatment or supervision). With respect to safety, there's no obvious reason why omega-3 can't be taken alongside stimulant medications like Ritalin, as (1) the doses that have shown benefits in controlled trials could be obtained through diet anyway, and (2) most of the ADHD children in these trials were already taking these kinds of medications, and no ill-effects were reported. Nonetheless, always be alert to possible reactions when introducing your child to any new food or substance. If possible, getting our nutrients from (natural) foods is always preferable to taking supplements in my view; but whichever approach you use, look carefully at how much omega-3 any food or supplement actually provides – and in which forms.

'How long will it take?' is another important question. Unlike most medications, omega-3s do *not* work rapidly to change behaviour or mood. It can take up to 3 months for any effects to show up fully, because of the slow turnover of these fatty acids in the brain. Some individuals do report clear benefits within a few weeks or even days, but in other cases the changes are much more gradual. Of course, not everyone can expect noticeable benefits from increasing their omega-3 intake. If you don't see any improvements within 3 months then it's reasonable to conclude that fatty-acid deficiency is not a major factor for your child. Other approaches to managing ADHD and related conditions should always be considered in any case. You've obviously taken advice on medication already, but other aspects of diet (see Chapters 6 and 7) and behavioural or other therapies can also be very helpful for some children.

Should my child take extra omega-6 as well as omega-3?

Not necessarily. Most people get plenty of omega-6 from their diets (it's in all vegetable oils as well as meat, eggs and dairy products), but not enough omega-3. It's true that the three studies to date showing benefits from fish oils (providing the omega-3 fatty acids EPA and DHA) did include a little evening primrose oil as well (providing the omega-6 GLA), simply because it came with the supplements used. However, early studies of evening primrose oil alone showed no real benefits for children with ADHD, and successful studies of omega-3 for mood and behaviour in adults haven't included any omega-6 at all. Having said this, some people (particularly those with very dry skin and hair, or eczema) may benefit from a little evening primrose oil in addition. The choice is up to you.

If I want to give my child supplements, which ones would you recommend?

As a scientific researcher I consider it extremely important to keep my work independent of commercial influences, so my studies aren't financed by any of the companies whose products I may choose; nor do I 'recommend' or 'endorse' any particular supplements. This is for you to decide (preferably in consultation with an experienced and knowledgeable practitioner who is similarly independent). If you want further information on what you should look out for when choosing fatty-acid supplements, please visit the FAB Research website which provides some detailed guidelines and explains the issues involved in more depth than I could do here (www.fabresearch.org).

What other nutrients could help to boost my child's omega-3 levels?

Vitamin E is an important antioxidant that helps to protect all the unsaturated fatty acids from breakdown, but vitamin E itself needs to be protected, and recycled when necessary, by other nutrients (especially vitamin C) and also other antioxidants. Once again, it's very important to make sure your child gets a good supply of natural antioxidants from her diet. This means fruits and vegetables, nuts and seeds and other whole, unrefined foods.

Many vitamins and minerals – notably vitamins B_1, B_3, B_6 and C and the minerals zinc, magnesium and manganese – are co-factors for converting essential fatty acids (EFAs) into highly unsaturated fatty acids (HUFAs), so make sure your child eats a good range of whole foods to provide these. If not, a multivitamin and mineral supplement may help.

Reducing your child's intake of foods rich in the omega-6 EFA (LA) can also help to improve omega-3 HUFA, as there is competition between omega-3 and omega-6 for the enzymes needed for EFA–HUFA conversion. Switch from ordinary vegetable oils to rapeseed (canola) which is richer in the omega-3 ALA, and include flax or walnut oils for salad dressings, or add them to smoothies, for the same reason.

How can I tell if my child would be helped by omega-3 supplements?

At the moment I'm afraid the only truly reliable test is to try this approach and see whether it helps. Benefits are more likely if your child's dietary intake and/or blood fatty-acid concentrations are low, but none of the current ways of assessing this (including blood tests) is necessarily reliable at the individual level. More research is still needed to find measures that may help to predict a good response to an increased dietary intake of fatty acids. Meanwhile, our studies and clinical impressions have suggested some possible indicators that we are now investigating further, as I've outlined above.

My son's a vegetarian – what kind of omega-3 supplements will work best for him?

First, let's be clear that omega-3 supplements will not 'work' for everyone. Some people already get all the HUFAs they need from their diet and/or their own metabolism. Individual differences in constitution, diet and lifestyle mean there can be no universal answers, but I hope the following points may help you and your son.

First, fish and seafood are almost the only natural foods that provide much of the omega-3 fatty acids EPA and DHA 'ready made'. Both are essential for optimal brain function. If your son doesn't eat fish (or take fish oil supplements), he's relying on making his own EPA and DHA from simpler omega-3 fats such as ALA, found in flax oil and green vegetables. The trouble is, this 'DIY' pathway isn't very efficient – particularly in males. Do whatever you can to help him reduce the other possible 'blocks' to this conversion pathway. The UK Vegetarian Society recommends 4 grams of flax oil per day for general use, but if you think your son may not be converting this very well, a good 'insurance policy' might be to eat foods fortified with EPA and DHA. These omega-3s are now added to some milks and eggs, for example, as well as some other foods, but do check how much these really provide – and make sure it's in the EPA and DHA forms.

What dosage is appropriate? Can you take too much omega-3?

We don't yet have clear answers to the dosage question when it comes to children's behaviour and learning, because no research studies in this area have yet compared different doses. What's more, we know that the 'optimal dosage' can vary between individuals (and even in the same individual over time), depending on differences in both diet and metabolism. As a guide, remember that 500mg per day of EPA and DHA is now recommended for everyone just to maintain a healthy heart. The successful treatment trials of omega-3 for children with ADHD, dyslexia or dyspraxia (DCD) haven't actually used much more than this (daily dosages have varied from around 550mg to 750mg of EPA + DHA combined).

Two controlled trials have compared different doses in adults with mental health problems, and both used pure EPA. In adults with depression, 1g of EPA (that's 1,000mg) was significantly better than placebo in reducing symptoms, and was also superior to either 2g or 4g of EPA.[23] For schizophrenia, a similar study indicated that 2g per day was the best of these doses.[24]

These findings illustrate clearly that 'more is not necessarily better' (particularly when it comes to any single fatty acid in isolation) – and yes, one can have too much of a good thing. No ill-effects have been reported in these studies – although high doses of fish oils can cause digestive upset in some people. Up to 3g per day of EPA and DHA is generally regarded as safe by medical experts, and much higher doses have been used in some treatment trials involving adults, but this is not advisable without expert monitoring. Personally, I would advise you to *check with your doctor before taking any supplements or making major dietary changes,* and not to take more than around 1g per day without expert advice and supervision. Just over 500mg EPA (and around 100mg DHA) is used in our current studies of dyslexia, dyspraxia and ADHD, but we already know that some children with severe mood swings or behaviour problems may need up to 1g EPA to achieve benefits.

Summary

1. Modern-day diets are relatively low in omega-3, but most children get plenty of omega-6s (and also, unfortunately, damaging trans fats from hydrogenated vegetable oils).
2. The incidence of childhood behavioural and learning disorders is increasing, along with many physical and mental health problems in which lack of omega-3 is implicated.
3. Theory and experimental evidence support a role for omega-3 in ADHD, dyslexia, developmental coordination disorder (DCD) and autism, although these are all complex conditions with many possible causes.
4. Physical signs consistent with fatty-acid deficiency are more common in individuals with ADHD, dyslexia and autism. Blood biochemical studies support this picture, but these kinds of studies can't provide definitive evidence of cause and effect.
5. Results from controlled treatment trials (which do address cause and effect) are mixed. Three studies have shown that supplementing with fish oils (providing EPA and DHA) can alleviate ADHD-related symptoms in children with ADHD, dyslexia or dyspraxia (DCD); the study of DCD children also found benefits for academic achievement. By contrast, two studies of ADHD children found no benefits from supplementing the diet primarily or exclusively with DHA.
6. Given their relative safety and general health benefits, omega-3 fatty acids may offer a promising complementary approach to standard treatments for child behaviour and learning difficulties. More studies in this area are still needed, however, before any firm conclusions can be drawn.
7. Ensuring your child's diet provides a good intake of omega-3 (preferably EPA and DHA) is sensible in any case purely for his physical health, and *may* help to improve mood, behaviour and learning.
8. If your child won't eat fish or seafood, many omega-3 supplements are available, but these can vary hugely in quality and content so check carefully and take expert advice if needed. Some foods are also fortified with omega-3, but look closely at the quantities and forms of omega-3 provided.

part three

the way ahead

transforming
your child's diet

chapter 10

top tips for you and your child

I hope that by now you'll understand why a good, balanced and varied diet plays a hugely important part in your child's well-being. Diet isn't a universal panacea, though, so in this chapter we'll look at some other things you can do to help your child, as well as how you can best prepare for making the necessary changes to what he eats.

> The most successful way to tackle any difficulties your child may be having is likely to involve using several different approaches in combination.
>
> Remember, too, that your child is unique. There is no 'one-size-fits-all' approach that will work with all children.

Before you start, talk to your child's doctor and any other professionals involved (teachers, health visitors, any specialist assessors or therapists), as well as relatives ... and your child!

If you carry on doing what you've always done, you'll always get what you've always got, as the saying goes. So if you don't like the way things are, you need to change something. Diet can actually be one of the easiest ways to start, and the first part of this chapter outlines some tips that should make your plans for healthier eating more likely to succeed. In the second part I've outlined some non-dietary strategies that may help, too. Then in Chapter 11 I've outlined a three-month, easy-to-implement plan that will enable you and your child to adopt a healthier, happier lifestyle.

Look at What You *Can* Have

Find out about what different foods, exercises and other activities can do *for* your child and '*against*' your child. When you've considered this information and decided what to do, *concentrate on what you* can *have* (and do) rather than on what is 'forbidden', and teach your children to do the same.

Mental and Emotional Attitudes

Having the right mind-set and approach can work wonders. Here are some strategies that may help.

Set an Example

You want your child to choose and enjoy a healthy diet and exercise, so you need to do so, too. Make sure you set a visible example. For children who are old enough to understand, a team effort can be very rewarding, so talk about what you're doing and why. If you can work together, you'll all feel better, sleep better, be more cheerful, have more energy, develop closer relationships, and be less hassled and stressed. You may well be tired and frazzled yourself, and find it hard to set an example. If so, start with yourself, try to stick with it, and you'll all benefit.

Inconsistency or Contradictions Will Prevent Progress

Ask yourself, 'Am I expecting my child to do what I don't do?' Be honest with yourself, and ask others for their opinions if necessary. Basically, if your tone of voice and actions don't match your words, your child won't believe the words – he'll believe your unspoken message.

Show Interest and Use Praise

No one likes to be ignored, and we all crave and need positive attention. If your child is eating or behaving badly and you react each time, ask yourself if that's the only way she's getting your attention. Children would prefer to

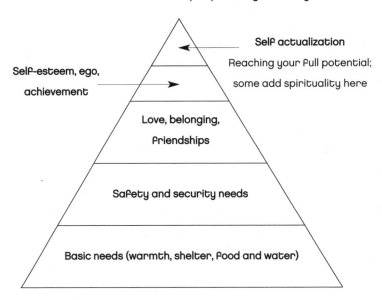

A Theory of Human Motivation

In 1943, Abraham Maslow introduced his 'needs theory', and it's still well-regarded today. The basis of Maslow's theory was that all humans have unsatisfied needs, and that's what motivates them to move on.

You can look at this from different angles; for example, in order to satisfy higher needs like achievement, you've got to have other 'lower' needs such as safety in place first. Put the other way around, when your need for safety is met, you'll want to move on to 'higher' levels. You may have attained a higher level when something happens, so you drop down a bit – our hierarchies are in flux.

A version of Maslow's 'hierarchy of needs' is shown here.

get 'nice' attention (through praise, cuddles, play, and being listened to or thanked), but will misbehave if they have to in order to get your attention. If you shout or grumble at your child habitually, you'll reinforce the very behaviour you don't like.

See Things From Your Child's Viewpoint

Look at things from your child's point of view and try to understand it. Your child will exhibit all sorts of behaviours, some of which aren't appropriate. If you focus mainly on his inappropriate behaviours, your child will feel criticized and under attack and he'll feel upset, defensive and maybe angry.

Make It Easy For Yourself

If you try to do too much at once, especially if you're tired or distracted, then you're more likely to give up and things will carry on as before. If something goes wrong one day, just shrug, do something to cheer yourself up, forgive yourself (or your child), and pick up where you left off later that day or the next morning.

Perfection Doesn't Exist

And if it did – there would be nothing to aim for! Perfection is an unattainable goal. Focus instead on measurable improvements. We all want people around us we feel happy and comfortable with, who won't judge us and who have our best interests at heart. If your children know you love them and that you're doing your best, then that's what matters most. If you point out something that's been done wrong, make sure it's voiced in a positive way and not as a criticism.

Look for the 'Positive Intention' Behind Your Child's Actions

If your child is misbehaving or refusing to eat 'good' foods, assume your child's behaviour has a positive intention, and try to discover what that is. For instance, has something happened recently that is bothering her? Also look at what your child has eaten and drunk recently, even if they're 'good' things, as a particular food type or additive could make her feel jumpy and irritable. She may be running around and shouting to try to get rid of the feeling, and not just to annoy you!

Whatever the cause, discuss alternative behaviours that would make both of you happy – or at least content. If possible, try to point out other situations where her current behaviour might be acceptable; this way your child can learn that different behaviours may be appropriate in different contexts.

Focus on Your Child's Behaviour

It's crucial to focus on your child's behaviour and not on the child himself. Your *child* is not bad, his *behaviour* is. Instead of saying, 'Jake, don't do that, you naughty boy!' try something like, 'Jake, you know I love you, but when you behave like that I feel upset. I'd like you to behave *this* way.'

Get Your Subconscious on Your Side

Be aware that your subconscious is very powerful, and you need to train it. If you're someone who says, 'I have no willpower,' the chances are your subconscious is working on a different goal to your conscious mind, and/or your blood sugar isn't properly regulated. Make your subconscious your ally, and not your enemy. Help yourself by eating properly and regularly so you keep your blood sugar balanced (see Chapter 7). If your child is exhibiting behavioural problems, chances are you're suffering too, so give yourself as much of an advantage as you can.

Healthy Eating Is Not about Going on a Diet

Don't tell your child she needs to 'go on a diet' – and don't do this yourself! When you 'diet', you'll both focus on what you *can't* have and do. Decide instead to become healthy, and you'll focus on what you *can* have and do. To help get your subconscious on your side, you need to aim and work towards a new goal, rather than running away from an old one.

If you say to yourself, 'I need to lose weight,' you'll focus on the weight itself. This will become the main issue and make it difficult for you. Similarly, if you say, 'I need to make Hannah behave,' then you're focusing on what she's doing now and not what you really want from her. Instead, focus on where you're going – towards being a slimmer, fitter parent with a happy and healthy child.

Set Goals

Successful people use specific goals. You can only benefit if you have specific goals, too. Keep repeating them and let your subconscious get to work. Instead of saying, 'I'll be slim and fit by the summer,' say, 'By May, I'll be 12 pounds lighter. By then I will also be able to walk for 45 minutes without having to stop.'

Be realistic and set attainable targets. Design goals that will work in relation to you and your children, write them down, and refer to them daily. If you want to amend them, then do so: it's your life.

Include your children in the process even if you think they're too young to understand; they'll pick up on your good intentions and enjoy the team feeling, and will react accordingly. If they refuse to have anything to do with the planning, just ignore the grumpiness and carry on so they can see you mean it. Casually elicit their opinions, and ask why they feel they disagree with what you're proposing or doing. Equally casually, ask if they have any questions, and answer them thoughtfully and without heat. If you don't know an answer, say that you can find out, and suggest you look it up together.

Be Flexible

Think carefully about any limiting beliefs you have ('I can't cook well', or 'I can't control Peter') and see how you can reframe them ('I can find some easy recipes and maybe take a cookery course', and 'I can help Peter control himself through talking, proper diet and setting a good example.'). If you have any limiting patterns of behaviour, look at how you can replace them with more choice and flexibility. For example, if you take your child shopping straight after school when he's tired and tetchy, try to do it at some other time, or give him a snack on your way there. Arguing about bed-time is better talked about calmly over breakfast at the weekend. Similarly, shopping *after* you've eaten rather than when you're hungry will help you buy food in a more informed and controlled way.

Visualize

Make your goals real in your mind: Close your eyes and *see* how you look, *feel* what it's like, and *hear* what you and other people are saying about the new you. Practise this daily, and teach your child to do the same. Make it a fun exercise together.

Remember, each person has his or her own reality and take on things. People always take the decision that they think is best for them, even if it may appear misguided or bewildering to you. But we all find it difficult to avoid short-term rewards at the expense of long-term goals. When Janice insists on eating yet another cheap burger, she's not doing this to spite you, or to put on weight. Rather, she may be unhappy about something, or the pain of (immediate) struggle with the cravings may seem worse than the (future) pain of weight gain, so she opts for the less painful route. Looking for, and working on, the root cause will be much more beneficial for you both, even if it takes time and patience. Teach your child to visualize a positive outcome, and let her work out how to attain it (you can guide her here, but be subtle about it).

Give Choices

Choices are good, and your child will like choosing (usually!). Letting your child choose takes away the 'you can't have'. For example, instead of saying, 'Sorry, Sam, you're not having chicken nuggets,' say, 'Would you like chicken strips or home-made fish cakes today? And would you like fresh green beans or juicy, tiny peas along with your sweetcorn?'

Let Go and Move On

If someone's behaviour has upset you, instead of suppressing your anger or tears, acknowledge the problem, let yourself feel it, and then give yourself permission to *let it go*. What happened was in the past, and you are in the present. The same goes if you've upset yourself; for example, eating a pile of doughnuts might leave you feeling appalled at yourself! It's done and in the past. Work out what conditions set you up for the doughnut-fest and work out a way to avoid the triggers in the future. You might find this 'acknowledge-feel-let go' approach a little difficult at first, but it becomes a lot easier with practice. Once you understand the process, teach your child.

That said, if you and your children have been through some trauma, suppressed feelings will be at work and can often undermine good eating habits. This can result in eating too much, eating the wrong things, or eating too little. If you or your child have begun to eat healthily and exercise properly, and you still feel tetchy or tearful, the chances are you haven't identified or worked through your other problems. If this is the case, ask for counselling or other help for you or your child. Ask your doctor about this first, although there are many other sources of help, too. If you're worried about cost, free or highly subsidized counselling is often available.

Don't Let Things 'Get to You'

Be relaxed and amiable. If something doesn't work, it doesn't. Run up and down the stairs a few times if necessary to dissipate the bad energy, take a deep breath, try to work out why your plan didn't work this time, and try again at a more appropriate time, or work out a different strategy. Remember Edison? When someone asked him what it felt like to fail so often as he was struggling to invent a lightbulb, he replied that, on the contrary, he'd merely found a thousand ways *not* to do it!

Get Outside!

Plenty of exercise in the fresh air is what our bodies and brains have evolved to expect. Sitting in front of TV and computer screens, being driven to and from school behind UV-proof windscreens, or leading the nocturnal existence that many teenagers and young people do are NOT acceptable substitutes. Sunlight is also needed to maintain mental well-being. (You and you child both need that vitamin D!) Get out there and enjoy it. If the days are short or very overcast, and your child suffers from feeling low at these times, consider trying a light box – these emulate sunlight (without the harmful bits), and many users claim an hour or so a day in the winter helps them get through it feeling 'normal' instead of depressed. Type 'light box' or 'SAD' (seasonal affective disorder) into a search engine and you'll find plenty of information on the subject, and lists of suppliers.

Just Eat

Choose to be aware of what you're doing, especially when eating. Instead of reading, watching TV or walking around while you're having your meal, sit down and consciously look at what you're eating: be aware of each mouthful, chew it thoroughly, and revel in the taste. If you're eating 'junk' food, you'll become sensitive to the 'plastic' and greasy taste and will start going off it. (Notice how many people fall into a trance-like state when eating? Don't be one of them, and don't let your child do this.)

Chewing thoroughly helps you to digest your food properly, and to feel full *before* you eat too much. Many of us were brought up to eat everything on our plates. This way of thinking doesn't do anyone any favours, especially if you've piled your plate a little high or your child has an issue with eating. If your child wants to leave some of his food, let him. If he wants to have seconds and isn't going through a growth spurt, ask him to wait for at least 5 minutes, and then see how he feels – he may find he now feels full. Use the 5 minutes to have a chat, as a good bond between you can help combat eating problems.

General Dietary Recommendations

You may need to read this book more than once before you take everything
on board. Forget what you were told as a child about not 'wrecking' books,
and highlight relevant bits and make notes in the margins. Keep a diary of
what's working. Remember, some things have a delayed effect, so a diary
really does help – it's quite difficult to recall the details a few days later …
especially if your brain is foggy from fatigue and a bad diet! Don't treat your
child as an isolated unit – you're an important part as well, and you need to
help yourself, too. See pages 278–83 for some tips on getting good food
into your children's mouths, and see the recipe chapters for some easy, tasty
and wholesome options.

Is Your Child Overweight?

If you or your child is overweight, you probably know it's not a good idea,
but don't panic about it! 'Going on a diet' doesn't work, but if you follow
the guidelines in this book, including the 12-week plan, you'll find weight
comes off anyway as a great side-benefit.

Being 'overweight' means having too much stored fat in proportion to the
rest of your body mass; it's not to do with total weight. Incidentally, too little
body fat is very damaging also, and if serious undereating (anorexia) or a
disorder like bulimia (binge-eating and vomiting) applies to you or your
child, you must seek medical advice. Being unfit is also unhealthy, and often
obesity and being unfit go together – but not always! I'll explain more shortly.

If you're overweight yourself, you're sending the wrong messages to your
child, and the chances are you aren't feeling as good as you could. In the
US, nearly two-thirds of adults are overweight, and a huge proportion of
their children are, too. The UK is doing its best to catch up, and that's not
good. Three Government watchdogs[1] said in February 2006 that red tape, a
lack of structure, training and communication, and hard-to-implement
strategies are jeopardizing efforts to tackle Britain's growing childhood
obesity crisis. In fact, it had taken 31 experts a full 18 months just to agree
on how obesity should be measured!

Fat Isn't Just a Feminist Issue

A report published early in 2006 has shown that Scottish children are among the fattest in the world: disturbingly, one in three is overweight, one in five 12-year-olds is classified as clinically obese, and one in 10 is severely obese. The causes? Poor diet and lack of exercise.

Aitken & Niven, Scotland's biggest retailers of school uniforms, are now stocking 'sturdy fit' lines, as children's waists and bottoms are expanding to adult sizes.

Basically, don't wait for the 'experts' in Government to give you the way forward – decide to take matters into your own hands, and start now.

- If your child is overweight now, and you let matters trundle along, chances are he'll carry on being overweight (probably more so) into adulthood.
- Obesity is recognized by the World Health Organization as one of the top 10 global health problems.
- Being overweight is a major factor for coronary heart disease – *and so is being inactive* (even if you're slim).
- Overweight or obese children (and adults) are more likely to suffer from depression (often associated with poor blood sugar level balance) and leaky gut syndrome, as well as diabetes, high blood pressure and cancer.

I think you'll know if you or your child is overweight, but there are various ways of measuring it: BMI, waist circumference, and waist–hip ratio.

BMI

BMI (or Body Mass Index) is not always an accurate measure of overweight or obesity, especially if your child is young, or you are pregnant. Many internet sites provide BMI calculators, and tables to help you judge whether your child's value (or yours) is in the 'normal' range. BMI has many limitations, and doesn't take into account either the actual percentage of body fat, or its distribution. Lean muscle weighs more than fat, so BMI could even improve as someone's fitness declines and their muscle turns into fat – clearly a very misguided indicator of 'health'. The distribution of body fat also turns out to be a more important indicator of risk than BMI when it comes to heart disease and related physical health problems. My advice would be to talk to your doctor, who will also take into consideration your diet, the amount and type of exercise you get, any family history of disease, and your waist circumference, blood pressure and blood sugar levels.

Waist and Hip Measurements

You may have heard the question, 'Are you an apple or a pear?' If a lot of your fat is around your abdomen (giving you an 'apple' shape), you're at greater risk of developing weight-related diseases. Men tend to be apples, but so do some women. Those who put weight on around their hips and thighs more than their abdomens ('pears'; generally pre-menopausal women) are a 'safer' shape. As a very rough guide, your waist shouldn't measure more than half your height.

The waist–hip ratio (WHR) takes body-fat distribution into consideration and is calculated simply by dividing your waist measurement by your hip measurement (your hips being the widest part of your bottom).

- Based solely on a WHR measurement, you're at low risk of weight-related diseases if your ratio is 0.8 or below for women, and 0.95 or below for men.
- If you fall into the 0.81–0.85 (women), and 0.96–1.0 (men) categories, you're at moderate risk.
- You're at a much higher risk if your WHR ratio is over 0.85 (women) or over 1.0 (men).

Food

Know Your Fats

- Avoid foods containing saturated fats or trans fatty acids and replace these with those containing either monounsaturated or natural polyunsaturated fats. (See Chapter 8 for details.) Cut down on animal fats and avoid fried or overly processed foods. Check carefully the contents of any margarines you may use, and avoid any with the words 'hydrogenated' or 'partially hydrogenated' on the labels.

- Try to include at least two portions of fish or seafood in your diet each week.
- Choose lean rather than fatty meats. Organic produce should contain fewer residues of drugs or growth hormones, and wild game and 'free-range' meat should have a healthier fat profile than the same kind of meat from a factory-farmed bird or animal (for the same reasons that exercise is good for you…!).
- Avoid most commercially baked cakes, biscuits and puddings as far as possible, as these usually contain saturated and trans fats.
- Use fresh seeds such as sunflower, sesame, pumpkin or linseed (flax) in salads, on cereals or as snacks, as these are a rich source of essential fatty acids. Fruit and nuts are also an excellent snack (but the latter should be fresh, and eaten only in moderation).

Eat Plenty of Fresh Fruit and Vegetables

These should ideally be included at every meal. Try to include a variety of the highly coloured fruits and vegetables, as these contain carotenoids and flavonoids (which have antioxidant properties) as well as many essential vitamins and minerals.

Avoid Too Many Sugary Foods and Refined Carbohydrates

Refined carbohydrates include white flour, white rice, many processed breakfast cereals and almost all cakes, pastries and sweets, etc. Choose wholegrain, unrefined starches instead where possible. You want 'slow-release' foods for sustained, balanced energy (see Chapter 7).

Top Eating Tips

Here are some tips to change your fussy eater into a child with an appetite for real food. So, in no particular order …

Babies

- Breastfeed rather than bottle-feed if you get the choice. If you use infant formula, try to make sure it has the highly unsaturated omega-3 and omega-6 in ready-made form (DHA and AA).
- Manufactured baby foods very often contain additives and added sugar as well as cheap 'fillers'. Whatever healthy foods you're eating (well, OK – not hot curries!), put some aside and blend it. Put the purée into ice trays and freeze, taking out what you need for your baby as and when.

Younger Children

- Leave the chocolate bars and the crisps out of the lunch box (see the Recipe chapters for alternative ideas).
- 'Healthy' lollipops? No – they may be sugar-free, but most contain synthetic substances.
- Enthuse about the healthy food you're eating – its appearance, texture, taste and content. Equally, discuss 'junk' foods: ask for your child's opinions, listen and accept them – but make sure they know yours, without argument.
- Have a policy that they try one to three pieces/spoonsful of whatever is on their plate.
- Don't use sweet things (e.g. pudding or sweets) as a bribe for finishing the main, savoury meal – the latter will be seen in a negative light and just something to be got through, and the sweet things will appear even more appealing.
- Instead of a junk snack when your child gets home from school, try toast with jam and then gradually move on to non-plastic bread (less refined flour and no additives) with a nut, real fruit or sesame spread.
- Worried about too much peanut butter? Try the delicious cashew and almond nut butters instead (they're available from healthfood shops and, increasingly, many supermarkets).
- Make fruit salads colourful and exciting. Take your children shopping with you to choose the ingredients and let them help make it.
- Don't give up! There may be resistance at first, but giving up quickly and labelling your child a picky eater won't help, and will become a self-fulfilling prophecy.

- Let your child help make at least one, and preferably more, meals a week.
- If your child has a childminder/carer, make sure he or she doesn't give your child foods and drinks you wouldn't give him at home.
- Make sure your child's school knows if she's affected by tartrazine and sugar, for example, and ask that she's not fed them.
- Younger children often don't like mixed food or luscious sauces. Let them have their ingredients separate on the plate, with the option of adding sauce or mixing them up if they want.
- Remember milk is a food, and not a drink. Encourage your child to drink plenty of water, and filter it if you can.
- Say, 'Well, you've tried it, and well done. Never mind you didn't like it just now – next week you might (be old enough to).'
- Advertising: Help your child see beyond the hype. *Which Online*[2] is a good place to start, as it shows you what children's food manufacturers are up to.

Older Children

- Make sure your child has breakfast before setting off for school, and encourage him to take a healthy break-time snack with him.
- Appeal to older children's vanity: They'll get fewer spots by eating 'healthy' foods and dumping the junk.
- If your child is too tired after school to do anything, explain she'll have much more energy with a good diet … and will find her schoolwork easier.
- Banning a food will have the wrong effect: They'll just want it more. Let them make their own informed choices – if they won't listen to you, point them to appropriate websites designed for teenagers (see the Resources chapter for ideas).
- Instead of crisps, try them out with hummus on good bread or as a dip for crudités (you can make this easily or buy it fresh and additive-free from the supermarket). Dairy not a problem? Then tsatziki is a good one, too.
- If you introduce your older child to new foods, she'll often try them, and enjoy them. Ask her to peruse your cookbooks and choose a meal or two a week.

- Allocate one meal a week to be made by your child, and help or not as requested. Offer to wash up, or he might not want to cook in the first place.

Supplies

- Keep fruit on display and encourage your child to eat it. For a slower sugar release, have a small handful of almonds, cashews or walnuts with it.
- When you make a lasagne, for example, make too much and freeze individual portions. These can be used by your teenagers in the same way as junk ready-made freezer meals – after all, what they're usually after is convenience rather than rubbish. The same goes for soups and casseroles.
- Going cold-turkey and chucking out all the junk food may backfire if you have lots of grumpy people on your hands. Unless you've got the family 'on side', gradually run down your supplies and introduce tasty and healthy alternatives at the same time.
- If your child's diet is varied and balanced, home-made cakes and biscuits in moderation are fine – as long as you keep an eye on what's going into them! Look for recipes in cookbooks for people with diabetes – but not the ones that tell you to add sweeteners.
- Buy small quantities of fruit and vegetables, as wrinkled apples, etc., lose their appeal as well as their nutrients.
- Buy organic if you can, and store in a cool, dark place.
- Grow beansprouts, cress or other simple vegetables if you can (tomatoes are a winner) – easy and nutritious, and something younger children like to join in with.

Meal Times

- Try to eat together at least three times a week. Yes, clubs get in the way, or your partner is back late from work, and, and, and … Talk with your family, say what you'd like and ask for some suggestions; if they're involved, they're more likely to comply.
- You don't have to wait for your partner to get home from work – eat with the children instead, and make them feel important.
- Remind everyone to chew. It's good manners to put down your cutlery between bits – I think that bit of etiquette came about so that people

would taste and chew their food properly, rather than bolt it down untasted and unappreciated (and, as you know now, setting themselves up for indigestion and leaky gut).

- When you're eating together, go for meals you'll all like (see Recipe chapters).

Eating Out

- Our society has become used to children having cheaper (and inferior) foods. Seek out restaurants that will let children have smaller portions of adult food rather than being palmed off with reformed grungy bits of mechanically recovered chicken covered with synthetics and hydrogenated oil.

General Notes

- Forcing and bribing won't work in the long term.
- Help your children develop their own judgement about what they're seeing and tasting. Don't tell them what they think or should think – but do give them some facts and figures when you can!
- Food tastes better over a shared story and a calm, unhurried atmosphere. Eat together when you can at a nicely set table (maybe with candles and background music?).
- View sweets, crisps and other sugary or salty snacks as things that make a very occasional showing – not 'banned foods', but certainly not treats.
- Processed 'low-fat' foods are not healthy. They contain a lot of sugars and processed ingredients, and no 'good' fats.
- Don't get too hung up on what's good and what's bad. Just aim to produce meals that are fresh and wholesome, and that look and smell great.
- Go for easy meals. The finicky stuff can come later if you have the time and interest.
- Accept you're up against junk food advertising for now. Campaign against it, and instil some cynicism into your children about these manufacturers' aims.
- It's *not* OK for your child to eat junk food just because he's exercising! Exercising alone does not make for health; if your child's body is badly fed,

it won't reward him with a good performance. Also, if exercise is difficult (because of his poor diet), your child is likely to give up and not exercise later in life – and that has all sorts of negative health implications.

- Processed food isn't cheap: a) it damages health (the most priceless commodity) and b) once you take out the additives and fillers you're really paying for, you're not left with a lot of the real stuff.
- Children will invariably refuse some foods when you start changing their diet. If you offer only a few new foods, and they accept half of them, you're left with a small repertoire. If over time you offer 60 new dishes, then even if only get a conservative one-third uptake, that's still 20 new things!
- Introduce your child to fruit and herbal teas – they can be an acquired taste, so it may take many attempts to find one he likes.

Non-drug Approaches

In my view, drugs should always be the last resort, rather than the first option. There are numerous different approaches that can be used to improve mood, behaviour and learning without the use of drugs. I can't possibly cover all of these here, but you can find out more for yourself using the same critical techniques I've been emphasizing throughout this book.

Social Skills

No human being exists in a vacuum, and the ongoing interactions your child has with other people are crucial to unlocking his potential. Social interactions with family members and close friends can help prevent depression. Good social skills will help your child in every aspect of life.

In early life, you as a parent are the most significant influence on your child's social and emotional development. Later on, people your child encounters in other settings – in the neighbourhood, at nursery, playgroup, school or elsewhere – will also play a major role. For older children and adolescents, a 'peer group' of friends and acquaintances (or a lack of these) can sometimes be more powerful than parental influences in many respects. Watch whom they're with, and try to involve 'mentors' (good and caring/teaching influences) in their lives.

Encourage your child into social situations such as swimming, football, tennis, Cubs and Scouts/Brownies and Guides, or chess club. A meal-and-play club (each week one parent of a group hosts the event) works well, and the children can be involved at all sorts of different levels. Board-game clubs and choirs are great for exercising your child's mind and teaching self-discipline; sports clubs mean they can let off steam, get fit and learn to work within a group; meal-and-play clubs help them to learn more about nutrition, social interaction and manners, and about play that doesn't involve TV or computers. Your child's school, local tourist information office and library will hold lots of useful information.

Sleep Hygiene

Sleep is a vital but often overlooked commodity. In the Appendix (page 395) you'll find a table of how many hours' sleep your child needs each night. At 2 years old this is about 11 hours, then this drops gradually with increasing age, to 10 hours a night at 9 years old and then 9 hours at age 15. In the Appendix you'll also find a template for a 'sleep diary' you can use to keep a record of your child's sleeping habits. This will help you spot what may be going on.

'Sleep hygiene' refers to the practices, habits and environmental factors that are critically important for sound sleep. Don't let your child's sleep problems ruin your quality of life as well as theirs. 'Behavioural' techniques really do work – and controlled trials have shown that even getting these from a booklet can often be just as effective as seeing a therapist,[3] although do seek help if you feel you need to.

Sleep *quality* is just as important as sleep *quantity*. A good diet and enough water throughout the day may help your child sleep better, as will a quiet time of 1–2 hours that doesn't involve the TV or computer (or screens of any other sort) before bed. Try to set a 'bedtime routine' prior to settling your child to sleep, and stick to it, even in the holidays.

A dark bedroom is essential, as melatonin (a critical sleep-inducing hormone) is only produced when it's dark. It's secreted by the pineal gland (a pea-size structure at the centre of your brain) when darkness falls. Lack of melatonin is heavily implicated in mood swings and aggressive behaviours. Melatonin:

- regulates your sleep–wake cycle
- may help with delayed sleep phase disorders
- is an important antioxidant
- is thought to help with jet-lag
- is thought to act as an immuno-modulator in cancer

Melatonin and Zinc

It's important for your child to have adequate zinc in her diet, as low zinc levels not only lead to susceptibility to infection and gut permeability, but zinc also regulates the synthesis of melatonin – the substance that helps to initiate sleep.

Eating and Sleep

It really does matter what you eat when! If you eat a high-protein meal shortly before bedtime, you won't have digested it properly before you go to sleep, thus interrupting your sleep cycle. It is better to:

- Eat a good protein meal at lunchtime or early evening – this will supply all the amino acids needed for the repair and building that take place at night. One important amino acid is tryptophan, which is needed for the production of serotonin (the feel-good chemical) and melatonin.
- Later in the evening have a light, low-GI carbohydrate-based snack – this will increase your blood sugar level and divert most of your amino acids (not the tryptophan) to tissues such as the muscles. Crucially, tryptophan gets the chance to cross the blood-brain barrier much more effectively when the other amino acids aren't around to compete.

Exercise

Exercise is an *essential* part of a healthy child's life, helping to improve not only movement coordination and energy levels, but general mind and body health. It's a good habit that your child can and should carry on into adulthood. Your child will not improve through diet alone, so look carefully at what kind of exercise may help. As well as helping sleep problems, a fun and balanced exercise programme will mean your child increases in:

- flexibility and suppleness
- stamina and strength
- core stability, balance and poise
- feel-good hormones (improving mood).

There are some ground rules: Never force your child; make the exercise fun; practise what you preach, and vary the exercise types to get all-round benefits.

If your child has dyspraxic tendencies (difficulties with coordination or balance), you may need specialist help and advice. Try to get your child to see that simply avoiding exercise is *not* the answer, and will make these problems (and others) worse in the long run.

A range of activities not only keeps boredom away (and gets your child away from the TV and computer) but also develops different sets of muscles and cardiovascular fitness. Walking is something every child should do. Ball games, swimming, cycling, working out at the gym and doing athletics can all have benefits – but find out what your child will most enjoy.

Consider Pilates and the Alexander Technique, too, and other things that help your child develop 'core stability'. Lessons are needed to begin with but, once mastered, the fun exercises (especially those on a big, blow-up ball!) can be carried on at home. Ask at your gym or leisure centre for more details, and check with your doctor before starting.

Physiotherapy and occupational therapy may be available if your child has special difficulties with movement and coordination. Ask your doctor and your child's teachers for advice. In addition, many special exercise programmes have been developed to help children with specific developmental problems, including dyspraxia, ADHD, dyslexia and related conditions, as well as more severe difficulties such as cerebral palsy. Some have more clinical evidence behind them than others, but evaluating these is beyond the scope of this book. As before, I would encourage you to keep an open but critical mind, find out what's available, talk to people who have tried things out before, and don't be fooled by unrealistic promises into paying large sums of money or subjecting your child to something that may not do her any more good than the exercise she can get in other ways.

The Importance of Emotions

Learning self-awareness (sensing and recognizing emotions, identifying and acknowledging feelings) is another critical part of your child's development. Acquiring the skills and techniques to do this will be an important tool for your child both now and in later life, particularly if he has specific difficulties such as ADHD, dyspraxia, dyslexia or autism which can often cause significant additional stress and frustration.

Antidepressant drugs have now been recognized by the National Institute for Clinical Excellence (NICE) as generally unsuitable for children, so it's well worth looking for alternatives to these and other medications. Having said this, don't rule out medication if this really does seem to be warranted, and always start by seeing your doctor if you think your child has undue emotional problems.

There are *many* forms of counselling and other therapies, and in the end only you and your child can decide if any of these will help. These kinds of approaches should supplement, and not replace, any other treatments your child may be having. No single mode of treatment is ever likely to be effective for all children (or their families), as each child is different. Look and ask around to find out what's available to help your child, but always start with a proper medical check-up.

Behaviour therapies and cognitive behavioural therapies (CBT) may be helpful, particularly if your child's suffering from serious relationship difficulties and low self-esteem. Your child's school may have a counsellor or special needs department, and along with seeing the doctor, that is a good place to start: ask for the school's SENCO (special educational needs coordinator) and take it from there. Either the doctor or your child's school may refer you to an educational psychologist, but be aware there's usually a long wait for this. In some areas, youth counselling is available on a free or subsidized basis. This can sometimes help if your child is unhappy because, for example, he is being bullied or feeling isolated and finds it hard to voice his concerns.

Anything that helps your child to learn 'emotional self-regulation' is likely to be more than beneficial. 'Emotional intelligence'[4] can often matter much more than scholastic ability or conventional 'IQ' when it comes to good health, productive employment and a satisfying personal life – all things you would want for your child.

Learning to control our emotions is of course part of normal 'growing up', but can often be a problem area in children's (and adults'!) development, particularly for those with special needs.

Specific physiological signs including brain-wave patterns are associated with an optimal, emotionally balanced state – and with focused attention, memory and problem-solving skills. Some programmes offer biofeedback (or 'neuro-feedback') to teach people to control either their heart rate variability – an excellent indicator of emotional self-regulation – or sometimes EEG (electro-encephalogram, a type of brain-wave recording). Biofeedback techniques of this kind are reported to help with some cases of dyspraxia, dyslexia and autism – but, as usual, more systematic research in this area is still needed. Always remember that, most of all, your child needs your unconditional love and support. If you are finding this difficult, then don't hesitate to seek help and advice for yourself first.

FAQs

I'm worrying that I won't be able to stick at this with my child. I fail whenever I try to do any diet or exercise plan – after two weeks it's usually abandoned.

If you want to, you *can* and will succeed this time. My guess is that you've rushed into a 'faddy' or strict diet whenever you've tried to lose weight, and pushed yourself too quickly on the exercise front. That way, you set yourself up to fail. When you follow this plan with your child, take your time. Focus particularly on stabilizing blood sugar levels (for both of you) and getting enough sleep, and I think you'll find that the rest begins to fall into place. Of course, you do need to want to do this (consider anything that might be causing you to sabotage your own efforts), and you'll also need to visualize and write out realistic goals.

I'm a single mum on Income Support and don't think I can afford to do this, especially as ready meals are so cheap and easy.

It's a myth that ready meals are cheaper – the highly processed ones, that is. Check the ingredients, which are usually lots of sugar or refined starch, so you get very little in the way of nutrients and plenty by way of additives. One woman I know was in the same position as you: she started going bargain-hunting with her child, hitting the supermarket and market just before closing time when fresh produce was discounted. The basics (local vegetables and fruit, brown rice, etc.) aren't expensive, and you can make nutritious meals easily. They don't have to be fancy, just tasty. She also grows her own lettuces, herbs and tomatoes in garden containers: cheap, easy and fun.

I want to take my son swimming, cycling and to play football but I'm depressed and overweight and find it hard and embarrassing to exercise, so how can I take my son out?

It's great that you want to take him out – you're already more than half way there. Try some of these steps:

1. Visualize where you want to be in three months' time, and work out what you need to be doing at two months in order to get there, and one month, two weeks and one week.
2. If you don't have friends who might join you, look online or locally for support groups – you are one of many, many people in the same situation.
3. Start eating healthily yourself, making sure you're getting enough omega-3 fatty acids and other essential micronutrients. Balancing your blood sugar and identifying possible food intolerances are also keys to weight control.
4. Ask at your local leisure centre when they run classes for the unfit (they're not all for people who can leap about non-stop!).
5. Start with your own activities and build up your confidence.
6. Explain to your son that you want to get better because you really want to play with him, and that you need his help. He may help take charge and walk with you for 'your' benefit – and at the same time benefit himself!

We always end up stressed and arguing at mealtimes, especially as we eat different things.

You need to work out what it is that's causing the stress. If it's simply because you're run off your feet, then you can do two things:

1. Prepare a few dishes separately such as fish/meat, carrots, green beans, etc., and put them in the middle of the table. Let everyone help themselves to at least something. If they won't eat, shrug, smile and change the subject. Refuse to argue, though allow debate as long as it's quiet and well mannered. Don't give in and get up to prepare something else; eventually they'll learn. Try to avoid pudding. Use any leftovers for lunch the next day (made into a soup, for example).

2. Sit everyone down and prepare the week's menu with them – if they choose something, they can't be fussy when it arrives. It helps to have cookbooks with luscious pictures in them to hand. At the same time, allocate who's going to help you cook on which day, and write it down for all to see and not deny later!

It's really hard to get my daughter to bed. We always end up arguing, and then she's tired the next day.

Choose a time other than bedtime to explain why you want her to go to bed at a particular time – show her page 395 in the appendix of this book to see how much sleep she should be getting. Have a tick sheet and offer rewards if she gets, say, 5 or 6 ticks in any given week. Ignore comments such as, 'All my friends stay up until this time' (or offer to phone their parents to discuss this; children often back down then!).

Make sure you have a good routine to follow and remember to keep proteins for earlier on in the evening (indigestion doesn't help sleep). If she wants to stay up to watch a programme on TV, offer to video it for her. Make sure she's getting plenty of exercise, as it's harder to sleep when you've just been sitting around all day.

Summary

1. This is a long-term, sustainable plan, not a quick fix.
2. Show your child what he *can* have rather than what he can't.
3. Make it easy for yourself, then you and your child will be able to follow the plan.
4. Healthy eating is a way of life; it's not about going on a diet.
5. Be aware of what you're eating and how you're eating it.
6. If your child is overweight, take steps to help him slim – without 'dieting'.
7. Know what foods are needed for what, and what they may do against you.
8. Look at which eating tips you can use with your child.
9. Eat together as often as you can.

10. Visualize your goals and write them down. Make sure they're achievable, and stay flexible.
11. Sort out, with professional help if necessary, any emotional issues from the past (for you and/or your child) and then move on.
12. Exercise is essential. Start moving with your child now.
13. Practise good 'sleep hygiene'.
14. Keep a sleep, food and mood/behaviour diary for your child.
15. Teach your child self-awareness.
16. Know where to go for advice and help, and find out what sorts of help there are in both conventional and complementary therapies.

chapter 11

your 12-week plan

This section contains everything you need to start on your own 12-week plan to help your child make the most of his or her potential. Each step builds on the next, so that within 12 weeks you'll have completed the framework needed to achieve lasting results.

That's not to say that the plan stops there – because it doesn't. The whole idea is that you and your child will be making some fundamental changes to your diet and lifestyle, so that things will not just go on like they did before.

> Remember: *if you always do what you've always done, then you'll always get what you've always got – so if you don't like it, change something!*

Changing ingrained habits is never easy, as you will know from your own experience. The brain is in fact a gigantically powerful habit-making machine – and old habits really do die hard if you've spent a lifetime practising and reinforcing them. In fact, most of your brain power is subconscious – so if you have a problem with 'willpower' at times, it's not lack of willpower; it's your subconscious sabotaging your efforts. This book and many others[1] can offer you some simple but very effective ways to deal with this, but if necessary counselling or other kinds of support might be helpful for your child, and you if necessary.

The good news is, creating new and better habits to replace the old, destructive ones really can be done. You simply need the determination and resources (energy and knowledge, and outside help if needed) to do things differently – and you will also need to convey this to your child. This is where an understanding of *why* those changes are so important, and *what real benefits* you can expect from making them, is crucial. It also helps to know what processes you are working with (and against) as you set about changing old, unhealthy habits into new, healthier ones.

Make It Easy For Yourself

If you make things hard to carry out, you'll set yourself up to fail. Identify things that might hold you back, work out how you might deal with them and put them behind you. These procrastination-causing items might include:

You're So Tired You Don't Know Where to Start
Ask friends, family, school and your doctor for help; people usually like helping and won't judge you as not being a perfect parent. (If they do, do you really want them in your life?) If you're really that tired, you need to find out what's causing it – it could be candida (a yeast infection), a virus, depression, poor diet, anaemia, not enough sleep, worry … all sorts. See your doctor and you'll find things start getting better once you make the first step.

You're Too Busy
List your goals, list the obstacles to be overcome, and prioritize them all. Now work out whom you can ask for help (family, colleagues, friends, health professionals), what things you could change, and what things really don't matter that much after all. A good question to ask yourself is, 'If I don't do that, will I look back in a year's time and regret it?' If you won't, then shelve it.

You're Convinced It Won't Work
Ask yourself why you think this: maybe it's something as simple as a family member or friend being derisory about your attempts, and you've taken their comments on board without realizing. It's your life, and not theirs,

and you must do what you feel is right. Become informed and act
accordingly. (You don't necessarily have to tell anyone anyway.)

It All Seems Too Much Effort

Look at your own needs. Chances are you're run down and tired, and used
to putting others first. Think of the aircraft safety drill: If oxygen masks
drop down, you have to don your own before giving one to your child, or
you'll pass out before either of you gets the vital oxygen. By the same token,
you not only deserve to be looked after by yourself and others, you also will
be able to help your family much more if you're feeling good about
yourself, and have more energy.

You Say, 'What Do I Know?'

Well, a lot actually. Never mind the people in the past who've belittled
your knowledge. It's your life, and if you've read this book then you're
quite capable of reading and investigating more, and then making your
own mind up having considered all the facts and opinions you can find.
Just because something's in the papers (or even books!), it doesn't mean
it's true – and similarly, just because your friend says something, it
doesn't mean she's right. Check, and check again, and you'll be more in
the know than most people. If you find some scientific articles over your
head, search for some more user-friendly sites that summarize their
findings.

Three Months Is Nothing

Ask yourself: *Are you prepared to start feeding your child's mind –
and your own – with more positive, healthy input, instead of more
of the same junk?*

Change Your Brain, Change Your Life was the compelling title of
one best-selling book in the US. Can you do it? Will you help your
child do it?

Twelve weeks is around three months – one quarter of a year. It can go by in no time – but equally, a great deal can be achieved in three months if you put your mind to it. Three months is:

- one trimester of pregnancy
- from Christmas time to spring
- a school term.

What are you going to do with your next three months?

Setting Goals

Obviously, all families are different, and you may be based at home, or out working much of the time. Use this plan as a guideline, and decide what you're going to do in each week, and when. Write it down and stick to the list wherever possible, as it'll make things easier to implement.

> **Start making different choices, for you and your child. You'd be surprised at how much difference it can make.**

All successful business people set goals, and it's good to learn from them. Goal-setting works better if you *identify the end you want (and the timepoint) and work back from there*, rather than aiming for some vague point in the future. Try doing this both for yourself and together with your child:

- Imagine where you want to be in a year's time, and what you want to be happening. For example, 'I want to be working two days a week, secure in the knowledge that Lettie is happy at nursery; and I would like mealtimes and bedtimes to be enjoyable affairs.' When you're doing this, visualize yourself there: see, hear and feel the situation. Identify anything that might get in your way, and look for a way around it.
- Now rewrite the goals in the present tense – they'll be easier to carry out: 'Lettie loves going to nursery and I'm enjoying going to work. I'm using my brain, meeting more people, and earning some money. We're sitting

down together at mealtimes at least three times a week – the children are helping with the cooking, chatting and sharing stories and trying out new foods.'

- Now write down where you'd need to be in six months' time if all this is going to happen in a year. Do the same for four and two months, and set targets for week seven, six, five, and so on, until you have clear plans for this next week.
- Write or print out your goals, and stick them up in sight.

Once you have clear targets, reward yourself and your child when you reach them. For your child, a reward might be going to the cinema, or on some special trip. *Resist using sweets or junk food as treats!*

- Accept that you'll fall off track sometimes. Shrug, take a deep breath and get back on – ditch the guilt. Equally, your goals aren't set in stone, and you should review them each week and month.
- Teach your child how to prioritize, even if it's as simple as making a list of three things and deciding what needs to be done first. Compare this with immediate temptations, and find a good compromise. Help your child to look at all the implications (good and bad) of a decision. If your child chooses to disobey your wishes (like not coming off the computer when asked, or leaving his clothes on the floor), explain that this is *his decision*, and so the consequences of the action (no computer the next day/less pocket money?) belong to him. Whatever you do, if you say there will be a consequence, then follow it through. And it's just as important to keep your promises of rewards.
- As soon as your child's old enough, stop taking responsibility for his actions. Different things will happen at different times. For example, soon he'll be old enough to put his shoes by the front door for the next morning, but he might not be asked to clean them until he's older.

Summary of Your 12-week Plan

Weeks 1 & 2	Arrange to see the professionals
	Start a diary
	Bone up
	Dump the junk
	Go shopping
	Replace vegetable cooking and drizzling oils
	Start establishing good sleep patterns
	Have a proper breakfast every day
Weeks 3 & 4	Supplements
	Make sure your child has healthy snacks
	Ease off on the squash
	Investigate and plan exercise options
Weeks 5 & 6	Eat together
	Vary the foods you eat
	Reward your child
	Start exercising
Weeks 7 & 8	Tell your children what they're eating
	Introduce another regular mealtime together
	Introduce essential fatty acids
	Your diary
Weeks 9 & 10	Stop smoking
	Cook with your child
	Do housework with your child
	Eat more fish
	Review the reward system
Weeks 11 & 12	Add another session of exercise
	Start a meal-and-play club
	Review goals and strategies

Weeks 1 & 2

Arrange to See the Professionals

Make a list of any concerns you have about your child's health, behaviour and learning, and go to speak to your doctor first about these, and the possible ways forward. Make an appointment to see the practice nurse for a hearing test and the optician's for a sight test if you think your child's hearing and/or vision might be affecting her progress.

Next, talk with your child's teachers or carers. Ask them for help, and also tell them what strategies you want to implement. Keep good communication and feedback going between all parties involved.

Start a Diary

This needs proper planning, and keeping to – it's harder than you might think to remember even yesterday evening, never mind three days ago. Keep a diary of your child's sleep patterns (see page 396), food eaten and when, and behaviour and activities. There's a suggested format in the Appendix. You can photocopy this or adapt it to your specific needs.

Bone Up

Start researching via the Internet (but treat what you find with caution). Visit your library and health centres for information on your child's condition (e.g. ADHD) and support groups. Find out more about diet and nutrition, and look for shops and websites selling wholesome foods (but don't just believe everything they tell you; remember their motives!). Build up a folder and don't be afraid to ask questions of the professionals. If there isn't a local support group, how about setting one up yourself?

Dump the Junk

Start with your fridge, then your kitchen cupboards. 'Dump the junk' (as the Food Commission's excellent campaign has been encouraging parents for some time). Do be warned that you may find you've little food left at the end of it! Most people are amazed at how much space is created once the dead, disgusting and inedible stuff they've been hoarding is thrown away.

Past It?

As you go through your stores of food and drink, you are going to throw out everything that is dead, decaying and past its 'use-by' date. You'll be replacing it with *smaller* quantities of fresh, live foods, full of nutrients and fibre.

If your instinct is not to waste things, then just put anything suitable onto your compost heap. Most foods will recycle nicely that way. (Exceptions include meat, fish and dairy products, which are more likely to breed maggots or attract stray animals – and possibly poison them.) However much it conflicts with your instincts for economy, please do *not* risk poisoning yourself or your family by eating perishable foods that have passed their 'use-by' date. It really isn't worth it.

This applies even to products that may look as though they keep for ever (if they do, they shouldn't be in your larder anyway), such as some types of flour, rice or other cereals. Not only will 'old, dead food' be lacking in nutrients in any case, but it may well harbour invisible moulds or other noxious microorganisms that can be at the root of many a mysterious stomach upset.

A Fatty Issue

Throw out all foods containing junk fats. (Look for the words 'hydrogenated' and 'partially hydrogenated'. 'Trans fats' are likely to be lurking in these, but are not usually identified explicitly.) You'll be replacing these with foods that provide the good fats and oils that your brain and body need – but please note, these usually have a much shorter shelf-life, so you'll only need to buy these as you use them. If the ingredients listed on any processed foods don't specify what kind of fat is in there – but you know there is some – err on the side of caution and throw it out.

Sweet Nothings and Preservation

Throw out foods and drinks containing artificial sweeteners, and bring in the natural sweetness of real food. Get rid of anything containing the other artificial additives listed in the 'Dirty Dozen' (see Appendix, page 389), which are mainly synthetic colourings and flavourings. Real food doesn't need artificial colours and flavours.

Check what kind of preservatives foods contain – and get rid of any that you suspect might be contributing to your child's problems. That said, some preservatives are needed to stop a food from deteriorating too quickly – if you're in doubt, check them out on one of the many Internet sites, such as Government department ones.

Eat food that spoils, but make sure you eat it before it does.

Go Shopping

Real food should be as fresh and whole as possible, but don't have a blanket ban on all things with a hint of 'not natural'. How 'close to nature' it should be depends on the food, and this is subject to some obvious conditions. For example, unpasteurized milk – and cheeses or yoghurt made from this – can be a possible source of TB or other bacteria such as listeria, so it's not suitable for anyone whose immune system may be unable to cope with this risk, including young children.

Replace Vegetable Cooking and Drizzling Oils

The common forms of vegetable oil such as sunflower, safflower or corn oil have been sold to us as 'healthy'. Well, they're not when they're heated up, as they can form harmful trans fats. What's more, as we saw in Chapter 8, too much of these oils can lead to an unhealthy excess of omega-6 relative to omega-3 fats, so:

■ Ditch your sunflower, safflower and corn oils. There are plenty of other sources of omega-6 fatty acids in a balanced and varied diet.

- Get rid of your margarines and 'spreadable butter', unless these are guaranteed trans fat free. If your child has a problem spreading butter (don't we all!), then make your own spread which you'll know won't have trans fats in it. I blend one part butter with one part olive oil; it keeps well in the fridge and spreads easily. Experiment with your child in making your own concoctions.
- Try olive, flax or walnut oil with bread instead of butter. Put some in a dish, drizzle in some balsamic vinegar, and dip fresh bread into it.
- Use saturated fats (in moderation) for roasting or frying. Butter or ghee (clarified butter), good-quality beef lard, goose fat or coconut oil are more stable when heated than polyunsaturated vegetable oils, which can form trans fats at high temperatures. Olive oil contains monounsaturates and is more stable than ordinary vegetable oils when heated, but add a small amount of water or stock if you're stir-frying with this, to keep the temperature down.
- Use olive, flax and walnut oils in dressings (see next chapter), or use special blends containing evening primrose oils (especially if your child has tendencies to dry skin and eczema, or you suffer with breast pain at those times of the month). You can even break open fish oil supplements and add these (if suitable for the taste of the dish!) – but if so, use it immediately. The highly unsaturated omega-3 in fish oils (EPA and DHA) will go off very fast as soon as they are exposed to light, heat and air.
- When it comes to omega-3 and omega-6 fatty acids, make sure you buy cold-pressed oils, and in small quantities. Bottles should be made from dark glass, and the contents kept away from heat and light. Refrigeration is best for omega-3 oils like flax (and essential for liquid fish oils), but olive oil is OK in a cool cupboard.

If that lovely, moist, soft-looking chocolate muffin, wrapped only in light cellophane, has a 'sell by' date of next year, then that's really telling you something! Let's face it: if it contained natural ingredients, then it would be 'past it' within days, not months or years. You can pretty much guarantee that this kind of luscious-looking item contains trans fats and other undesirable additives.

Start Establishing Good Sleep Patterns

Getting enough sleep can be much easier said than done – but that's no excuse for allowing your child to stay up too late. Children need far more sleep than many adults realize (see Appendix, page 395). Their brains are still developing, and sleep is essential for consolidating any learning that goes on during the day (and there should be plenty of that). A sleep diary can help, and there's one for you to copy in the Appendix (page 396). See also the list of tips in the table below.

- Eat a balanced, varied nutritious diet.
- Avoid sugar and refined carbs at bedtime (no processed cereal!). If your child's blood sugar rises too quickly, insulin will kick in and blood sugar may drop too low, so she might wake up and have a problem going back to sleep.
- Rather than the sugary snack at bedtime, let your child have a high-protein snack several hours beforehand (providing the amino acid tryptophan that's needed to produce melatonin and serotonin). A slow-release carb snack at bedtime – a small serving of porridge, wholemeal toast with butter, or a piece of baked potato in its skin – can then help raise blood sugar gently (and help the tryptophan that's there to get into the brain).[2]
- Make sure your child drinks plenty during the day, but less in the three hours before going to sleep; if your child wakes up needing to urinate, she may find it hard to go to sleep again – especially if she's turned the light on to go.
- Keep the bedroom dark (use a black-out blind if you need to). If your child wants to go to sleep with the light on, get one of those that gradually fades out. (Most also fade in – which can help with waking up in the mornings, especially in winter.)
- Avoid TV (or computers) just before bedtime, and try to have it out of your child's room altogether – it stimulates the brain too much.
- A bedtime story or reading is great – but try to keep this gentle and relaxing, not a thought-provoking, adrenaline-producing adventure.

- If a book doesn't appeal, try listening to some gentle classical or 'healing' music, or a relaxation CD. Sounds of the sea can be soothing (save birdsong for the mornings!).
- If your child's feet get cold in the night, get her to wear socks to bed, as cold feet could wake her up.
- That said, keep the bedroom cooler than the other rooms. As long as the bed is warm, your child should sleep better (and it'll save on your heating bills).
- Electro-magnetic fields may affect sleep, so try to keep any electrical equipment away from the bedside, or switch it off at the mains at night.
- Exercise helps your body relax enough to go to sleep. Keep it for earlier in the day and not just before bedtime, as that can have the opposite effect.
- A bath before bedtime can be warming and relaxing, and conducive to settling down. If a younger child doesn't like baths, instead of saying 'Would you like a bath?' (guess the response and the subsequent argument!), say something like 'Which bubble bath shall we use tonight? The green or the pink one?'
- If night waking is an issue, help your child to view being awake as a chance to relax and daydream without interruption, rather than something to fret about.
- Establish good 'sleep hygiene': use routine and timetables and try to stick to them.

Establish a sensible bedtime routine, and stick to it. Behavioural training works. Get into the habit of doing the same, relaxing things, in the same order; ideally start a good hour or two before your child's bedtime, so that he knows what's coming next, and has a chance to prepare for (and accept) it.

Set whatever alarm is needed to get you and your child out of bed half an hour earlier than needed. *Yes, that's right, half an hour earlier.* You are going to spend that half-hour getting properly prepared for the day ahead – both of you.

Have a Proper Breakfast Every Day

Have breakfast *every day*, and make sure this contains some protein. Choose from any of the breakfast ideas provided in the next chapter, but make sure that you vary these throughout the week. Your child should not be eating exactly the same foods each day, every day.

Weeks 3 & 4

Supplements

If your child has had a limited diet, or is under the weather, then you may want to consider using omega-3 and multi-vitamin and mineral supplements. If so, make sure these are high quality and don't contain artificial sweeteners or other undesirable ingredients. (Most supplements sold in big stores and supermarkets just can't be top quality owing to the huge profit margins these stores demand from suppliers. Seek expert advice if you're not sure.)

Make Sure Your Child has Healthy Snacks

If you suspect that blood-sugar swings are a factor for your child (see Chapter 7), you would both benefit from planning, a day in advance, a timetable of meals and snacks that will fit in with the next day's activities. Make sure your child never goes for more than two to three hours without easy access to something healthy and palatable to eat. There are all sorts of healthy snacks, for example an apple and some cashew nuts, a fruit smoothie with yoghurt, or an almond-and-raisin mix.

Good Snacks

Fruit and either nuts or seeds are ideal snack foods (unless of course your child has any allergies or intolerances to these). Fruits and unroasted nuts/seeds are particularly useful in combination.

Fresh fruit usually has a reasonably low GI rating, and will provide vitamins, minerals and antioxidants as well as fibre and water. But some fruits will 'dump' their sugar into the bloodstream quite quickly. The protein, fat and fibre from nuts and seeds will slow down the release of sugar, and also provide a range of other micronutrients.

Make sure your child nibbles at them slowly and chews properly – it's tempting to cram them all in at once, and to swallow them after only a couple of perfunctory chews, especially if your child is hungry.

Ease Off on the Squash

Proper hydration is vital for all brain and body functions, and drinking enough water is essential. If your child eats a lot of fruit and vegetables, she may not need to drink quite so much. You may well have dumped the fizzy drinks last week, but hung on to the squash – especially if your child is used to sweet drinks. You now need to start getting these down and out.

Soft Drink Damage

This is why it's a good idea to dump soft drinks:

- They cause large blood-sugar fluctuations.
- The sugars and acids (carbonic and phosphoric acids) help rot teeth.
- Phosphates from the drinks can reach your bloodstream and cause calcium to leach from your bones.

- The additives can cause health and behavioural problems.
- They usually have little or no nutritional value.
- Any vitamin C they contain can react with the preservative sodium benzoate to form the cancer-causing benzene.

You can do this step by step:

1. First, make sure you only have squash that has sugar rather than sweeteners, and only have one bottle.
2. Buy in some fruit juices – sweeter ones initially, like pineapple or mango rather than tart ones like orange, grapefruit or cranberry. Make sure you buy juice, and not 'fruit drinks'.
3. Mix a bit of squash with a bit of fruit juice, and add water.
4. Dilute some fruit juice, leaving out the squash.
5. Start using tart rather than sweet diluted juices.
6. Just offer water (filtered if you can: it tastes better and some of the impurities are taken out).

Get your child to be aware of how much water she drinks (keep a tick chart?). Tell her to look at the colour of her urine: if it's dark yellow (and smells strong), she needs to drink more water. It should be pale and clear.[3]

Investigate and Plan Exercise Options

Exercise: the Benefits

Moderate exercise benefits you and your child:

- increases flexibility, strength and endurance
- boosts your immune system
- burns calories
- increases your metabolic rate
- helps control insulin levels
- decreases incidence of illnesses
- alleviates depression

- helps control appetite
- helps control cravings
- increases energy
- adds muscle and tone
- decreases excess fat
- helps you feel better
- helps you look better
- helps you to think more clearly.

Start looking into what forms of exercise are available for your child; some will be through clubs, and some you can do together. Be aware that places like leisure centres have vending machines stocked with crisps, sweet things and fizzy drinks – and that bottled water can be charged at a premium. Take your own snacks and water with you!

Weeks 5 & 6

Eat Together

If you don't often eat together, commit to doing this at least twice a week. Use a kitchen wall calendar so your family is prepared for it to happen. Choose a time when it's least likely there'll be arguments (not when everyone's trying to do something). Sit at the table and make an occasion of it. Talk about the importance of chewing – and practise it!

Vary the Foods You Eat

Found some foods your child likes? Great! Now's the time to start adding to them. Not only will your child have a better range of nutrients, but there will be less chance of a food intolerance building up.

Libraries and 'remainder' bookshops have lots of cheap recipe books, and you'll also find them online (see Resources chapter). Jamie Oliver, for example, offers good and interesting twists on food that children (as well as adults) will like. Take your child shopping with you when you can. If you can't, go through a cookbook together and ask him to choose something new to try this week. He needs to understand that as long as he tries it, he won't necessarily have to finish it. Many cookbooks designed for children are dominated by cakes and puddings, so be careful here. Look at the many cookbooks designed for students; they may not have lots of mouth-watering illustrations, but most good ones teach basic, step-by-step, wholesome cooking.

Reward Your Child

Start designing a reward system for your child. For example, if she goes to bed each night for a week on time and without fuss, then she could have X (you decide between you) as a reward, and $X + Y$ if she hangs up her clothes/puts her toys away, too.

Charts often work well, even with older children: Give them a tick list of what to do when, and you can add your own comments at the end of the day, or give that day a ranking (a star or smiley). Avoid black marks or cross faces: Rewards and compliments always work better than negatives or punishment.

Start Exercising

Commit to exercising at least twice a week (you'll build this up later). Much depends on the time of the year, but an example to start with might be walking to and from school together (if you live miles away, park a mile from school and walk the rest). Take the time to observe your surroundings and talk about them, or things going on in your lives. Girls will talk away happily in most situations, but boys like to chat when they're 'doing' something side by side with the other person. You could also enrol your child for swimming, football, athletics or tennis – whatever takes her fancy.

Yes, it may take ages to get your child ready, but practice will help – just keep cool and look upon each outing as one more than you've done before; it's not a failure if you're late. Write in your diary what you think might have precipitated any mishaps (and indeed, what helped things go well).

Weeks 7 & 8

Tell Your Children What They're Eating

Talk about micronutrients (vitamins are a good one to start with) with your child – at the table is a good time, or when cooking together. Make a game of it. Say what we need them for, and what we can find them in. Have quizzes.

Vitamin C is a good one to start with: vital for general health and immune function, and lack of vitamin C can cause scurvy. There are plenty of resources[4] with stories of sailors (and how the British got the name, 'Limeys'), along with gruesome pictures of scurvy. Make sure your child knows he won't suffer from this when he's eating well.

Even if your child's young, you can introduce the concept of antioxidants in story form: the antioxidants are 'goodies' that will protect him.

This could be a good opportunity to explain why all orange drinks aren't the same: They'll taste different (some 'synthetic'), many have virtually no vitamin C in them, and many have additives (like tartrazine), added sugar or sweetener. Buy a selection and do a proper taste-test (rinse your mouth out between each one). Talk about how eating the whole citrus fruit (minus peel!) or vegetable is a better way of doing it. Talk too about shelf-life, storage and vitamin deterioration. Save orange peel for the bath; the essential oil in it gives off a lovely fragrance.

Avoiding 'Meltdowns'

Remember, 'Preparation and Planning Prevents Poor Performance'.

Keep in mind the three Es: Eating, Exercise and Emotional self-regulation.

If negativity takes over your child's mood and behaviour (and he seems to forget everything he ever learned), just don't join in! Try instead to be an example of what kind of mood and behaviour you'd like to see your child mirror back to you. If you're stressed, she will be stressed. If you resort to shouting (without good cause, such as warning of some immediate danger) your child is unlikely to calm down and control her own behaviour.

Some children can't read the emotions of others very well, *especially those who have ADHD, dyspraxia, bipolar tendencies or autistic spectrum disorders, so you need to bear this in mind.*

Introduce Another Regular Mealtime Together

… And make sure it's at the table and not in front of the TV.

Introduce Essential Fatty Acids

Now's the time to start planning to introduce fish into your child's diet. If he balks at whole fish (it looks gruesome/is too fiddly/the bones are difficult to get out), buy some fillets to serve up – or make fingers or cakes. White fish is less strong-tasting and a good addition to your child's diet, but try also to introduce omega-3-rich oily fish such as trout, mackerel, herring, sardines, salmon and tuna steaks (canned tuna has a lot of the good oil squeezed from it, but is better than nothing).

At the same time, start cutting back on saturated fats and deep-fried foods. Chips and takeaways aren't totally banned (you need a realistic lifestyle here!), but these should be an occasional thing rather than the norm.

This isn't going to happen overnight if your child isn't used to fish – and some just may not like it! (If so, supplements may be a better option.)

Your child needs omega-6 fatty acids too, but these are plentiful in most diets. Meat, dairy products and eggs provide highly unsaturated omega-6, ready-made. The simplest omega-6s are often consumed to excess from vegetable oils and margarines, which is why you've already started replacing these. Use sunflower seeds, pumpkin seeds and pine nuts in his diet (in salads, cereals or as a snack). Flax seeds are particularly good, as they're the only one with more omega-3 than omega-6. Add these ground up, in oil form, or sprinkled on food. (Flaxseed is an excellent source of dietary fibre and will swell up, so make sure your child keeps drinking plenty of water.)

Your Diary

Keep it going! You'll find it's an invaluable reference. Look through it carefully and see what patterns are emerging.

Weeks 9 & 10

Stop Smoking

If you smoke, not only are you hurting yourself, but your child can be harmed by it too – both by the second-hand smoke, and by the messages she'll carry into later life. Now's a great opportunity to think about giving up, as you should be beginning to feel the physical and social effects of your healthy eating, planning and exercise programme with your family. If it's not just a matter of stopping (some can), look into what therapies are available, like acupuncture, hypnotism or nicotine patches. Your doctor will be pleased to help. Decide the day you're going to start (not when you have a lot going on), put it on the calendar/goal list, and go for it.

Cook with Your Child

Even if you only do it once a week to begin with, let your child help you cook. Depending on his age and abilities, it could be toast (with good bread) with butter or peanut butter; scrambled eggs or a stir-fry, for example. Make sure others in the family know he cooked it, and while he's basking in the praise, ask what he'd like to do next time.

Do Housework with Your Child

Your children may be tired, but I bet you are, too! Get them helping out, even if it's only putting things out ready for school the next day, and a whiz around with a feather duster. Make sure it's on the list, and perhaps add a bit of pocket money (or a comic or magazine) for each time it's done properly.

Eat More Fish

Add more oily fish to the menu (as home-made fingers and cakes, or as fillets, or grilled/baked/barbecued whole). Take your child to the fishmongers (you can but try!) and encourage her to try a new type.

Review the Reward System

Is it still going, and is it still working? Review it if necessary, bringing your child into the discussion. Remember you deserve rewards too, and let your child see your chart as well as his.

Weeks 11 & 12

Add Another Session of Exercise

This can be something big, like a new sport, or finding somewhere to ride regularly together, or just a turn around the block or the park after school or at the weekend.

Start a Meal-and-Play Club (MPC)

This can involve anything from two to six families (anything over that can get too much). Each week, one family hosts a meal-and-play session – a simple, nutritious meal or picnic (weather permitting!) and a board game can be enough. Encourage the children to help out and to eat together at the table, with you there. You only need do this once a month if there are four or five families involved.

Review Goals and Strategies

Your needs and aims may well have begun to change by now, so sit down to review them. Look over what you've done and congratulate your child (and yourself!) on your progress. Ask him about what he'd like to do differently, and explore why.

Remember, this is a plan for life, not just a quarter of a year. Enjoy the progress you're all making, and look upon your efforts as one of the best investments you can make for your child.

FAQs

How long is the clear-out going to take?

This will probably be a big clear-out, but most people find they can do it in less than half a day – or in bursts over one weekend. It obviously depends on the size of your kitchen (and just how much food and drink you keep in your fridge and food cupboards), how you decide to go about it, and the number of people you may be able to recruit to help with the task.

If your life really doesn't allow you more than the briefest intervals of 'free time', then it really doesn't matter if you do this 'clear-out' in shorter sessions over a few weeks – you'll achieve the same result. Do it in 10-minute intervals (you can throw out quite a lot of junk in 10 minutes); if you set a timer, somehow it focuses your efforts more. All that matters is that you do it!

What about essential reserves? Surely it doesn't make sense to have an empty larder?

No, you're right. Of course you should make sure you have some reserves of food in the house. And if you can't bear not to have stocks enough to withstand a nuclear winter, you may well want to invest in some healthy replacements first – but ideally, apart from some basic staple foods that you can acquire fairly cheaply and easily as you need them, it's probably better to keep the re-stocking until you've experimented with what works best for you and your child.

No way will the rest of the family put up with this. How shall I approach it?

Domestic arrangements may prevent you from throwing out some foods (and drinks) that other family members are simply not prepared to give up. That's obviously a matter for you to negotiate, and this is why clear, unheated discussions of what you are going to be doing – and why – need to have taken place with every other person likely to be affected by the diet and lifestyle plan you've chosen.

Everyone is entitled to make their own choices, and obviously, if your partner or other adults in the household want to carry on as before, then that has to be up to them. One would hope that they have enough respect for your needs and wishes that some compromise can be arranged – and do make clear that it's not going to be all or nothing: home-made cakes and biscuits, for example, will be replacing the junk ones. (Get the 'complainers' to help you make some!)

Where children are concerned, I'd say that it's a slightly different matter. You as parent or caregiver have the ultimate responsibility (in law) for overriding any choices your child might make that could compromise her health or safety. So you could have a case for arguing that certain foods and drinks just should not be available – or at the very least, should not be kept within easy reach – just as you wouldn't allow your child free access to the alcohol or to drugs you might have in the medicine cabinet.

Use Reverse Psychology

A great example of this came from a highly intelligent girl who worked for us one summer as a student helper. Apparently, her mother had played an unusual trick that had worked perfectly – namely, to make sure that the cod liver oil was loudly proclaimed as delicious, but was not offered to the children, because it was an 'acquired taste – only for grown-ups'.

Alcohol was similarly locked away, but unlike the cod liver oil this was brought out for the whole family on rare special occasions, and a 'taste' of gin, whisky, rum and other spirits was always freely offered to the kids if they wanted to try it. 'No way!' 'Disgusting.' 'Yeeuucchh – how can you drink that stuff?!' were the general reactions of Jane and her sisters to the alcoholic drinks. The cod liver oil, however, they were not even allowed to try … although it was kept in a cupboard opened with a key that the children could reach.

Of course when the parents weren't around, it wasn't the alcohol cupboard that they 'raided' … it was the cupboard with the precious cod liver oil. Jane said, 'Actually, it didn't taste very good at all, but we all pretended it did, because we wanted to do what the adults did, and what they kept to themselves was obviously the most desirable thing. So we used to creep to the cupboard and steal ourselves a teaspoon or more on most days, whenever our parents weren't around. There were four of us, so it must have been very obvious to Mum that the level in the bottle went down much faster than expected. But she never let on until much later, when we all had a good laugh about it. To this day, I actually quite like the taste of cod liver oil, because of the associations.'

Very Important Note: I would actually say **'Don't do this with cod liver oil'** – because taking too much of this at once really could lead to vitamin A poisoning. Given its taste, drinking this to excess would probably be unlikely – as with Jane – but it's a risk not worth taking. Try the 'reverse psychology' with something safe if you're going to do it at all.

Summary

1. Make goals and review them periodically.
2. Dump the junk.
3. Get your child on board.
4. Relax and make it as easy for yourself as you can; enjoy the process.
5. Do things together.
6. Exercise with your child.
7. Eat a fresh and varied diet.
8. Establish good sleep patterns.
9. Keep a food, sleep and behaviour diary and look for telling patterns (bad and good).
10. Keep researching, learning and questioning, and enjoy your new life!

Make sure you have a good look through our recipes chapters, and enjoy making the delicious things there.

I look forward to hearing your stories.

With very best wishes for a healthier and happier future.

Dr Alexandra Richardson
Food and Behaviour Research
www.fabresearch.org
Registered charity number SC034604
Telephone: 0870 756 5960
email: info@fabresearch.org
snail mail: FAB Research, Unit 1, The Green House, Beechwood Business Park, Inverness IV2 3ED, Scotland.

chapter 12

recipes

ground rules, breakfasts, snacks and packed lunches

The main rule here is, *enjoy* yourself preparing and consuming your delicious and nutritious breakfasts, snacks and sweet treats, safe in the knowledge that your child is eating well. Just follow the guidelines and try out the tried-and-tested, easy and delicious recipes.

General Ground Rules

1. **Choose fresh, whole, unrefined foods** whenever possible, and try to make sure that the meals and snacks your child eats are made from these. Incidentally, this really can save you money.
2. **Plan ahead** whenever you can; it gets easier with practice. Make larger quantities than you need, and freeze spare batches. If you're making sandwiches for packed lunches, make a week's worth at once, and just take one lot out a day; by lunchtime they're defrosted.
3. **Shop little and often.** To feed your child better, it can help to go shopping more regularly (particularly for fresh fruit and vegetables). If this just isn't practical, there's no need to despair. Just a little planning will make all the difference – and can save you a great deal of money and time. Incidentally, canned or frozen fruit and vegetables can often be

'fresher' and more nutritious (as well as cheaper) than the ones you buy as 'fresh' – and they will give you much more flexibility.

Freezer Tips

- If you don't have a freezer – think about getting one. Instead of filling it with packaged, store-bought 'ready meals' and processed 'convenience' foods, use it to store foods, meals and snacks that you yourself have bought and prepared.
- It's much cheaper to make many simple meals in large quantities.
- Buy some good containers and labels, and store meal- or snack-sized portions.
- Perfect foods for freezing include most soups, casseroles, potato or vegetable mashes, pancakes, home-made breads, cakes, biscuits and flapjacks, fruit smoothies, purées and puddings … the list is almost endless.

4. **Involve your child in choosing and preparing foods.** If you take your child shopping, explain in advance why some foods and drinks are just NOT going to be on the menu (they contain harmful substances that can damage your health and make you feel bad; they are too expensive; there are better, tastier, healthier alternatives). Invite your child to help you find those alternatives.

- 'We're not going to have fizzy pop this week – because it's made of sugar, additives and water. Those drinks can rot your teeth, make you fat and make you feel bad. Let's find some fruit juices and drinks that don't do that. Can you help think of some?'
- It's very important to eat *at least* five portions of fruit and vegetables every day, so ask, 'Can you think of five fruits and vegetables that you might like? Let's see if we can make a list. Do you prefer sweetcorn or peas? Cherry tomatoes or cucumber? Apples or pears?' (The 'two-alternative forced choice' can be a very effective tactic. Don't take 'none' for an answer – and if your child won't agree to one of your suggested options, get them to use their imagination to think of an alternative that fits the same category.)

- Invite your child to help you with preparing meals and snacks.
- Fruit smoothies are usually a winner with children – especially if they get to choose what goes into these, and test their results.

This list shows you foods that most children can tolerate:

What's OK to Eat?

Even 'healthy' foods can sometimes cause allergy or intolerance reactions in some individuals (see Chapter 6). If you suspect this for major food groups such as milk and dairy products, or wheat and other grains, get expert help and check out the many good books and other resources with recipes avoiding these. The foods listed below are fine for most people.

- **Vegetables:** There are lots to choose from (veggies in the corn or potato family can cause problems for some individuals). Buy fresh vegetables in small quantities.
- **Fruit:** All except citrus fruits, or sometimes tomatoes (yes, they are fruits) rarely cause problems. Buy fresh fruit in small quantities and keep some in the fridge, placing in the fruit bowl when it begins to empty.
- **Nuts and seeds:** Almonds, walnuts, cashew nuts, hazelnuts; pumpkin, sesame and sunflower seeds, and pine nuts; nut and seed spreads like almond nut butter and tahini (made from sesame seeds). Peanut is the most common allergic trigger, though other nuts can also be problematic.
- **Legumes (beans):** Haricot, borlotti, chick peas
- **Cereals and grains:** Good alternatives to wheat can include oats, millet, quinoa, rice, pearl barley, kashi, amaranth and buckwheat (which isn't a member of the wheat family!).
- **Bread:** Rice bread, specially made gluten-free bread, rye bread, pitta bread (yeast-free), spelt bread (this is an older version of wheat and is fine for some who have wheat intolerance)
- **Flour:** Rice, chickpea, potato and buckwheat flour

- **Oils:** Cold-pressed extra-virgin olive oil, flax and walnut oils. Reduce/avoid sunflower, safflower and corn oils, as these can raise the omega-6 to omega-3 ratio, and don't cook with these (use saturated fats sparingly for this).
- **Fish and seafood:** The main direct source of important omega-3 fats, but some children may have adverse reactions to these.
- **Milk and dairy products:** Goats' milk or sheep's milk may be tolerated better than cows' milk by some people. Rice, almond, quinoa or soya milk are alternatives (although soya milk in particular may not suit some children).
- **Eggs:** Highly nutritious, but watch for possible sensitivities
- **Meats:** Choose low-fat, unprocessed meats – organic if possible.

5. **Don't be afraid to experiment.** Variety really is the spice of life! And a lack of variety is one the unhealthiest aspects of most people's diets. We're all creatures of habit, so when we find a few foods or particular meals that we like, we tend to eat them again, and again … and this is NOT healthy.

   If your child always eats pretty much the *same* foods every day, then (a) this reduces her chances of getting all the essential nutrients she needs, and (b) it can also exhaust her body's ability to digest them properly, increasing her chances of developing food allergies or intolerances. To give just one example, wheat and milk products (usually with sugar, 'bad fats' and additives) are often found in almost every meal or snack eaten by children whose diets rely on processed and 'convenience' foods.

   A healthy diet needs to be **VARIED** (as well as 'balanced' in the sense of providing appropriate proportions of the major 'macronutrient' groups: protein, fat and carbohydrate).

Breakfast

This really is the most important meal of the day. It should set your child up for the morning, providing both a steady source of energy and the essential nutrients needed for brain and body health. 'No time' for breakfast? You need to make some. Your child 'isn't hungry' in the mornings? (He would be if he had been out of bed and doing something for any length of time … ideally some exercise!)

Getting your child up earlier (and probably getting him to bed earlier, too) may be something you need to tackle first. In my experience, the children who are most 'untogether', infuriatingly slow, moody/irritable and 'not hungry' in the mornings are precisely the ones who can least afford to miss out on breakfast. However, none of us really can skip breakfast without paying a price, which includes functioning below par for the rest of the day, and probably bingeing on sugary foods later on. If you do this yourself, then you'll know exactly what I'm talking about. Take time to read the very well-written book *Only Fat People Skip Breakfast* by Lee Janogly; it's written for adults who want to lose weight, but describes very well what lack of breakfast can do to anyone.

What Sort of Breakfast Should You Give Your Child?

Traditional British Cooked Breakfast?

A fry-up of bacon, sausage, egg and fried bread (with or without mushrooms, tomatoes, baked beans and other options) is the traditional British cooked breakfast – often described as a 'heart attack on a plate'. Is it really that bad? As usual, that depends … It will have too much saturated fat for most people, and frying foods in hydrogenated and trans fats is good for no one; but this kind of breakfast would 'traditionally' have been eaten by workmen engaged in heavy physical labour (farmers, bricklayers, etc.) and only after they had already been up and working for an hour or two.

Even if your child were willing to eat this, the full array is unlikely to be a healthy option and you'd probably find it a pain to prepare on a regular basis. Some components might, however, be suitable. Try: eggs (scrambled or poached); bacon or good-quality sausage (grilled – or substitute with smoked salmon or soya/quorn if you want a vegetarian option); tomatoes (grilled or tinned); mushrooms (preferably grilled or steamed); toast (made from good, wholegrain flour); beans (they don't *have* to be in a sugary sauce, or you could make your own).

A Continental Breakfast?

Sadly, the modern so-called 'continental breakfast' is often a nutritional horror story, usually made up of lots of refined starch and sugar, along with heaps of saturated or hydrogenated fats (and of course caffeine, in the adult version). It usually consists of:

- a token glass of fruit juice (acceptable – but eating whole fruit, either in a fruit salad or as a fruit smoothie, would be more nutritious and less likely to upset blood sugar balance)
- refined, highly processed 'breakfast cereals'. These are expensive, and have usually been stripped of the dietary fibre and vital nutrients that whole grains should contain. They are typically laden with sugar (as much as 40 per cent in some cases) and also with artificial additives (some of which are often synthetic forms of just a few of the natural vitamins that were removed in the refining process! It's almost laughable …)
- white bread and toast with high-sugar jams (as above – foods that mainly consist of refined sugars and starches are 'empty calories')
- highly sweetened breads, pastries or croissants (and these sugary, fatty snacks should *not* be blamed on the Danish or French, whose traditional breakfast fare is actually very different indeed!).

This kind of breakfast is the sugar addict's dream – and nightmare. Although it may give your child (or you) an initial 'energy buzz', it is likely to set him up for mood swings, brain fog, irritability and fatigue within a short space of time (the initial 'high' will probably wear off just as he has got to school and supposedly settled into the first lessons of the day …).

The real, traditional 'continental breakfast' is in fact a totally different thing:

- fresh fruit salad, served with home-made yoghurt and sprinkled with nuts and seeds

- wholegrain breads, rolls and crispbreads, usually served with real butter (in moderation)
- an assortment of cold fish, meats and cheeses, accompanied with salad vegetables (tomatoes, cucumber, sweet peppers, etc.).

The Ideal Breakfast
At Least 1 or 2 Servings of Fruits and Vegetables
This provides vitamins, minerals, antioxidants and other essential nutrients + fibre and water)

Aim to find at least 7 different ways of getting fruits and vegetables into your child in the mornings. One for each day of the week! Be inventive – and remember, there are no rules about what is or is not a 'breakfast food'.

- A fruit smoothie is often the ideal way to do this. The variety of fruit and juice combinations you can use for these is endless – and other nutritious ingredients can often be smuggled into your child's diet this way. Examples include:
  - essential fatty acids (a tablespoon of flax oil, with or without evening primrose oil, or even some deodorized fish oils can be disguised in a jug of freshly made fruit smoothie, which can be kept in the fridge and consumed throughout the day)
  - yoghurt
  - protein powder (if all other methods of getting some protein into your child's breakfast fail, this can be a useful tactic that may not even be detected, although it will thicken the mixture).
- Tomatoes or mushrooms (preferably grilled or lightly sautéed and not fried to death) are a good accompaniment to many cooked breakfast foods – such as scrambled eggs or baked beans on toast.
- Don't be conservative – any vegetables your child will eat can be brought out at breakfast time – including coleslaw, or perhaps apple, carrot and cucumber sticks with a 'dip' that your child likes.
- The tomato sauce with a portion of baked beans can count towards the daily fruit and veg here – but the combination should only count as one serving. (The beans themselves are a useful source of protein, carbohydrate and fibre; look for low-sugar and low-salt varieties.)

Some Good-quality Protein

This provides the essential amino acids needed to build and repair brain and body tissues, and to make key enzymes and transmitter molecules. Protein is essential to the structure and function of brain and body, and its slow digestion helps maintain blood-sugar balance.

Please note, the portion of protein-rich food does not need to be huge; a matchbox-sized piece of cheese, or one egg, would do if your child is 'not hungry' in the mornings. Examples of proteins to use at breakfast are:

- eggs, cheese, meat, pâté, fish, and/or a glass of milk or some yoghurt
- scrambled eggs (with smoked salmon pieces if you can)
- smoked haddock/kippers. Some children love these – others hate them – but as with most foods, children often follow *your* likes and dislikes here.

A Good Serving of 'Slow-release' Carbohydrates

This provides energy (calories) for fuel. Unrefined wholegrains are ideal.

Wholegrain breads and unrefined, wholegrain cereals should be on offer – *not* the refined versions (which include many of the cereal bars that are packaged and promoted as though they are 'healthy options' when they often aren't). Look at the sugar content – in all of its possible disguises. Look at the fat content: how much is saturated fat or 'hydrogenated' vegetable oils? Avoid anything containing the latter. What artificial additives are in there? Check against the 'Dirty Dozen' (page 389).

Porridge oats are hard to beat, but get the real thing – not the expensive, processed, sweetened, dried, mushy varieties. As well as being suitable even for most people who avoid gluten-containing grains, oats are often hailed as a natural 'super-food'. They'll give your child a steady release of energy throughout the morning, provide a valuable source of dietary fibre to soothe and smooth digestion (and encourage the right kinds of gut flora), and the effects on cholesterol and other fats can be beneficial for heart health.

- Try soaking oats overnight in fruit juice (or water) – for a delicious breakfast that can be eaten hot or cold. Dried fruits can be soaked with it (apricots, raisins or dates will absorb the liquid and will soften and swell in the process, which can make them more palatable to children).

- Or prepare porridge the traditional way – using milk or water and heating it carefully to boiling point before allowing it to stand for a few minutes. To sweeten it, try some alternatives to refined sugar. Again, raisins, dates, sultanas or apricots can do the trick – or see if your child will try molasses for a treacly taste (and some vitamins and minerals), or try honey (not the cheap, more processed stuff).

Alternatively, choose other cereals that are wholegrain with as little added sugar as possible.

Try home-made flapjacks, muffins or fruit breads. These can be made in batches, stored in the freezer and very quickly reheated in the oven in the morning. They're delicious, nutritious and have no added ingredients that you don't know about. See below for recipes.

Essential Fatty Acids

Omega-3 fatty acids are much more likely to be lacking from your child's diet than omega-6 ones (which are found in meat and dairy products as well as grains and ordinary vegetable and seed oils). Ideally, you want to provide the omega-3 fats that your child's brain needs (EPA and DHA) in a ready-made form.

- A portion of fish – if your child will eat this – is ideal here. Try kedgeree, kippers, smoked salmon, roll-mop herring or sardines on toast. If not, good-quality supplements are another way to provide EPA and DHA directly.
- Flaxseeds can be sprinkled onto breakfasts (they swell up, so give your child plenty of water or juice when she gets up, or later, once the food has had time to 'settle'). Flax oil can be drizzled onto breakfasts or added to smoothies, and/or you can add walnuts or walnut oil.

Breakfast Menu Plan

- Fruit smoothies (next page)
- Boiled or poached eggs

- Scrambled eggs (with or without cheese) in a pitta envelope with some sliced tomato and a sprig of fresh basil leaves (grow them on your window sill). Add smoked or tinned salmon to give some extra essential fatty acids.
- Home-made muesli (below)
- Stuffed pancakes (next page)

Smoothies

This is a great one for children to help with. For the liquid part, use fruit (or even carrot) juice, water or natural yoghurt, or a combination of the three.

Bananas are tasty and thicken smoothies, so are a good ingredient to have. As I write this, my local market sell 4 pounds of loose bananas for £1 when they start to pack up.

There are no hard-and-fast rules here: Take whatever soft fruits you have to hand and try out different combinations. Pop the whole lot into a blender, and serve it as a 'milk shake' or smoothie.

You can add protein powder, wheat germ and ground flax, pumpkin and sunflower seeds, and a little walnut oil.

Throw the whole lot in a blender and whiz around for 10–20 seconds.

Here's a very easy one I've just made: it took me less than 2 minutes and was enough for four glasses:

- 140ml/¼ pt milk
- 2 small bananas
- 1 kiwi fruit

Incidentally, you can make vegetable ones as well:

- carrot and avocado (add caraway seeds)
- pepper, carrot, cucumber and tomato
- apple juice, watercress, cucumber and avocado.

Muesli

Make up a batch in advance: plenty of large oat flakes (add quinoa and millet flakes if you want); mixed nuts; chopped, dried fruit (apricots, raisins, etc.) and coconut flakes. When you serve it up, add a bit of natural yoghurt (sweetened with a teaspoon of honey if necessary) and a chopped, fresh apple.

Stuffed Pancakes

These are quick and easy to make, and children like to help toss the pancakes.

You can make up pancakes in advance and freeze them in batches by separating individual pancakes with greaseproof paper and putting in a freezer bag. They defrost pretty quickly.

For the pancake batter:
1 free-range egg

115g/4oz flour (use rice, corn or almond flour for a change or if your child's intolerant to gluten: the texture is different, but the taste is interesting!)

170ml/6 fl oz milk (use goats' milk or unsweetened rice or soya milk if your child has a casein intolerance; rice milk looks watery, but it tastes good). Or use fromage frais.

1 tsp baking powder

1 tsp powdered cinnamon or a few drops of vanilla essence

a tiny bit of lemon, lime or orange zest (optional)

1 tbsp extra-virgin olive oil, butter or ghee

For the filling:
Nut butter or grated cheese

Scrambled egg and salmon

Slightly warmed summer fruits

Stewed apple or stewed pears

- Beat the egg and then add in all the other ingredients except the oil.
- Lightly oil a heavy-based pan or griddle (if a child is helping you, an omelette pan is fine), pour in a ladle-full of the batter and cook until bubbles begin to appear on the top. Flip over and cook the other side for 1 minute.
- Slide onto a plate, place some filling in the middle, roll up and serve.

Add cinnamon or mixed spice to taste, and maybe some mixed chopped nuts. When you use sweeter fillings, add some lemon juice to bring down the glycaemic load of the pancakes and fillings, or have some fromage frais or Greek yoghurt to add protein.

Snacks

Avoid biscuits and go for something like the things listed here. Make sure your child remembers to chew them slowly and properly.

- A couple of oatcakes spread with cream cheese and topped with ham and gherkins, or smoked salmon.
- Celery, carrot, pepper and breadsticks dipped into hummus or pâté (fish, liver or vegetable). You can make these easily yourself, or buy them from the supermarket (look out for freshly made versions with no additives).
- An apple and a handful of nuts (almonds/walnuts/cashews).
- A handful taken from a container of pre-mixed seeds (pumpkin and sunflower), pine nuts (optional, as they are expensive), mixed nuts, chopped dried fruits (like apricots and raisins).
- Good-quality wholemeal bread spread with butter (optional), peanut butter (wholenut and no sugar), and/or blackcurrant or blueberry jam (use a 'fruit spread' as jams have added sugar, whereas fruit spreads just use fruit).
- Flesh of half an avocado spread onto pumpernickel bread. You could add a little paprika, pepper or lemon juice. If your child finds pumpernickel too strong in taste, use oat cakes.

- A banana smoothie (banana, kiwi and milk, blended together; add a spoon of protein powder to the mix, or have a piece of cheese at the same time).

Packed Lunches

A survey by the Food Standards Agency found that nine out of ten children's packed lunches contain too much saturated fat, sugar and salt. Don't let your child be a bad statistic! In your child's lunchbox, aim to include a non-sugary drink (water or cold herbal tea), a portion of protein (meat, fish, beans), a portion of starch (good bread, pasta, rice, potatoes), one or more portions of vegetables and a portion of fruit.

One of my friends makes up a week's worth of sandwiches at once and freezes them (this doesn't work with tomatoes, cucumber or lettuce!), taking out one lot a day. By lunchtime they're defrosted – good on a summer's day, too, for keeping them cool. It's best to put packed lunches in an insulated lunch-bag with an ice block (the plastic, gel-filled ones that freeze), especially in the summer.

Sandwiches

Use pitta, wholemeal, granary, ciabatta, focaccia or sour dough breads, tortilla wraps, or large lettuce leaves for the outside. Spread with olive oil, butter (or a home-made 50:50 spread), or mayonnaise.

For the fillings:
- ham (off the bone) and tomato
- tuna and sweetcorn mayo (home-made if you can)
- egg and cress (moistened with mayo if you want)
- fish, vegetable or meat/liver pâté, or hummus
- peanut butter (or almond or cashew nut) and dates or banana or dark fruit spread

- cheese and apple
- bits of lettuce, tomato, apple, ham, cheese and hummus (best in pitta or a wrap)
- avocado and lettuce

Green and Pasta Salads

Make up a container of mixed vegetable or wholemeal pasta salad (more ideas in the next chapter); if you choose the latter, add some peas, peppers and sweetcorn. Avoid rice, as if it's not kept well chilled and eaten promptly it can cause food poisoning.

Other Savouries

Pack a pot of dip and add some crackers (oat cakes are good), home-made bread sticks, and sticks of raw celery (yes, kids can like it a lot!), carrot, cucumber, cucumber and red/yellow pepper. Also try:

- cherry tomatoes
- some small home-made quiches and pizzas that have a lot more topping than bottom
- a small packet of unsalted nuts (vary the type) mixed with pumpkin and sunflower seeds. Pine nuts are good too, if you can afford them.
- cheese pieces
- vegetable juice
- hard-boiled egg

Sweet Bits

- a whole fruit (vary this) or a fruit salad (fresh or tinned in juice); you can toss chopped fruit like apples in a bit of lemon juice to stop them browning
- home-made fruit smoothie
- malt loaf (if you make your own, add cinnamon) and butter, or fruit cake

- fruit bar (see recipe on page 346) or flapjack (better to make your own, so you know what's gone into them)
- natural yoghurt with a bit of honey and chopped nuts, or stir in some dark fruit spread (rather than 'jam')
- dried fruit (go easy on this, as the sugar is concentrated)

Start slowly, and over time your child should begin to want the sweet stuff less and less.

chapter 13

recipes

light meals and sweet stuff

As with breakfast, the same general guidelines apply to light meals and lunches: Include protein, complex carbohydrates and essential fatty acids. Have plenty of vegetables, and if you want to go for a pastie, make your own; at least that way you know what's in it.

Soups

Make use of soups for nutritious and delicious meals at all times of the year; they're a great way of getting vegetables and (and some fruit) down children. For a more filling meal you can add cheese, rice, pasta, sweetcorn or tinned beans. Soups freeze well and can be thawed and reheated quickly. Keep some potato cakes or pitta bread in the freezer, too. Whip them out to defrost at the same time and have them with the soup.

Soups are not in the slightest bit complicated and are fun and tasty to make. That said, if you're stuck for time, try some of the fresh ready-made soups that use only good ingredients, and no nasty additives. (Avoid the cheaper supermarket versions: read the labels and you'll see why.)

Follow these rules and you'll be fine.

1. Put in the flavour bits first and fry them gently: onions, garlic and herbs. Add bits of chicken or fish at this stage of you're using them.
2. If you're planning on a thicker soup, stir in a bit of flour.
3. Add fish, chicken or vegetable stock and keep stirring until the flour is incorporated if you've used it.
4. Bring to the boil, add chopped vegetables and simmer for a while.

If you find it's too salty, add a whole potato to cook with it for a while: the potato will absorb much of the salt. Just discard it at the end.

Try these variations:

- leek, bacon and potato
- tomato, pepper and onion
- broccoli, celery and Stilton
- carrot and orange or apricot (perhaps with ginger or cinnamon?).

To Make Stock

If you can make your own stock, that's better, as bouillon cubes are very salty. Home-made stock is cheap and easy to make and very nutritious. It smells wonderful, too. You use leftovers to make stock before throwing them out. You can also use stock as a base for a casserole/hot pot.

VEGETABLE STOCK

You can use all sorts of vegetables, but unless you're making cauliflower, broccoli or cabbage soup, avoid these as they make a strong-tasting stock. Use peel, corn cobs, vegetables that you don't feel you'll use before they get old. Potatoes (white and sweet), celery, carrots, squash, onions, parsley, green vegetables, shallots, leeks, peppers, herbs, peppercorns, bay leaf ... whatever you have.

Use about one part solids to one part water, and make sure the solids are covered. Bring to the boil and simmer for an hour or so. Cool and strain.

FISH STOCK

Use cheap white fish scraps, trimmings and bones. You can even add crab, lobster and shrimp shells. Have about 500g (1 pound) of scraps to 1¼ litres (2 pints) of water. You can use a glass of dry white wine as part of the liquid content.

- Gently sauté two chopped onions and garlic (and maybe celery) until they're soft.
- Add the scraps and water, and simmer for about an hour. Periodically skim off any foam during cooking, then cool and strain.

POULTRY STOCK

Use the poultry bones left over from your roasts, or buy cheap parts. Include some vegetables such as garlic, onion, carrot, celery and black peppercorns. If you want a darker and richer stock, roast the meat bits, bones and vegetables at 230°C/450°F/Gas Mark 8 for about 45 minutes before adding them to the water (make sure the solids are covered). While your stock is cooking, foam will form, which you need to skim off with a spoon. After cooking, strain the stock and discard the solid bits.

RED MEAT STOCK

This uses a similar method to the poultry stock: use roasted meat and vegetables for a rich flavour. You'll need to simmer it for closer to 4 hours, stirring occasionally, and adding water if the bits aren't covered. Strain, chill and take off the fat layer that forms.

Reduce stock (simmer it) by half for easier freezing. Add water when you use it. Meat stock, when cooling, will form a layer of fat – either skim it off or use it as a handy seal when freezing the stock.

Here are two soup recipes supplied for us by Ian Smith. See his site www.supper-tonight.co.uk for more.

Minestrone

A favourite with the ready-meal industry, but out of a tin really bears little resemblance to the real thing. And, to be authentic, it should be made with rice, not pasta; useful if you need to be gluten free. And please, please promise me you will not use the ready-grated Parmesan cheese sold in little tubs.

150g/5oz dried borlotti beans

200g/7oz Savoy cabbage

50g/2oz unsalted butter

2 tbsp olive oil

2 medium-sized onions, diced

50g/2oz pancetta, diced

2 medium-sized carrots, diced

2 celery stalks, finely sliced

200g/7oz ripe tomatoes, skinned and deseeded

2L/3 pints 10fl oz stock

300g/11oz potatoes, cut into chunks

100g/4oz French green beans, diced

100g/4oz peas

150g/5oz short-grain Italian rice

salt and pepper

50g/2oz Parmesan cheese, freshly grated

- You'll need to soak the borlotti beans for about 12 hours or overnight, and the cooking time is around 3 hours, so a little forward planning is needed for this recipe. After you have soaked the beans, drain them and give them a rinse in fresh water.
- Finely shred the Savoy cabbage leaves. The best way to do this is to cut out the stem from the centre, roll the leaves so they resemble a cigar, then slice them across, as finely as you can.
- Put your saucepan on a low heat, melt the butter in it and add the olive oil, onions and pancetta. Sauté gently until the onions are soft, but do not brown – 10 minutes, say, before adding the carrots and celery.
- Now add the borlotti beans, coat them well in the oil and butter; cook for about another 5 minutes, and then add the tomatoes. Cook slowly while stirring so that the tomatoes break down to form a sauce. Add a dash of your stock to help it along.
- Now add the rest of the stock. (Traditionally you would use a meat or beef stock, but if you need to, you can use vegetable stock.) Bring to a simmer, turn down the heat, put the lid on the pan and leave for around 2 hours.
- Add the potatoes, green beans and peas, put the lid back on and continue to simmer for about 40 minutes.
- After that you need to mash the potatoes to thicken the soup. Either take them out of the soup and mash them in a bowl, or crush them against the sides of the pan.
- Add the rice: Arborio will do, or Vialone Nano, if you can find it.
- Simmer again until the rice is cooked, 10 to 15 minutes.
- Check the seasoning, add salt and freshly ground black pepper to taste.
- Stir in the Parmesan and serve.

Gazpacho (Cold Tomato Soup) Serves 4

Very simple and very refreshing on a hot day. (Not that we get too many hot days where we live! Whatever happened to global warming?) It is very easy to make an indifferent gazpacho by not using the best ingredients. You must use good extra-virgin olive oil, good sherry vinegar and ripe, sweet, good-flavoured tomatoes.

2 slices white bread, slightly stale
2 cloves garlic
1kg/2¼lb tomatoes
½ medium cucumber, peeled and sliced
1 small onion, grated
1 green pepper, deseeded and sliced
20ml/3 dessertspoons sherry vinegar
30ml/2 tbsp olive oil
salt and freshly ground black pepper

- You will need a food processor for this recipe.
- Cut the crusts off the bread slices and roughly crumble it. If you only have fresh bread, not stale, then cut the crusts off as before and whiz it up in the food processor to make breadcrumbs, and the take them out until later.
- Sprinkle a pinch of salt on your chopping board and crush the cloves of garlic on the board with the back of a heavy knife. Keep crushing it until it becomes a paste. The salt helps as a sort of abrasive.
- Put the peeled and sliced vegetables into your food processor and give them a good blitz.
- Add the breadcrumbs and blitz the gazpacho some more.
- Add the sherry vinegar, olive oil and salt and pepper to taste. Blitz it again.
- At this point the gazpacho will still be fairly chunky, so rub about three-quarters of it through a sieve to give it a finer texture. Mix it back in, pour all the gazpacho into a suitable container or containers and chill in your fridge for at least 2 hours.
- You can serve it in bowls as a soup, or in glasses as a drink.

Pasta

Pasta is available in wheat, corn, buckwheat, seaweed and rice versions, and is great when tossed with a tablespoon of pesto and a dash of walnut oil. Stir in some vegetables (peas can be cooked with the pasta in the last few minutes) and top with Parmesan or any other cheese. (For a tasty and nutritious tomato sauce recipe, see next page.)

Pancakes

These are great made with a savoury filling such as nut butter or cheese and tomato. See page 328 for recipe.

Parcels

Fish parcels are quick and easy to make, and provide lots of vital nutrients.

- Place fish fillets (or whole fish) on a plate-sized piece of foil.
- Squirt with lemon or lime juice, and add some mashed-up or sliced garlic, slivered almonds, herbs and ribbons of carrots and courgettes.
- Close up the foil and cook for 10–15 minutes at 175°C/340°F/Gas Mark 4.
- For a white sauce recipe to accompany the fish, see next page.

Sauces

To accompany light meals, learn to use quick and easy sauces and marinades to add a nutritious zing.

Sauces are so easy to make, especially ones for pasta. Much of what you need will be in your cupboard or fridge anyway. Once again, just experiment.

Tomato Sauce

- Gently fry some finely chopped onion in some olive oil (or butter or ghee).
- When they've softened, add some crushed garlic and shredded basil and oregano leaves and stir a bit.
- Tip in a tin of chopped tomatoes (or a carton of passata), and add a squidge of tomato purée – sun-dried if you can – and simmer for 10–30 minutes, depending on how thick you want it.
- If you forget about it and it thickens too far, just add some water.
- For a variation, add courgettes or peppers or spinach.
- A creamy tomato sauce can be made by gently frying the onions in butter, adding a tin of chopped tomatoes, simmering for 10 minutes then stirring in three lightly beaten eggs.

White Sauce

- This easy-to-make sauce is thin but tasty.
- Simply mix together some crème fraîche (full-fat, as fat reduced has additives), chopped basil, ground black pepper, the juice of half a lemon and some Parmesan shavings.

Marinades

Marinades can tenderize and add flavour to your fish, meat or vegetables. Experiment: they rarely go wrong.

Use an oil-based marinade for low-fat foods (poultry and white fish, and lean red meat) as this helps keep them moist while cooking.

Game and oily fish are best marinated in wine- or vinegar-based mixtures, as the acid starts tenderizing the meat before cooking.

You can use any of these for vegetables, or do something simple like combining oyster sauce with a smidgen of honey.

Oil-Based Marinade

- Take some olive oil (with a bit of walnut oil if you want an interesting variation) and mix in crushed garlic and shredded herbs.
- Add some chopped chilli for a kick.

Wine- or Vinegar-Based Marinade

- To wine or vinegar, add ingredients such as plain yoghurt, herbs, chopped or puréed tomatoes, and black pepper.
- A mixture of yoghurt, lemon juice and rosemary or thyme also makes a lovely marinade.

Eggs

Use the breakfast ideas (see previous chapter), and serve with salad or other vegetables. Or make an omelette. Try this recipe:

Ian Smith's Tortilla Española (Spanish Omelette)

Should you order a Spanish omelette in England, you will probably get a vegetable omelette with some potato in it. Not that we're complaining; it can be very good. But the real thing is hearty comfort food – for keeping the workers going. Here is our version with potatoes and onion. You can eat it hot or cold.

500g/1lb waxy potatoes
280ml/10fl oz olive oil
100g/4oz onion, thinly sliced
4 eggs
salt

- Peel the potatoes and cut them into chunks, about an inch (2.5 cm) thick.
- Put the olive oil in a saucepan and warm it over a moderate heat. Add the potatoes and onion and cook very gently for about 20 minutes until the potatoes are cooked. The idea here is to simmer them gently in the oil. You do not want to fry them. Stir them from time to time to prevent them from sticking together.
- When the potatoes are ready, pour off the oil and reserve it. Beat the eggs together with some salt, then add the potatoes and onion to the egg mixture.
- Heat 2 tablespoons of the reserved oil in your frying pan over a high heat, and add the egg/potato mixture. Turn the heat down to moderate and fry for about 4 minutes. The underside will turn golden brown, and all the egg should be just about set.
- Now for the slightly tricky bit. You need a plate the same size as the frying pan. Put the plate on the frying pan and turn the pan and plate over (don't worry: it's easier than it sounds!). Put the pan back on the heat. You should now have a plate with your tortilla on it, golden brown side up. Slide the tortilla off the plate back into the frying pan, and fry for another 3 to 4 minutes, or until it is golden brown on both sides.

- If you can bear to, let the tortilla stand to cool on a plate for about 15 minutes, or leave to go completely cold. We never can – it gets eaten straight away!

Salads

These go down well in summer. Bagged salads lose some of their nutrients, so go for chopping up your own if you can – but if you're in a hurry …

For a crunchy and nutritious salad, chop up tomatoes (or use whole cherry ones), cucumber, peppers, apple, dates and cheese, and also add sunflower and pumpkin seeds, pine nuts, fresh leafy herbs and watercress. Maybe add some chopped ham (off the bone, not reformed gunk). Toss in a dressing made from olive or walnut oil and balsamic vinegar (ordinary or raspberry). Serve in warmed-up pitta bread or with some boiled new potatoes and fish.

Or, for a Greek version:

Ian Smith's Greek Salad

This appears on all the Greek menus we have ever seen, and can be used as a side salad, a starter or a meal on its own. When eaten in Greece, the one thing that is constant is that the tomatoes appear to have been chopped by a blindfolded chef with an axe. You will know what we mean if you have been there.

So here is our version. Best eaten under a blue sky on a terrace overlooking the Mediterranean, if you can arrange it!

It's not really possible to be exact about quantities with this salad. How big is a medium onion? Do try and use good-flavoured tomatoes if you can. The vine tomatoes which have appeared recently seem very good. And if you can find them, kalamata olives are the best. Stone them and leave them whole.

1 small cucumber
3 medium-sized tomatoes
1 medium-sized onion
1 small green pepper
handful of black olives
salt
ground black pepper
2 tsp dried oregano
200g/8oz feta cheese

For the dressing:
olive oil
red wine vinegar

- Wash the cucumber and then slice off all the green skin.
- Roughly chop the tomatoes. Not blindfolded, please.
- Slice the cucumber, onion and pepper into rings.
- Put these together with the olives into a bowl and sprinkle to taste with seasonings and oregano.
- To make the dressing, mix 5 parts olive oil to 1 part red wine vinegar, pour over the salad and mix.
- Put the feta cheese on top in one piece. Sprinkle on a little more olive oil and oregano, then leave for 15 minutes so the flavours develop.

Sweet Stuff: Fruit Bars, Desserts and Cakes

Try to make desserts an occasional thing rather than something that appears every day. If you need to use sugar, try to reduce the amount and maybe add more fruit instead; you will soon get used to the new, less sweet taste. Experiment. Use brown sugar or molasses instead of white table or caster sugar if you can, but NEVER use sugar substitutes like aspartame.

If you do need to buy sweets and puddings rather than making your own, make sure they're from a source that guarantees no processed fats or additives.

A good squeeze of lemon juice will decrease the glycaemic value of a pud, as will the addition of cinnamon. Use them liberally!

Fruit Bars

Easy, and don't necessarily need cooking.

85g/3oz rolled oats
85g/3oz raisins
85g/3oz stoned dates
85g/3oz dried apricots
85g/3oz walnuts
85g/3oz desiccated coconut
2 tbsp ground pumpkin seeds
2 tbsp ground sunflower seeds
2 tbsp ground sesame seeds
2 tbsp ground flaxseeds

- Pop the lot in a blender (set for coarse cut) and mince. Work the mix together until it binds and form into small bars. If you need liquid, add a couple of tablespoons of water or mint tea.
- Refrigerate for an hour, then keep in an air-tight container (if there are any left …).
- For a cooked version, soaking the fruits for a few hours (doing this over a low heat speeds up the process), mix with a couple of tablespoons of water/fruit juice or mint tea, and add 30–55g (1–2oz) coarsely ground mixed nuts. If this mixture won't hold together, add in a beaten egg. Form into bars, brush with a little olive oil, and bake at 180°C/350°F/Gas Mark 4 for 20 mins or so (but check after 10).

Cocoa (or Carob) Delight

Serves 4

Quick, easy, nutritious and delicious.

85g/3oz ground up cashew nuts

30g/1oz ground almonds

140ml/¹/₄ pint rice milk

3 medium-sized bananas (slightly green bananas have a lower glycaemic index than browning ones)

1 tsp ground cinnamon

¹/₂ tsp nutmeg (optional)

1 tbsp cocoa or carob powder

- Pop the whole lot into a blender (maybe in two parts) and whiz for 2 minutes.
- Spoon into four small dishes.
- If you want, decorate with some split almonds. You can lightly toast them in a dry, heavy pan – but be careful you don't burn them.

Baked Apples

Serves 4

Easy to prepare, you can serve these with a bit of cheese or a dollop of
fromage frais so you get some protein as well. Protein helps slow down the
rate of absorption of sugar into the blood. That said, don't have apples (or
any fruits if you can help it) after a protein-heavy meal. This is because the
protein sits in your stomach for a while; fruit, however, digests more
quickly, and it can start fermenting on your stomach before it gets out.
That's why melon (sprinkled with ground cinnamon) is often used as a
starter rather than a pud.

4 crisp eating apples

grated rind (zest) of a lemon or half an orange

juice of the lemon or half orange

1/4 tsp powdered ginger or 1/2 tsp grated fresh ginger

1/2 tsp mixed spice

55g/2oz dried mixed fruit or finely chopped dried apricots (use organic if you
   can)

55g/2oz chopped mixed nuts

30g/1oz pumpkin seeds, ground or chopped finely in a blender

- Preheat oven to 200°C/400°F/Gas Mark 6.
- Core the apples with a sharp knife or corer and place them in a deep
  baking tray lined with oiled foil or greaseproof paper.
- Combine all the other ingredients and stuff the apples with the mix.
  You'll have some left over, so sprinkle it around the base of the apples.
- Cook in the middle of the oven until softish rather than very soft – about
  half an hour.

Fruit Crumble

This can be made all year round, using whatever fruits are in season; in the summer it's nice cold. I've chosen mostly dark fruits, as they're high in nutrients. Serve with a dollop of Greek yoghurt, fromage frais, home-made ice-cream or cream (not the synthetic type), as their protein helps slow down the absorption of sugar into the body.

For the filling:
Use 500–700g (1–1½lb) fruit such as blackberries, blueberries, blackcurrants and sliced par-cooked apples or pears. I find it handy to keep a bag of summer fruits in the freezer so I can whip them out when needed.
cinnamon or nutmeg to taste (optional)

For the topping:
55g/2oz ground almonds
30g/1oz ground rice (or rice flour if you can't get the ground stuff)
55g/2oz oats (steel rolled rather than the quick cook variety)
handful of seeds (like pumpkin and sunflower), coarsely ground

- Preheat oven to 200°C/400°F/Gas Mark 6.
- Cook the fruit gently in a pan until it begins to soften. You don't need to add sugar.
- In the meantime, blend the topping ingredients.
- Spoon the fruit into a deep dish, adding some cinnamon and nutmeg if you like. Gently spread the topping over the fruit.
- Place in the middle of the oven for about half an hour.
- Serve hot (but let it cool for 5–10 minutes first) or cold.

If you're finding it hard to come off the sweet stuff, add some very finely chopped dried organic apricots or dates to the topping.

Carrot Cake

1 free-range egg

115g/4oz wheat, rice or millet flour (for a richer mix, use almond flour)

30g/1oz finely ground oats

170g/6oz grated carrots and or courgette (grate them finely)

3–4 tsp baking powder

1 tsp cinnamon, nutmeg or mixed spice (use whatever you have to hand)

1 tbsp extra-virgin olive oil

90ml/3fl oz water (slightly warm is better)

- Preheat oven to 200°C/400°F/Gas Mark 6.
- If you're doing this by hand, beat the egg first and then add the rest of the ingredients, and mix well. If you have a food processor, you can pop the lot in all at once.
- Grease a small loaf tin with olive oil (or use greaseproof paper) and pour the mixture in.
- Place in the middle of the oven for about 35 minutes (check it's just going brown and feels firm to the touch).
- Serve in slices, hot or cold. I like to heat up a slice under the grill having first sprinkled it with cinnamon. If you're not trying to watch your weight, spread with a bit of butter or drizzle some walnut oil on.

If there's any left, make sure you eat it within a couple of days (remember, there are no preservatives in this!); store it in an airtight container.

Ice-Cream

The only real effort here is remembering to stir the setting ice-cream halfway through the freezing process (or you end up with large crystals in it). If you or your family are big ice-cream fans, it might also be worth investing in an ice-cream maker which does a lot of the stirring work for you! You also need to get the ice-cream out at least 30 minutes before serving it – as it has no nasty additives, you don't get soft scoop!

2 large ripe mangoes or equivalent volume of soft dark fruits
water
570ml/1 pint natural yoghurt
concentrated apple juice to taste (optional)

- Liquidize the fruit along with a few tablespoons of water.
- Push it through a sieve to get rid of bits, then add the yoghurt. If it's not quite sweet enough, add a little concentrated apple juice.
- Place the mixture in the freezer and, when it's icy and half frozen (about 2 hours), take it out, whisk or process it well, and pop it back in to freeze. Repeat this process when it's almost solid.

chapter 14

recipes

main meals

Paprika Pork

500g/1¼lb lean pork fillet
olive oil for frying
3 peppers (a mix if you can – choose from red, yellow, green or orange)
tomato sauce
2 heaped tbsp paprika
300ml/1½ pints water
black pepper to taste

- Cut the pork into strips (about adult finger size) and fry in olive oil on a medium heat for 5 minutes.
- Add the peppers, tomato sauce, paprika and water, and black pepper if you want it.
- Simmer for 30 minutes.
- Serve with new potatoes and some green vegetables.

If you have time, grill or roast the peppers for 20 minutes or so, as this brings out their sweetness. For the tomato sauce, use a jar (look out for additives), or make your own (see page 340). The paprika is mild, so your children should enjoy the taste. If you want the sauce to be a little sweeter, add a scant tbsp of apricot spread/jam.

Casserole/Hot Pot

You can use quorn/pork/lamb/kidneys/chicken/turkey for this – whatever you have in the fridge. Likewise, vary the vegetables with the season. Use what you have.

675g/1¹/₂lb lean meat, cut into small chunks or fingers
2 large carrots, peeled and sliced (in discs or fingers)
1 small turnip, peeled and sliced
2 large onions, peeled and sliced
1 leek or 2 courgettes, sliced
seasonings
450g/1lb potatoes, sliced (peeled if you want)
25g/1oz butter
up to 450ml/³/₄ pt water or stock

- Preheat oven to 200°C/400°F/Gas Mark 6.
- Layer the meat and all the vegetables except the potatoes into a casserole pot.
- Season to taste (pepper, herbs).
- Place the sliced potatoes in a layer over the top, and dot the butter over. If you don't want the potato topping, use mashed swede or turnip instead. You can also put the potatoes into the casserole itself (but cut into cubes first).
- Cover with the water or stock and cook in the oven for about 2 hours.

A slow cooker would be a great investment if you tend to have more time/energy in the morning: stick the food in (a recipe book comes with most slow cookers), go out for a few hours, and feed the hungry hordes when they come in or when it suits you.

Easy Roast Meal

The Meat

A roast chicken takes about 1½ hours to cook, and 10 minutes to stand. It does vary with size, though: Allow 20 minutes of cooking time per lb (45 minutes per kg) plus an extra 20 minutes.

Make a couple of nicks in the skin and pop some garlic cloves and/or stuffing under the skin, and squirt in a bit of lime or lemon juice, too.

Baste your chicken with butter or olive oil, and rebaste a couple of times during cooking, using the juices and fat that have run into the roasting tin.

Make sure the juices run clear (stick a thin, sharp knife in) before you take it out of the oven.

The Vegetables

Choose from potatoes (wedges), leeks, shallots, onions, peppers, broccoli, cauliflower, parsnips, squash, pumpkin, carrots, aubergines, courgettes, peppers, baby sweetcorn, sugar snaps. If you have a sprig or two of rosemary, pop that in too for a delicious flavour and smell. While the chicken is roasting, cut them up into chunks and toss them in olive oil and herbs. Allow about 45 minutes for them to cook.

Burgers

You can make these from fish, pork, chicken, turkey, beef, quorn or beans. I find it's easier and less messy to use a burger maker (cook shops sell them). Use greaseproof paper between the burgers, put in a bag and freeze, and use when you want.

Burgers can be used as a main meal – served with rice, salad and a variety of vegetables, rather than in a bun.

There's no hard-and-fast recipe – experiment with what you have around. If your burger mix is too dry, add a teaspoon of olive oil or a beaten egg to bind the mix. Use herbs that you have to hand, remembering that you need half as much dried herbs as fresh.

If you don't have a mincer, buy minced meat, as finely chopped meat isn't the same. Go for the leaner varieties.

Meat Burgers

1 medium onion, finely chopped
450g/1lb lean meat, minced
a large handful of breadcrumbs
fresh herbs, chopped
1 inch (2.5cm) root ginger, grated (optional)
olive oil

- Mix all the ingredients except the oil together in a large bowl. Divide into four, and make a pattie from each portion. Refrigerate for an hour, brush with oil and then cook slowly (grilling or frying), turning often.

Vegeburgers

The great thing is, these are so easy. If a mixture gets too gloopy, add some more beans/lentils/breadcrumbs, and if it's too dry, add egg or oil. If you don't have time to cook beans and lentils, use tinned varieties.

For the bulk, choose from: lentils, any cooked beans, chickpeas, peas, sweetcorn, tofu, breadcrumbs, toasted buckwheat, carrot, walnuts, mushrooms.

To 'season', choose from: onions, miso, soy sauce, ginger, garlic, ground seeds, grated vegetables, chilli, black pepper.

Choose 1–3 items from the 'bulk' list, and mash them up with some items from the 'seasoning' list. Two tins of beans or lentils is a good place to start for 4–6 burgers. Form into patties, brush lightly with olive oil, coat with oat flakes if you want, and cook slowly (grilling or frying).

You might find it easier to use one of those wire barbecue food holders (designed for fish and crumbly foods).

Top with some cheese and grill lightly.

Meat Fingers

Never mind the shop-bought 'nuggets' that have very iffy ingredients – it's just as easy, cheaper and more nutritious to make your own.

- Slice 3–4 fillets of chicken, turkey, pork or beef into fingers (narrower for the beef).
- Dip into a mix of beaten egg and pepper (optional).
- Dunk into some seasoned flour (optional).
- Fry on a high heat for a few seconds either side to sear the meat, and then on a low–medium heat for 5–10 minutes in olive oil, turning frequently.

Now, you could:

- Serve with some stir-fried vegetables (buy ready made, or use thinly sliced carrots and courgettes, and mangetout, baby sweetcorn, sprouting broccoli and mushrooms).
- When the meat has finished cooking, make it into a stroganoff: On a very low heat, stir in some cream (or 50:50 cream: crème fraîche) and mushrooms that you've previously sliced and fried gently in butter. Serve with green vegetables and quinoa (which only takes about 10 minutes in all to cook).
- Pander to your child's whims if he has a burning desire for baked beans, and add them to the plate instead (and also some green veg if you can). Maybe include some roasted potato wedges (yours, not the shop-bought ones). The occasional tin of baked beans isn't going to hurt – just avoid the ones that contain lots of salt, aspartame and the like.

Comforting Pasta

You can make this into a whole meal, or serve it with a tomato and feta salad, or a range of green vegetables (go for watery rather than starchy ones, to balance the pasta). Make them while the pasta is cooking, so that the whole meal preparation and cooking shouldn't take more than 20 minutes. If wheat intolerance is a problem, use corn or rice pasta – but cook it for a couple of minutes less than it says on the packet.

350g/12oz dried pasta – wholemeal if you can
2–3 eggs
peas or spinach
400-g/14-oz tinned fish
tinned sweetcorn
small handful of Cheddar, or blue cheese or Parmesan
one tub (250g/9oz) mascarpone or crème fraîche

- Cook up the pasta of your choice (about 10 minutes).
- Add the eggs (still in their shells) to the cooking pasta so they hard-boil.
- Add the peas or spinach about 3 minutes before the end of the cooking time.
- While the pasta is cooking, flake some tinned fish, drain a can of sweetcorn, and grate the cheese.
- Drain the pasta, putting the hard-boiled eggs and peas/spinach to one side. Rinse the pasta with boiling water.
- Shell and chop the eggs up into chunks.
- Mix all ingredients together, except for the cheese.
- Put into an ovenproof pot, top with the cheese, and grill until the cheese is beginning to brown.

The recipes that follow were kindly supplied for this book by Ian Smith. His recipes – written in his own inimitable style – are proof that you can make nutritious and interesting meals easily. You use a variety of ingredients for each dish, and once you have them, the making of the dishes is very straightforward. You can see plenty more of Ian's delicious and easy-to-make meals from around the world on www.supper-tonight.co.uk.

Salad Niçoise

It's very difficult to give a recipe for salad Niçoise, as there are many variations. As a general rule, it should contain anchovy fillets, eggs, lettuce, tuna and black olives – preferably the small French Niçoise olives. It's also not easy to give quantities, but as a general guide, use at least one egg and four anchovy fillets per person.

new potatoes

eggs

1 tuna steak

olive oil

lettuce

tomatoes

black olives

anchovy fillets

For the dressing:

olive oil

white wine vinegar

clove garlic, chopped

- Boil the potatoes first, as they will take the longest to cook, 15 to 20 minutes say. Dice them when they are cooked.
- While this is going on, put the eggs in a pan with cold water, bring to the boil and simmer for 5 minutes or so. We want the eggs to have slightly soft yolks.
- Sear the tuna in a hot pan with some oil, on both sides for about 2 to 4 minutes each side, depending on how thick the steak is. When it has cooled, cut it into strips.
- Chop the lettuce and tomatoes.
- Combine the lettuce with the tomatoes and black olives.
- Make a dressing with 5 parts olive oil to 1 part vinegar and the clove of garlic.
- Mix the salad with the dressing, and then arrange all the other ingredients artistically!

Patatas o lo Pobre
(Poor Man's Potatoes)

There is nothing poor about this recipe. A classic Spanish recipe for potatoes, there are, of course, many variations. You could use green instead of red pepper, and we do know of one very famous chef who omits the pepper altogether. Whatever ingredients you use, it is the slow cooking of vegetables in olive oil which makes this so good.

The cooking time may be a bit lengthy, but it doesn't need much attention. In fact, we wrote this recipe down while cooking it. As we write, we've just put the pepper in, and it's starting to smell absolutely wonderful.

170ml/6fl oz olive oil
1 large Spanish onion
salt
1 red pepper
2 cloves garlic
2 bay leaves
340g/12oz waxy potatoes
freshly ground black pepper

- Cover the bottom of a large saucepan with a bit of the olive oil. Thinly slice the onion, and when the olive oil is warm add the onion together with a pinch of salt. Simmer very slowly, stirring occasionally, until the onion turns golden – about 20 minutes.
- While the onions are cooking, take out the seeds from the pepper and roughly chop it.
- Slice the garlic thickly.
- When the onions are golden, add the pepper and garlic, together with the bay leaves.
- Continue simmering until the pepper is soft, about 15 minutes.
- After the pepper has been cooking for about 10 minutes, peel the potatoes, cut them into chunks and sprinkle them with a little salt. Leave for about 5 minutes.
- When the pepper has softened, add the rest of the olive oil, and when it has warmed up, add the potatoes. Keep simmering gently, stirring occasionally, until the potatoes are tender, about 15 to 20 minutes.
- When the potatoes are cooked, drain everything in a sieve, keeping the olive oil aside to use again in another recipe (bearing in mind it will be flavoured).
- Check the seasoning, add salt if necessary, and a little freshly ground black pepper, and serve.

Paella

Paella takes its name from the two-handled pan in which it is cooked. If you don't have one, use a large frying pan.

There are many variations of this classic Spanish recipe; basically you can use whatever you want. In a similar way to risotto, the secret of a good paella is good stock and the appropriate rice. We are using Arborio rice and fish stock.

1.2L/2 pints fish stock
450g/1lb mussels
2 wine glasses dry white wine
450g/1lb fresh cockles
olive oil
100g/3½oz pork, cubed
100g/3½oz chicken breast, cubed
400g/14oz onions, chopped
1 heaped tbsp garlic, chopped
400g/14oz Arborio rice
good pinch saffron
225g/½lb prawns, unshelled
225g/½lb peeled prawns
110g/4oz cod fillet, cubed
1 lemon
3 heaped tbsp flat leaf parsley, chopped

- Simmer the fish stock gently in a pan.
- Wash the mussels in plenty of cold water, scrape off any barnacles and pull off the 'beards'. Discard any mussels which are open and refuse to close when rapped with the edge of your knife.
- Put the clean mussels in a large pan with half the white wine over quite a high heat, and put a lid on the pan. When all the mussels have opened, strain off the liquid and reserve the mussels, discarding any which have refused to open.

- Wash the cockles in plenty of cold water, and discard any which are open and refuse to close when rapped with the edge of your knife. Cook the cockles in the same way as the mussels and reserve both the cockles and the liquid.
- Heat the paella pan on a fairly high heat and then add a generous amount of olive oil. Heating the pan before adding the oil helps to stop the meat sticking to it.
- Add the pork and fry for a few minutes until sealed. Take the pork out of the pan and keep to one side.
- Now do the same with the chicken.
- Now put the chopped onions in the pan, followed by the garlic after a couple of minutes, and sweat them down, which should take about 10 to 15 minutes. We need them soft and translucent.
- Now add the rice, and stir to make sure it is well coated with the oil. Keep stirring for a minute or two and then add the paprika.
- Add about ¾ pint of fish stock, the reserved liquor from the cockles and the mussels, and the pinch of saffron. If you have a timer, set it for 10 minutes at this point. Keep an eye on the rice, stirring from time to time and adding more stock when you think it is getting too dry. We don't want the rice to stick to the pan. Not yet anyway.
- After 10 minutes, add the cooked pork and chicken. The paella will now need your full attention. Set your timer for 5 minutes and keep stirring and adding stock when needed.
- After 5 minutes add the unshelled prawns, set the timer for another 5 minutes, and keep stirring and adding stock when needed.
- Nearly there now. Add the reserved mussels and cockles, the peeled prawns and the cod. Give it all a final stir and leave on the heat for a final 5 minutes without stirring. This time, we *do* want the rice to stick to the pan. If it happens, the bottom of the paella becomes golden and crunchy (we think it is the best bit!).
- Take the pan off the heat. Cut the lemon in half and squeeze over the paella. Sprinkle with the chopped parsley and serve.

Risotto di Peoci

Please use the right rice for this. We use Arborio as it is readily available.
You could also use Baldo, Carnaroli, Vialone Nano or Roma if you can find
it. Do not use long-grain rice or the famous American rice where the grains
are guaranteed to separate each time.

The method is also important. Don't be tempted to add all the stock at
once. Continuous stirring not only prevents the risotto from sticking to the
pan, it also helps to bring out the starch from the rice to make the creamy
consistency we are looking for.

170g/6oz finely chopped onion
2 cloves garlic, finely chopped
olive oil
a little red chilli, chopped
840ml/1½ pints vegetable stock
28ml/2 tbsp dry white wine
455g/1lb mussels
water
170g/6oz Arborio rice
salt and freshly ground black pepper to taste
juice of half a lemon
15g/½oz unsalted butter
3 tbsp grated Parmesan cheese
2 tbsp parsley, finely chopped

- Have everything you need to hand – vegetables all chopped and ready.
- In a large pan, gently fry the onion and garlic in the olive oil. We need them to be soft and translucent, not brown. Also add the chilli. BE CAREFUL! We want very gentle background heat here. We would rather you leave the chilli out than add too much.
- In a separate pan, bring the vegetable stock to simmering point.
- Now it's time to cook the mussels. Put the wine in a large pan over a high heat and add the mussels – which should, of course, be cleaned and debearded first. Any open mussels which refuse to close when tapped with a knife should be discarded. Put the lid on the pan and cook for 2 or 3 minutes until they are all open. Discard any mussels which do not open.
- Take the mussels out of their shells and put them in a bowl of water, which will help to stop them drying out. The liquor from the mussels is used at the start of the risotto; don't throw it away.
- Now add the rice to the onions and garlic and stir so the grains are well coated with the oil, which should take only a couple of minutes.
- Add the mussel liquor (leaving out the last couple of tablespoons, which will be gritty) and stir until absorbed.
- You can now start adding the hot stock one ladle at a time, waiting until each ladleful has been absorbed before adding the next. Stir continuously. It is important that the stock is hot, otherwise the rice will stop cooking when you add it.
- After about 15 minutes the rice should be cooked and the risotto should have a soft, creamy consistency.
- Season to taste with salt, if needed, and freshly ground black pepper and add the lemon juice.
- Add the butter and Parmesan and stir vigorously to incorporate. The risotto should look creamy and shiny. Add the cooked mussels and the chopped parsley, and warm through.

Romesco de Peix (Catalan Fish Stew)

Very simple and very good indeed. This is a recipe with lots of preparation which can be done in advance, and the actual cooking takes minutes only. We are using the very Spanish method of preparing a sauce and thickening it with almonds; the fish is then cooked in the sauce. You can use whatever fish you chose. Monkfish would be good, or any other firm-fleshed fish. We are using cod for this version. Small clams such as palourde or carpet shell clams are also very good, but we couldn't find any, so we are using mussels. I think we need to have a serious discussion with our fishmonger!

1 Spanish onion

olive oil

455g/1lb mussels

2 glasses dry white wine

1 red pepper

2 cloves garlic

1 tbsp rosemary

3 medium-sized tomatoes, skinned, deseeded and chopped

vegetable stock

saffron

2 bay leaves

1 tsp smoked paprika

dash of sherry vinegar

1 heaped tbsp ground almonds

salt to taste

455g/1lb cod

flat leaf parsley

- Chop the onion, then select a pan big enough to hold all your ingredients, cover the bottom of the pan with olive oil, and gently fry the onion until it is soft and golden, stirring from time to time. This should take about 15 to 20 minutes.
- Wash the mussels in plenty of cold water, scrape off any barnacles and pull off the 'beards'. Discard any mussels which are open and refuse to close when rapped with the edge of your knife.
- Put the clean mussels in a large pan with half the white wine over quite a high heat, and put a lid on the pan. When all the mussels have opened, strain off the liquid and reserve. Discard any mussels which have refused to open. Take most of the mussels out of their shells, but leave a few so you can use them in their shells as decoration later.
- Quarter and de-seed the red pepper, and slice it thinly. Also thinly slice the garlic. Finely chop the rosemary.
- The onion should be ready now, so add the red pepper, garlic and rosemary, and continue cooking gently until the red pepper has softened. About 10 minutes, say.
- Now add the second glass of white wine and allow the alcohol to bubble away. Add the tomatoes, stock, saffron, bay leaves, paprika and the mussel liquid, turn up the heat a bit and let everything bubble away merrily. It should all cook down to make a sauce. Another 10 minutes, say.
- Finally, add a dash of sherry vinegar, and stir in the ground almonds. This will thicken the sauce. Taste, and add salt if you need to.
- Just before you are ready to eat, put the cod in the sauce, skin side down. Add the reserved mussels, and scatter the mussels still in their shells over the top.
- Leave 5 minutes until the cod is cooked, and serve. Scatter a bit of chopped parsley over the top.

Seafood Gumbo

An American idea born of necessity. What do you do as a good European when you find yourself in a strange land and you can't get the ingredients to cook your usual dishes? You adapt what you can find. Essential ingredients for a gumbo are celery, onion, green pepper and okra. You can use whatever seafood you can find, but don't leave out the okra, which when cooked will help to thicken the gumbo.

Traditionally you would eat gumbo with some long-grain rice.

225g/¹/₂lb mussels

225g/¹/₂lb cockles

3 tbsp light olive oil

4 slices pancetta (or streaky bacon), chopped

840ml/1¹/₂ pints stock

2 celery sticks, sliced

1 onion, chopped

1 green pepper, sliced

225g/¹/₂lb okra, thickly sliced

1 green chilli

1 bay leaf

sprig of thyme

2 tbsp spring onion, chopped

1 tbsp parsley, chopped

455g/1lb tomatoes, chopped

8 king prawns, shell off and de-veined

cod fillet, skinned and cut into chunks

salt and pepper to taste

- Wash the mussels in plenty of cold water, scrape off any barnacles and pull off the 'beards'. Discard any mussels which are open and refuse to close when rapped with the edge of your knife. Wash and scrub the cockles.
- Put the olive oil in a large pan over a medium heat and gently fry the pancetta or bacon for 3 minutes or so.
- Slowly add the stock, stirring as you do, then add the celery, onion, pepper, okra, chilli, bay leaf, thyme, spring onion, parsley and tomatoes. Bring back to the boil and simmer for about 20 minutes. The vegetables need to be quite soft and well cooked.
- We are now 4 minutes from the end. Add the king prawns, mussels and cockles. Give the gumbo a stir and then add the chunks of cod. Put the lid on the pan and wait for the cockles and mussels to open.
- Check the seasoning, adding salt and ground black pepper to taste. Discard any of the shellfish which haven't opened. Serve.

Thai Red Chicken (or Quorn) Curry

Life is much easier these days when it comes to Thai ingredients. You can get most things in the supermarket, although the only Thai ingredients in this recipe are the fish sauce and the curry paste. Don't let the smell of the fish sauce put you off!

You can make this curry as spicy as you like. When we have had friends round who do not like spicy food, we make it with as little as half a teaspoon of curry paste. Should you use the amount in the recipe, it will be hot.

2 medium-sized chicken breasts or quorn fillets

water

1 clove garlic, chopped

olive oil

1 tbsp red Thai curry paste

2 400-g/14-oz tins of coconut milk

1 red pepper, thinly sliced

grated zest of 1 lime

2 tbsp Thai fish sauce

1 tsp sugar

2 tbsp chopped coriander leaf

- Put the chicken breasts in a pan of cold water, and slowly bring to simmering point. As it reaches simmer, take the pan off the heat, put the lid on the pan and leave for 10 minutes.
- While this is going on, gently fry the garlic in the oil until it just begins to colour. Keep an eye on it to make sure it doesn't burn.
- Now add the curry paste and stir-fry until it begins to smell aromatic and to 'split'.
- Add three-quarters of the coconut milk (1½ tins) and the red pepper; bring to the boil.
- Add the lime zest, fish sauce, sugar and 2 or 3 ladles of the water in which the chicken breasts have been cooking, and bring to a brisk boil.
- Taste. The sugar should balance the heat of the chilli, and the fish sauce should balance the lime.
- Slice the cooked chicken breasts and add to the curry.
- Serve sprinkled with chopped coriander leaf, and with some plain boiled rice.

Bigos (Polish Hunter's Stew)

We are not sure, but we suspect that this recipe is really designed to use up odds and ends of leftover roast meat. Two days might sound like a lengthy cooking time, but the Bigos will not need any attention for most of this time, and there is something very satisfying about starting to cook something on Sunday to eat on Tuesday.

We have found numerous recipes for Bigos, but this one seems to work well. One of our Polish friends was kind enough to say it was the best Bigos she had eaten.

2 tbsp goose fat

2 large onions, chopped

900g/2lb sauerkraut, drained and chopped

900g/2lb white cabbage, finely chopped

500ml/18fl oz vegetable stock

200g/7oz smoked ham or bacon in small dice

115g/4oz polish pork sausage in small dice

200g/7oz beef in small dice

1 apple, peeled, de-cored and sliced

8 dried prunes, pitted and chopped

115ml/4fl oz full-bodied red wine

1 tbsp marjoram

2 bay leaves

a few dried mushrooms

- Melt the goose fat in the bottom of a large saucepan and gently fry the onions until they start to turn golden.
- Add the sauerkraut, cabbage and vegetable stock and bring to a simmer.
- Add the diced meats. If you cannot find Polish sausage, use a continental style pork sausage … not an English banger!
- Add the rest of the ingredients, bring back to simmer and leave for around 2 hours, then turn off the heat and leave for 24 hours.
- Reheat the next day and simmer for an hour and a half. The Bigos will start to turn a dark colour. You could eat it now, but you must resist. Leave it another day, even though it smells wonderful.
- Again, reheat, this time with the lid off, for about 1 hour. The idea here is to reduce down the liquid; we need the Bigos to be fairly dry. Check the seasoning, remembering that sauerkraut is salty anyway, and serve.

Nasi Goreng

This is a brilliant recipe. It takes only a few minutes to cook, and tastes much better than you think it will. If you have one, cook this in a wok; it's much easier than a frying pan.

2 eggs

½ tsp salt

1 tsp sesame oil

2 tbsp groundnut oil

2 cloves garlic, finely chopped

2.5-cm/1-in piece fresh root ginger, finely chopped

6 spring onions, finely chopped and separating the white part from the green

¼ tsp cayenne pepper

1 heaped tbsp fresh coriander (stalks and leaves), chopped

170g/6oz cooked basmati rice

100g/4oz peeled prawns

- Beat the eggs together with the salt and the sesame oil.
- Heat the groundnut oil in the wok or frying pan, and fry the garlic, ginger and the white spring onion until they start to turn colour.
- Add the cayenne pepper. Be careful here! We are looking for gentle heat to complement the ginger.
- Now add the beaten egg mixture and stir fry it until it starts to 'scramble'.
- Add the cooked rice and the prawns and stir until heated through.
- Finally, add the green spring onion and chopped coriander, and serve.

appendix

determining cause and effect: the need for randomized controlled trials (RCTs) – and their limitations

When it comes to deciding what you can do to get the results you want for your child, all kinds of information is available to you. These notes are intended to try to help you make sense of the information you may come across, in this book and elsewhere, about different kinds of 'evidence'. The trouble is, judging its reliability – or even what it means – can be very difficult for any parent. Generally speaking, the most important evidence that you need to be able to weigh up and judge for yourself concerns 'cause and effect'.

'If I do this, what will happen?' What you really mean when you ask yourself this question is, 'What will happen *as a result of my action?*' We all make 'cause-and-effect' predictions all the time (for better or worse). We couldn't survive without doing so. We base our judgements on what we've picked up from our own past experience or observations, or what we've learned from other people. In many areas we can't experiment or even observe for ourselves, so we have to use the evidence other people present us with – things that we hear about, read about, see on TV or look up on the Internet. Unfortunately, not all of this 'evidence' is equally reliable. So if you don't want to waste your time and money (or worse), then it's always worth taking a critical stance and always bearing a few basic points in mind.

Correlation Is Not Causation (Even if A and B both 'Go Together', This Doesn't Mean A causes B)

Even if two things usually go together ('co-relate' or correlate) – such as eating fish and not suffering from depression, for example – this doesn't necessarily mean that one *causes* the other. We'd always need additional evidence for that conclusion to be justified. Newspaper articles and even scientific journal reports frequently make this very fundamental error, assuming that just because two things go together, the relationship must be one of cause and effect. This isn't so. The apparent association could just be down to chance (pure coincidence) – or there may be another, independent reason why the two things go together.

- *'The survey showed that people who took vitamin pills had fewer hospital admissions than those who didn't.'*

This doesn't necessarily mean that taking vitamins prevented the hospital admissions (although it might have done). There are plenty of other possible explanations, so always ask yourself what those might have been. In this case, how about:

- People who take vitamin pills may have higher incomes/a higher level of education/more knowledge about the importance of diet/may eat more healthily.
- They may take more exercise/get more holidays in which to relax.
- They may be more likely to look after themselves (or be looked after) in other ways.

Any or all of these other things *could* help to explain why these people have fewer hospital admissions. The fact that they take vitamin pills may have nothing to do with it. (In fact, if they have higher incomes, this might even explain both of the observations. If so, this would be what's called a *tertium quid* – a 'third thing which' is the real reason for the apparent link between two others.)

Always think about other possible explanations. Ask yourself what information you *haven't* been given that would help you to get a fuller picture.

Does It Really Follow? (If A Causes B, then B Should Reliably Follow A.) If So, How Might a Link Work?

To decide whether one thing actually causes another, the very first thing we need to establish is 'which came first?' Effects follow causes, not the other way around! Plenty of long-term studies – especially those concerning diet and well-being – can't even tell us this.

It's also worth asking yourself if there's any reasonable *mechanism* that could help to explain the link. (Miracles don't count here, by definition!) Just how exactly might one thing be causing the other?

Many of the most 'convincing' stories that lead us to believe one thing causes another have no trouble meeting both of these criteria, but unfortunately they still don't actually give us firm evidence of cause and effect. For example:

- *'The number of police on the town's streets was reduced by 20 per cent, and rates of crime doubled over the next three months.'*
- *'I stopped my son drinking Superfizz and his school grades the following term were better than they've ever been.'*

The trouble with these examples – plausible though they are as cases of cause and effect – is that there could actually be many other reasons for the second thing happening. With the crime rates, perhaps a new gang happened to move into the area. With your son's grades – maybe the teaching improved, or the friend who was distracting him in class left.

Again, always ask yourself what *additional information* (that may not be put in front of you) could explain the link between two things. It doesn't have to be simple cause and effect. Use your imagination. Could there be a different explanation?

Don't Put Your Trust in Anecdotes (One Swallow Doesn't Make a Summer)

You'll have heard numerous stories of individuals who've apparently 'benefited' from all kinds of 'treatments'. These may be first-hand accounts (from people you know), or second- or third-hand ones (from them, or from people they know). 'Miracle cure' stories are also reported all the time in the media, because of course these are very useful for commercial purposes. Remember where most newspapers, magazines and TV channels get a large share of their revenue from …? Yes – it's from advertising. The most effective advert of all is one that makes you think it's a news story. Our papers and TV are full of them.

Although these kinds of personal reports (or preferably, proper 'single case studies' published in peer-reviewed journals) can sometimes be helpful in suggesting whether a particular treatment *may* be of any value, further studies are always needed to check this out.

These 'anecdotal' reports can often be highly misleading – but they're extremely convincing, because they're personal. You can identify with them. For that reason, you'll notice I've used them in this book to illustrate various points. But that's all they can do – illustrate. They can never provide firm evidence for anything – let alone 'proof'. Apparent 'benefits' can easily arise for many, many reasons other than the supposed 'treatment'. If any effects are genuine, they should stand up to formal, 'systematic' investigation.

Be Systematic

To find out whether one thing really does cause another, we always need to do some testing. We need well-designed 'intervention' studies – where something is changed deliberately and systematically (you intervene) and the consequences of this change are actually observed, not just assumed. What's more, we ideally need to compare at least two groups of people, each of which is treated in a different way, and measure what happens to each group (the outcomes).

'Open' and 'Uncontrolled' Studies

I long ago lost count of the ridiculous number of 'research trials' (all apparently investigating the effects of fish oils on children's behaviour and learning) that journalists and many other people have kept ringing me up about, or emailing or writing to ask me to comment on. Almost always, it turns out that they've seen some wonderful report in the newspapers or on TV. Each time, the 'trial' has turned out to be one where a group of children were simply given some fish-oil capsules, and 'results' were presented describing how much they'd improved on this or that measure. (Oddly enough, in almost every case there would be a particular supplement named, too. Might these stories have come from the kind of company press releases I warned you about in Chapter 2? In fact, in many cases friendly journalists actually sent me the press releases first! Forewarned is forearmed, I suppose …)

This kind of 'study' doesn't tell us anything at all about cause and effect. At the very best, any 'results' may be a useful pointer for further research – and then only if some thought went into designing the study so that it might actually tell us something new.

- If there's no comparison group of people given an alternative treatment (or even no treatment at all), then the study is completely 'uncontrolled'. All kinds of things quite apart from the treatment could have been the real cause(s) of any supposed 'effects' observed. Media attention – and particularly the lure of being on TV – is often enough to generate the most marvellous 'improvements', but few later stand up to scrutiny.
- If everyone knows what kind of treatment is being tested, then the study is said to be 'open' (or 'open-label'). It might or might not be 'controlled' (there may be two different treatments being compared, for example, but all the people involved know who's receiving what). Once again, this kind of study is prey to numerous confounds. Expectations are extremely powerful, so if people know what treatment they are receiving, their beliefs and expectations alone could produce apparent 'results'.

Randomized Controlled Trials

In general, *randomized, double-blind, placebo-controlled* trials are the only kind of studies that can provide unequivocal evidence of cause-and-effect relationships. They are often called randomized controlled trials (RCT) for short. These kinds of studies are the best we have when it comes to determining cause and effect – although they do have plenty of limitations of their own.[1]

A Placebo Control is Essential

A 'placebo' is a 'dummy' treatment given to some participants, and it must be *indistinguishable* from the one being tested. Giving a placebo treatment to some of the people taking part really is essential if we're to be sure that any changes observed are not simply the result of beliefs and expectations (on the part of participants, researchers, or both), the extra attention involved in taking part in the study, or numerous other possible confounding factors. The point is that placebo treatments alone really can 'work'. (In fact it caused quite a stir when data presented to the US Food and Drug Administration showed that 80 per cent of the supposed effects of anti-depressant drugs could equally well be explained by placebo effects.)[2]

No One Must Know the Identity of the Treatments

The standard 'double-blind' procedure is also crucial if we're to prevent expectations, or bias from other sources, from influencing the results. When a study is 'double-blind', this means that until it has been completed (and all of the data have been collected, checked and verified; and the preliminary analyses carried out) nobody who is involved in the research can know who received which treatment. (In a 'single-blind' study, the researchers may know, but the participants don't – or very occasionally, vice versa.)

Everyone Must Have an Equal Chance of Getting Each Type of Treatment

'Random allocation' to treatment groups means that each individual has an equal chance of receiving the so-called 'active treatment' (the one being tested). This helps to control for other influences that could affect the results. The actual method of randomizing the treatments must also be concealed, to prevent any bias that might otherwise occur in allocating the treatments. (If the sequence of codes identifying which treatment is which could be guessed, then the people delivering the treatment could be tempted to give the 'real' treatment to the people they think most likely to benefit.)

If the number of participants is large enough, random allocation should also ensure that the different treatment groups are well matched for any other factors that could affect the outcomes –such as age, sex, height, weight, symptom profile or even hair colour! Individual differences that might sway the results should all 'come out in the wash' if enough people are studied.

So … if the *only* difference between the two groups is the type of treatment they received, and the outcomes (what actually happens to each group) turn out to be significantly different, then it's quite reasonable to conclude that these differences really are caused by the treatment. Everything else should have been 'controlled' by the strict randomization and blinding procedures.

RCTs Also Have Their Limitations

Although they're the best we have, RCTs have plenty of limitations themselves. First, they're just not suitable for testing certain kinds of treatments or 'interventions' – so other systematic methods need to be found instead. How can we ensure 'double-blind' conditions if we want to test a behavioural programme, delivered face-to-face by a therapist? Or if treatments need to be individually tailored? With great difficulty, or not at all, is the answer. The RCT is best suited to drug treatments (and it's why much research into the effects of nutrients involves food supplements rather than real foods, which is not an ideal situation, as discussed in Chapter 4).

What's more, the actual reporting of RCTs is a highly complex topic in itself. Omission of any key details (such as how many people dropped out of the trial at any stage – and why this happened) can lead to misleading interpretations. The key question these days is whether the reporting followed 'CONSORT' guidelines – used by the leading scientific journals to make sure

382 they are what you feed them

that all relevant facts are reported.[3] As usual, nothing is perfect, but RCTs are still the best single tool we have if we want to determine cause and effect.

'Meta-analyses' of RCTs

The only kind of evidence that is more powerful than RCT evidence comes from 'pooling' (combining) the results of many different RCTs of the same kind of treatment in a so-called 'meta-analysis'. These kinds of studies (if they are the product of a truly systematic review by people with appropriate expertise) come at the very top of the so-called 'hierarchy of evidence' – but again, they still need to be treated with caution.

We saw one example of this in Chapter 6, where:

- an early meta-analysis of RCTs investigating possible effects of food additives or particular food substances on the behaviour of hyperactive children concluded that there was no overall effect
- a later meta-analysis, which focused just on artificial food colourings (AFCs) and also included some more recent studies, found that there *was* an effect of these additives on children's behaviour. (This got worse in children who received AFCs.)

With meta-analyses, everything depends on the methodology used, and particularly on which studies are included or excluded. In this case the first study not only included fewer trials, but was combining different things: apples, pears and even bananas, as they say. The second one just included apples – and had more of them.

Another very recent example was a 'new' meta-analysis of studies investigating the effects of omega-3 fatty acids on deaths from heart disease and other causes such as cancer. Whether you see yourself as a scientist or not, it's really worth skim-reading for yourself some of the e-correspondence that this article rapidly generated in the *British Medical Journal*, which chose to publish it.[4] Unfortunately, the real scientific details are – as always – highly technical, but if we just focus on the question of what studies were included in this particular meta-analysis (and which ones were left out), I think it's fair to say that the authors chose to throw in one extremely large and rather rotten watermelon, which served to squash the otherwise highly consistent picture that came from the assortment of cherries, strawberries, redcurrants and grapes – along with the odd banana – that's been reviewed on many previous occasions. UK journalists had a field day, of course, but in my view it's worth completely ignoring (as usual) the dramatic headlines concocted by editors whose job it is to sell their newspapers. Sadly, many of them really wouldn't know a good study from a hole in the ground.

'The Demon-Haunted World: Science as a Candle in the Dark'

The message I've tried to convey throughout this book is that you *do* need to see yourself as a scientist – and that simply means being curious, observant, systematic and open-minded, but above all, sceptical. As I said in Chapter 1, I've actually met many parents who are far better scientists than some of those who get paid for the job. Getting their children well has been their motivation, and to that end they've observed, studied and experimented until they've found out for themselves what 'works' for their children.

The title I've used for these closing paragraphs is that of a simply superb book by Carl Sagan, which I would recommend to anyone.[5] (He was a leading scientist whom the US government once asked to look into the apparent phenomenon of 'abduction by aliens' which seemed to sweep across America before people became more obsessed with earthly terrorism instead. This he did with extraordinary sensitivity and rigour – and he explains some of his methods and findings in this book.) He was also an extraordinarily good writer, and this is probably the best book I've come across for explaining to anyone what 'the scientific method' really is about (including his special 'Baloney Detection Kit'). Science is something you really can use – and teach your children to use. In fact, children often tend to adopt scientific principles quite naturally as they try to make sense of their world – until the adults get fed up with their endless questions (let alone home-made experiments) and tell them to shut up and watch TV instead.

All I would emphasize is: *please* don't just believe everything you hear or read without questioning it. It's not just your health and well-being, and that of your children, which is at stake. It really is the future of humanity.

384 they are what you feed them

Essential Minerals

These are the minerals known or thought to be essential to humans – and some of the reasons why each is needed.

These minerals are easily obtainable from a healthy diet that includes meat, fish, eggs, vegetables, fruit, nuts, seeds, beans and pulses, dairy products and whole grains. If you don't get enough of these minerals then you can end up with deficiency diseases and disorders. Too much of a mineral can be poisonous, and may inhibit the uptake of other minerals and vitamins.

Mineral	Needed for
Arsenic	Yes!
	■ possibly helps with metabolism of phospholipids (part of the cell membranes)
Boron	■ bones
Calcium	■ bone and tooth formation
	■ blood clotting
	■ regulation of heart rate
	■ nerve transmissions
Chloride	■ water balance
	■ body pH (acid–alkali balance)
Chromium	■ blood-sugar regulation
	■ metabolism of fats and carbohydrates
Copper	■ myelin sheaths (outer coating of nerve fibres)
	■ collagen
	■ skin pigments
	■ red blood cells
Fluoride	■ teeth
	■ bones
Iodine	■ thyroid gland operation
	■ cell metabolism
Iron	■ red blood cells (the iron part 'picks up' and 'carries' the oxygen around your body)
	■ immune defence cells

Mineral	Needed for
Iron ...	■ white blood cells
	■ brain function
Magnesium	■ metabolism of carbohydrates, lipids, proteins
	■ nerve transmission
	■ muscle contraction
	■ the conversion of vitamin D to its active form
Manganese	■ normal utilization of several vitamins, and a variety of other biochemical roles in the body
	■ fat metabolism
	■ skeletal and connective tissues
	■ energy production
	■ making cholesterol and DNA
	■ brain function
	■ processing blood sugar
Molybdenum	■ important in many biochemical reactions
	■ aids in the metabolism of iron
	■ removal of uric acid from the body
	■ helps the body burn fat
	■ for healthy bones, teeth, kidney and liver
	■ helps the body use its iron reserves
Nickel	■ fat metabolism
	■ blood-sugar regulation
Phosphorus	■ energy production
	■ metabolism of protein, carbohydrate and fat
	■ strengthens bones and teeth
	■ muscle contraction
	■ kidney function
	■ nerve function
Potassium	■ release of energy from food
	■ synthesis of protein
	■ regulation of water balance
	■ nerve and muscle function
	■ regulation of blood pressure
Selenium	■ antioxidant (works with vitamin E to protect the body from free-radical damage)

Mineral	Needed for
Selenium ...	■ fat metabolism
	■ immune system
	■ male fertility
Silicon	■ body tissues
Sodium	■ water balance
	■ the passage of substances in and out of each cell
	■ maintenance of a normal body pH
	■ nerve signals
	■ muscle contraction
	■ regulation of blood pressure
Vanadium	possibly:
	■ energy production and other biochemical reactions
	■ blood sugar
	■ fat metabolism
	■ bones and teeth
Zinc	■ for proper growth of skin, hair and nails
	■ cell division and replication
	■ healing wounds
	■ immune system
	■ taste and smell
	■ metabolism of carbohydrates

'Food Pyramids' and Healthy Eating

More than a decade ago, the US Department of Agriculture created a 'food pyramid' which was meant to embody a healthy diet in one picture. The concept was great, but the content wasn't. Even their recently updated version ('My Pyramid') shows many holes in their dietary knowledge. Or are they holes? As well as scientific consultants, various representatives of the food industry had their say in building it.

I much prefer this one by the Harvard School of Public Health. Details for each part are given on their website: www.hsph.harvard.edu/nutritionsource/pyramids.html.

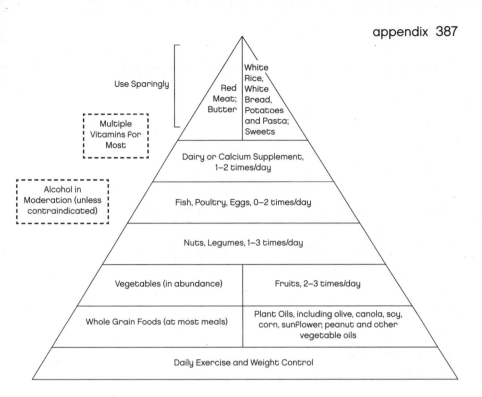

In my opinion, however, even this pyramid doesn't emphasize omega-3 oils enough, or the dangers of trans fats – which may be found in hydrogenated or partially hydrogenated vegetable oils (and can be created if ordinary vegetable oils are used for cooking).

Food Additives

European Food Additive Categories and Code Numbers

Category	E number
Colours	E100–E180
Preservatives	E200–E290
Antioxidants	E300–E322
Emulsifiers, stabilizers and sweeteners	E400–E483
Mineral hydrocarbons	E905–E907
Modified starches	E1400–E1442

Additives Commonly Associated with Allergies and Hyperactivity

Colourings

E102 Tartrazine	*Banned in Norway and Australia*
E104 Quinoline Yellow	*Banned in Australia, Norway and US*
E110 Sunset Yellow	*Banned in Norway*
E122 Carmoisine or Azorubine	*Banned in Sweden, US, Austria and Norway*
E124 Ponceau 4R or Cochineal Red A	*Banned in US and Norway*
E132 Indigo Carmine or Indigotine	*Banned in Norway*
E155 Brown HT	*Banned in much of Europe and US*

Preservatives

E210 Benzoic acid

E211 Sodium benzoate

E220 Sulphur dioxide

Flavour Enhancer

E621 Monosodium glutamate

Artificial Sweeteners

E950 Acesulphame K (potassium)

E951 Aspartame

E954 Saccharine

Note that this is only part of a very long list of E numbers! Many appear to be very safe, but many can have side-effects – which can differ between individuals. Essentially, if the product you're looking at has a whole load of E numbers or chemical names listed on it, and you know you could make the product at home without additives, think carefully about buying it.

What's in the Food You Buy Your Child?

Copy or photocopy this table and keep a tally for a week or more of the foods you usually buy for your child. While there are many more additives, it can get too complicated and time consuming to jot them all down. The additives shown here form Dr Lizzie Vann's 'Dirty Dozen'. See her website (www.organix.com) for further details.

Additive Day	1	2	3	4	5	6	7	Comments
Colourings								
E104 (Quinoline Yellow)								
E133 (Brilliant Blue)								
E110 (Sunset Yellow)								
E122 (Carmoisine)								
E124 (Ponceau 4R)								
E132 (Indigo Carmine)								
Artificial Sweeteners								
E951 (Aspartame)								
E954 (Saccharine)								
E950 (Acesulphame K)								
Flavour Enhancer								
E621 (Monosodium glutamate)								
Preservatives								
E211 (Sodium benzoate)								
E220 (Sulphur dioxide)								

Different Names for Sugar on Food Labels

Acesulfame***	Glucose	Potassium sweetener***
Amazake	Glucose-Fructose	Rapadura
Aspartame***	High Fructose Corn	Raw Sugar
Beet Sugar	Syrup**	Saccharine***
Brown Sugar	Honey	Sorbitol*
Carob Powder	Hydrolysed starch	Sorghum
Concentrated Fruit Juice	Invert Sugar	Stevia***
Corn Syrup	Maltose	Sucrose
Dextrin	Maltodextrin	Syrup
Dextrose	Malitol*	Turbinado
Evaporated Cane Juice	Manitol*	White Sugar
Fructose	Maple Syrup	Xylitol*
Galactose	Molasses	

* These are naturally 'sweet' alcohols or polyols. They can occur naturally in fruit, but are commercially produced from sources such as dextrose.
**This is made from 50 per cent fructose and 50 per cent glucose.
*** These are artificial sweeteners.

Omega-6 and Omega-3 Fatty Acids – Making Your Own HUFA from EFA

- The truly essential fatty acids (EFAs) that can't be made within the body are linoleic acid (LA), of the omega-6 series, and alpha-linolenic acid (ALA) of the omega-3 series.
- The longer-chain, highly unsaturated fatty acids (HUFAs) that the brain needs can in theory be synthesized from these EFAs – via processes of desaturation (insertion of a double bond) and elongation (adding two carbon atoms to the fatty acid chain).

- *However*, the conversion of EFA to HUFA is relatively slow and inefficient in humans, so pre-formed HUFA from dietary sources may be needed to ensure an adequate supply of these vital nutrients.

OMEGA-6 SERIES		ENZYMES INVOLVED IN HUFA SYNTHESIS	OMEGA-3 SERIES	
Linoleic Acid (LA)	18:2		Alpha-linolenic Acid (ALA)	18:3
⇩		*Delta 6-desaturase*	⇩	
Gamma-linolenic Acid (GLA)	18:3		Stearidonic Acid	18:4
⇩		*Elongase*	⇩	
Dihomogamma-linolenic Acid (DGLA)	20:3		Eicosatetraenoic Acid	20:4
⇩		*Delta 5-desaturase*	⇩	
Arachidonic Acid (AA)	20:4		Eicosapentaenoic Acid (EPA)	20:5
⇩		*Elongase*	⇩	
Adrenic Acid	22:4		Docosapentaenoic Acid (DPA)	22:5
⇩		*Elongase, Delta 6-desaturase, Beta-oxidation*	⇩	
Docosapentaenoic Acid (DPA)	22:5		Docosahexaenoic Acid (DHA)	22.6

Four HUFAs are particularly important for brain development and function:

1. DGLA (from the omega-6 series)
2. AA (from the omega-6 series)
3. EPA (from the omega-3 series)
4. DHA (from the omega-3 series).

- AA and DHA are major structural components of neuronal membranes (making up 20 per cent of the dry mass of the brain, and more than 30 per cent of the retina).
- EPA and DGLA are also crucial, but they play functional rather than structural roles.
- EPA, DGLA and AA (but not DHA) are needed to manufacture *eicosanoids* – hormone-like substances including prostaglandins, leukotrienes and thromboxanes. These play a critical role in the moment-by-moment regulation of a very wide range of brain and body functions, including *hormone balance, immune function and blood flow.* (DHA gives rise to other substances whose functions are not yet fully known).

Omega-3 and omega-6 can't be converted into each other within the body. However, *both* are essential, and the balance of omega-3 and omega-6 fatty acids is very important, as they play complementary roles in many biological functions.

For example, substances made from AA include the 'pro-inflammatory' series 2 prostaglandins, while DGLA and EPA give rise to 'anti-inflammatory' prostaglandins (series 1 and series 3 respectively). Similarly, thromboxanes derived from AA will constrict blood vessels, while those derived from EPA will relax blood vessels and improve blood flow.

Randomized Controlled Trials of Treatment with Omega-3 Fatty Acids in Children with ADHD and Related Conditions

Investigators	Diagnosis (+ ascertainment)	N (male, Female)	Active Treatment: Daily doses of omega-3 + other constituents	Trial design	Duration of treatment in parallel groups	Outcome
Voigt et al., 2001	DSM-IV ADHD with minimal or no comorbidity (psychiatric clinic, US)	54 (42, 12)	DHA 345mg (from algae)	RCT, double-blind, parallel groups; adjunctive to pharmacotherapy	4 months	No effect of treatment on a wide range of behavioural and computerized measures of ADHD-related symptoms
Richardson & Puri, 2002	Dyslexia + ADHD features (special school, UK)	29 (25, 4)	EPA 186 mg, DHA 480 mg (from fish oil) Omega-6 (GLA 96 mg, AA 42 mg) Vitamin E 60 IU	RCT, double-blind, parallel groups (+ one-way placebo-active crossover); monotherapy	12 weeks (+12 weeks)	Active > placebo for changes in parent ratings of ADHD-related symptoms

Investigators	Diagnosis (+ ascertainment)	N (male, Female)	Active Treatment: Daily doses of omega-3 + other constituents	Trial design	Duration of treatment in parallel groups	Outcome
Stevens et al., 2003	ADHD-type difficulties + physical signs consistent with EFA deficiency (community-based sample, US)	47 (41, 6)	EPA 80mg, DHA 480mg (From Fish oil) Omega-6 (GLA 96mg, AA 40mg) Vitamin E 56 IU	RCT, double-blind, parallel groups; adjunctive to pharmacotherapy	16 weeks	Active > placebo for changes in teacher-rated attention, parent-rated conduct, and per cent meeting clinical criteria for oppositional defiant disorder
Hamazaki et al., 2004	ADHD (special summer camp, Japan)	40 (32, 8)	EPA 100mg approx DHA 510mg approx (From Fish oil & Fermented soybean oil)	RCT, double-blind, parallel groups; adjunctive to pharmacotherapy	2 months?	No effect of treatment on a wide range of behavioural and psychometric measures
Richardson & Montgomery, 2005	DSM-IV DCD (mainstream schools in one UK geographical region)	117 (78, 39)	EPA 558mg DHA 174 mg (From Fish oil) omega-6 Omega-6 (GLA 60 mg) Vitamin E 15 IU	RCT, double-blind, parallel groups (+ one-way placebo-active crossover); monotherapy	12 weeks (+12 weeks)	Active = placebo for changes in motor function Active > placebo for changes in teacher-rated ADHD-related symptoms and age-standardized measures of reading and spelling achievement

How Much Sleep Does Your Child Need?

Age	Night-time Sleep (hours)	Daytime Sleep (hours)	Total Sleep (hours)
1 month	8.5 (many naps)	7.5 (many naps)	16
3 months	6–10	5–9	15
6 months	10–12	3–4.5	14.5
9 months	11	3 (2 naps)	14
12 months	11	2.5 (2 naps)	13.5
18 months	11	2.5 (1–2 naps)	13.5
2 years	11	2 (1 nap)	13
3 years	10.5	1.5 (1 nap)	12
4 years	11.5	0	11.5
5 years	11	0	11
6 years	10.5–11	0	10.5–11
7 years	10.5	0	10.5
8 years	10–10.5	0	10–10.5
9 years	10	0	10
10 years	9.5–10	0	9.5–10
11 years	9.5	0	9.5
12–13 years	9–9.5	0	9–9.5
14 years	9	0	9
15 years	8.5–9	0	8.5–9
16 years	8.5	0	8.5

Sleep Diary

Date		
Time woke/woken		
Time got up		
Any problems on waking?		
Time and length of daytime naps or times during the day when your child felt sleepy		
Time to bed		
Time to sleep		
Any problems going off to bed/getting to sleep? Please describe, including what your child did, what you did, and how and where your child eventually fell asleep.		
Time and length of all waking in the night. Please describe what happened – why your child woke, what he did, what you did and how your child eventually fell asleep.		
Any other events of note during the night? For example snoring, twitching, etc. Please describe.		
Times of breakfast (B), lunch (L) and dinner (D)	B L D	B L D
Anything else of importance?		

references and resources

References

Chapter 1

1. By no means all of my publications are about food and diet. My early research involved exploring the biology of temperament and personality in dyslexia and related conditions, as well as the role of visual and auditory perception, and genetic factors, and I still do some work in these areas. A full list of my publications can be found on the University of Oxford website, or via the charity FAB Research, at www.fabresearch.org
2. Gregory *et al.*, *National Diet and Nutrition Surveys* (London: HMSO, 2000).
3. The latest WHO predictions of trends in the global burden of disease can be found at http://www.who.int/healthinfo/statistics/bodprojections2030/en/index.html. By 2030, depression is now predicted to be by far the single biggest cause of disability in high-income countries (accounting for almost 10 per cent of the total), while dementia and diabetes will both tie with heart disease at 5.5 per cent each, followed by alcohol-use disorders at 4.4 per cent. Diet is a risk factor in all of these disorders.

Chapter 2

1. Anyone wanting to find our more about the real state of our food should read:
   - *Not on the Label: What Really Goes into the Food on Your Plate* by Felicity Lawrence (Penguin Books Ltd, 2004)
   - *Fast Food Nation: What the All-American Meal Is Doing to the World* by Eric Schlosser (Penguin Books Ltd, 2002)
   - *The Great Food Gamble* by John Humphrys (Coronet Books, 2002)
   - *The Politics of Food* by Geoffrey Cannon (Ebury Press, 1987)

And visit:

- Jamie Oliver's site (www.feedmebetter.com) and read his books
- the Food Commission website (www.foodcomm.org.uk).

2. These need to be randomized, double-blind, placebo-controlled trials, as explained in the Appendix (page 375).

3. Gesch, C. B., Hammond, S. M., Hampson, S. E., Eves, A. and Crowder, M. J., 'Influence of supplementary vitamins, minerals and essential fatty acids on the antisocial behaviour of young adult prisoners. Randomised, placebo-controlled trial', *British Journal of Psychiatry* 181 (2002): 22–8

4. Natural Justice – and now the Wellcome Trust.

5. In February 2006, the National Institute for Health and Clinical Excellence (NICE) issued guidance that all hospital patients should be routinely screened for malnutrition and offered specialist nutritional support if required. As many as 40 per cent of hospital patients are at risk, and malnutrition is estimated to cost the NHS £7.3bn a year. See http://news.bbc.co.uk/1/hi/health/4733278.stm

6. For more detail on these pernicious influences, read the excellent book *Toxic Childhood* by Sue Palmer – an education specialist with many years of experience in working with children, parents and schools.

7. Examples of pioneering parents who have led much of the science include Vicky Colquhoun and Sally Bunday of the Hyperactive Children's Support Group – who first suggested that deficiencies in essential fatty acids may contribute to ADHD and related conditions. In the field of autism, special credit is due to Brenda O'Reilly, who first founded the charity Allergy-Induced Autism and then the charity Autism Unravelled. Some others put their own medical training to good effect when they found conventional medicine couldn't help their children and grandchildren – see the excellent books by Dr Natasha Campbell MacBride (*Gut and Psychology Syndromes*) and Jaqueline McCandless MD (*Children with Starving Brains*). And the same is true of many of the leading researchers in the biomedical treatment of autism and related conditions – including Professor Paul Shattock (OBE) of the Autism Research Unit in Sunderland, and Dr Gordon Bell of the University of Stirling, to name but a few.

8. There are some exceptions. For example, see Felicity Lawrence's excellent book *Not on the Label*, where she expands on information about the food industry and its practices that she first discovered when doing research for her articles in the *Guardian*.

9. There are many other ways in which corporate interests influence the content of supposedly independent scientific journals. See the essay published in the open-access Public Library of Science by Richard Smith (former editor of the *British Medical Journal* for 25 years) entitled 'Medical Journals Are an Extension of the Marketing Arm of Pharmaceutical Companies': http://medicine.plosjournals.org/perlserv/?request=get-document&doi=10.1371/journal.pmed.0020138. His opening paragraph

quotes from other editors of leading medical journals who had already arrived at the same conclusion: "'Journals have devolved into information laundering operations for the pharmaceutical industry," wrote Richard Horton, editor of the *Lancet*, in March 2004 [1]. In the same year, Marcia Angell, former editor of the *New England Journal of Medicine*, lambasted the industry for becoming "primarily a marketing machine" and co-opting "every institution that might stand in its way" [2].' This essay is well worth reading in full – as are many of the references it contains.

10. I know that finding a suitably qualified practitioner can be very difficult. Many 'nutritional therapists' have had only minimal training – so do beware, and don't be afraid to ask any practitioner about exactly what qualifications and experience they have. From my own experience in research, I very much favour practitioners with a medical background and training, although I am aware these are in short supply – and relevant personal experience can sometimes count for more (both are the ideal). See the Resources section for details on the different kinds of practitioners and the organizations that try to regulate these professions. If you're having difficulty, the FAB Research charity *may* be able to point you to a specialist in your area. If you're a UK practitioner with relevant qualifications and experience, please get in touch!

Chapter 3

1. A range of excellent books on these syndromes, and links to other websites you may find useful, can be found on the FAB research website at www.fabresearch.org. See also the Resources chapter for contact details for some of the main charities and support groups in the UK, only some of which are knowledgeable about dietary approaches to these conditions.

2. The British Dyslexia Association estimates that 5 per cent of UK children have severe dyslexic difficulties, while a further 5 per cent are more moderately affected. Severe ADHD similarly affects around 5 per cent of children, and the mild to moderate cases add another 5–10 per cent. Dyspraxia has a similar prevalence, and rates of autistic spectrum disorders, while still somewhat lower, have been increasing dramatically in recent years. Even allowing for overlaps, these estimates are consistent with figures showing that 20 per cent of UK primary school children are informally listed by schools and Local Education Authorities as having Special Educational Needs (SEN) – although official SEN Statements are limited to only a fraction of this by the system.

3. This particularly applies to ADHD, where girls are relatively more likely to show attentional difficulties without hyperactivity-impulsivity. (See Arnold, L. E., 'Sex differences in ADHD: conference summary', *Journal of Abnormal Child Psychology* 24 [1996]: 555–69.) However, concerns have also been raised

about the usual diagnostic criteria for dyslexia, because boys will be diagnosed more readily using any 'unisex' cut-off for poor reading, simply because girls are – on average – better readers than boys at any given age.

4. In the UK, examples include the financier Guy Hands, the entrepreneur Richard Branson, and Lizzie Vann OBE, founder of the Organix company, although there are many others. Branson and several top US entrepreneurs were interviewed for an article about 'Overcoming Dyslexia' in *Fortune* magazine in 2002 – see http://money.cnn.com/magazines/fortune/fortune_archive/2002/05/13/32287 6/index.htm

5. These difficulties exceed those expected from age, education and abilities in other areas, and can't be explained by any obvious sensory (visual or hearing) problems. In education, the term Specific Reading Difficulties (SRD) is often preferred to distinguish these children from so-called 'garden-variety' poor readers whose difficulties are more general.

6. Motor difficulties are not due to a medical condition such as muscular dystrophy or cerebral palsy, or part of any generalized developmental problems.

7. The leading UK experts in the treatment of ADHD do not take such a narrow approach. Thus a few years ago, experts at the Institute of Psychiatry published a systematic, evidence-based and auditable protocol for the clinical management of ADHD. This includes explicit mention of evidence-based dietary approaches as well as the options for behavioural therapies. See Hill, P. and Taylor, E., 'An auditable protocol for treating attention deficit/hyperactivity disorder', *Archives of Disease in Childhood* 84.5 (2001): 404–9

8. Buitelaar, J. K., Van-der-Gaag, R. J., Swaab-Barneveld, H. and Kuiper, M., 'Prediction of clinical response to methylphenidate in children with attention-deficit hyperactivity disorder', *Journal of the American Academy of Child and Adolescent Psychiatry* 34.8 (1995): 1025–32; DuPaul, G. J., Barkley, R. A. and McMurray, M. B., 'Response of children with ADHD to methylphenidate: interaction with internalizing symptoms', *Journal of the American Academy of Child and Adolescent Psychiatry* 33 (1994): 894–903; Pliszka, S. R., 'Effect of anxiety on cognition, behavior, and stimulant response in ADHD', *Journal of the American Academy of Child and Adolescent Psychiatry* 28 (1989): 882–7; Taylor, E., Schachar, R., Thorley, G., Wieselberg, H. M., Everitt, B. and Rutter, M., 'Which boys respond to stimulant medication? A controlled trial of methylphenidate in boys with disruptive behaviour', *Psychological Medicine* 17 (1987): 121–43.

9. Papalos, D. and Papalos, J., (Broadway Books, 2001).

10. Aaron, Elaine, *The Highly Sensitive Child: Helping Our Children Thrive When the World Overwhelms Them* (Broadway Books, 2002; HarperCollins, 2003).

11. In using this phrase – and the diagram showing the different levels at which we all operate – I must pay tribute to my colleague Dr Alan Watkins, author/editor of *Mind-Body Medicine* (Churchill Livingstone, 1997), who uses this formula to extremely good effect in his highly successful coaching programmes for reducing stress and boosting 'emotional intelligence' in both adults and children. For more details of his work, see the conference profile at http://www.nlpexecutivecoaching.com/conference/2005/people/watkins.php

12. Ibid.

13. Campbell-McBride, Natasha, *Gut and Psychology Syndromes*, is discussed further in Chapters 5 and 6 – also see the Resources section (page 420) for more details.

14. We will be returning to this topic in Chapter 5, but the likelihood that the mother's gut flora may themselves be abnormal, and the problems could therefore be multiplied down the generations, is discussed in more detail in Natasha Campbell-McBride's book *Gut and Psychology Syndromes*.

15. See the reports by Sustain and the Mental Health Foundation: 'Feeding Minds: the impact of food on mental health' and 'Changing Diets, Changing Minds: how food affects well-being and behaviour' – both available at http://www.mentalhealth.org.uk/page.cfm?pagecode=PRFM

16. The leading research in this area has been carried out by Professor John Stein, Dr Sue Fowler and colleagues at Oxford University's Department of Physiology, Anatomy and Genetics. Their pioneering research showed that subtle visual and auditory perceptual problems are common in dyslexia and related conditions and can actually play a causal role in some of the associated difficulties. See the Resources section page 420 for details of how to contact them via the Dyslexia Research Trust, the charity set up to support their research and clinical work.

Chapter 4

1. The Harvard School of Public Health has done an excellent job in pointing out the extent to which government guidelines on 'healthy eating' are often subverted by the influence of the food industry. See their excellent *Nutrition Source* website at http://www.hsph.harvard.edu/nutritionsource/, and the book by the Chair of their Nutrition Department, Walter Willett: *Eat, Drink, and Be Healthy* (Free Press, 2005).

2. For more details of the protein content of various foods – and a very sensible review on the topic of dietary protein, see the information on this topic from the Harvard School of Public Health *Nutrition Source* website http://www.hsph.harvard.edu/nutritionsource/protein.html

3. 'Spelt' is a much older variety of wheat than we use now and contains all the essential amino acids (it does contain gluten, however, so avoid this if your child is gluten-intolerant). Quinoa is a complete protein grain, and the 'pseudo grains' amaranth and buckwheat are rich in amino acids.

4. If you or your child is vegetarian (and even more so if she is vegan) it's essential that you get informed about food. It is possible to remain healthy on these kinds of diets – but you need to know what you're doing, and I've met many vegetarians and vegans (especially children and young adults) who are putting their health at risk by their ignorance. See the resources section for the contact details of the UK Vegetarian Society, and the Vegan Society. In my view, anyone taking up a vegetarian or vegan diet should read the superbly well-researched book by Stephen Walsh: *Plant-based Nutrition and Health* (The Vegan Society, 2003).

5. For a very readable review of the evidence that omega-3 may help – and some other non-drug approaches to stress, anxiety and depression – see David Servan-Schreiber's wonderful book: *Healing without Freud or Prozac: Curing Stress, Anxiety and Depression without Drugs, and without Talk Therapy* (Rodale International Ltd, 2005). It's available from the FAB research website (www.fabresearch.org) and bookshops everywhere (it's been a best-seller in more than 18 countries).

6. If your child has autistic-type symptoms, do have a look at the very insightful papers by Dr Mary Megson on the nature of the visual perceptual problems many of these children have, and the potential importance of *natural* (not synthetic) vitamin A in helping to alleviate autistic symptoms in some cases. Given the importance of vitamin A to your child's immune system and the health and integrity of the lining of his gut, this theory has some obvious implications for the much-debated 'vaccine reactions' that many parents are convinced played a part in triggering their child's autism. See www.megson.com

7. Gregory *et al.*, *National Diet and Nutrition Survey*, volumes 1 & 2 (London: HMSO, 2000). By 'dietary deficiency' I mean less than the so-called 'Lower Reference Nutrient Intake', which would be expected to meet the needs of only a tiny minority (2.5 per cent) of the population. By 'less than recommended' daily intake, I mean less than the so-called 'Reference Nutrient Intake' – which would be expected to meet the needs of around 97.5 per cent of the population. These measures are only based on statistical averages, and there can be wide variation in individual needs. However, none of our dietary standards has ever taken into account the nutritional needs of our brains, or the potential effects of nutrients on behaviour.

8. See the very impressive website of the not-for-profit Vitamin D Council, run primarily by a group of bright and dedicated doctors who are determined to get the message out to the public as well as governments and a medical profession who don't seem to listening yet. http://www.vitamindcouncil.com/

9. See *Sunlight Robbery* by Oliver Gillie, who has painstakingly assembled and summarized the evidence that vitamin D deficiency is now a major health problem in the UK and many other countries. This can be found from the website of the Vitamin D Council (see above).

10. Krishna Vaddadi, a specialist in neurology and psychiatry, has been a pioneer in this field, showing that deficiencies of fatty acids and vitamin E can contribute to motor symptoms in both schizophrenia and Huntington's disease. His early controlled trials include Vaddadi, K. S., *et al.*, 'A double-blind trial of essential fatty acid supplementation in patients with tardive dyskinesia', *Psychiatry Research* 27.3 (1989): 313–23; and Vaddadi, K. S., *et al.*, 'A randomised, placebo-controlled, double blind study of treatment of Huntington's disease with unsaturated fatty acids', *Neuroreport* 13.1 (2002): 29–33. Further details can be found on the FAB research website.

11. Always seek reputable sources of information – preferably by people or organizations with academic and/or medical qualifications or other relevant knowledge and experience – but beware ones that are trying to sell you something, and be alert to sponsorship by vested interests. Good basic nutrition sites with information on vitamins include the Harvard School of Public Health (HSPH):
http://www.hsph.harvard.edu/nutritionsource/vitamins.html
and the UK Food Standards Agency (FSA):
http://www.eatwell.gov.uk/healthydiet/nutritionessentials/vitaminsandminerals/.
The FSA takes a very conservative line, while the HSPH is rather more critical of the status quo – and I've already recommended Walter Willett's book *Eat, Drink and Be Healthy*. For a truly radical (and in my opinion honest and accurate) view of modern-day malnutrition, Dr Paul Clayton's book *Health Defence* (Accelerated Learning Systems, 2004) is simply a tour de force, offering the most easy-to-read synthesis of the latest scientific and medical knowledge about nutrition and health that I've ever come across.

12. Gesch, C. B., Hammond, S. M., Hampson, S. E., Eves, A. and Crowder, M. J., 'Influence of supplementary vitamins, minerals and essential fatty acids on the antisocial behaviour of young adult prisoners. Randomised, placebo-controlled trial', *British Journal of Psychiatry* 181 (2002): 22–8.

13. Eves, A. and Gesch, B., 'Food provision and the nutritional implications of food choices made by young adult males, in a young offenders' institution', *J Hum Nutr Diet* 16.3 (2003): 167–79.

14. Schoenthaler, S. J., 'Diet and delinquency: a multi-state replication', *Int J Biosocial Res* 5.2 (1983): 99–106.

15. Omega-3 deficiency can produce similar symptoms owing to the interactions between B_3 and these vital fats. This was noticed and commented on by one of the earliest researchers into omega-3 for mental disorders. Rudin, D. O., 'The major psychoses and neuroses as omega-3 essential fatty acid deficiency syndrome: substrate pellagra', *Biol Psychiatry* 16 (1981): 837–50.

16. These drugs are 'selective serotonin reuptake inhibitors' – the idea being that they might help you to make more of the little serotonin you've got. For children, almost all of these have now been ruled unsuitable by the UK

Committee for the Safety of Medicines owing to their potential side-effects, but the evidence of these took longer than it should have done to come to light. See http://www.publications.parliament.uk/pa/cm200405/cmselect/cmhealth/42/4 111105.htm

17. This quote comes from the *Merck Manual of Diagnosis and Therapy: Section 1 Nutritional Disorders*. See
http://www.merck.com/mrkshared/mmanual/section1/chapter3/3m.jsp

18. B_{12} injections can usually bypass absorption problems, and are recommended for some people. Ask your doctor about this if you're concerned.

19. It's good to see this kind of research going on, but in my view it would be so much better if studies could drop their obsession with single nutrients in isolation. Sadly, both 'reductionism' within the medical sciences and the patent-profit motives that drive and fund most research still seem to dictate otherwise. See the FAB research website for more details, but examples of the best systematic reviews include Taylor, M. J., Carney, S., Geddes, J. and Goodwin, G., 'Folate for depressive disorders', *Cochrane Database Syst Rev* 2 (2003): CD003390; Malouf, R. and Areosa, Sastre A., 'Vitamin B_{12} for cognition', *Cochrane Database Syst Rev* 3 (2003): CD004326; Malouf, R. and Grimley Evans, J., 'The effect of vitamin B_6 on cognition', *Cochrane Database Syst Rev* 4 (2003): CD004393; Malouf, M., Grimley Evans, J. and Areosa, S. A., 'Folic acid with or without vitamin B_{12} for cognition and dementia', *Cochrane Database Syst Rev* 4 (2003): CD004514.

20. Bernie Rimland of the Autism Research Institute in San Diego has summarized the evidence on vitamin B_6 and magnesium for autism, and the safety issues. See http://www.autism.org/vitb6.html and http://www.autisme.net/b6safe.html

21. Gregory *et al.*, op cit. 'Deficient dietary intake' here means less than the 'Lower Reference Nutrient Intake', which is unlikely to meet the needs of more than 2 or 3 people in every 100.

22. Beri-beri is the classic thiamine deficiency disease, involving unpleasant neurological and physical symptoms, and was first observed when grains such as rice started to be highly refined and 'polished' – thus robbing them of many valuable nutrients. Wernicke Korsakoff's syndrome is the version that alcoholics get – including irreversible memory problems and that stumbling, uncoordinated gait – because excessive drinking will serious deplete B_1 (along with almost every other essential nutrient).

23. Benton, D., Fordy, J., and Haller, J., 'The impact of long-term vitamin supplementation on cognitive functioning', *Psychopharmacology* 117.3 (1995): 298–305; Benton, D., Griffiths, R. and Haller, J., 'Thiamine supplementation, mood and cognitive functioning', *Psychopharmacology*, 129.1 (1997): 66–71.

24. Lonsdale, D. and Schamberger, R., 'Red cell transketolase as an indicator of nutritional deficiency', *Am J Clin Nutr* 33.2 (1980): 205–11.

25. Gregory *et al.*, op cit.

26. Konofal, E., Lecendreux, M., Arnulf, I. and Mouren, M. C., 'Iron deficiency in children with attention-deficit/hyperactivity disorder', *Archives of Pediatric and Adolescent Medicine* 159.8 (August 2005): 788.

27. Chen, J. R. *et al.*, 'Dietary patterns and blood fatty acid composition in children with attention-deficit hyperactivity disorder in Taiwan', *Journal of Nutritional Biochemistry* 15.8 (2004): 467–72.

28. Kotagal, S., Silber, M. H., 'Childhood-onset restless legs syndrome', *Annals of Neurology* 56.6 (2004): 803–7.

29. Some excellent advice for vegetarians can be found in Stephen Walsh's book *Plant-based Nutrition and Health* (The Vegan Society).

30. 'Gut dysbiosis' and how to remedy this is dealt with in expert detail in *Gut and Psychology Syndromes* by Natasha Campbell-McBride, available via the FAB Research website. As she is a medical doctor with qualifications in both neurology and nutritional medicine, your doctor shouldn't dismiss this book out of hand if you show it to him or her.

31. Galland, L., 'Magnesium, stress and neuropsychiatric disorders', *Magnesium and Trace Elements* 10.2-4 (1991): 287–301; Fehlinger, R. and Seidel, K., 'The hyperventilation syndrome: a neurosis or a manifestation of magnesium imbalance?', *Magnesium* 4.2-3 (1985): 129–36; Kozielec, T. and Starobrat Hermelin, B., 'Assessment of magnesium levels in children with attention deficit hyperactivity disorder (ADHD)', *Magnesium Research* 10.2 (1997): 143–8.

32. Starobrat Hermelin, B. and Kozielec, T., 'The effects of magnesium physiological supplementation on hyperactivity in children with attention deficit hyperactivity disorder (ADHD). Positive response to magnesium oral loading test', *Magnesium Research* 10.2 (1997): 149–56.

33. Gregory *et al.*, op cit.

34. Ibid.

35. Mayer, Anne-Marie, 'Historical changes in the mineral content of fruits and vegetables', *British Food Journal* 99.6 (1997).

36. Gregory *et al.*, op cit.

37. Beach, R. S., Gershwin, M. E. and Hurley, L. S., 'Gestational zinc deprivation in mice: persistence of immunodeficiency for three generations', *Science* 218.4571 (1982): 469–71.

38. There is evidence that in some circumstances increasing dietary zinc intake at the expense of copper may cause a *deterioration* in cognitive function. In a 1994 paper in *Science*, it was noted that zinc supplements made Alzheimer's disease worse, so fast that the trial had to be stopped in a matter of days. Bush, A. I. *et al.*, 'Rapid induction of Alzheimer Aß amyloid formation by zinc', *Science* 265 (1994): 1464–7. In another study, rats given extra zinc showed cognitive impairment and decreased brain copper, which the researchers suggested were related. The dose of extra zinc was extraordinarily small, only

one-third of the normal intake. Flinn, J. M. *et al.*, *Physiology & Behavior* 89 (2005): 793. Cognitive decline also correlated with low plasma concentrations of copper in patients with mild to moderate Alzheimer's disease, suggesting that copper deficiency might be contributing to their symptoms. Pajonk, F. G. *et al.*, *Journal of Alzheimer's Disease* 8 (2005): 23–7. In my opinion, if such small doses of zinc could have the effects noted in the Flinn study – let alone the other evidence that's mounting – supplementation with zinc alone should *not* be recommended for Alzheimer's disease or other forms of dementia, and should also be treated with caution in any other groups until more data are forthcoming. In fact, a randomized controlled trial of *copper* supplementation in Alzheimer's is now under way, to see if this many have any benefits. With luck, the results may help to shed some more light on this important but clearly complex issue.

39. Schrauzer, G. N., Shrestha, K.P., 'Lithium in drinking water and the incidences of crimes, suicides and arrests related to drug addictions', *Biol Trace Elem Res* 25.2 (1990): 105–113.

40. Many, if not all, drugs can have effects on nutrient status or metabolism. These are not usually made clear to patients (for example, I was never told that the contraceptive pill could alter B_6 metabolism; and my mother and father were never told that the powerful antibiotics I was regularly prescribed as a child would help to wipe out my natural gut flora). I can't possibly deal with other important potential interactions in this book – but in addition to asking your doctor to check, you can use the Internet to get what information there may be.

41. Always seek information sources that are more likely to be reliable and *as free as possible from commercial bias.* The US National Institutes of Health website on dietary supplements might be a good (and conservative) place to start – and this includes information on how to spot 'health fraud'. See http://ods.od.nih.gov/health_information/health_information.aspx

42. It can be very difficult to find individuals with appropriate formal qualifications and training to advise you on nutritional issues – and especially in relation to behaviour. See the resources section for useful contacts, or visit the FAB Research website.

43. This is now recommended by the Nutrition Department of the Harvard School of Public Health, in recognition that many key nutrients may be lacking from modern diets. I would agree – and I also think there's a good case to be made for basic supplementation with omega-3 fatty acids, discussed further in Chapters 8 and 9.

44. Gesch, C. B. *et al.*, op cit.

45. Benton, D., 'Micro-nutrient supplementation and the intelligence of children', *Neuroscience and Biobehavioral Reviews* 25.4 (2001): 297–309.

46. I don't think I'm wrong in saying that the vitamin and mineral recipe being trialled in the following studies originally arose from a chance conversation

between a psychiatrist and a vet, as the latter was well used to correcting behavioural problems in animals using specific nutrients. If I am, I'm sure that the authors – or the company now making the supplement – will correct me. See: Kaplan, B. J., Crawford, S. G., Gardner, B. and Farrelly, G., 'Treatment of mood lability and explosive rage with minerals and vitamins: two case studies in children', *J Child Adolesc Psychopharmacol* 12.3 (2002): 205–19; Kaplan, B. J., Simpson, J. S., Ferre, R. C., Gorman, C. P., McMullen, D. M. and Crawford, S. G., 'Effective mood stabilization with a chelated mineral supplement: an open-label trial in bipolar disorder', *J Clin Psychiatry* 62.12 (2001): 936–44.

47. Some of this research was in fact carried out more than 100 years ago – when Robert McCarrison, an enterprising army doctor serving in India, noticed that the town-dwellers who ate a refined, processed diet were suffering from a whole array of 'modern' diseases (like cancer, heart dieases and diabetes) that the rural-dwelling Indians, eating the traditional whole food diet, were still free from. He went further – and did his own experiment in which he showed that rats fed on the 'urban diet' developed the entire range of the same diseases (and antisocial behaviours including attacking their own young), while the rats fed on the rural diet remained healthy. See the McCarrison Society website at http://mccarrisonsociety.org.uk/

Chapter 5

1. There are obvious benefits to us of hosting bacteria that can do this, because we need a regular supply of both the B-spectrum vitamins (which are water soluble and can't be stored) and amino acids (which also can't be stored) for many basic functions that provide us with energy and/or support the processes of cell repair and maintenance – and we need vitamin K for the vital function of clotting our blood in case of injury. As we saw in Chapter 4, this is why your child should ideally eat wholesome foods at regular intervals *throughout the day* that provide both B vitamins and good-quality protein. Regular meals certainly couldn't be guaranteed during most of our evolution, so the fact that our 'friendly' gut bacteria can produce these nutrients for us is more than useful, and not just coincidence. If you or your child suffer from 'energy dips' during the day, the wrong balance of gut flora might be one reason why.

2. As usual, though, some of the products most heavily advertised to you aren't necessarily all they're made out to be. Do watch out for how much sugar these kinds of products may contain – which could defeat the whole object – and likewise, any undesirable flavourings and additives.

3. *Gut and Psychology Syndromes* by Natasha Campbell-McBride (Cambridge: Medinform Publishing, 2004). I'd recommend this book to anyone whose child has autism (or one of the related conditions such as ADHD, dyslexia or any mental health problems), or who has digestive problems and/or wants to

learn more about these. It's available via the special FAB Research website that accompanies this book.

4. As Natasha explains in her book, without the right gut flora, the programming of certain 'naïve' immune cells so that they become either Th1 or Th2 cells – involved in cell-mediated and antibody-mediated immunity respectively – can become unbalanced, with allergies or autoimmune disorders thought to reflect relative Th2 dominance. I would add that the dietary balance of omega-3 and omega-6 fatty acids (discussed in Chapter 8) is also thought to affect this immune-system balancing act, and may interact with gut bacteria in doing so. See Das, U. N., 'Essential fatty acids as possible enhancers of the beneficial actions of probiotics', *Nutrition* 18 (2002): 786.

5. The recognition that what we call 'the immune system' affects the way our brains and minds work has spawned a whole new field of science called 'psychoneuroimmunology'. I say 'what we call "the immune system"', because we refer to this as though it's a single entity, which of course it isn't. All kinds of different cells and processes play a part in defending us from attack by 'foreign' substances – which include bacteria, viruses, fungi, parasites and other things that could do us damage. The rather artificial distinction we make between 'mind' and 'body' also leads us to forget that these are inextricably linked. If you come down with influenza or some other virus, your body's immune response will include the production and release of specialized cells designed to attack and eradicate the virus, as well as raising your body temperature (which helps to activate many of these cells). In addition to physical aches and pains, you will usually suffer from intense fatigue and 'brain fog' until the immune response starts to lessen. Some of the mental symptoms can be directly attributed to the effect of certain immune cells on your brain. It is not at all far-fetched to suggest that, in some cases, symptoms resembling 'ADHD' or 'depression', for example, might reflect the effects of ongoing immune responses to pathogenic substances that are never identified. Indeed, many of these symptoms overlap with those of 'Chronic Fatigue Syndrome' – another purely descriptive diagnosis that has replaced the older terms of 'myalgic encephalitis' (ME) and post-viral fatigue syndrome. Although often dismissed by the media with terms like 'yuppie flu', these kinds of conditions are all too real – even if modern medicine hasn't done too well in identifying their causes. That's because they're highly complex and 'systemic' (meaning they reflect a disorder of your whole system), and therefore don't usually respond to 'magic-bullet' pharmacological approaches. Professor Michael Maes from Belgium was one of the first scientists to draw attention to the potential role of immune dysfunction in depression and related conditions, and his extensive list of publications on this topic can be accessed via PubMed (see http://www.ncbi.nlm.nih.gov/entrez/) or any other scientific database. An excellent guide for clinicians and others interested in psychoneuroimmunology

can be found in the book *Mind-Body Medicine* by Dr Alan Watkins (Churchill Livingstone, 1997).

6. This 'cupped hands' rule – along with many other practical tips for improving your digestion – is recommended by practitioner Gudrun Jonsson in her very popular and highly readable little book *Gut Reaction* (London: Vermilion Books, 1999).

7. Paul Shattock of the Autism Research Unit at Sunderland University has pioneered the so-called 'Opioid Excess Theory of Autism'. For more information and other resources, see their website at http://osiris.sunderland.ac.uk/autism/

8. Your stomach lining doesn't usually suffer from the highly acidic contents because it's covered in a protective coating of mucus. Sometimes this protective barrier fails, and the walls do become damaged and painful – that's when you have an ulcer. And it's only quite recently that it was realized that some particularly nasty bacteria are usually responsible for these – of which more later.

9. Or in the US, if your child should consume products made with the artificial fat-substitute 'Olestra', which the body cannot digest. Do look this one up on the Internet if you don't know about it already. Read the views on both sides (it's a very good example of how different sources give you different information!) and see whether you think that the FDA put corporate interest over public health. This substance was not, however, approved as a foodstuff by authorities in the UK or the rest of Europe – which in my personal opinion was definitely the right decision.

10. The established belief that no bacteria could withstand the stomach's acidity delayed for a long time the acceptance of the fact that the bacterium *Helicobacter pylori* plays a key role in most stomach ulcers. In fact, it survives partly by producing its own little alkaline 'cloak' – but low stomach acidity will favour the growth of this and other 'bad' bacteria.

11. *Clostridium difficile* – which can cause severe diarrhoea – is the version that appears to be causing problems in many of our hospitals (see http://news.bbc.co.uk/1/hi/health/4612779.stm). Several strains of Clostridia have been identified significantly more often in stool samples from autistic children than controls; see Parracho, H. M., Bingham, M. O., Gibson, G. R. and McCartney, A. L., 'Differences between the gut microflora of children with autistic spectrum disorders and that of healthy children', *J Med Microbiol* 54.10 (Oct 2005): 987–91.

12. For an excellent explanation of how alcohol is processed, and many other potential sources of 'adverse reactions' to food and drink, see *Was It Something You Ate?* by John Emsley and Peter Fell (Oxford University Press, 2001).

13. A baby's gut is effectively sterile from birth – so the bacteria that colonize this and other membranes (for example in ears, nose, throat and skin) will be the

ones to which he is first exposed. These *should* be beneficial bacteria picked up primarily from Mum – both during his entry into the world and from feeding at her breast. In our modern age of antibiotics, contraceptive pills, and the decline in breastfeeding, however (all of which have already been going on for several generations) there is no guarantee that the 'right' bacteria will be the ones to which baby is fist exposed. Natasha Campbell-McBride makes this point very clearly indeed in her book *Gut and Psychology Syndromes* – and the family histories she describes, in which Grandma may have some mild health issues, Mum has allergies and often Irritable Bowel Syndrome, and the child presents with autism or related conditions, is one with which I am all too familiar. In these cases, things seem to get worse down the generations, and the baby may have picked up a wealth of 'bad' bacteria, compromising both his digestive and his immune system from the outset. If this sounds like your family – despair not. Natasha's book contains all the information needed to deal with even this 'worst-case scenario'. Get it and read it now!

14. The relatively new science of 'psychoneuroimmunology' acknowledges the role of diet and digestion in shaping the way the immune system affects both mind and body, but we still know far too little about this. Natasha Campbell-McBride's new term 'gut and psychology syndromes' was chosen carefully, describing and capturing as it does the problems faced by the many, many children and adults who are falling through the 'GAPS' in our current knowledge.

Chapter 6

1. Also see their website at http://www.hsph.harvard.edu/nutritionsource/ for an explanation of different types of foods and nutrients and what these can do for you.
2. Lau, K., McLean, W. G., Williams, D. P. and Howard, C. V., 'Synergistic interactions between commonly used food additives in a developmental neurotoxicity test', *Toxicol Sci* 90 (1), 2006: 178–87. Epub 2005 Dec 13.
3. Howard, V., 'Synergistic effects of chemical mixtures – can we rely on traditional toxicology?', *The Ecologist* 27.5 (September/October 1997).
4. See 'Diet, ADHD and behavior: a quarter-century review', Center for Science in the Public Interest, 1999. This review is freely available online, and provides details of most of the studies published up to this time. (Other studies since then are discussed in this chapter and more details can be found on the FAB Research website.) It also includes: 'Scientists' letters to the department of health and human services', and 'A parents' guide to diet, ADHD and behavior'. See http://www.cspinet.org
5. Schab, D. W. and Trinh, N. H., *Journal of Developmental & Behavioral Pediatrics* 25.6 (2004): 423–34.
6. Bateman, B., Warner, J. O., Hutchinson, E., Dean, T., Rowlandson, P., Gant, C., Grundy, J., Fitzgerald, C. and Stevenson, J., 'The effects of a double blind,

placebo controlled, artificial food colourings and benzoate preservative challenge on hyperactivity in a general population sample of preschool children', *Archives of Disease in Childhood* 89 (2004): 506–11.

7. www.fabresearch.org

8. Ward, N. I., Soulsbury, K. A., Zettel, V. H., Colquhoun, I. D., Bunday, S. and Barnes, B., 'The influence of the chemical additive tartrazine on the zinc status of hyperactive children – a double-blind placebo-controlled study', *Journal of Nutritional Medicine* 1 (1990): 51–7.

9. Rowe, K. S. and Rowe, K. J., 'Synthetic food coloring and behavior: a dose response effect in a double-blind, placebo-controlled, repeated-measures study', *Journal of Pediatrics* 125 (1994): 691–8.

10. Interestingly enough, a few weeks later some soft drinks with excessive levels of benzene were withdrawn from sale in the UK – and at the time of going to press, results of the FSA's own tests on benzene levels in soft drinks in the UK are still awaited.

11. Dr Rosemary Waring from Birmingham University and her colleagues have pioneered much of the work in this area, having been encouraged to do so by the observations of parents and support groups – particularly Brenda O'Reilly of Autism Unravelled. See Alberti, A., Pirrone, P., Elia, M., Waring, R. H. and Romano, C., 'Sulphation deficit in "low-functioning" autistic children: a pilot study', *Biological Psychiatry* 46.3 (1999): 420–24 (and see Resources for contact details of Autism Unravelled and how you can benefit from their ongoing research and information activities to help your child). A difficulty with sulphation could have widespread effects on the gut, brain and immune system, in keeping with many features of autism and related conditions. One very simple practical tip that may be of some help (according to parents who've tried this) is to add Espom Salts (magnesium sulphate) to your child's bath! This may also help by delivering additional magnesium to anyone who may be lacking in this key mineral (as we saw in Chapter 4, this may be quite a lot of people). For an example of parents sharing their practical tips and personal research on this topic, see http://www.bbbautism.com/epsom_condensed_plaintext.htm

12. See http://www.babyorganix.co.uk/report2/ for full details, in the special 'Carrots or Chemistry' report by the Organix company.

13. www.foresight-preconception.org.uk/summaries/frames/lead-nf.html

14. This contentious issue was discussed in depth at the 6th Congress of the International Society for the Study of Fatty Acids and Lipids (ISSFAL), following data presented in the keynote lecture by Dr Joseph Hibblen of the US National Institutes of Health. Further information on the 'fish and mercury' is available from the FAB Research website – including links to other places where consumers can find the most up-to-date information on the most safe and sustainable sources of fish.

15. See www.ocfp.on.ca/English/OCFP/Communications/CurrentIssues/Pesticides
16. Emsley, John and Fell, Peter, *Was It Something You Ate?* (OUP, 2001).
17. Brostoff, Jonathan and Gamlin, Linda, *The Complete Guide to Food Allergy and Intolerance* (Bloomsbury, 1998).
18. Campbell-McBride, Natasha, *Gut and Psychology Syndromes.*
19. This is not always easy, but see the Resources for some tips on how to find a suitably qualified and experienced practitioner.
20. Arnold, G. L., Hyman, S. L., Mooney, R. A. and Kirby, R. S., 'Plasma amino acids profiles in children with autism: potential risk of nutritional deficiencies', *Journal of Autism and Developmental Disorders* 33.4 (2003): 449–54.
21. Kefir is a special kind of fermented milk containing helpful gut bacteria, as well as beneficial yeasts that can help fight off the harmful yeasts like candida. It's easier to digest than ordinary yoghurts, so it's good for babies, invalids and the elderly – and if you're suffering from some digestive disorder.
22. See http://osiris.sunderland.ac.uk/autism/
23. Millward, C., Ferriter, M., Calver, S. and Connell-Jones, G., 'Gluten- and casein-free diets for autistic spectrum disorder', *Cochrane Database of Systematic Reviews* 2 (2004): CD003498.
24. Bushara, K. O., 'Neurologic presentation of celiac disease', *Gastroenterology* 128.4 Pt 2 (2005): 92–7; Wills, A. J. and Unsworth, D. J., 'The neurology of gluten sensitivity: separating the wheat from the chaff', *Current Opinion in Neurology* 15.5 (2002): 519–23; Volta, U., De Giorgio, R., Petrolini, N., Stangbellini, V., Barbara, G., Granito, A., De Ponti, F., Corinaldesi, R. and Bianchi, F. B., 'Clinical findings and anti-neuronal antibodies in coeliac disease with neurological disorders', *Scand J Gastroenterol* 37.11 (2002): 1276–81.
25. Haas, Elson M., *The False Fat Diet* (Bantam Books, 2001).

Chapter 7

1. To stay healthy, vegetarians do need to learn more about which foods provide which nutrients than omnivores do – simply because animal products are the richest sources of many key nutrients, and also tend to provide these in the forms that are easiest for humans to absorb. We saw this in Chapter 4 with respect to 'haem' versus 'non-haem' forms of iron, for example. As another, neither active vitamin A nor vitamin D is found in vegetarian foods, although the first can be made from beta-carotene, the second from sunlight – as long as enough of these is available and these pathways are working efficiently. Similarly, some very important omega-3 fatty acids aren't provided directly by vegetarian foods, and therefore need to be made in the body from simpler ones that are. This process requires many vitamin and mineral 'co-factors' – so these need to be available in the diet, and properly absorbed. In the case of protein, different vegetarian foods eaten together can easily provide the full range of amino acids found in 'complete' animal protein (lentils with rice, for example,

or beans with toast). Vitamin B_{12} is generally acknowledged to be the only nutrient that vegetarians *must* get from a supplement source – but an awareness of other nutrients and how they work together is important. For information and advice on being or becoming vegetarian, see the websites of the Vegetarian and Vegan Societies (provided in the Resources section).

2. Both the 'Food Pyramids' devised by the US Government's agencies and the advice given by the UK Government fail to reinforce this distinction. (The FSA's website says 'Starchy foods such as bread, cereals, rice, pasta and potatoes are a really important part of a healthy diet' – and although it does add the advice: 'Try to choose wholegrain varieties whenever you can,' that doesn't strike me as offering you much incentive! In the Appendix you'll find the 'Healthy Eating Pyramid' drawn up by the Nutrition Department of the Harvard School of Public Health, which does a much better job of making the distinction between refined and unrefined starches clear – with one at the top, and the other at the bottom of the pyramid.

3. Dr Robert McCarrison conducted the experiments to show this while serving in India with the British Army. Having observed health differences between the urban Indians (eating a diet of refined foods) and the rural Indians (eating the traditional whole food diet), he studied rats given either one diet or the other, and the results were very clear. See the McCarrison Society website, where Professor Michael Crawford gives an overview of the findings of this remarkable man, and their implications.
http://mccarrisonsociety.org.uk/content/view/19/52/

4. Peet, M., 'International variations in the outcome of schizophrenia and the prevalence of depression in relation to national dietary practices: an ecological analysis', *Br J Psychiat* 184: 404–8.

5. Molteni, R. *et al.*, 'A high-fat, refined sugar diet reduces hippocampal brain-derived neurotrophic factor, neuronal plasticity, and learning', *Neuroscience* 112.4 (2002): 803–14.

6. The books *Pure, White and Deadly* by John Yudkin (now out of print) and *Sugar Blues* by William Duffy (Warner Books, 1975) spell out very clearly what sugar is about. And that was then. This is now – and you'll find many more books on this topic – including *The Sugar Addict's Total Recovery Guide* by Kathleen DesMaisons, and her version for children, *Little Sugar Addicts: End the Mood Swings, Meltdowns, Tantrums, and Low Self-Esteem in Your Child Today*. Along with her website at http://www.sugaraddict.com/ this has all the information needed if you or your child want to kick the sugar habit.

7. Gottschall, E., *Breaking the Vicious Cycle: Intestinal Health Through Diet* (Kirkton Press, 1996). See also the website that Elaine Gottschall has set up to help parents and professionals worldwide. http://www.breakingthevicciouscycle.info/

8. *The Management of Celiac Disease* by Dr S. V. Haas and M. P. Haas was published in 1951, before the recognition that a very specific immune reaction

to gluten was the cause of classic coeliac disease. True coeliac disease affects only around one person in every 1,500 – but the diet developed by Dr Haas and his colleagues was successful in treating a much wider range of problems, involving severe digestive and sometimes psychiatric or neurological symptoms.

9. Natasha's own dietary plan is based on Elaine Gottschall's Specific Carbohydrate Diet™ (itself based on the one devised by Dr Haas and colleagues). Elaine's book and website are noted above. Natasha's dietary advice can be found – with recipes – in her book *Gut and Psychology Syndromes* (see the Resources chapter for details).

10. See Colantuoni, C. *et al.*, 'Evidence that intermittent, excessive sugar intake causes endogenous opioid dependence', *Obesity Research* 10.6 (2002): 478–88.

11. Spangler *et al.*, 'Opiate-like effects of sugar on gene expression in reward areas of the rat brain', *Brain Research and Molecular Brain Research* 124.2 (May 2004): 134–42.

12. Molteni, op cit.

13. This was her first book – and her programme has been revised in the later books on sugar addiction and how to beat this – cited in note 6.

14. Again – this is Rule Number One in Kathleen DesMaison's programme for beating sugar addiction. Why not make it easy for yourself and your child instead of setting yourselves up to fail? The same rule is captured in the title of another best-selling book aimed at the weight-loss market (most failed dieters have sugar-sensitivity problems): *Only Fat People Skip Breakfast* by Lee Janogly (HarperCollins, 2004).

Chapter 8

1. Gregory *et al.*, *National Diet and Nutrition Surveys* (London: HMSO, 2000).

2. Read about this issue in the superb book *The Omega Diet* by Professor Artemis Simopoulos and Jo Robinson (HarperPerennial, 1999), available from the FAB Research website. In addition to explaining the science behind the health benefits of omega-3, this book contains recipes and a complete dietary plan for you to follow, as well as very useful appendices showing the omega-3 content of different foods.

3. At his untimely death in 2003, David Horrobin had 939 scientific research publications to his name, and a further 114 patents on which he was a named inventor. You can find his bibliography – assembled as a tribute and resource by one of his old colleagues – via the FAB Research website. With respect to controversy – you can look up the vicious obituary published by the *British Medical Journal* only two weeks after his death. No article published in the *BMJ* has ever attracted so much correspondence – either before or since – and the emails that flooded in are on the website still, but these tell only something of the tale of this remarkable man. For those interested to read David Horrobin's own story about his scientific research and the curiosity that drove much of his

life's work – see *The Madness of Adam and Eve* (available from the FAB Research website). He wrote this book for the general public, at the request of the Schizophrenia Association of Great Britain for whom he served as President for many years.

4. John Stein gave an extremely moving 'memorial lecture' in honour of David Horrobin at a conference shortly after the latter's death, conveying as probably no one else could have done the extraordinary vision, courage and sheer creativity of the man and his life's work. In my view, these are all qualities that John himself shares. You can find his tribute to David Horrobin via the FAB Research website, or in *Prostaglandins, Leukotrienes and EFAs* 70 (2004): 339–43.

5. Puri, B. K. and Richardson, A. J., 'The effects of olive oil on omega-3 fatty acids and mood disorders', *Archives of General Psychiatry* 57 (2000): 715.

6. For the technically minded – in the natural, so-called 'cis' forms of polyunsaturated fats, all the 'missing hydrogen' corresponding with the double bonds is usually on the same side of the molecule. In trans fats, the missing hydrogen is on both sides (*trans* means 'across'). This changes the shape of the molecule, so that it will no longer 'kink' in the right places. It also changes the way these fats behave in the body and brain – with potentially very damaging consequences.

7. Alarming levels of these dangerous trans fats in fast foods are highlighted in a recent study in the *New England Journal of Medicine*. See http://www.newscientist.com/article/dn8989-fast-food-awash-with-worst-kind-of-fat.html

8. The Campaign Against Trans Fats in Food is a UK organization run by volunteers, seeking to provide information, raise awareness and persuade individuals, companies and government agencies to take action to reduce consumption of these dangerous fats. Visit their website at www.tfx.org.uk/

9. This issue is of huge practical concern, as it has important implications not only for people following vegetarian or vegan diets, but also for our global food supply and its environmental impact. Seminal papers showing the poor conversion of the simplest forms of omega-3 and omega-6 to the highly unsaturated forms most important to the brain and body health are: Pawlosky, R. J., Hibbeln, J. R., Novotny, J. A. and Salem, N. Jr, 'Physiological compartmental analysis of alpha-linolenic acid metabolism in adult humans', *Journal of Lipid Research* 42.8 (2001): 1257–65; Salem, N. Jr, Pawlosky, R., Wegher, B. and Hibbeln, J., 'In vivo conversion of linoleic acid to arachidonic acid in human adults', *Prostaglandins Leukotrienes & Essential Fatty Acids* 60.5-6 (1999): 407–10.

10. Burdge, G. C., Jones, A. E. and Wootton, S. A., 'Eicosapentaenoic and docosapentaenoic acids are the principal products of alpha-linolenic acid metabolism in young men', *British Journal of Nutrition* 88 (2002): 355–63; Burdge, G. C. and Wootton, S. A., 'Conversion of alpha-linolenic acid to

eicosapentaenoic, docosapentaenoic and docosahexaenoic acids in young women', *British Journal of Nutrition* 88 (2002): 411–20.

11. See Simopoulos, A. P., 'The importance of the ratio of omega-6/omega-3 essential fatty acids', *Biomed Pharmacotherapy* 56.8 (2002): 365–79; Haag, M., 'Essential fatty acids and the brain', *Canadian Journal of Psychiatry* 48 (2003): 195–203.

12. Recommendations of the International Society for the Study of Fatty Acids and Lipids (ISSFAL) – see www.issfal.org.uk/ The UK Joint Health Claims Initiative (JHCI) has also reviewed the studies on omega-3 and heart health, and food producers in the UK can now make limited health claims if their products make an appreciable contribution towards the JHCI daily recommended intake, which is 450mg of EPA + DHA. See http://www.fabresearch.org/view_item.aspx?item_id=822

13. Facchinetti, F., Fazzio, M. and Venturini, P., 'Polyunsaturated fatty acids and risk of preterm delivery', *European Review of Medical and Pharmacological Sciences* 9.1 (Jan/Feb 2005): 41–8.

14. Logan, A. C., 'Omega-3 fatty acids and major depression: a primer for the mental health professional', *Lipids in Health and Disease* 3 (2004): 25.

15. Willatts, P. and Forsyth, J., 'The role of long-chain polyunsaturated fatty acids in infant cognitive development' *Prostaglandins Leukot Essent Fatty Acids* 63.1-2 (Jul/Aug 2000): 95–100.

16. Stordy, J., 'Docosahexaenoic acid for dark adaptation in dyslexia', *Lancet* 346.9871 (1995): 385.

17. Maes, M., Mihaylova, I. and Leunis, J. C., 'In chronic fatigue syndrome, the decreased levels of omega-3 poly-unsaturated fatty acids are related to lowered serum zinc and defects in T cell activation', *Neuro Endocrinology Letters* 26.6 (Dec 2005): 745–51.

Chapter 9

1. According to the latest UK National Diet and Nutrition Surveys, the average intake of children of all ages is way below the 500mg day of EPA and DHA recommended for heart health. Unfortunately, the data don't distinguish between the different types of omega-3, but the total daily omega-3 intake from fish and fish dishes (the only appreciable dietary source of ready-made EPA and DHA) was only 110mg for children aged 1.5 to 4.5 years, and less than 90mg for boys or girls aged 4–18 years. The main source of 'omega-3' for all age groups was actually the broad category of 'vegetables, potatoes and savoury snacks' – but vegetables and vegetable oils only provide ALA, not the more important EPA and DHA.

2. Peet, M., Glen, I. and Horrobin, D. F. (eds), *Phospholipid Spectrum Disorders in Psychiatry and Neurology* (Carnforth: Marius Press, 2003).

3. Colquhoun, I. and Bunday, S., 'A lack of essential fatty acids as a possible cause of hyperactivity in children', *Medical Hypotheses*, 7 (1981): 673–9.

4. Baker, S. M., 'A biochemical approach to the problem of dyslexia', *Journal of Learning Disabilities* 18.10 (1985): 581–4.
5. It is important to note that these kinds of physical signs are typically associated with deficiencies in *both* omega-3 and omega-6 essential fatty acids.
6. Stevens, L. J., Zentall, S. S., Abate, M. L., Kuczek, T. and Burgess, J. R., 'Omega-3 fatty acids in boys with behavior, learning, and health problems', *Physiology and Behaviour* 59 (1996): 915–20; Taylor, K. E., Higgins, C. J., Calvin, C. M., Hall, J. A., Easton, T., McDaid, A. M. and Richardson, A. J., 'Dyslexia in adults is associated with clinical signs of fatty acid deficiency', *Prostaglandins Leukot Essent Fatty Acids* 63 (2000): 75–8; Richardson, A. J., Calvin, C. M., Clisby, C., Schoenheimer, D. R., Montgomery, P., Hall, J. A., Hebb, G., Westwood, E., Talcott, J. B. and Stein, J. F., 'Fatty acid deficiency signs predict the severity of reading and related difficulties in dyslexic children', *Prostaglandins Leukot Essent Fatty Acids* 63 (2000): 69–74.
7. Stevens *et al.*, op cit.
8. These papers are too numerous to reference in full here, but see the FAB Research website for details. In ADHD children, reduced blood concentrations of key HUFAs (including AA, DHA and total omega-3) have been reported in several studies: (Bekaroglu *et al.*, 1996; Burgess *et al.*, 2000; Burgess and Stevens, 2003; Chen, J. R., *et al.*, 2004; Mitchell *et al.*, 1987; Stevens, L. J. *et al.*, 1995), but not all (Burgess and Stevens, 2003). Reductions of omega-3 were also found in adults with ADHD (Young *et al.*, 2004). In children and adults with autistic spectrum disorders, fatty acid abnormalities have been reported in both plasma (Vancassel *et al.*, 2001) and RBC membranes (Bell *et al.*, 2004a; Bell *et al.*, 2000). Findings include particular reductions in omega-3 HUFA, an elevated ratio of AA:EPA (consistent with tendencies towards inflammation) and an apparent increased susceptibility to breakdown of membrane fatty acids, possibly reflecting increased oxidative stress.
9. Bell, J. G., Ross, M. A., Cyhlarova, E., Shrier, A., Dick, J. R., Henderson, R. J. and Richardson, A. J., 'Membrane fatty acids, reading and spelling in dyslexic and non-dyslexic adults', *ISSFAL 6th International Congress* (2004b), Brighton, UK; Ross, M. A., Cyhlarova, E., Shrier, A., Henderson, R. J., MacKinlay, E. E., Dick, J. R., Bell, J. G. and Richardson, A. J., 'Working memory and schizotypal traits in relation to fatty acid status in dyslexia', *ISSFAL 6th International Conference* (2004), Brighton, UK.
10. MacDonell, L. E., Skinner, F. K., Ward, P. E., Glen, A. I., Glen, A. C., Macdonald, D. J., Boyle, R. M. and Horrobin, D. F., 'Increased levels of cytosolic phospholipase A2 in dyslexics', *Prostaglandins Leukotrienes and Essential Fatty Acids* 63.1-2 (2000): 37–9; Bell, J. G., MacKinlay, E. E., Dick, J. R., MacDonald, D. J., Boyle, R. M. and Glen, A. C., 'Essential fatty acids and phospholipase A2 in autistic spectrum disorders', *Prostaglandins Leukotrienes and Essential Fatty Acids* 71 (2004a): 201–4.

11. Aman, M. G., Mitchell, E. A. and Turbott, S. H., 'The effects of essential fatty acid supplementation by Efamol in hyperactive children', *Journal of Abnormal Child Psychology* 15 (1987): 75–90; Arnold, L. E., Kleykamp, D., Votolato, N. A., Taylor, W. A., Kontras, S. B. and Tobin, K., 'Gamma-linolenic acid for attention-deficit hyperactivity disorder: placebo-controlled comparison to D-amphetamine', *Biological Psychiatry* 25 (1989): 222–8.

12. Voigt, R. G., Llorente, A. M., Jensen, C. L., Fraley, J. K., Berretta, M. C. and Heird, W. C., 'A randomized, double-blind, placebo-controlled trial of docosahexaenoic acid supplementation in children with attention-deficit/hyperactivity disorder', *Journal of Pediatrics* 139 (2001): 189–96; Hamazaki, T. and Hirayama, S., 'The effect of docosahexaenoic acid-containing food administration on symptoms of attention-deficit/hyperactivity disorder – a placebo-controlled double-blind study', *European Journal of Clinical Nutrition* 58 (2004): 838.

13. Stevens, L. J., Zentall, S. S., Deck, J. L., Abate, M. L., Watkins, B. A., Lipp, S. R. and Burgess, J. R., 'Essential fatty acid metabolism in boys with attention-deficit hyperactivity disorder', *American Journal of Clinical Nutrition*, 62 (1995): 761–8.

14. Richardson, A. J. and Puri, B. K., 'A randomized double-blind, placebo-controlled study of the effects of supplementation with highly unsaturated fatty acids on ADHD-related symptoms in children with specific learning difficulties', *Progress in Neuropsychopharmacology and Biological Psychiatry* 26 (2002): 233–9.

15. Richardson, A. J. and Montgomery, P., 'The Oxford-Durham study: a randomised controlled trial of fatty acid supplementation in children with developmental coordination disorder', *Pediatrics* 115 (2005): 1360–66.

16. Whether fatty acids could actually improve motor coordination remains an open question. Some of the individual children showed dramatic transformations of their handwriting over the treatment period that clearly deserve further investigation, but this kind of apparent benefit remains at the 'anecdotal' level for the time being.

17. Before we had a chance to publish the results in a peer-reviewed journal, this trial was featured on the flagship episode of Lord Winston's hugely popular BBC1 series on *The Human Mind*. You can find some of the best media articles and other discussion that followed via the FAB Research website.

18. See the FAB Research website for more information on this important issue.

19. FDA, U., Letter regarding dietary supplement health claim for omega-3 fatty acids and coronary heart disease. US Food and Drug Administration, Center for Food Safety and Applied Nutrition, Office of Nutritional Products, Labeling, and Dietary Supplements, October 31, 2000.

20. Controlled trials had provided enough evidence of benefits that EPO was available on prescription for atopic eczema until recently. This is no longer the case – not because of any problems with the original data, but because the

amount of evidence required has increased since the original trials were done. See Horrobin, D. F., 'Essential fatty acid metabolism and its modification in atopic eczema [review]', *Am J Clin Nutr* 71.1Supp (2000): 367S–72S.

21. Hamazaki, T., Sawazaki, S., Itomura, M., Asaoka, E., Nagao, Y., Nishimura, N., Yazawa, K., Kuwamori, T. and Kobayashi, M., 'The effect of docosahexaenoic acid on aggression in young adults. A placebo-controlled double-blind study', *Journal of Clinical Investigations* 97 (1996): 1129–33.

22. See the FAB Research website for details of this research, particularly the full text of the excellent review: Logan, A. C., 'Omega-3 fatty acids and major depression: a primer for the mental health professional', *Lipids in Health and Disease* 3 (2004): 25.

23. Peet, M. and Horrobin, D. F., 'A dose-ranging study of the effects of ethyl-eicosapentaenoate in patients with ongoing depression despite apparently adequate treatment with standard drugs', *Archives of General Psychiatry* 59 (2002): 913–19.

24. Peet, M., Horrobin, D. F. and E-E-Multicentre-Study-Group, 'A dose-ranging exploratory study of the effects of ethyl-eicosapentaenoate in patients with persistent schizophrenic symptoms', *Journal of Psychiatry Research* 36.1 (2002): 7–18.

Chapter 10

1. The National Audit Office, the Healthcare Commission and the Audit Commission.
2. www.which.net/campaigns/food
3. Montgomery, P., Wiggs, L. and Stores, G., 'The relative efficacy of two brief treatments for sleep problems in young learning disabled (mentally retarded) children: a randomized controlled trial', *Archives of Disease in Childhood* 89.2 (Feb 2004): 125–30.
4. See the books *Emotional Intelligence* by Daniel Goleman (Bloomsbury, 1996), *Tapping the Healer Within* by Dr Roger Callahan (Contemporary Books, 2002), and Professor David Servan-Schreiber's best-selling book *Healing Without Freud or Prozac* (Rodale International Ltd, 2005).

Chapter 11

1. See Tony Buzan's book *Headstrong* (HarperCollins, 2001) for an explanation of how your brain really works – and how to form new, good habits by getting your 'subconscious' on your side.
2. If 'sugar-sensitivity' is an issue in your family, look up the books by Katherine DesMaisons – *Little Sugar Addicts* (for your child) and *The Sugar Addict's Total Recovery Program* (for you or other adults with this syndrome). You can find them via the FAB Research website, along with more information on sugar cravings and mood swings.

3. Excess B vitamins can make urine more yellow when excreted; harmless, but worth knowing. Some medications or highly coloured foods – like beetroot – may also cause unusual coloured urine, but so can certain diseases. There's plenty of information about what urine should look like – and even colour charts – on the Internet, but if you are in any doubt at all, ask your doctor.

4. This child-friendly site makes a good starting point: http://askabiologist.asu.edu/research/scurvy/

Appendix

1. See the article on this topic by Slade, M. and Priebe, S., 'Are randomised controlled trials the only gold that glitters?', *British Journal of Psychiatry* 179 (2001): 286–7.

2. Kirsch, Irving, Moore, Thomas J., Scoboria, Alan and Nicholls, Sarah S., 'The emperor's new drugs: an analysis of antidepressant medication data submitted to the U.S. Food and Drug Administration', *Prevention & Treatment* 5.1 (2002): 23.

3. See http://www.consort-statement.org/

4. http://bmj.bmjjournals.com/cgi/eletters/332/7544/752#131534

5. Sagan, Carl, *The Demon-Haunted World: Science as a Candle in the Dark* (Headline Book Publishing, 1997; available from the FAB Research website)

Resources

Further Information

If you have any enquiries or would like further information on issues raised in this book, please visit these websites:

- www.theyarewhatyoufeedthem.com (an interactive resource where reviews can be read and posted and questions answered)
- www.fabresearch.org (Food and Behaviour Research)

Finding a Nutrition Practitioner

In general, 'nutritionists' don't usually offer advice to individuals on health issues (most are more likely to be working in public health or industry), but 'nutritional therapists' usually do, and 'dietitians' may.

Neither 'nutritionist' nor 'nutritional therapist' is yet a protected professional title.

By contrast, the title 'dietician' is protected, and only those who are registered as such with the Health Professions Council can use it.

Dieticians

Dieticians are trained to university degree level (4 years BSc or 2 years postgraduate study on top of an existing healthcare qualification), and receive practical training in hospitals and the community. Their job involves interpreting and communicating the science of nutrition so that people can make practical and informed choices about food and lifestyle. Dieticians can help to diagnose health problems and devise appropriate dietary treatments. Some work in the NHS alongside doctors or other health professionals. Others may be in private practice, and any may work in one or more specialist areas.

If you can, try to find a dietician who specializes in mental health, allergies and intolerances, child behaviour problems, infant nutrition or child health – whatever your particular needs may be. You can seek referral to a dietician working with the NHS through your local hospital or GP surgery. To find details of registered dieticians working in private practice in your area, contact the British Dietetic Association at the address below or visit: http://www.dietitiansunlimited.co.uk/

The British Dietetic Association (BDA)
5th floor, Charles House
148/9 Great Charles Street
Queensway
Birmingham B3 3HT
tel: 0121 200 8080
fax: 0121 200 8081
info@bda.uk.com
www.bda.uk.com

Nutritionists

As noted above, most nutritionists don't work with individuals as practitioners to solve health problems (although a few do). Rather, they are more likely to work in academia, public health, industry or other capacities.

The Nutrition Society is a well-established academic and professional association that wants to see the title of 'nutritionist' protected (which it currently isn't). They have their own register of nutritionists, with four different 'levels', each of which requires at least degree-level training in nutrition or its equivalent.

The Nutrition Society
10 Cambridge Court
210 Shepherds Bush Road
London W6 7NJ
tel: 020-7602-0228
http://www.nutsoc.org.uk

Nutrition Therapists

This is by far the largest group working in private practice offering nutritional advice to members of the public.

Unfortunately, use of this title is not restricted, so 'nutrition therapists' can vary extremely widely in their levels of training, experience and professional competence. Some have little or no formal training, many have done brief courses to obtain a 'certificate' or 'diploma' that may not be recognized by most professional or academic bodies. Others may have rigorous qualifications, including degree- or postgraduate-level training in nutrition or related areas.

It's a lottery unless you find out more about the qualifications and experience of each individual. Beware of any who may advertise their services to you in a 'pushy' way, or tell you that certain diagnostic tests or supplements are essential for your child. (Many will be on commission to the companies selling you these things, even if that may not be obvious. Always ask.)

The British Association for Nutritional Therapists (BANT) is working with the Nutritional Therapy Council (www.nutritionaltherapycouncil.org.uk) to devise and maintain a registration and accreditation system for nutritional therapists. BANT can provide you with a list of registered therapists in a given UK region.

British Association for Nutritional Therapists (BANT)
27 Old Gloucester Street
London WC1N 3XX
tel/fax: 08706 061284
http://www.bant.org.uk

Information on Vegetarian or Vegan Diets

The Vegetarian Society of the United Kingdom
Parkdale
Dunham Road
Altrincham
Cheshire WA14 4QG
tel: 0161 925 2000
fax: 0161 926 9182
http://www.vegsoc.org

The Vegan Society
Donald Watson House
7 Battle Road
St Leonards-on-Sea
East Sussex TN37 7AA
tel: 01424 427393
fax: 01424 717064
http://www.vegansociety.com

Information on ADHD, Autism, Dyslexia or Dyspraxia

The following are just a few of the many UK charities and support groups addressing the needs of parents and others who care for individuals with these conditions. You can find many more on the FAB Research website. Look also for local groups in your area.

Hyperactive Children's Support Group

Offers information and support based on many years of practical experience, primarily to parents of hyperactive children, but also to schools, health professionals and policymakers. HACSG can provide a full list of additives, colourings, sweeteners and flavourings to avoid, and other dietary advice.

HACSG
71 Whyke Lane
Chichester PO19 7PD
tel: 01243 551313
www.hacsg.org.uk/

The Overload Network

A Scottish-based charity providing advice and support to parents of children with ADHD-type difficulties and campaigning for alternatives to medication. They can be contacted at:

141 Norman Rise
West Lothian
Livingston EH54 6NN
tel: 01506 205919

Autism Unravelled

A charity that provides excellent newsletters on the latest research and its practical implications with respect to diet, allergies and related issues in autism and related disorders:

Brenda O'Reilly, Director
Autism Unravelled
3 Palmera Avenue
Calcot
Reading
Berkshire RG3 7DZ
www.autism-unravelled.org/

Autism Research Unit, University of Sunderland

Directed by Paul Shattock, provides information on biomedical research, including the 'Sunderland Protocol' – practical strategies for managing autistic spectrum disorders.

Autism Research Unit
School of Health, Natural & Social Sciences
University of Sunderland
Sunderland SR1 3SD
tel: 0191 510 8922
autism.unit@sunderland.ac.uk
http://osiris.sunderland.ac.uk/autism/

The Dyslexia Research Trust

An Oxford-based charity set up by Professor John Stein to support and promote scientific research into the nature and causes of dyslexia and related conditions, and to provide clinical services to children and adults with these conditions. With Dr Sue Fowler, John Stein pioneered the research showing that visual treatments can help many children and adults with dyslexia and related conditions.

Mrs Clarice Davies, Administrator
Dyslexia Research Trust
Sherrington Building
Dept of Physiology, Anatomy and Genetics
University of Oxford
Parks Road
Oxford
Oxon OX1 3PT
www.dyslexic.org.uk

British Dyslexia Association

The BDA provides information and support for parents, education and health professionals and policymakers. They also provide a national framework for the many regional associations affiliated to the BDA.

> The British Dyslexia Association
> 98 London Road
> Reading
> Berkshire RG1 5AU
> Helpline: 0118 966 8271
> General enquiries: 0118 966 2677
> www.bdadyslexia.org.uk

The Dyspraxia Foundation

A UK charity that exists to help people to understand and cope with dyspraxia. They are a resource for parents, for teenagers and adults who have the condition, and for professionals who help all of them. They also provide a national framework for their many regional associations.

> Dyspraxia Foundation
> 8 West Alley
> Hitchin
> Herts SG5 1EG
> Helpline: 01462 454 986 (10 a.m. – 1 p.m. Mon – Fri)
> Admin tel: 01462 455 016
> dyspraxia@dyspraxiafoundation.org.uk
> www.dyspraxiafoundation.org.uk

Further Information

This is only a small sample of the kinds of books available covering some of the topics described in this book. We keep the FAB website updated with new book suggestions, so please visit us there.

Bali, Karen, Child, Sally K., Craze, Richard (ed) and Jay, Roni (ed), *The Art of Hiding Vegetables: Sneaky Ways to Feed Your Children Healthy Food* (White Ladder Press Ltd, 2005)

Blythman, Joanna, *The Food Our Children Eat: How to Get Children to Like Good Food* (Fourth Estate, 2000)

Campbell-McBride, Natasha, *Gut and Psychology Syndromes* (Medinform Publishing, 2004)

Chaitow, Leon, *Candida Albicans* (Thornsons,1996)

Clayton, Paul, *Health Defence* (Accelerated Learning Systems, 2004)

DesMaisons, Kathleen, *Potatoes Not Prozac* (Pocket Books, 2001)

Emsley, John and Fell, Peter, *Was it Something You Ate?* (OUP, 2001)

Erasmus, Udo, *Fats that Heal, Fats that Kill* (Alive Books, 1996)

Good Food Magazine '101 Simple Suppers' (BBC Books, 2003)

Green, Christopher and Chee, Kit, *Understanding ADHD* (Vermillion, 1997)

Haas, Elson M., *The False Fat Diet* (Bantam Books, 2001)

Jackson, Jacqui, *Multicoloured Mayhem* (Jessica Kingsley Publishers, 2004)

Jackson, Luke, *A User Guide to the GF/CF Diet for Autism, Asperger Syndrome, and AD/HD* (Jessica Kingsley Publishers, 2003)

Janogly, Lee, *Only Fat People Skip Breakfast* (HarperCollins, 2004)

Lawrence, Felicity, *Not on the Label* (Penguin Books, 2004)

McCandless, Jacqueline, *Children with Starving Brains* (www.autism-rxguidebook.net/)

Palmer, Sue, *Toxic Childhood* (Orion, 2006)

Schlosser, Eric, *Fast Food Nation* (Penguin Books, 2002)

Schmidt, Michael, *Smart Fats* (North Atlantic Books, 1997)

Servan-Schreiber, David, *Healing without Freud or Prozac* (Rodale, 2004)

Simopoulos, Artemis P. and Robinson, Jo, *The Omega Diet* (HarperPerennial, 1999)

Stevens, Laura, *10 Effective Ways to Help Your ADD/ADHD Child* (Avery Publishing Group, 2000)

Stordy, Jacqueline and Nicholl, Malcolm J., *The LCP Solution: The Remarkable Nutritional Treatment for ADHD, Dyslexia and Dyspraxia* (Ballantyne Books, 2000)

Watt, Fiona, *The Usborne Beginner's Cookbook* (Usborne Publishing Ltd, 1999)

Walker, Caroline and Cannon, Geoffrey, *The Food Scandal: What's Wrong with the British Diet and How to Set It Right* (Arrow, 1986)

Walsh, Steven, *Plant-based Nutrition and Health* (The Vegan Society, 2003)

Watkins, Alan (ed), *Mind-Body Medicine: A Clinician's Guide to Psychoneuroimmunology* (Churchill Livingstone, 1997)

Weil, Andrew, *Eating Well for Optimum Health* (Warner Books, 2001)

Wilkoff, William G., *Coping with a Picky Eater: A Guide for the Perplexed Parent* (Prentice Hall & IBD, 1998)

Willett, Walter, *Eat, Drink, and Be Healthy* (Free Press, 2005)

Websites with Information on Food and Diet

All links listed on this page are for information purposes only and do not necessarily reflect my opinions or those of FAB Research.

This is only a sample list. For more links that you may find helpful, please visit our own websites (listed at the start of this section, page 420).

www.hsph.harvard.edu/nutritionsource/
The website maintained by the Department of Nutrition at the Harvard School of Public Health, providing accessible, up-to-date and evidence-based information on food and diet, including practical information on healthy eating.

www.childrensfood.org
Home of the Children's Food Advisory Service.

http://chewonthis.org.uk
An interactive site for children explaining what's in their food and how it's marketed to them.

www.nu-intelligence.com
A site whose aim is to assist with practical steps that parents and the wider population can take in their daily lives to improve their understanding and knowledge of essential nutrition. They have some great links.

Sustain and the Mental Health Foundation produced two reports in January 2006 on the links between diet and mental health:

- *Feeding Minds: The Impact of Food on Mental Health*
- *Changing Diets, Changing Minds: How Food Affects Mental Well-being and Behaviour*

Both can be downloaded from
www.mentalhealth.org.uk/page.cfm?pagecode=PRFM

www.mind.org.uk/Information/Booklets
The UK mental-health charity Mind has produced a booklet called *The Mind Guide to Food and Mood*.

www.teachernet.gov.uk/wholeschool/healthyliving/foodanddrink
Aims to help schools support children in leading a healthy lifestyle and to make the most of the resources which already exist. It links to information on food and drink in schools and provides guidance on many aspects of school food.

www.bantransfats.com
A US campaign to ban partially hydrogenated fats – and see www.tfx.org.uk for the UK campaign.

www.foodcomm.org.uk
The Food Commission's excellent website, providing straightforward information on food issues and many other useful links.

www.parentsjury.org
The Parents Jury is an independent jury of over 1,300 parents which seeks to improve the quality of children's foods and drinks in the UK. The Jury is co-ordinated by the Food Commission.

www.fedupwithfoodadditives.info
A site run by Sue Dengate offering 'independent information about the effects of food on behaviour, health and learning ability in both children and adults'.

www.foodlaw.rdg.ac.uk/additive.htm
Has a list of all the additives listed in three EU directives: colourings, sweeteners and 'miscellaneous' additives, and their e-numbers and chemical or English names.

www.food.gov.uk/multimedia/pdfs/elist_numbers.pdf
Has a similar list in a pdf file or html, but divided into smaller categories, including antioxidants – only 15 of these listed.

www.veggieglobal.com/nutrition/non-vegetarian-food-additives-no-e.htm
Has a list of non-vegetarian additives.

index

and bad carbs 177
and candida 126
and food allergies and intolerances
34–5, 165
and mineral deficiencies 93
omega-3 treatment trials 258
and sugar addiction 192
morphine 114
mouth 111–12, 180
muesli 327–8
multi-vitamin/mineral supplements
99–100, 305
'IQ' studies 100
prison study 18, 81–2, 121–2

Nasi Goreng 374
National Diet and Nutrition Surveys 8
Natural Justice 81, 102
nervous system
and dietary fats 73, 245
mercury effects 154
micronutrient needs 76, 79, 80, 88,
89, 93, 94
neurotransmitters 73, 93, 149, 159,
211–12, 236
nutrients, essential 67–107
nuts and seeds 278, 304, 311–12, 320,
329
micronutrients in 79, 83, 87, 88, 89,
90, 95, 107
monounsaturated fats in 73, 221, 222
omega-3 in 230
omega-6 in 229, 234
polyunsaturated fatty acids in 223
protein in 72, 174
nystatin 126, 127

obesity see overweight and obesity
oestrogen 83, 96
older children
eating tips 280–1
and tartrazine 147
oleic acid 221

oligosaccharides 179
olive oil 73, 221, 234, 302, 321
Oliver, Jamie 8, 15–16, 100, 308–9
omega-3 fatty acids 53, 57, 159, 210,
212, 218, 219, 223, 227–8, 243,
245–64, 390–4
in ancestors' diets 103
balance with omega-6 232–4, 245–6,
262, 301
biochemical studies 249–50
and brain development and function
16, 35, 85, 100, 203, 236, 244, 245
dietary sources 73, 155, 230, 233,
311, 326
essential for health 203, 235–41
in infant formula 237, 279
low levels in boys 249
and other nutrients 79, 92, 93, 261–2
signs of deficiency 59, 257–9
supplements 261, 264, 302, 305, 326
assessing need 262
cod liver oil 242, 257
combining with Ritalin 260
controlled treatment trials 16, 59,
213, 246, 250–4, 258, 264, 393–4
dosage 263
fish oils 255–7
vs food 254
in pregnancy 155
risks 255
vegetarian 232, 262–3
and vision 60, 237–8, 245, 258, 259
omega-6 fatty acids 218, 219, 223,
227–8, 243, 390–4
balance with omega-3 232–4, 245–6,
262, 301
and boys' physical health 249
and brain health 203
dietary sources 73, 229–30, 311, 326
essential for health 203, 235–41
in infant formula 237, 279
and other nutrients 79, 92
supplements 260–1